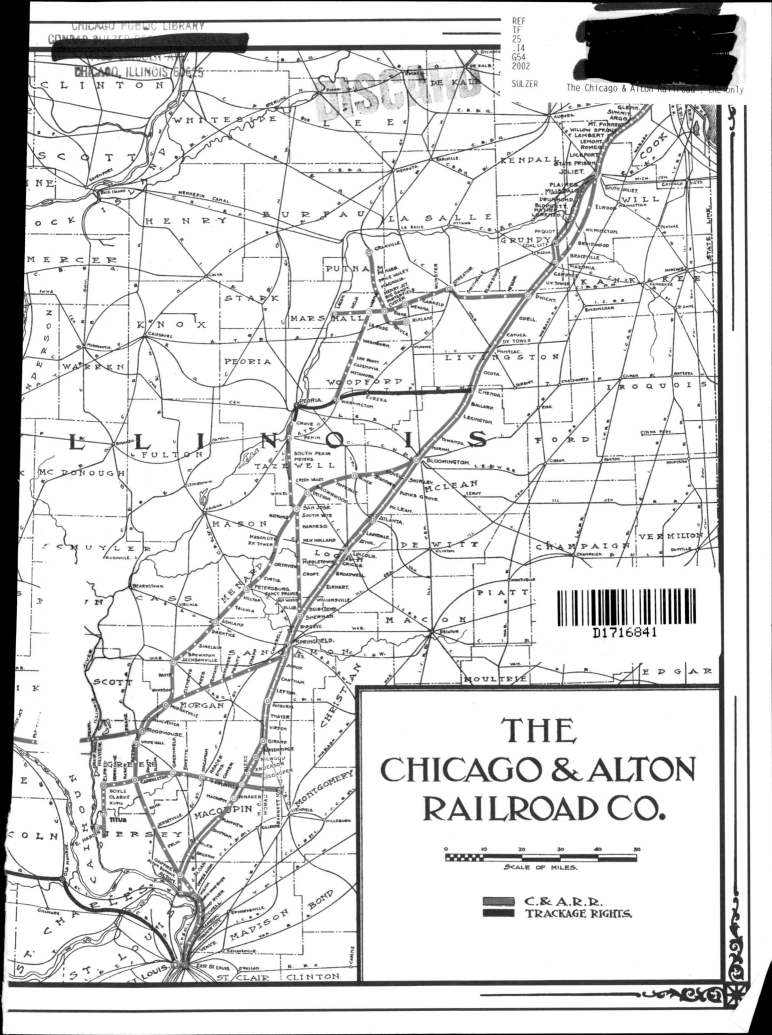

THE
CHICAGO & ALTON
RAILROAD CO.

0   10   20   30   40   50
SCALE OF MILES.

C. & A. R.R.
TRACKAGE RIGHTS.

The Chicago & Alton Railroad

The Chicago & Alton Railroad

The Only Way

GENE V. GLENDINNING

Northern Illinois University Press / DeKalb

© 2002 by Northern Illinois University Press

Published by the Northern Illinois University Press, DeKalb, Illinois   60115

Manufactured in the United States using acid-free paper

All Rights Reserved

Design by Julia Fauci

Library of Congress Cataloging-in-Publication Data

Glendinning, Gene V.

The Chicago & Alton Railroad : the only way / Gene V. Glendinning.

    p.   cm.

Includes bibliographical references and index.

ISBN 0-87580-287-7 (alk. paper)

1. Chicago and Alton Railroad Company—History. 2. Railroads—Illinois—History. I. Title.

TF26.I4 G54 2002

385'.09773—dc21   2001052126

Frontispiece photograph courtesy of the William Raia collection.

Contents

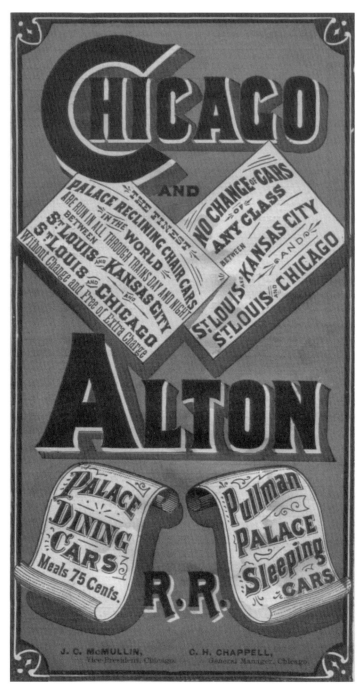

From the collection of Robert Jones.

Acknowledgments

Growing up as the son of a Gulf, Mobile & Ohio switchman within blocks of Glenn Yard on the southwest side of Chicago certainly had a lot to do with my writing this book. I spent many hours observing the servicing of diesels, classification of cars, dispatching of freight trains, and—the highlight of most days—the passing of the *Alton Limited* and the *Abraham Lincoln*. Admittedly, as a youth, I never associated the name Chicago & Alton with the Gulf, Mobile & Ohio until I came across the long expired road's name in a wonderful story of early railroading called *Singing Rails* I had found on a shelf of my high school library. The author, Herbert L. Pease, mentioned the C&A by name only eight times in the 304 pages of his wonderful telling of his years as an agent at the turn of the century, but I recognized some of the station names where Pease worked as being the same as those I found in expired GM&O employee timetables my dad brought home. My interest grew.

During my teenage years and throughout my early adulthood, I was an avid reader of railroad-oriented magazines, especially *Railroad* and *Trains*. Though the stories in each fascinated me, I found little related to the C&A or, for that matter, its successor, the GM&O. Nor did I learn much from the general railroad histories then circulating that made only oblique reference to the C&A in discussions usually dealing with Pullman's first sleeping car or Lincoln's funeral train. Frustrating as the dearth of C&A coverage was, I became committed to putting the facts together. Though my job required considerable travel and the raising of a family left little time for serious research, I was inspired to learn everything I could about this once important railroad about which so little had been published.

Arthur D. Dubin's now legendary volumes, *Some Classic Trains* and *More Classic Trains,* and William Kratville's *Steam, Steel, & Limiteds* appeared in the late 1960s and were revelations to me. The copy and photos these two superlative railroad historians devoted to the C&A's famous passenger trains were my first exposure to what was developing as a consuming avocation. In the early 1970s, a friend, Donald J. Heimburger, gave me a photocopy of a 1945 article written by D. W. Yungmeyer titled *An Excursion into the Early History of the Chicago and Alton Railroad.* Don's timing could not have been better. That early work proved a catalyst to get seriously involved in research. Yungmeyer's essential overview of the C&A's early days was the first that exposed me to the railroad's origins. About the same time, Arthur D. Dubin gave me a bound volume the railroad itself published that included its charters, leases, mortgages, and similar legal documents. Arthur's thoughtful gift proved the source for nearly everything I eventually used related to the railroad's corporate structure through 1900 and led me to sources for the actual documents.

In 1972 the Gulf, Mobile & Ohio Historical Society was founded, and Richard R. Wallin began editing its publication, the *GM&O Historical Society News.* He published many C&A photos I had never seen. James Windmeier's extensive series of articles on C&A steam locomotives proved invaluable. He made his subjects, the massive machines I knew nothing of, come alive. I have relied on Jim's efforts and thank him for his pioneering work. I too began contributing articles based on my accumulated research, and much of my earlier work became the basis for parts of this book.

From the resources housed in libraries throughout Illinois and elsewhere, I gathered the background and facts needed to knit this narrative together. In the many hours spent poring over original and secondary materials, I came to appreciate and admire those who had collected the material and so efficiently produced for me the local, county, and state histories, genealogy collections, directories, biographies, almanacs, general business-oriented titles, original documents, and thousands of pages of microfilmed newspapers I examined. I extend my thanks to the staffs of the Arlington Heights Memorial Library, Barrington Public

Library, California State Railroad Museum Library, Chicago Historical Society Library, Des Plaines Public Library, Dwight Public Library, Harold Washington Library Center of Chicago, Hayner Public Library, Hinsdale Public Library, Illinois State Archives, Illinois State Geological Survey, Illinois State Library, Joliet Public Library, Lake Forest College, Lemont Public Library, Lincoln Library of the Springfield Public Library, Lockport Library, McLean County Historical Society Stevenson-Ives Library, National Archives–Great Lakes Region, New York Public Library, Newberry Library, Northwestern University Library of Transportation, Park Ridge Public Library, Pontiac Public Library, Southern Illinois University at Edwardsville Elijah P. Lovejoy Library, Wilmington Township Public Library—all of whom assisted my work—and especially the staffs of the Illinois State Historical Library, St. Louis Mercantile Library, and DeGolyer Library at Southern Methodist University who provided exceptional help and courtesies. Thanks especially are extended to Kay Bost, Charles Brown, John Hoover, Patricia O'Neill, and Evelyn Taylor.

After a few years of solitary research, I realized I needed assistance if I was ever going to move on to writing this story. Volunteering to help was David Johnson who, over the course of four years, devoted many hours scanning microfilmed newspapers, in the process demonstrating a particular knack for spotting essential information. He sent me reams of photocopied newspaper stories regarding the railroad. Thank you, David, for your outstanding effort and devotion to the project.

Robert Fiedler made known to me a source of information I might never have stumbled upon when he invited me to join him at the National Archives–Great Lakes Region on the southwest side of Chicago. There are housed the court documents filed during the period of receivership from 1922 to 1931, which proved invaluable. A meticulous researcher, Bob also shared his work on the Litchfield, Carrollton & Western as well as fascinating details of other obscure Illinois railroads, his specialty, many of which I used. I also benefited from his perceptive insights of why things happened the way they did.

Many have contributed photos, timetables, and other matter from their collections, and I would be remiss if I did not acknowledge them:

David C. Bearden; Sam Bell; Larry J. Brandt; John P. Brown; Mary Ann Clark; Kenneth Donnelly; Darren Doss; Marty Gundelfinger; Frank Herman; Trent R. Johnson; Robert Jones; Marc Liberta; Michael Matejka; William Molony, who has made the study of Will County railroads a passion; James Mischke; Steve Mueller; Gary Osing; Stephen T. Parsons, who provided essential original company correspondence shedding light on events of the 1940s; Richard Peterson; William Raia; Paul Rodie; Mike Schafer; Douglas A. Shehorn; Keith Sherman; Steve Smedley; Donald Snoddy; Charles M. Smith; Paul Stringham; David Wagner; Richard R. Wallin, who generously shared his enormous collection of photos; Elizabeth Pearson White, whose published research on Benjamin Godfrey and his early involvement with the railroad proved invaluable; Hubert Walton; Russ Wilcoxson; Jeff Wilson; and Wayne Wesolowski, an expert on the Lincoln funeral train who selflessly shared his information with me. I apologize if I have overlooked anyone. If I have, please know nonetheless how appreciative of your help I am.

I was fortunate to have four knowledgeable men read all or portions of the manuscript. For their corrections, comments, and suggestions and for their time and dedication to this project, I extend thanks to George Broughton, William K. Dunbar, Paul Stringham, and Richard R. Wallin. Needless to say, any errors of fact or judgment that might appear are mine alone.

My thanks also go to the director, Mary Lincoln, and staff of Northern Illinois University Press who have brought this book to fruition, but especially to Kelly Parker, my editor, who gave shape to the final manuscript.

Thanks are also extended to everyone who encouraged me through the long process. Many politely suffered through my sometimes uninvited, extemporaneous, and extended discourses about the C&A as I made each new discovery. Thank you for your patience and understanding.

To my father, whose railroad career instilled my lifelong interest; to my mother, who taught me the love of books; to my sister, who was always supportive; and to my three children, who tolerated Dad's side trips to see some abandoned right of way, I fondly dedicate this book.

The Chicago & Alton Railroad

The famous *Alton Limited* is southbound pounding across the Wabash and out of Springfield, Ill. past Iles Tower, in the autumn of 1941. (Walter Peters Photo, Richard R. Wallin Coll.)

The State Sets Its Course

In 1818, the year Illinois was admitted to the Union as the twenty-first state, fewer than 50,000 white settlers populated its 56,000 square miles. Most of these intrepid pioneers had come from Virginia, the Carolinas, and Kentucky to settle in the state's southern extremes, which were rich in forests and rolling hills. The central and northern regions, composed of vast expanses of uninterrupted prairie, saw practically no settlement at all. The few who did take up residency there experienced nearly solitary existences, living among the native Sauk, Fox, Potawatomi, and Illini.[1]

Over the next 30 years, nearly 800,000 others settled in Illinois. While some came from southern states, even more journeyed from eastern states, especially New York, lured by reports of cheap, fertile soil covering an almost flat surface—ideal conditions for planting grains and raising livestock. Many from Pennsylvania and Ohio made their way to central Illinois over the National Road. They erected crude cabins and began cultivating the land. Immigrants from more distant places—Ireland, England, Germany, and Scandinavia—arrived in the northern sector of the state by boat through the Great Lakes from Buffalo. They liked what they found in Illinois: many staked their claims on the open prairie and began farming, and some took jobs in the Galena lead mines. Many others never went further than Chicago: there, the immigrants—especially the Irish—found work digging the canal, dredging the river, erecting piers, and building wharves for the mercantile houses along Water Street.

By 1847 Illinois was the fastest growing state in the Union and ranked eleventh in population but was still a place of unrealized potential on the edge of the country's western expansion. Despite its remarkable population growth and burgeoning agrarian economy, there was still a major deficiency: safe and reliable transport. Steamboats began plying the Ohio River westward from Wheeling, Cincinnati, and Louisville as early as the 1820s. As the West expanded, the number of boats steadily increased. Within a few years, they were making regular calls along the Mississippi River at St. Louis, Alton, and Hannibal and as far north as Ft. Snelling (today's St. Paul). Steamboats made travel and shipping easier for those settlements situated along the two great waterways, the Ohio and Mississippi Rivers, and to some extent, the Wabash and Illinois Rivers, but were of little benefit to farmers and merchants in the state's interior.

Settlements did emerge, nevertheless, along the state's interior rivers. Supplies were brought in and surplus products moved out on slow moving, crudely built, flat-bottomed boats. These were propelled by one or two men pushing poles into the soft riverbeds. But the process was unreliable and sometimes dangerous: all too often hazards such as submerged stumps and floating branches, or seasonal threats—such as spring freshets, summer droughts, and winter freezes—threatened safe passage. Overland travel was only slightly less precarious. Roads, more often than not, were paths simply marked by wagon ruts in the thick and tall prairie grass. In spring and autumn, the traces became little more than quagmires of sodden soil. Winter's blowing and drifting snow obliterated them. Except for essential travel, there was little movement throughout Illinois during all but the driest seasons.[2]

Illinois's backward condition in the late 1840s was in sharp contrast to those of states like New York, Pennsylvania, Ohio, and Maryland, which already had canals and railroads connecting major towns and cities. Illinois's long-anticipated Illinois and Michigan Canal, designed to connect Lake Michigan at Chicago with the Illinois River at LaSalle, had been started more than a decade earlier but was still not completed. As for railroads, the only two in Illinois were hopelessly primitive and separated by hundreds of miles of prairie. The Galena & Chicago Union (G&CU) was started to bring lead shipments from the mines at Galena to the boats at Chicago, but construction had progressed for only a few miles west of Chicago.[3] The Northern Cross was opened in 1842 between Meredosia, on the Illinois River, and Springfield but had already fallen into deplorable shape as a result of inferior materials and poor construction techniques.[4]

Proposals for a man-made water route between Lake Michigan and the Illinois River had been circulated in Congress as early as 1810, when Illinois was still part of the Northwest Territory. A canal, it was suggested, would furnish a complete water route from the Atlantic Ocean (via the anticipated Erie Canal), across the Great Lakes, to the Mississippi River, and down to New Orleans. In 1816, a year before digging of the 364-mile Erie Canal commenced, Congress directed Illinois's territorial governor, Ninian Edwards, to negotiate a treaty with the American Indian tribes for the purchase of a strip of land 20 miles wide and 100 miles long from the mouth of the Chicago River southwest to the Illinois River through which the canal would be cut. Over the course of the next 20 years, Congress and the Illinois General Assembly argued over whether the canal should be a private venture or one undertaken by either the federal or state government. It wasn't until Independence Day 1836, the traditional start date for the country's improvement projects, that the ceremonial spade of dirt was turned for the first 10-mile segment from the Chicago River's south branch at Canalport (now Bridgeport) to Summit on the outskirts of Chicago.[5] Little more was accomplished before the panic of

1837, the worst economic depression in the nation's young history, commenced. After a futile start, work was suspended.

The early development of railroads in the East began in the 1830s. The success of the early ventures quickly captured the imagination of Illinois's more progressive citizens, who saw railroads as the answer to Illinois's desperate transport needs. As early as 1832, Speaker of the Illinois House, Alexander Jenkins, proposed a "central" railroad that would run practically the length of the state, from Cairo to LaSalle (the projected end of the Illinois and Michigan Canal). He predicted the railroad's opening would accelerate settlement of the intermediate prairies. He was right, of course, but like so many visionaries, he was well ahead of his time. Had his central railroad been built, it would have exceeded in length the nation's then total railroad mileage, 350 miles.[6]

The Speaker was not alone, however, in advocating railroads for the state. His idea was embraced by several others, including the young and politically ambitious Abraham Lincoln who, during his campaign for the General Assembly the same year, wrote: "No other improvement that reason will justify us in hoping for can equal in utility the railroad. It is a never-failing source of communication between the places of business remotely situated from each other. Upon the railroad then, regular progress of commercial intercourse is not interrupted by either high or low water or freezing weather, which are the principal difficulties that render our future hopes of water communication precarious and uncertain."[7] For Lincoln and others living in the state's interior and enduring tedious travel on horseback and aboard flat-bottomed boats, the promised speed and comfort of a railroad would be a remarkable advance. Their calls led to a movement for railroads that arose throughout the settled portions of the state. In 1835 the legislature issued charters for the Chicago & Vincennes and the Jacksonville & Meredosia, the first charters for railroads granted in Illinois. In the next year, responding to the public clamor, the General Assembly chartered another 15.[8]

Enthusiastic predictions of success for these early ventures, however, did not result in the laying of track. The promoters' vision was greater than their resources. The aggregate capitalization of the proposed companies was $15 million, a sum that far exceeded the available wealth in the entire state. And there was little support beyond the state's borders. Eastern capitalists in Boston, New York, and Philadelphia were finding in their own regions opportunities with more assured futures in which to invest and showed little or no interest in the Illinois ventures. Illinois projects were seen by easterners as little more than ventures with little potential—short lines to reach insignificant river outlets from the remote interior.[9]

The campaign for Illinois railroads paralleled the earlier push for the Illinois and Michigan Canal. There was a consensus that railroads should be built, but whether railroads should be privately or state funded could not be resolved. John Krenkel, in his seminal study *Illinois Internal Improvements: 1818–1848,* concluded that "The failure of private interests to raise the capital required for undertaking the various internal improvement projects led directly to the adoption of a general system by the state in 1837. It gave to the friends of state ownership a most decisive argument."[10] One Democrat, Sidney Breese, somewhat broke ranks with his fellow party members in promoting the idea of state development of internal improvements (for it was the Whigs who philosophically supported public spending). Breese was at the time an influential judge of the Second District Court in Vandalia. He realized that if the state's infrastructure was to be built, the interests of all the state's citizens had to be addressed.

In 1835 Breese wrote a letter published by partisan newspaper editors: "Having some leisure from the labors of my circuit, I am induced to devote a portion of it giving to the public a plan . . . by which the north may get their long-wished-for canal, and the southern and interior counties a channel of communication quite as essential to their prosperity. . . ." Breese urged the state to pledge the funds needed for construction of both the canal and the railroad—especially the central railroad proposed by Jenkins. He also called on the federal government to grant land along the railroad's right-of-way, which could be sold to

settlers in much the same way canal land was being sold. "It will make the southern and interior counties, cause them to settle, raise the value of their lands . . . and furnish the means of transportation for their products, whether to a northern or southern market, of which they are now destitute." To make certain all interests were satisfied, he proposed:

> To avoid jealousies and heart-burning, let the expenditures on both works commence at the same time, and be prosecuted with equal energy; and when this main artery is finished, it will not be long before similar ones, branching off to the Wabash and upper Mississippi will be constructed. Then Illinois will rival any other state in our vast confederacy. . . . Let then the south, the north and the interior unite. Let the project be submitted at the coming session, let the loan be authorized, and let us all enter upon it with the determined spirit which should characterize all great undertakings, and success is certain.[11]

Breese's stirring words had their intended effect in the 1836 elections. Voters that year overwhelmingly favored candidates who supported state-sponsored internal improvements. The futility of earlier attempts to raise private capital had persuaded a majority that if so major an undertaking as a railroad—or canal—was to be accomplished, it would have to be publicly financed. A consensus developed, and calls rang out for a convention where a state-sponsored improvements package would be hammered out. Such a gathering in December 1836 at the state's capital, Vandalia, nicely coincided with that year's session of the Tenth General Assembly. After just two days of discussions, with no formal surveys or cost estimates, the delegates passed spending resolutions totaling $10 million for the canal, a network of railroads, and river and road improvements.[12]

Though the convention may well have been, in retrospect, the most irresponsible gathering in the state's history, other states, such as Michigan and Indiana, were passing similarly ambitious programs.[13] The internal improvement movement had built momentum in many of the northern states. The nation's inflated economy was booming. The federal government was running a surplus. President Jackson and his fellow Democrats in Congress had plans for returning part of the largess back to the states, giving each confidence that their projects could be funded.[14]

Members of the Illinois legislature correctly sensed the public's mood and, after three months of subdued debate in early 1837, passed an "Act to Establish and Maintain a General System of Internal Improvements." The legislation was breathtaking, even by standards of today's megaprojects. To appreciate the size of the program, one must imagine the construction of all of Illinois's existing interstate highways being started at the same time. Relatively speaking, that's how big the 1837 plan was, and such was the unbridled confidence of the state's early leaders. The legislature was venturing into uncharted waters, fully confident of success but with neither the experience nor the resources to successfully steer a correct course.

At the heart of the proposed railroad system, like a tree's trunk, was the Central Railroad, intended to run from Cairo up the middle of the state to LaSalle and beyond to Galena. Like branches, other roads were to cross the state: a route from Alton to Shawneetown, Mt. Carmel, and Paris (called the Southern Cross); a route from Quincy to Danville by way of Jacksonville and Springfield (the Northern Cross); and a route from Warsaw to Bloomington via Peoria with a connection to the Central.[15] No railroad was planned for the territory further north. There the Illinois and Michigan Canal would serve as the main commercial artery.

With internal improvements enacted, the legislature took up another matter that had been on the state's agenda for several years: the relocation of the capital. In 1820 the state's first capital at Kaskaskia (Randolph County) on the Mississippi River had been moved to Vandalia (Fayette County), a desolate place with little to recommend it but its centrality. In what was considered a controversial decision, the 1837 legislature selected Springfield over rivals Alton, Jacksonville, and Peoria. Two years later, in 1839, the state's affairs were transferred to Springfield.[16] Homeward-bound legislators certainly must have felt a sense of pride in what they had ac-

complished. They had fashioned a comprehensive improvements program that was responsive to citizen wishes, and they had settled on the location of a new capital, making it more central and accessible to the state's expanding population. It appeared that Illinois was about to enter a new and promising era. There seemed to be no reason the state would not flourish.

The timing, however, could not have been worse. Within a few months of the enactment of the Internal Improvements Act, the nation's economy collapsed, all but dooming the state's program. By the end of 1838, $4.9 million of state bonds had been sold, but $4.6 million had already been spent with little to show for it. A small number of bonds were sold in 1839, but on very unfavorable terms, and, after interest, they netted the state very little. Realizing there was little hope of succeeding, the General Assembly threw in the towel and repealed the Internal Improvements Act in 1840. By 1841 Illinois faced bankruptcy.[17]

One of the most unlikely of men, Thomas Ford, a Democrat from Monroe County, inherited the crisis. He was elected governor in 1842, defeating his Whig opponent, Joseph Duncan—governor when the Internal Improvements Act was passed. Although a strong proponent of the canal, Duncan had opposed most of the other aspects of the act (the legislature overrode his veto). Nevertheless he and most members of the Tenth General Assembly—blamed by the voters for the failed program and the state's huge new debt—either were turned out of office or chose not to run.[18] The deficit handed Ford had escalated to almost $15 million, up from $217,276 in 1834 before the improvements frenzy began. Some wanted Ford to repudiate the state's obligations, but instead he resolved to return the state to fiscal soundness, even though he estimated there was only "$200,000–300,000 of good money" in the entire state.[19]

Ford persuaded the General Assembly to make legal tender out of depreciated state-issued bonds acceptable in lieu of cash payments for state debts. He raised taxes and used the revenues for interest payments on the improvement bonds. He canceled a 400-ton order of English rail and sold much of what was already on hand. Though liquidating railroad supplies, Ford directed work on the canal be resumed. Using canal corporation land as collateral, he borrowed $1.6 million ($600,000 from English interests, the rest from New York capitalists) and placed the funds in the canal treasury. Ford reasoned that an operating canal would generate tolls, providing funds to repay the borrowed capital. Unless work proceeded, he argued, the state would be left with nothing more than a worthless ditch.[20]

Irish immigrants were recruited to dig the canal. They worked 10 to 12 hours a day, 6 days a week, for wages of 72 cents a day. They labored in disease-ridden, wet marshes that turned into lakes for part of the year. Their tools included little more than blasting power, picks, shovels, and wheelbarrows. At the end of an exhausting day, in the early hours of darkness, they returned to their crowded Bridgeport boarding houses. Back on the job early in the morning, they pressed on, digging a channel 60 feet wide that sloped to 36 feet at the bottom, within stone-lined walls 6 feet deep. More workers arrived, employed either as stonecutters, shaping the blocks for the canal's walls, or as carpenters assembling one of the 15 sets of locks.

Ford's decision to proceed with the canal was vindicated six years later in 1848 when the packet *General Fry,* loaded to capacity, slowly made its way north to Chicago from Lockport with the first revenue load. The long-anticipated water highway was finally opened. After years of wrangling over its merits and a cost of $6.5 million, Illinois had something to show for its presumed intemperance.[21] What formerly had been the state's one-way southern flow of traffic—thanks to the canal—became a two-way street of commerce. To Chicago from New Orleans came sugar, flour, and finished goods. From the Illinois River Basin came corn and wheat. From Galena, lead; from Chicago, lumber. Chicago quickly emerged as the most important market for the crops and livestock of Illinois and the sur-

rounding states. The canal's opening brought sharp drops in freight charges. Lumber, for instance, moved at a $30 per thousand feet rate, half of the previous $60 rate. Wheat was shipped at four cents a bushel, half the eight cents teamsters charged. During the first 10 years of operation, the canal saw annual volumes of more than a million tons.[22]

By the late 1840s, as economic stability replaced depression, the General Assembly once again—this time more cautiously—began considering railroad charters. Unlike earlier efforts, these petitions were for private companies. The bitter lesson had been learned. If railroads in Illinois were to be built, it would be through the enterprise and fortitude of its citizens.

The Fifteenth General Assembly, meeting in the yet-to-be-finished capitol in early December 1846, began dealing with the state's affairs in what was described as an "exceedingly quiet and orderly" session.[23] The legislature authorized a convention at which a new state constitution was to be written, then drafted legislation for the state's first effort at universal education (though for males only), before electing from their ranks Stephen Douglas of Jacksonville as the state's senator to Congress. Once those and other public matters were settled, the legislature turned its attention to private matters—the issuance of charters for the formation of private companies, including railroads. The first railroad charters passed were renewals of the G&CU, the Mt. Carmel & Alton (Mt.C&A), and the Liverpool, Canton & Knoxville, railroads which dated from the 1836–1837 period and were about to expire. Then on Saturday, February 27, 1847, new railroad charters were granted for the Nauvoo & Warsaw, the Rock Island & LaSalle, and the Alton & Sangamon.[24] It is from that date that the history of the Chicago & Alton is marked, for it was the projected 72-mile A&S from which the St. Louis—Chicago—Kansas City triangle of service evolved.

2

A Railroad Emerges from the Prairie

The prosperous farms of Madison, Macoupin, and Sangamon Counties produced considerable tonnage in the railroad's early days, but the majority of revenue was derived from travelers and the transport of mail. (Courtesy of Illinois State Historical Society)

As with other places in Illinois's interior, Springfield's greatest impediment to growth in its early days as the state's capital was the absence of cheap and reliable transport. The handful of pioneering settlers were, of necessity, self-sufficient. The Sangamon River did provide Springfield a tenuous water outlet to the Illinois River, but it was usually too shallow to accept anything except flat-bottomed boats. Postal delivery riders had forged two-rut "roads" early on but only to Edwardsville to the south, Decatur to the east, and Peoria to the north.

A stagecoach system was started in the 1820s by John Frink and Martin Walker. Their service worked reasonably well during the summer and autumn months. It was the wet spring and frozen winter months when trips became less reliable. Would-be passengers could be stranded for several days. In the spring, when accumulated run-off filled creek and riverbeds, stages often had to be held at their starting point—the Globe Tavern on Adams Street—until the waters receded, for not a single bridge existed in all of Sangamon County.[1]

Most of what freight there was—surplus grain and hogs—farmers turned over to teamsters. Their ox-drawn wagons plodded across open prairie northwest to Petersburg then west to Beardstown, where cargo was transferred to boats for the remainder of the journey to St. Louis. When winter arrived and the Illinois River froze, an overland trip to Alton,

32 miles and several days longer, had to be made. Merchants faced similar less-than-ideal conditions. Virtually everything they sold came from the East through New Orleans, up the Mississippi River to Alton or Beardstown, then by wagon to Springfield. The burdensome shipping charges forced merchants to charge higher prices than shopkeepers in river towns like Alton, Beardstown, and Peoria.[2]

It was probably Sangamon's Democratic state senator, George Forquer, who first publicly proposed a railroad for Springfield. In 1834 he suggested one be laid from the Wabash River at Danville, through Decatur, Springfield, Beardstown, and Rushville, to the Mississippi River at Quincy. His proposal met with predictable enthusiasm from those who would be served by it, but a dissenting voice was raised in Alton. The editor of the *Alton Spectator* dismissed Forquer's announcement as little more than a ploy to enhance Springfield's chances for being named the new state capital, then a hotly contested issue. Forquer protested and denied the charge, but his political opponents seized the issue.[3]

Among those expressing muted enthusiasm for the route Forquer proposed was Abraham Lincoln. He thought Forquer's railroad would do little to help his hamlet of New Salem, located northwest of Springfield on the Sangamon River. Lincoln had piloted boats on the Sangamon and had firsthand knowledge of how precarious such a trip could be. He favored dredging the river as a better way for the state to spend its money. For Lincoln, New Salem—situated about 10 miles north of Forquer's planned route—was too far off-line to benefit his community.[4] He did not dismiss the idea of a railroad outright, however. He just had a different route in mind. While serving his first term in the General Assembly, Lincoln wrote a letter, which appeared in Springfield's *Sangamo Journal,* that spelled out his vision. Lincoln wrote: "A railroad from Springfield to Alton would do ten times more toward building up the latter town, than the seat of government, the national road, the loan office and the state prison [all either sought by or already located at Alton] added together. If Alton could be made the depot of the productions of the Sangamon country, she would of necessity become an important town, and in our opinion she cannot be with-

out it."[5] The article struck a responsive cord, for in March 1835 an estimated 1,000 citizens gathered in Springfield to determine not how to get the Danville-Quincy line built, but how to build one from Springfield to Alton and the Mississippi River.[6]

Forquer, having recognized the shift in the political breezes, attended the meeting. He now eloquently addressed the issue, coming out in full support of an Alton-Springfield line. Others also spoke before chairman William Elkins appointed a nine-member committee of prominent Springfield men to meet with representatives of Macon, Macoupin, and Madison Counties to explore the railroad's feasibility. In May 1835 the delegates of the four counties met at Carlinville and, among other actions, named W. B. Mitchell, a civil engineer originally from Pennsylvania, to survey a route. This was a major step, one indicating that citizens of both Alton and Springfield (and the territory in between) were already receptive to the project.[7]

Assisted by a few others, Mitchell started a survey at Alton and, working north, spent the next four months on the project. In September his findings were published.

The general face of the country presents uncommon facilities for the construction of a railway, and were it not for the necessity of crossing several streams where considerable excavation and embankment are required, the cost of grading would be reduced to a very small amount.

The exception was at Alton.

In commencing the location at Alton, the greatest difficulty presented itself at the outset, the Mississippi bluffs approaching the river at an elevation of 200 feet above its waters at medium height, afforded but little hope of acquiring sufficient distance to attain the summit by an admissible grade.

Much labor and time was bestowed upon the examination of every supposed practicable pass, which resulted in a conviction of the necessity of adopting an incline plane to remove the alternative as unobjectionable as possible. The location was made along the little Piasa Creek as far as the valley of that stream [that] would accommodate the grade, being a distance of one mile. From this point, an incline plane having an elevation of

Above all others, Benjamin Godfrey, Madison County's most prominent entrepreneur, was the driving force behind formation of the Alton & Sangamon Railroad. (Courtesy of Illinois State Historical Society)

112 feet, with a base line of 1,844 feet reaches the elevation of the first bench of the table lands. From whence a grade at the rate of 30 feet per mile passes the summit at Howard's.

The situation and inclination of the plane is such as to admit its being used advantageously by animal power, or a reciprocating rope may be employed so as to allow the descending teams to draw up those ascending, and for the accomplishment of this object the coal banks in the immediate vicinity of the head of the plane, and the inexhaustible beds of limestone at Alton, which is much in demand in the interior, will furnish constant and profitable means of acquiring the requisite preponderance in either direction.[8]

It was Mitchell's engineering experience in Pennsylvania that undoubtedly led him to recommend an incline plane for scaling the bluffs. The forbidding heights of the Allegheny Mountains were being conquered in this fashion. Such an arrangement at Alton would have been a remarkable sight in contrast to the otherwise nearly flat operations across the open prairie.

Mitchell's report stated the railroad could

be completed for under $500,000, an average of $6,831 per mile, reduced by about $400 a mile if, to avoid high shipping charges, a steamboat were purchased to bring materials up from New Orleans. Mitchell also suggested more could be saved if timberland—and a steam-driven sawmill to cut it—were purchased.

Once the report was made public, land speculators started moving in. A rash of "towns" were laid out on the open prairies along the railroad's probable route, and, amazingly, eager buyers were found. Lots in Woodburn ("And where is Woodburn?" the *Sangamo Journal* sarcastically asked) sold for $30 each, an extraordinary sum when land was still available for a few dollars an acre.[9]

In February 1836 at the offices of the Alton State Bank, five of the two towns' leading businessmen—Stephen Griggs, Winthrop Gilman, and Benjamin Godfrey of Alton and Elijah Iles and Thomas Mather of Springfield—met to review Mitchell's report.[10] Godfrey, 42, was, without question, the most prominent of the five and, as later events would reveal, the most steadfast in organizing a railroad company. He and Gilman had come to Alton from New Orleans in 1832. The two had opened a warehouse and started other enterprises. Later they gained control of the Alton branch of the Illinois State Bank. Godfrey, the father of 15 children (eight of them daughters), later founded the Monticello Female Seminary and platted the town around it. He purchased vast tracts of Madison County land (as many as 10,000 acres). He was an eager benefactor of most social and civic projects. They and his numerous Alton area business interests gave him wide-ranging connections and a reputation as perhaps the state's most successful entrepreneur.[11] This man of considerable accomplishment was about to begin his crowning achievement, albeit at devastating personal sacrifice.

It was Godfrey who offered the start-up capital for the projected railroad. A few others bought stock, but after a brief initial flurry, there were no other buyers. It quickly became apparent that local interests could not produce the needed capital. But there might be other sources. The Vandalia Convention gave Godfrey hope that the state might incorporate an Alton-Springfield line into its planned railroad system. As Alton's delegate to the convention, Godfrey tried to interest his peers in his railroad, but, despite the magnitude of the eventual network, the 72-mile Alton-Springfield line was not included. Alton was instead made the terminus of the Southern Cross, and Springfield was designated a mid-point on the Northern Cross route—then thought far more strategic for the state. Satisfied that Alton would get a railroad, Godfrey was nevertheless dismayed that his Alton-Springfield link was not to be part of the state's vast system. He returned home determined to push on with what by now had become his obsession.

Several public meetings in both Alton and Springfield over the next few years were held in hopes of starting a railroad, but to no avail. As one might expect, the various fund-raising committees found few willing subscribers. Devastated by the effects of the 1837 panic and disillusioned with the state's failed internal improvements program, citizens had little confidence and even less capital. Godfrey and the others continued to beat the drums, but few were hearing their sound.

Springfield's political leaders had gotten what they wanted (relocation of the capital), but those expecting a functioning railroad (Sangamon's farmers and merchants) were soon disappointed. Despite economic woes, a portion of the Northern Cross had been laid and, after reaching Springfield, held some promise, but the line quickly turned into an embarrassment. Its track—strap iron over wooden stringers—was so poorly built that after just a few years of operation, trains could not make a trip from Jacksonville to Springfield without incident. The two simple locomotives that had been purchased frequently failed even with so light a load as one or two small carriages. The state had spent a fortune building the line, but Sangamon farmers and merchants were little better off after its completion than they would have been had it never been started.[12]

It had been three years since the first meeting on the Alton-Springfield railroad, and still there was no visible progress. The 1837 panic and its lingering aftermath lessened the level of interest in the line in Springfield, leaving it up to the business interests in Alton and Madison Counties to generate new momentum. In late 1838 another public meeting in Alton was called, chaired by Madison County's state senator, Cyrus Edwards. Out of that meeting came a resolution that called for a committee named by Edwards to meet in Vandalia with Springfield and Carlinville representatives to determine "the best possible disposition that can be made of the stock so as to secure a speedy completion. . . ."[13] What Edwards proposed was that, in return for Alton-Springfield railroad stock, the state would release what remained of its now useless rail and spikes, as well as parts of rights-of-way of at least two lines that would be used by the Alton-Springfield railroad. It took a while for the concept to catch on, but during the 1840–1841 legislative session, Abraham Lincoln—as steadfast a proponent of improvements as ever (especially those that benefitted his district)—introduced a bill that indeed made the state a partner in the Alton-Springfield railroad project.

Included in the bill was authority to take ownership of the rights-of-way the state had provided the now defunct Mt.C&A up to the junction with the Alton & Shelbyville—part of the ill-fated Southern Cross—and rights over the Northern Cross from New Berlin to Springfield. The materials on hand would also be transferred. The bill allowed the proposed railroad "to use so much of the railroad iron now owned by the state as will be sufficient to lay down a single or double railroad track, from the end or diverging point of the state works on the Alton & Shelbyville railroad, to the point of intersection with the Northern Cross railroad contemplated in this act."[14] In other words, in exchange for stock in the new company, the state would barter supplies and land to allow construction of the Alton-Springfield line to begin. In the legislature Lincoln argued that the state's property would be wasted if the principle that "no one should have any for fear all should have some" prevailed.[15] It was a clever way to allow legislators, like Edgar County's Leander Munsell, who objected to state property being given away without conditions, to vote for the bill. Munsell wasn't alone in finding state-sponsored projects abhorrent. The overwhelming mood throughout the state was against a resumption of them.

With the value of the state's supplies and land on the company's books, it was assumed local citizens would be more inclined to invest. Then, with the show of local support, the much larger sums needed for the line's completion could be secured from eastern capitalists, encouraged by the value of the state's transferred assets and local investment. There was little in the scheme for the state to lose. If the railroad succeeded, the state could see a large dividend for its relinquished land and materials (the act allowed other operators to use the completed railroad, so there was potential for added income from operating leases). If the project failed, the land and material the state turned over would simply revert back to it.

On February 27, 1841, Governor Thomas Carlin signed Lincoln's bill, providing a charter for the Springfield and Alton Turnpike Company.[16] Two months later, interested citizens gathered in Alton's courthouse to listen to a report on the railroad's financial prospects. The worth of the rights-of-way and materials the state would donate was placed at $200,000. For another $300,000 (no doubt based on Mitchell's projections), it was estimated the road could be finished. The group was told combined annual revenues would reach $160,000. Half that sum would be in expenses, leaving $80,000 in annual earnings, a handsome 50 percent return before interest was paid on the borrowed capital.[17] The report was entered into the minutes. Then Edwards, again serving as chairman, appointed another group to seek stock subscriptions. With all the positive projections, who could resist investing? As it turned out, nearly everyone. Despite the prestige and influence of the project's backers, partnership with the state, and an improved economy, few shares were sold. The Springfield & Alton Turnpike was only one of a string of failed attempts to get a railroad started. None of the privately proposed lines, chartered in the 1835–1836 frenzy, had reached fruition either. Only the Northern Cross had thus far been built, and it had been less than a sterling success.

Four years passed before another effort to start a railroad at Alton was mounted. By 1845 prosperity had returned. The state's crop yields were at all-time high levels, and there was a growing demand in Europe for the state's corn, wheat, oats, and other grains. Immigration, which had all but ceased after 1838, had resumed. Reports from Lockport indicated the canal commissioners expected the Illinois and Michigan Canal to be finished within two years. Though still not out of the woods, the state was in much better financial shape than it had been a decade earlier. It was time for proponents of an Alton-Springfield railroad to try again, but this time it wasn't Alton or Springfield businessmen, but regional politicians, leading the charge.

By 1845 the Northern Cross had all but ended its limited usefulness. The entire line needed complete rebuilding. The railroad's two failed engines had been withdrawn from service the year before. Mules and horses now pulled trains. Over the course of its existence, several lessees had tried to profitably operate the road, but all had failed. In frustration, the legislature had directed Governor Augustus French to sell what was left of the Northern Cross, but no buyers had been found, even with a selling price that was a fraction of its construction cost.[18]

To solve the Northern Cross dilemma and to figure out a way to get an Alton-Springfield line started, high-powered politicians from Madison, Morgan, and Sangamon Counties met at the U.S. District Court House in Springfield in the spring of 1845. The consensus reached at the meeting was that plans for the Alton-Springfield line would likely continue to languish as long as it was promoted as a singular entity. If, on the other hand, an Alton-Springfield railroad were made part of a larger scheme—one that combined it with the Sangamon & Morgan (S&M; as the legislature had renamed the Northern Cross earlier that year)—then not only would the interests of the citizens of the affected counties be better served, but the greater goal of selling the S&M might be made easier too. Eastern investors, it was assumed, would then view the combined railroads as a more viable investment. No merger of charters would be involved (the two railroads would remain separate corporations), but it was understood they would ultimately be brought together as unified components of a larger, eastward-directed system.[19]

None attending knew if the plan would work, but it seemed a logical plan of action. Near the end of the Fifteenth General Assembly, a bill for an Alton & Sangamon charter and another facilitating the S&M's sale were signed by Governor French two days apart on February 27 and March 1, 1847.[20] The A&S charter, like the one earlier granted the Springfield & Alton Turnpike, called for a route from the Alton public landing to New Berlin by way of Carlinville, then to Springfield. Also as before, certain rights-of-way were to be assumed, including parts of the Mt.C&A and Alton & Shelbyville, but there was no mention of leasing operating authority as the turnpike charter allowed.

The sale of the S&M was completed in April 1847 to a Springfield merchant, Nicholas Ridgely; the road's contractor, James Dunlap; and state senator Joel Matteson. They bid $21,000 and paid the sum with state scrip, presumably Matteson's. State records reveal no cash whatsoever was paid for the railroad.[21]

A&S stock subscription books were opened for the first time in May 1847 at both ends of the proposed line. Raising capital was the foremost task confronting the commissioners since $500,000 had to be on the books before the company could be formally incorporated. After a few days, 480 shares were posted in Alton's books, and 350 shares were recorded at Springfield, including two shares bought by Lincoln (who would later buy four more).[22] Though the sales represented, at par value, purchases of $83,000 of stock, only $4,150 in actual cash was taken in. It was the practice at the time for railroad stock to be purchased with a down payment of $5 with incremental payments collected as construction progressed.

The sales had been a hesitant start, one far short of what was needed. It was realized that eastern financiers would have to be visited. A delegation comprising Alton's state senator, Robert Smith; Simeon Ryder (a former sailing captain and brother-in-law of Godfrey); and two Springfield merchants, Virgil Hickox and John Williams, was formed. They left for Boston to present their case.[23] Since Boston capitalists had reputedly already earned excellent returns from investments in Michigan, Ohio, and Indiana railroads, it was assumed the same men would welcome a chance for added wealth further west. Meanwhile, local stock sales continued, promoted through two letters—written by Lincoln on behalf of the Springfield Railroad Committee—placed in local newspapers.

. . .The *chief* reliance for taking the stock must be on the Eastern capitalists; yet, as an inducement to them, we, here, must do something. We must stake something of our own in the enterprise, to convince them that we believe it will succeed . . . .

Increase of business would naturally follow the building of a good road in any country; and this applies especially to this road, by the facts that the country of its line is unequalled in natural agricultural resources, is new, and only yet very partially brought into cultivation. Not one tenth of the land fitted for the plough has yet been subjected to it. Add the *new* fact that the use of Indian corn has, at length, been successfully introduced into Europe, under circumstances that warrant the hope of its continuance, and the amount of means of transportation which the people of this country must need, is beyond calculation. . . .

Again, at no distant day, a railroad, connecting

In the Illinois legislature and in private legal practice, Abraham Lincoln was outspoken in support of development of Illinois's early railroads, including the Springfield & Alton Turnpike and the Alton & Sangamon. (Courtesy of Illinois State Historical Society) the Eastern cities with some point on the Mississippi, will surely be built. If we lie by till this be done, it may pass us in such a way as to do us harm rather than good; while, if we complete, or even begin, our road first, it will attract the other, and so become, not merely a local improvement, but a link in one of a great national character, retaining all its local benefits, and superadding [sic] many from its general connection. . . .

In view of the foregoing considerations, briefly stated, is it not the interest of us all to *act,* and to act *now,* in this matter?[24]

Lincoln's second letter read in part:

. . . Constructing a railroad from Alton to Springfield, is viewed but as a link in a great chain of railroad communication which shall unite Boston and New York with the Mississippi. Whatever interest Illinois has in this great improvement, and whatever advantages this particular route through Illinois may possess, is necessarily connected with the proposed work from Alton, on the Mississippi, to Springfield. . . .

Since the abandonment of the internal improvement system by the state, several acts of incorporation have been passed by the Legislature, the object of which was to secure to the people of the state, if possible, the construction of the most important of these works by individual enterprise and capital. These acts of incorporation have looked to no general plan, such as is now contemplated, and the great work of connecting the Mississippi with the Eastern cities, through Indiana and other states, can now be commenced only by blending some two or three charters. Of these acts of incorporation, one was passed last winter to construct a railroad from Alton to Springfield. . . .[25]

Lincoln employed smart public relations to characterize the railroad as a purely local endeavor yet a part of a greater system. The purpose of the A&S was no longer to be that of just securing reliable transport to and from the Mississippi River for Springfield, but rather to become an integral part of a system to connect the Mississippi with the East Coast—a far more expansive and ambitious objective. Illinois was then effectively the western border of the country's development (besides Missouri and Arkansas, only Iowa and Texas had become states west of the Mis-

sissippi). It was logical for the organizers to look eastward. The idea of pushing north toward Chicago was not yet a consideration.

The possibility of extending a line across the state to Chicago only began to surface after downstate delegates attended a convention on rivers and harbors held in Chicago in July 1847. The convention was organized to protest President James Polk's veto of an 1846 appropriation bill (sponsored by Chicagoan and Illinois Congressman John Wentworth) that would have allocated federal funds for marine improvements throughout the West, including Chicago and St. Louis. Polk and his fellow Democrats saw expansion of the country as a far less divisive issue than development of the existing states that the Whigs advocated. He and his party were intent on annexation of new land—later labeled Manifest Destiny—especially of the Oregon Territory. Instead, with his veto of the Rivers and Harbors Appropriation Act, Polk had polarized the country.[26]

It isn't known how many of the other Alton or Springfield delegates had visited Chicago before the river and harbor convention (probably none), but it is certain that it was delegate Abraham Lincoln's first look at the city and that it was an eye-opening experience. He and the other downstate delegates were impressed by the number of ships docked along the river and by the cargos assembled there. They could see many more ships anchored offshore in Lake Michigan. They saw crowded boardwalks filled with busy people and dusty streets jammed with wagons and carriages. They were shocked at the prices paid for real estate. The experience convinced them of the city's importance, and they came away realizing Chicago had a future and those doing business there would prosper. There were more than 200 miles of open land between the Mississippi River at Alton and the Great Lakes at Chicago, but the opportunities presented through a rail connection could not be ignored.

Before such expansion could be considered, however, financing the first segment still had to be accomplished. Godfrey and his associates faced disappointment when the team sent to Boston returned empty-handed. The only thing they had to show the monied interests was Mitchell's 10-year old report with its plan for an incline plane at Alton's bluffs and support data of outdated prices and projections of revenues. Their presentation failed to impress would-be investors. A new survey and business plan was needed before another attempt at raising eastern capital could be mounted. In early February 1848, a group gathered in Alton's council room and passed a resolution—offered by Edward Keating, then Alton's mayor—for a new survey which would "command the confidence of the capitalists of the country."[27] It was resolved that two engineers from New York State, Frederick Harback and another named Child, should carry out the work, but Ryder, as chairman of the meeting, proposed instead an engineer he had met in Boston, William Crocker.

Crocker, with an assistant and a crew of rodmen, spent three months on the project. The team first explored the Alton Bluffs for a suitable route up and out of the flats of Alton, eventually choosing the Piasa Creek Valley. Over the past decade, locomotive design had advanced considerably, and Crocker no longer saw the need for Mitchell's incline plane. For the first two and one-half miles from the Market House in Alton, grades would average from 53 to 60 feet to the mile, proving to be the most troublesome for northbound train crews for some 35 years, but far more efficient than what Mitchell had proposed. From the creek's origin, Crocker's team offered two options. Both would use the graded right-of-way of the Alton & Shelbyville for about eight and one-half miles from a point about three miles north of Alton. From there, one route would cross Coup's Creek and, from the Lick Creek crossing, pass over open prairie to the S&M at New Berlin. From that point Crocker's road would use 16 miles of the S&M into Springfield. The second routing would run across the prairie on a line somewhat to the east of the first, directly to Carlinville, then almost due north to New Berlin.[28]

With projections of generous profit margins and the promise of healthy dividends, the pace of local stock sales quickened. In March 1849 the city of Alton invested $151,000. A month later the city added $26,000 more. Sangamon and Madison Counties subscribed to $250,000, and Greene County took $5,000 more.[29] Armed with the new survey, revenue projections, and in-creased local investment, Ryder and Godfrey departed for New York.

Before getting his start in warehousing and trading at New Orleans, Godfrey had captained a merchant ship out of Baltimore for nine years, calling on ports in Europe, the Caribbean, and Mexico. The contacts he made led Godfrey to Henry Coit, one of New York's wealthy capitalists who had made part of his fortune in the West Indies trade. He bought a large block of stock. So did another New York financier, J. B. Danforth. Through dogged perseverance, Godfrey sold more shares and in October 1849 sent reports back to Alton that he had raised the needed capital.[30]

Although the funds needed to incorporate were now in hand, construction money was needed. For this Godfrey approached Augustus T. Cowman of Hyde Park, New York. In June 1850 the two formed a partnership, the A. T. Cowman Company. They agreed Godfrey would manage construction while Cowman would supply the capital.[31] While Godfrey finalized arrangements with Cowman, Ryder had returned to Alton with an offer from Crocker and two of his associates to build part of the railroad. Meanwhile, the other commissioners in Alton had received an offer from John Shipman, a resident of Long Island, New York, to supervise construction of the entire line in return for stock in the completed railroad. Though he would have preferred Crocker, Shipman's offer was a deal Ryder, on behalf of the railroad, could hardly refuse. "I very much regret," Ryder wrote Crocker, "that we could not have so arranged as to have brought you out here to build the road. But as things have turned I suppose we shall have to give it up. I am very much obliged to you for the interest you have taken in our cause and am sorry that your efforts did not result so as to employ you and your friends." Crocker nevertheless was employed by Cowman and supervised construction out of Alton under Shipman.[32]

It had taken a little over two and one-half years to raise enough capital to bring about incorporation, but in February 1850 documents were filed with the state, naming the first officers of the company: Henry Coit, president; J. B. Danforth, acting director; John Shipman, chief engineer; C. F. Jones (formerly of the New York & Erie and New York &

Harlem railroads), resident engineer; and Issac Gibson, secretary.[33]

A flurry of activity was evident at Alton during the spring and summer of 1850. Engineers had completed surveys for the Alton terminus. Eager to work, men were lined up outside the construction tent of Joseph Gilmore of Dayton, Ohio. Gilmore had been hired as a sub-contractor to prepare the first four miles of line from the terminus on Seventh Street to Coal Branch. Stone and timber for the planned depot and engine house were being stockpiled at Alton's public landing. Stacks of ties were nearby. By now there were fewer state-owned rails available. Much of the state's supply had been sold to avoid mandated payment of duties to the federal government if the rails were not used by the end of 1843 (a price extracted from Washington for receiving the state's share of the government's surplus). Five hundred tons of the rail had been purchased with $45 worth of canal scrip by state senator Matteson. He then sold the rail for a quick profit to the state of Michigan for its railroad, the only one in the United States still using flat rail.[34] That autumn, 3,000 tons of 56-pound, 18-foot-long sections of iron rail and 200 tons of spikes manufactured by Bailey Brothers & Company of Liverpool, England, had been brought up from New Orleans. Another 600 tons was at New Orleans, waiting to be moved north.[35] At the height of the summer's heat in August, Gilmore began the difficult task of digging through the bluffs of the Piasa. By late autumn, grading crews, made up of more than 150 men, were employed. Another 200 were about ten miles north at Brighton, and similar-sized gangs were at Coups Creek and Carlinville.[36]

Cowman purchased the *Newton Waggoner,* a recently launched stern wheeler packet, along with two barges bought expressly for transporting ties and other supplies. The packet arrived at Alton's public landing with its first cargo of 5,200 cedar ties. The load had been brought from the Cumberland River Basin.[37] In October Cowman signed a contract with Thomas and Charles Wason, brothers who five years earlier had formed the Wason Manufacturing Company of Springfield, Massachusetts. Cowman ordered 34 freight cars, made up of 24 26-foot-long, eight-wheel boxcars and 10 gravel cars "of the usual length, made to dump both ways"; five 56-passenger coaches "equal to the first class passenger cars . . . in use on the Hudson River Railroad"; and "two 28-foot-long, eight-wheel baggage cars."[38] In January 1851 J. W. Zacharie, a New Orleans business associate and friend of Godfrey's employed as the railroad's New Orleans agent, reported receipt of a consignment of "pieces and packages said to compose nine gravel cars." Two Wason craftsmen were in Alton awaiting the arrival of the kits, ready to assemble them.[39]

The stockpiling of supplies at the public landing at Alton continued. Meanwhile, in Washington passage of legislation to create the long-awaited Illinois Central (IC) was being deliberated. Since Senator Sidney Breese's attempts to get Congress to grant federally owned land in Illinois to the new company had failed, Senator Stephen Douglas, who succeeded Breese in 1850, took up the crusade. Douglas was successful in getting the federal government to create a land grant program by joining forces with Alabama senator William King for a similar subsidy for a railroad to run from the opposite side of the Ohio River at Cairo to the Gulf of Mexico, the Mobile & Ohio (M&O). Theirs was a major achievement, one skillfully handled by Douglas over considerable sectional opposition and the philosophical objections of his own Democratic Party. Contributing to his victory was his designation of Dunleith (opposite Dubuque, Iowa) instead of Galena as the northern terminus to give access to Iowa and the addition of a branch to Chicago, fast becoming an important city to the nation.[40]

Coit and Danforth knew very well why the Chicago branch was added to Douglas's legislation. Articles in newspapers and firsthand reports of those returning from business trips made clear what a dynamic place Chicago was becoming. The canal was fulfilling the promises made of it, and it was apparent by the numerous ships docked there that Chicago was emerging as the commercial center of the northern reaches of the West. It was Coit and Danforth who proposed the route to New Berlin be abandoned in favor of a more direct route to Springfield. Nine fewer miles of track would be required, and four fewer streams would have to be bridged, but more importantly, dependence on another railroad would be eliminated. After the realignment, one could draw an almost straight line on a map from Alton to Joliet with Springfield and Bloomington as midpoints.

The state's rapidly developing economy and population growth also encouraged Coit and Danforth. Over the past 10 years, Illinois's population had increased 79 percent. While Madison County had added 6,000 citizens, Macoupin 5,529, and Sangamon 4,508, places to the north were seeing even faster gains. Will County, where Joliet was located, had added 6,536 residents during the same period. And the most impressive gains of all were in Cook County. The county's population had grown to 33,184, and 90 percent lived in Chicago.[41] The growth in the state's number of livestock and quantities of crops paralleled that of the state's population. The value of livestock was $912,036, up almost $300,000 from 1840 levels. Hogs were valued at $1.9 million. The 1850 wheat harvest totaled 9.4 million bushels against 3.3 million a decade prior; oats reached 10 million bushels versus 4.9 million; and corn totaled 57.6 million bushels against 22.6 million. Potatoes, buckwheat, and hay harvests also showed increases. Even more impressive was the state's new industrial base, something that hardly existed 10 years earlier. Illinois now had 3,164 manufacturing establishments, including 29 iron foundries, two pig iron producers, 16 woolen mills, and 52 breweries and distilleries that together employed more than 16,000 workers. Most of the new industry was located in Chicago.[42]

In early 1849, discussions concerning connecting Alton with Chicago were held with interested Chicagoans. While leaders in that city had promised no financing, they encouraged the road's officers to push their idea forward. Ryder, in a letter to Crocker that year, stated: "Our road will connect with the [Great] lakes in three years. The Chicago folks have agreed to meet us at Springfield and the Lafayette road [the Terre Haute & Alton (TH&A)] will be commenced next summer and the Terre Haute folks are anxious to connect in Alton with this road. All of which will feed our road . . . and make it very profitable."[43]

Sangamon's senator, John Stuart, whose close ties to the A&S dated from his time as a member of the Springfield Railroad Committee during the Springfield & Alton Turnpike period, introduced the needed legislation for the railroad's extension from Spingfield to Chicago. Stuart was one of the more active members of Springfield's affairs, both political and social, and it was therefore Stuart's task to advance the railroad's and Springfield's interests. He introduced his bill in the General Assembly of 1849–1850 and succeeded in getting it through the Senate, but after it was read in the House, a one-term senator from Macon County, Edward Smith, rose to object to the bill's passage. He argued that not only was the bill approved in his absence, but also that the building of Stuart's Springfield-Chicago railroad would interfere with the extension of the S&M and the IC, both projected to run through Smith's district. Smith, as should have been expected, was being protective of "his railroads" when threatened by "their railroads." In deference to Smith, the House returned Stuart's bill to the Senate where it was tabled. For the time being, the A&S's plans were stalled.

By this time the legislature had taken up consideration of an IC charter. Passage of it was the Seventeenth General Assembly's dominant issue. In January 1851 Senator Ashley Gridley of Bloomington—whose district included the counties of DeWitt, Logan, Macon, and Tazewell as well as his own county of McLean—introduced the enabling legislation.[44] Numerous route adjustments were proposed by various legislators generally favoring their districts, but Gridley saw to it that they were tabled or defeated. He wanted a divergence of no more than 17 miles from a straight line between the terminals of Cairo and Dunleith, thus making certain that the main line would pass through Bloomington, Clinton, and Decatur, county seats of McLean, DeWitt, and Macon Counties.[45] After passage only Logan and Tazewell Counties would be left without a railroad, at least for the time being.

While seemingly all attention was focused on IC matters, Stuart made his second attempt at getting extension of the A&S passed. He first introduced an amendment to the road's charter allowing the route change north of Carlinville directly into Springfield. In light of the attention paid the IC, Stuart's amendment became a minor act few saw any reason to oppose. His bill easily passed.[46] Stuart then introduced a bill for a charter for a railroad from Springfield to Bloomington. He worked closely with his colleague, Gridley. By limiting the A&S's extension to Bloomington, they adroitly allayed the concerns of those protective of the IC. Again, his bill met little opposition.[47]

Gridley's district, so sparsely populated that it included five counties, had been ably served by him. He had provided railroads for all but one county of his district, Tazewell. He now corrected the matter. On February 17, 1851, six days after passage of the Bloomington extension amendment, Gridley's added legislation passed, permitting the A&S to lay a branch off the Bloomington extension into Tazewell County through Pekin to Peoria, an important Illinois River town of 5,000 residents and the site of several manufacturing and mining operations.[48]

The Seventeenth General Assembly was particularly active in railroad affairs. A Springfield correspondent for the *Joliet Signal* described the times: "The railroad excitement throughout the country continues to increase. Judging from present indications the period is not very distant when the entire West will have railroads constructed at convenient distances apart to carry to market the products of the soil."[49] Sixty-two railroad bills or amendments were enacted during the 1851–1852 session, one of them—for rights to build a line from Jacksonville to Alton (a 60-mile distance)—introduced and guided through the legislature by Morgan County's senator, Newton Cloud. On February 15, 1851, the bill for a charter for the Jacksonville & Carrollton Railroad (J&C) was signed.[50] It was common for railroad charters then being issued to include start and completion dates (usually 10 years), but the J&C's contained neither, a fortunate circumstance since it would take 15 years for it to be finished. Why this planned railroad among the several organized that year was important for the A&S is found in the first of 16 sections of the bill. Specifically permitted was the uniting of the J&C with the A&S at or near Brighton, eliminating the obligation of the J&C to lay its own tracks between Brighton and Alton, in effect making it a branch of the A&S.[51]

The formality of approving the A&S's extension to Bloomington and Peoria was the main agenda item at a stockholder's meeting held in Alton in April 1851. It was at this same meeting that the company's first five directors were named: Henry Coit, J. B. Danforth, and J. D. Dankin of New York; Virgil Hickox, a prominent Springfield businessman and local political figure; and Edward Keating, a lawyer and former mayor of Alton.[52]

Because the 1851–1852 autumn and winter seasons proved to be relatively mild, work on the A&S progressed at a steady pace. In January 1851 Shipman reported that 779 men and 64 horses were at work grading near Alton and that masons were constructing bridges and culverts at various places along the line.[53] He had divided the right-of-way between Alton and Carlinville into 36 sections, and all were in some stage of preparation with 14 nearly finished. Twenty-three miles of right-of-way had been graded with another ten miles about half-finished. Foundations and walls for the engine house and machine shops at Alton were nearly completed, as were the walls of the depot. The eighteen-inch-thick walls of locally quarried stone would support a roof of large wood beams, making Alton's Piasa Street depot larger and more impressive than the more modest depots along the line.[54] To aid the fledgling company's efforts, the Springfield City Council passed an ordinance granting a right-of-way up Third Street plus a donation of property for a depot between the First Presbyterian Church and Jefferson Street, a few blocks from the town's square and the new capitol. Eight additional lots, two blocks north of the proposed depot site, were also donated to be used for the erection of a machine shop.[55]

Though progress was evident up and down the line, masked from public view was the resistance of some disgruntled subscribers to pay for the stock to which they had subscribed. In 1851, when calls for the first added stock payments went out, three defaults in particular proved troublesome: those of John Burkhardt, James Barret, and Joseph Klein. They refused to complete their contracts. The A&S hired Abraham Lincoln, who by now had a thriving legal practice and had developed a reputation as a successful litigator, to represent the company. Before trial Burkhardt relented, or "caved in" as Lincoln described it, but Barret and Klein persisted.

Barret was one of Sangamon County's better known farmers who owned considerable acreage, including some 4,200 acres near Island Grove, about halfway between Jacksonville and Springfield in Morgan County. He had subscribed to 30 shares of A&S stock. Barret claimed the provision in Stuart's amendment that entitled stockholders expecting the railroad's route to follow one of Crocker's original routes to a full refund applied to him. Barret contended that since the railroad's route was removed from the vicinity of his property, the railroad was worthless to him, and thus he was no longer obligated to pay the balance owed.

To counter his claim, Lincoln established that Barret had not fully paid for his stock—just a little more than half—and thus Barret was not entitled to a refund. On the contrary, Lincoln contended, he should be made to pay the stock's entire cost. Virgil Hickox, as a witness for the railroad, testified that Barret expected to be named the railroad's treasurer, and when that didn't happen, he refused to pay. Others testified that Barret had promised payment 15 to 20 times but each time reneged. When both sides had finished presenting their cases, Judge David Davis, in Springfield Circuit Court, ruled that the railroad had a right to change its routing and by so doing did not void a contract for stock purchased. He awarded $1,351 to the railroad. Barret appealed to the Illinois Supreme Court, but again, Lincoln's arguments prevailed. Justice Treat affirmed Davis's decision. There was no fraud, and the subscription was nonconditional, Justice Treat ruled.[56] The case, the first of 19 Lincoln argued on behalf of Illinois railroads before the Illinois Supreme Court, became the precedent that later protected other railroads similarly threatened by subscriber default.

Klein's contention was not that he owned property adversely affected by the railroad's routing change but that by signing a promissory note, rather than paying cash, he was not bound to pay for the rest of the stock. He was willing to forfeit the 5 percent down payment if he were allowed to be released from further payment. His argument was rejected, both by Judge Davis and later on appeal before Justice Treat, both using the Barret case as precedent.[57]

A third legal matter involving stock confronting the A&S was a bit more bizarre, since it was brought before the Madison County Circuit Court by none other than Simeon Ryder, former president of the commissioners. He wanted his 50 shares repurchased by the company. Ryder, likely feeling his chances for an important position in the company's management were thwarted after Coit was named president, had disassociated himself from the company and joined those organizing the TH&A. Ryder's argument was that, in effect, preferred shares had been created when the City of Alton agreed, in return for an annual 6 percent interest payment, to give New York investors the city's proxy for the 1,000 shares it owned. The value of the stock he owned and his percentage of ownership, Ryder contended, were diluted. Facts brought out during the trial showed that Ryder did not actually own the stock he claimed since he had turned his shares over to Godfrey. The court found Ryder's defense insufficient, stating the agreement between the city of Alton and New York investors was not binding on the corporation or the other stockholders but was only an understanding between the two parties, a decision upheld by the Illinois Supreme Court on appeal.[58]

Meanwhile, Shipman was out examining the country for suitable routes for both the Bloomington extension and the Peoria branch. He concluded the line to Bloomington could be laid to run from Springfield north about 35 miles, cross Sugar Creek (near Funks Grove), and then run in the divide between Sugar Creek and the Kickapoo Creek. The Peoria branch could split about one mile north of Rocky Ford, cross Sugar Creek and Prairie Creek, then extend on a straight line past Delavan, through Circleville, crossing the Mackinaw River there, before reaching Pekin. He didn't report on how the line would cross the Illinois River to Peoria, presumably leaving that for another visit, but did predict that 60 miles of track toward Bloomington could be in running order by December, with work on the 100-mile Peoria branch carried out simultaneously.[59] That, however, was the last heard of the Peoria branch. With limited capital, the directors decided everything was to be poured into the Bloomington extension.

There was considerable excitement at

Alton's public landing when the first two engines, the *B. Godfrey* and *Alton* (by today's standards diminutive), were carefully transferred to the landing from a steamboat that brought them up from New Orleans. A month later the *Springfield* was unloaded, and in September the *E. Keating* arrived. The *B. Godfrey* and *E. Keating,* each with five-foot drivers, were the intended passenger engines. The *Alton, Springfield,* and *Macoupin* (which arrived a few months later) had four-foot drivers for heavier freight service.[60]

In August, after four months of hard labor in the bluffs, grading crews were scraping the relatively flat topography of the prairies almost within sight of Carlinville. Other crews were working on a six-mile stretch north of there, pushing their way toward Springfield. Meanwhile, masons were building bridges, some with spans up to 40 feet, while carpenters were erecting a 100-foot-long trestle across Macoupin Creek.[61] With so much progress evident everywhere, it was easy for warning signs of impending trouble to go unnoticed, but for several months Cowman had been receiving troubling reports from the field. Early in 1851 one of the construction engineers, J. F. Barnard, sent a telegram from his Alton office. "Men not paid . . . cannot keep going . . . everything depends on my paying promptly and fully. Exerting useless without money."[62] About the same time, Shipman reported to Cowman that if the construction schedule was going to be met, the number of workers would have to be increased. Cowman advanced the wages and reluctantly approved the additional hiring, for construction was consuming cash faster than he could generate it. He had already invested about $670,000 and had reached his limit.[63]

In September 1851 Cowman shocked Godfrey in telling him he could not continue and intended to dissolve their partnership. He suggested Godfrey meet with one of those from whom Cowman had obtained support to get more funding. With no other choice, Godfrey agreed to take over Cowan's interests as well as his obligations.[64] Godfrey then met with 32-year-old financier, Henry Dwight, Jr., who had achieved considerable success and who, at the time they met, claimed to be the agent for some 100 New York banks. Dwight had learned the banking business at his father's

Geneva, New York, bank. In 1839 he had moved to New York City and started his own investment firm and had established business relationships with New York and New England investors, including a few in Connecticut who were keenly interested in railroads.[65]

Godfrey admitted to Dwight he did not have the money needed to complete the contract and that if he failed he stood to fall hopelessly in debt, taking with him several close friends who had also invested in the fledgling company. "If I do this thing," Dwight told Godfrey, "I must have the whole of your property and everything I can make from it; I can make no conditions with you; but you must put yourself entirely in my hands."[66] Godfrey had little choice. At the same time, Dwight persuaded Godfrey that to conveniently carry out the needed negotiations, Godfrey should accept Dwight as his New York financial agent. In that capacity Dwight would perform the "general supervision of the financial transactions."[67] Their agreement, signed in September 1851, averted the A&S's immediate cash crisis, but there was no way of knowing how dreadful the deal Godfrey struck with Dwight would be for the company or for himself. It was the beginning of a tenuous and tumultuous period in the A&S's history.

For arranging the funding, Dwight had demanded control of the company. Consequently, Coit, Danforth, and Dankin resigned as officers and directors. In their place Dwight appointed one of his clerks, Orestes Quintard, and an associate, William Platt, to join him in filling the vacancies. Keating was retained as a director and was named the railroad's superintendent. Hickox also remained a director and was named the railroad's Springfield agent.[68]

The speed with which the railroad was being built astounded observers. Brief local newspaper reports on the progress of other railroads then under construction periodically appeared, but none of those reports compared with the long and detailed accounts of the A&S's progress. Even dispatches from the nation's capital describing the erection of an impressive monument to George Washington were given far less notice than the frequent reports Shipman and other railroad officials gave the newspapers. At least once a month, an update on A&S matters appeared. Despite the newspapers' limited circulations, what they published about the railroad's progress was passed on to citizens by word of mouth during courthouse conversations, visits to town, or after church services. The locals were more excited by the coming of the railroad than nearly any other event in their lives.

By April 1852 grading was finished to Virden (51 miles north of Alton), and some 1,200 men were now at work on the railroad, including 250 in Sangamon County just south of Springfield. Ties, spikes, and rails brought up the Mississippi and Illinois Rivers were being unloaded at Naples, then reloaded onto S&M cars. The loads were moved to a 400-foot section of track off a switch at a junction of the two roads about two miles south of Springfield at a place later named Iles.[69] Bridges at Lick Creek and Sugar Creek had neared completion, and the news that the *B. Godfrey* was running 12-mile trips from Alton to Brighton pulling loads of supplies caused considerable interest. By mid-May, track was in place from Alton to Coup's Creek. Newspaper notices sought contractors to dig water wells at Carlinville, Auburn, Chatham, and Springfield and a pit for a turntable at Carlinville.[70]

While most of the events surrounding the railroad were drawing applause, some in Springfield were questioning whether the size and appearance of the depot planned for the state's capital was imposing enough. About mid-year, the *Illinois Journal* raised the issue in an editorial criticizing the design. The writer called for a second story to be added to the 5,590-square-foot, flat-roofed structure's planned 15-feet-high walls to give it more bulk and, symbolically, to give the capital more stature. Though smaller in overall dimensions, the S&M depot on the other side of town was two-storied and pleasing in appearance. "We should like to see this building an ornament to the place . . . it can be made so, at so trifling an expense," the writer declared.[71] Apparently the railroad's management was persuaded, at least partially. When built, the station's ends were peaked to provide at least a sloping roof, but the wooden structure essentially remained single-storied, indeed hardly comparable in appearance to the company's more impressive stone depot at Alton.

Just a year after guiding enabling legisla-tion through the General Assembly for the IC as well as for the Bloomington extension and Peoria branch, Gridley returned to the Illinois Senate to introduce yet another important piece of A&S legislation. In the second session of the Seventeenth General Assembly, convened in early June 1852, he initiated a bill, passed June 19, that effectively doubled the railroad's projected length by permitting the company to extend its line from Bloomington to Chicago. The northward thrust was to be achieved either by a connection with the Chicago & Rock Island (C&RI; formerly the Rock Island & LaSalle) at a point somewhere between Ottawa in LaSalle County and Joliet in Will County or by a route via Joliet over its own rails. To reflect the expansion, the bill also changed the name of the A&S to the Chicago & Mississippi Railroad (C&M).[72] Gridley's amendment also extended the road to St. Louis, albeit by boat rather than by rail. The C&M was permitted to operate its own steamboats between Alton and St. Louis, giving the company control over passenger schedules and preferred space for its freight. Although relatively short-lived, the company's boat operations were important. Owning its own boats removed dependence on independent operators for transfer of its St. Louis–bound passenger and freight traffic.

The first two craft the railroad bought and put into service were the 255-foot *Altona,* built at St. Louis in 1852, and the same-sized *Cornelia,* constructed at McKeesport, Pennsylvania, in 1851. Both were side-wheelers. Because of its enormous 32-foot wheel and 13-foot buckets, the *Cornelia* was a particularly fast boat, making the upstream St. Louis–Alton run on at least one occasion in 1 hour and 37 minutes, a record that stood until 1915. Operation of the two craft, however, became an adventure. In December 1853 the *Cornelia* sank, not an uncommon occurrence for steamboats at the time. More than 30 boats had already been destroyed on Alton–St. Louis passages. After being raised it was returned to service but again sank in 1856 at the Chain of Rocks, where it was left. The *Altona* too had a short life; it also sank at the Chain of Rocks during December and was not recovered. Replacing the boats were the larger, 358-ton *St. Paul,* the *Winchester,* and the *Reindeer.* All three were side-wheelers. The *St. Paul* proved to be unprofitable, and the *Reindeer* sank near Wood River in November 1857. Their replacements were the veteran *Baltimore,* a 275-foot side-wheeler with a 36-foot wheel holding 10-foot buckets, and the 347-ton *York State,* built that year in Brownsville, Pennsylvania. Both of these packets sank in 1859 at the Chain of Rocks.

Other boats were pressed into service until 1860, when the 283-foot side-wheeler *City of Alton* began to ply the Alton–St. Louis route. After trackage rights over the TH&A were secured to Illinoistown (later East St. Louis), the somewhat smaller side-wheeler *B. M. Runyan,* built in 1858, was operated until December of that year, when it sank in shallow water below Alton. It was raised and repaired at St. Louis in the spring of 1864 but replaced by the *Tatum.*[73] Though short-lived, the steamboat period provided a colorful chapter in the railroad's history.

In June 1852 Oliver Lee and three assistants—James Spencer, Henry Gardner, and Richard Morgan, Jr.—arrived in Bloomington. Lee opened an office there and another in Springfield. He had been hired by Dwight as the chief engineer of the Bloomington-Springfield extension. Lee was a well-qualified railroad engineer, having spent five years with the Hudson River Railroad, most recently as secretary of the company, and before that as superintendent and division engineer.[74] The young crew Lee brought with him spent a month and a half examining two lines before settling on the one eventually laid. Except for a formidable rise about 20 miles south of Bloomington, they found the undulating prairie ideal for a relatively flat, straight right-of-way. The biggest obstacle facing them: bridging the Sangamon River north of Springfield. While the extension surveys progressed, construction to the south of Springfield continued.[75]

On July 1 tracklayers reached Carlinville. Crews had laid 35 miles of track out of the Alton Bluffs and across the open prairies before reaching the first town of any size along the route. This was cause for a celebration—heralded as "The Great Rail Road Festival"—the following Saturday, July 5. An estimated 6,000–7,000 persons gathered, many brought in by trains made up of all the cars the company could press into service. It was the largest gathering the county had yet seen.

Residents of St. Louis, Alton, and the surrounding counties attended, as did Governor French and some of the state's well-known speakers.[76]

Just before midday the following Monday, a borrowed S&M engine (probably the *Phoenix*), two passenger cars, and "some burden cars" with an estimated 300 riders left Springfield on a 10-mile excursion over the completed line to Lick Creek, near Chatham, for an equally joyous celebration. The train passed over the Lick Creek trestle without incident. This added considerably to the public's confidence in the road's construction. Orations were delivered, the Declaration of Independence was read, and, after dining and socializing, the passengers boarded the train and returned to the capital. At the S&M crossing, that road's evening train was held so the special could pass. Hearty cheers of those on both trains rang out, celebrating the near completion of the new railroad. "Our citizens seem scarcely to realize that within forty days," an editorial in the *Illinois Journal* enthused, "we shall be able to take breakfast in our city, dine in St. Louis, and return the same night. But it will be done!"[77]

Notices appeared in Alton and Springfield newspapers announcing service between Alton and Carlinville. "Until the completion of this road, the contractors will run a passenger car in connection with the materials train, between Alton and Carlinville—leaving Alton at 30 minutes past 9 A.M., on arrival of St. Louis mail; and leaving Carlinville at 5 P.M." The first trains were carrying an estimated 50 to 60 passengers and Carlinville mail. Within days passenger and freight service was extended to Girard, 13 miles north of Carlinville, a 47-mile run from Alton. Only nine miles of rails remained to be laid to join the line up from Alton with that being built south from Springfield.[78]

As the shadows of late summer lengthened on Thursday September 9, 1852, the distinct sound of an engine's whistle and bell could be heard throughout Springfield. Citizens left what they were doing and started lining the single track along Third Street. The first train through from Alton approached to the accompaniment of cannon fire and citizens' cheers. The train's arrival was affirmation that what a few years earlier had been but a dream had been realized. The aspirations of those who had organized the company, the hopes of those who would benefit, and the confidence of those who had recently taken up residency with the promise of a railroad were simultaneously fulfilled by the train's appearance. One who witnessed the event was Springfield's James Matheny, who later wrote: "The most important event to Springfield was the completion of the Alton and Sangamon Railroad. The completion of that road breathed into us new life. . . ."[79]

A celebration was appropriate, and both Alton and Springfield bid to host the event. It was decided the state's capital would enjoy that honor. Early on the morning of October 7, a gathering of 400 guests, some originating in St. Louis and brought to Alton aboard the *Cornelia,* boarded a special train at the Alton depot headed for Springfield and a firsthand look at the railroad. A sense of pride filled both those on board and those along the line. "It was a glorious sight—the careening of the passenger train over prairies," a Springfield journalist gushed.[80] After the group disembarked about two o'clock, with hundreds of Springfield citizens joining them, they walked the few blocks to the company's still-unfinished machine shop, where they were seated for a meal. After Hickox's introduction, Godfrey delivered what most considered a fine speech, filled with enthusiastic predictions of a great future for the two towns now that the railroad had arrived. Others too addressed the gathering, including St. Louis's mayor, Luther Kennett, as the warmth of the afternoon sun's rays washed over them.

Regular passenger and freight runs between Alton and Springfield began immediately after the first ceremonial trip. An every-day-but-Sunday passenger train was scheduled to leave Alton for Springfield at eleven o'clock with a stop at Virden for meals, and Springfield for Alton at ten o'clock with a meal stop at Carlinville. One rider reported passage from Alton to Springfield as "a comfortable ride" of four to five hours, an average of about 15 mph, including stops—a vast improvement over trips that formerly took much longer, sometimes days, by stage or horseback.[81] Freight trains began running whenever there were engines available to pull the collected cars.

Both cities experienced immediate rewards.

Alton was already southern Illinois's most significant city on the Mississippi River, a passionate rival of Missouri's older and larger St. Louis about 20 miles south. Alton was one of the state's earliest commercial centers, strategically located above the confluence of the Missouri and Mississippi Rivers and below the Illinois. Some of the state's first newspapers were published there, and the state's penitentiary had been built in the town's bluffs. Its boat landing was active; five flour mills were operating (the first group of several more that would later make up a significant Alton industry); commission houses dealt in beef, pork, lard, whiskey, furs, flour, and lead; a sawmill was thriving; and coal was mined in the general vicinity. Warehouses storing products that supplied the needs of much of southern Illinois lined the river's bank.[82]

Springfield had come into prominence as the new center of the state's government though it wasn't a very attractive place. The streets in most seasons were quagmires of mud through which hogs freely wandered. In summer the stench from manure piled beside stables and trash and garbage collected in gutters was often overpowering. The rooms of the American House, Joel Johnson's City Hotel, and Torrey's Temperance Hotel, however, were usually filled by those with state business to conduct. Since returns home on weekends were difficult, if not impossible, visitors stayed over for several weeks of General Assembly and court sessions. The money spent added considerably to the local economy. Politics was Springfield's primary interest.

The promised rewards brought to the area by the railroad were being fulfilled. Demand for business sites at Alton increased, and a mini-boom in building ensued. Retail sales at Springfield rose, as did new housing. Land prices in both places climbed, and there was outward expansion of each city's borders. Other town sites along the railroad prospered as well. Within three weeks of the laying of rails through Carlinville, it had been reported that "all the lots on the west side of the square, and south of Carrollton Street, were sold . . . at good round sums, ranging from $450 to $900." Lots in Virden enjoyed brisk sales. A new town, Shipman, was platted.[83]

Within a month of the C&M's opening, newspaper advertisements, placed jointly with the Michigan Central (MC)—which had reached Chicago just weeks earlier—announced the "Great Northern Route" between St. Louis and New York, the "safest, cheapest and most expeditious route to New York, Boston, and Philadelphia, via Alton, Springfield, Bloomington or Peoria, to LaSalle, and by stage and railroad, via Aurora, or by packet to Chicago," and the advertisements promised the trip could be made in five days.[84] Others capitalized on the railroad's opening too. The Western Stage Company promoted triweekly service between Bloomington and Springfield with connections to the road's trains. S&M advertisements that had been running for some time showing schedules between Springfield, Jacksonville, and Naples now appeared with an added line calling attention to connections at Springfield to Alton.[85]

The pent-up demand for a railroad became evident at once and exceeded expectations. One train in mid-September was reported to have carried 15 freight and two passenger cars, filled to capacity, no doubt with two or three engines employed. An average of 110 passengers a day were being carried, and the first month's revenues exceeded $14,000. By the end of 1852, trains of 20 to 25 freight cars were operated while the passenger trains of a mail car, baggage car, and three coaches, capable of seating 180 passengers, "went out, filled to capacity." By year's end daily revenues were approaching $600, nearly $200,000 on an annual basis.[86]

Disturbing, however, was the final tally of the railroad's cost, $1.3 million, $17,361 a mile, more than $400,000 over expectations. The fundamental cause of the excess was the hasty pace of construction and what Godfrey viewed as interference from Keating after Dwight appointed him superintendent. From Godfrey's perspective, Keating made unwise commitments, often without consulting Godfrey, running up costs and straining their relationship.[87] Certainly higher costs for everything contributed as well. The price of rail, spikes, and connectors had risen substantially since the earlier estimates had been made. English mills could hardly keep up with American orders for railroad iron. They demanded and got premiums for their products.

Dwight was not pleased when Keating's reports of final costs reached him. He had anticipated advancing somewhat under $500,000 but was now confronted with bills totalling more than $1 million. He and William Platt, president of the City Bank of New Haven and the person Dwight named as president of the railroad, refinanced the company. A prospectus issued in November stated all bonds issued before October 1852 would be canceled and replaced. The $2 million issue of C&M bonds was sold to English, New York, and Connecticut investors.[88] At Dwight's urging, in December Hickox and Keating resigned as directors though both retained their management positions—Hickox as the road's agent at Springfield and Keating as the road's superintendent. Dwight contended the business of the company was largely being conducted in the company's New York William Street office, and it was important that the full board be available for meetings, something neither Hickox nor Keating could easily manage. Named to replace them were two more of Dwight's clerks, John Kelso and Herman Herwig.[89] Dwight was now in sole control of the C&M.

Deception and Default

3

Swinburne delivered 38 American type locomotives in 1854 such as no. 31 seen here. Because of the C&A's failure in the late 1850s, Swinburne went largely unpaid and failed. (Thomas Norell Photo., E. L. DeGolyer, Jr. 5 x 7 Photo. Coll., P727.1154, courtesy of DeGolyer Library, SMU)

In the autumn of 1852, attention was quite naturally focused on the bustling activity associated with the building of the C&M through Madison and Macoupin Counties. But north of Springfield, clues that work was about to begin on the Bloomington extension became apparent when small newspaper advertisements soliciting grading and masonry bids and offers to buy bridge timbers and white oak ties started appearing. No doubt remained after Oliver Lee hired six contractors to complete the 26 sections of the 51-mile Springfield-Bloomington route.[1] They would raise a grade and lay track through nearly virgin territory.

William Carson's 100-man crew was the first to start. His objective was to keep at it as long as weather permitted, which, as it turned out, was about eight weeks before an unusually wet, early winter set in. Workers had to quit when their loaded carriages and wagons bogged down in the soaked ground. Others found the grade they were raising impossible to stabilize. Before the rains arrived, however, masons had finished 30-foot-tall cut stone piers, and William Chase, of O'Tously & Company, had installed pilings in the Sangamon River for three, 100-foot spans and two trestles—one 450 feet long at the north end and another 800 feet long at the south end. The bridge was the most costly and challenging work on the entire extension. More than 450,000 feet of timber and nine tons of iron would be consumed before its completion.[2]

In February 1853 Peter Badeau and a couple of rodmen started a survey of the 88-mile distance between Bloomington and Joliet. By March contracts for all segments had been let. Later that spring carpenters had the walls for a depot at Bloomington erected, and masons at Joliet had begun laying stone for an engine house and shops.[3] With late spring breezes and warmer temperatures drying the prairies, grubbing and grading crews began work north of the Sangamon River, penetrating deep into the vast, open prairies of Logan County. The projected route north to Bloomington had been set as a nearly straight line through Logan and McLean Counties over some of the richest, though sparsely populated, land in the state. In a matter of days, a 15-car work train reached Fancy Creek, nine miles north of Springfield. The train provided rough sleeping and eating accommodations.[4] It moved like a ship through a sea of tall grasses and colorful wildflowers.

With few settlements along the route, it was left to railroad officials to designate convenient station sites. These were laid out about every 10 miles, the practical distance a farmer could expect to cover in the same day.[5] About 18 miles north of Springfield, John Gillett, a farmer and cattle raiser, had staked out a settlement he called Elkhart. A rudimentary depot was erected there. About 12 miles further north was a place settled by Russell Post in 1835. He named his hamlet Postville, and it became the Logan County seat. After the government was moved to Mt. Pulaski in 1848, the tiny county jail and the somewhat larger courthouse at Postville sat vacant. What activity remained at Postville centered at the hotel, where Frink & Wagner stagecoach passengers on the Chicago–St. Louis route stopped for meals.[6]

Mt. Pulaski, in the southeast corner of the county, was less centrally located than Postville, and residents—especially in the northern and central areas—resented the far

longer trips they had to endure to reach it. Postville's 100 residents assumed the railroad would pass through their town, enabling them to reclaim the county government and to restore the town's future. Lee's projected route, however, placed the track about a mile east. As an official of the railroad, Virgil Hickox knew this and, after a search of county records, learned that Pennsylvanian Isaac Loose owned the land through which the railroad could be laid. Loose had bought the land during an 1839 government sale but from all reports had never visited the site, content to hold it as a long-term investment. Hickox decided to buy the site before anyone else got the idea.[7]

Hickox recruited two friends, John Gillett of Elkhart and Robert B. Latham of Mt. Pulaski, to form a land company. Abraham Lincoln, an acquaintance of all three, was hired as their legal counsel. Latham was designated to make the long and tiring trip to Pennsylvania to personally secure title to the property. During his absence, Gillett and Hickox enlisted state representative Colby Knapp to introduce legislation to remove the county government once again to the land the three acquired. Eleven days after Latham met with Loose and a sale was agreed to, Knapp's bill was enacted.[8]

The property was surveyed and platted with provision for a free right-of-way for the railroad. The three named the place for Lincoln, the only town to bear the future president's name before he became nationally prominent. Survey stakes already marked off lots and streets by the time tracklaying crews reached the place in mid-August. Newspaper advertisements for a "great sale of lots in the town of Lincoln" had been placed, and a week after the line was opened a special train was run up from Springfield for prospective buyers. In that single day, 90 lots were sold. The highest priced, of course, were those that paralleled the railroad, along Chicago Street. There lots sold for as much as $150. Other property further from the track fetched somewhat lower prices, closer to $40 per lot. The partners had paid only $1,350 for the property sold that day but had netted $6,000, and they still had more land to sell. As the train headed back to Springfield that evening, Gillett, Hickox, and Latham shared congratulations on their success.[9]

It was not long before the settlement of Lincoln began to flourish. The C&M erected a water tank and a woodshed, part of which served as an office. The county constructed an imposing new government building for its offices and courts. The number of retail stores increased, and soon commercial blocks emerged. The merchants and craftsmen saw their businesses flourish, and their prosperity was converted into impressive residences. As more were attracted to the town, Lincoln's borders pushed outward and its population grew (to some 5,700 by 1860). The settlement of Postville was annexed as Lincoln's fourth ward.[10] The coming of railroads transformed vacant Illinois prairie into new communities.

The northern extension almost immediately resulted in higher passenger traffic. One day's count at Alton off the southbound train in the autumn of 1853 showed 235 arrivals, 135 originating at Lincoln.[11] The strong patronage was evidence that travelers had abandoned the uncomfortable and less reliable stages for speedier and more convenient trains. Track continued to be laid northward at a steady pace. Xenia, named for an early settler's former Ohio hometown 11 miles north of Lincoln, was a thousand-acre site platted by R. T. Gill just before the railroad's arrival. A freight house and modest depot were erected there. Within months some 500 persons took up residency. Later the town was renamed Atlanta. By October rails reached Funks Grove, just nine miles south of Bloomington. At the same time, tracklayers out of Joliet had laid 15 miles of rails as far as the Kankakee River.[12]

Bloomington was now within sight, but the C&M was not the first to reach the town. That distinction was claimed by an IC train out of LaSalle that had arrived at Bloomington in May 1853. Three of Bloomington's most fervent promoters, Illinois Supreme Court judge David Davis; McLean County's first lawyer and founder of Bloomington's first successful newspaper, Jesse Fell; and state senator Ashley Gridley, had been instrumental in convincing the IC's management to make the railroad's entry into Bloomington on the east side of town. Now the three persuaded Lee to locate his line through Bloomington's west side, reasoning that with railroads on either side of the town's borders, development between the two railroads would follow. And so it did. Later, when it became known that Lee was looking for a place to locate the railroad's shops, as an inducement for the railroad to choose Bloomington the three men offered seven acres (owned by W. H. Allin) for the minimal cost of $3 just to the north of where the C&M's depot was being erected.[13] Their foresight paid off handsomely, for over the years the railroad's shops were greatly expanded and became Bloomington's largest employer. Over time Bloomington became more closely identified with the railroad than any other city on the line.

Seven months after the laying of the first rails north of Springfield, the first revenue train made the entire 131-mile run to Bloomington from Alton on October 18, 1853.[14] Unlike the fanfare that accompanied the arrival of the first IC train six months earlier, there was no official ceremony to mark the event. Already accustomed to the daily arrival of trains, Bloomington citizens took scant notice.

Two miles of track were hurriedly laid beyond the Bloomington depot to Bloomington Junction (later Normal), where the town's two railroads intersected. Once the short stretch of main line was opened, passengers were able to make across-the-platform connections with LaSalle-bound IC trains, where they transferred once again to C&RI trains headed for Chicago. There passengers again transferred to eastbound trains, completing a trip to New York City in "only sixty hours."[15] In today's world of two-hour flights between St. Louis and New York, a two-and-a-half-day journey might seem amusing, but in the 1850s such travel speed was a marvel.

Though open, the Middle Division, as the Springfield-Bloomington segment was designated, had been hastily constructed and was far from finished. Eight hundred thousand dollars, somewhat more than $13,500 per mile, had been spent constructing it, and the high costs were creating enormous pressure on Dwight in New York.[16] What could be seen—the extension of the main line—disguised what could not be seen—the financial problems Dwight and Godfrey faced. With his personal assets pledged to Dwight, Godfrey could not meet a payment on the $16,000 of notes held by Wason for the cars his company had delivered in 1851. It was not the first payment missed, and in late 1852 Wason sued Godfrey and his former partner, Cowman, in United States District Court at Springfield. Neither Godfrey nor Cowman appeared at the hearing to argue their case, so by default a judgment of $13,534 was awarded Wason, but he remained unpaid. Saddled with Cowman's debts as well as his own and not yet reaching a settlement with Dwight, Godfrey was close to failure.[17]

Despite his considerable business interests, Dwight, in early 1852, became caught between a rock and a hard place when the New York credit market suddenly tightened. He had to scramble to raise funds to satisfy repayment calls not just on his railroad obligations but on his other business ventures as well. Desperate for cash, Dwight began a series of outlandish dealings that mixed his personal affairs with those of the C&M. His fraudulent acts began with the theft of some bonds. One of the banks for which he served as New York agent was the Massillon Bank of Ohio. When the credit crunch hit, Dwight owed the Massillon bank over $300,000. Among the bank's assets were $230,000 worth of Cleveland & Pittsburgh bonds held as collateral. With no authority whatsoever, Dwight convinced the cashier of the bank, a brother of Dwight's close friend William Platt, to transfer the bonds to him. No one else at the bank, least of all its officers or its executive committee, knew of the transfer. Dwight later claimed he took possession to provide for the bonds' "safekeeping," though he never had any claim on them.[18] Once he had them, Dwight offered the bonds as collateral for a $230,000 personal loan he obtained from the British Bank of North America.[19] Though this fraud had nothing to do directly with the C&M, it marked the start of Dwight's criminal actions that led him to prison and the railroad to near ruin.

Dwight had raised enough cash, albeit illegally, to temporarily stave off personal bankruptcy, but he still had the growing railroad debt to face. In June 1853 with the Bloomington extension under way, Dwight influenced the road's board of directors to authorize issuance of $2 million worth of C&M bonds, secured by a second mortgage, which Dwight successfully placed with various lenders. The lenders demanded two stipulations—that half

the bonds would be issued only "for the purpose of defraying the expense incident to the construction of a double track along the line" and that the total value of the bonds issued would not exceed the value of subscribed capital stock.[20] Dwight saw his next chance to cash in, again with the compliance of his handpicked cronies on the board, by delivering to himself in August 1853 a $6 million construction contract for the two extensions—Springfield to Bloomington and Bloomington to Joliet. Half of his compensation was to be paid in C&M stock, the other half in bonds. Incredibly, the $6 million figure was more than three times Lee's estimate for finishing the Springfield-Joliet segment, fully furnished with superstructure, depots, land, fencing, engineering expenses, and contingencies.[21]

At the same meeting, Dwight's lackeys passed a resolution that called for "a double track along the line" and ordered $1 million of the company's bonds to be issued to Dwight immediately. Of course, the resolution was totally contrary to the lenders' stipulation that bonds would be issued only after a double main line was finished. The action also contradicted terms limiting issuance of bonds to the level of capitalization because the value of bonds issued now reached $3.5 million—$500,000 greater than the par value of the common stock.[22]

Dwight then initiated yet another scheme with not even a pretense of legitimacy, drawing an unwitting Godfrey into his tangled affairs. When the two men had agreed on Dwight's loan allowing completion of the Alton-Springfield segment, Dwight suggested that one of his staff be appointed to act in Godfrey's stead as his financial agent since most of their business would be conducted in New York. Godfrey agreed, thinking the move merely a matter of convenience. Dwight, however, had other ideas. Having previously secured a sizeable personal loan from Nathan Peck, president of the Merchants' Bank of New Haven, and now in need of capital again, Dwight returned to the banker for another loan. This time Peck declined. The bylaws of his bank prohibited loans in excess of 10 percent of the bank's capital stock to a single individual or company, and the additional sum Dwight sought would have exceeded that figure. Though Dwight's role as Godfrey's financial agent in September 1852 was nearly at an end, and though he had no authority whatsoever, Dwight told Peck he was the agent for "Benj. Godfrey & Co." He described Godfrey as a "contractor on the lower end of the railroad" and told Peck that Godfrey "was good for the loan." On the strength of Dwight's assurances, Peck accepted the Godfrey paper and accepted others months later. What Dwight did not tell Peck was that the company was completely fictitious; there never was a Benj. Godfrey & Co.[23]

Dwight's need for capital was seemingly insatiable. Elisha and Edwin Litchfield of New York had emerged as important controllers and builders of railroads in the West. Two of their roads, the Michigan Southern (MS) and the Northern Indiana (NI), were rapidly pushing west to Chicago. Dwight, it can be assumed, had prior business dealings with the brothers, for in October 1853 they lent him $250,000 in what were known as the MS's "Jackson Branch Bonds," secured by second mortgage C&M bonds, with a promise to repay them in six months. As it turned out, the C&M bonds were invalid since they were numbered beyond those allowed under the $3 million limit.[24]

Despite his desperate attempts to keep himself financially afloat, Dwight could not stave off failure and in November 1853 was declared bankrupt. His assets, including Godfrey's pledged property, were taken over by the Metropolitan Bank of New York. At this point, Dwight owed his creditors $2 million.[25] Given his personal circumstances and the economy's weakness, amazingly, the resourceful and persuasive Dwight was able to fashion a syndicate of lenders for the railroad. They included Brown Brothers, one of New York's leading commercial lenders; Henry Hotchkiss (both personally and as president of the New Haven County Bank); the City Bank of New Haven and Merchants' Bank of New Haven; the Phoenix Bank of Hartford; the Seneca (New York) Bank; Henry St. John, a wealthy New Englander; Dwight's brother, Edmund, a New York attorney; and William Swinburne of Paterson, New Jersey, who held a contract for 38 locomotives for the railroad. Collectively, the participants agreed to put up $500,000 of the $800,000 principal needed to complete the Bloomington-Joliet segment.[26] For the balance Dwight returned to the Litchfield brothers, this time through Charles Gould of the NI.

On Christmas Day 1853, Edwin Litchfield and two NI officers, George Bliss and John Stryker, met with Dwight and his brother, Edmund, at a hotel opposite Gramercy Park in New York City. Both sides exchanged proposals, but neither proved acceptable to the other. After a week of negotiations, however, a deal was reached. In return for appointment of three directors, it was agreed the MS would extend the deadline for Dwight's return of the Jackson Branch Bonds to March 1855, would immediately advance the C&M $30,000 for payment of the interest then due on the second mortgage bonds, would loan $300,000 in exchange for Dwight's stock and rights to vote for two years, and would lease some equipment to Dwight's road. A stipulation to the agreement was that Dwight had first to return for cancellation the excess $500,000 worth of second mortgage bonds and accept a readjustment of the debts Dwight claimed he was owed by the company.[27] With no leverage whatsoever, Dwight had little choice but to agree to the terms.

Three days after the deal was struck, Dwight and three of the board members—Platt, Quintard, and Kelso—met ostensibly to put the company's affairs in order, but their real purpose was to approve payment of $1.6 million in bonds and stock for claims Dwight submitted, though none were supported by vouchers. They also issued $3.5 million of stock as settlement of Dwight's earlier agreed to construction contract.[28]

By the end of the week, to comply with the lenders' stipulations and to make room for Litchfield-appointed directors, Dwight, Platt, Quintard, Kelso, and Herwig resigned. Replacing them were Edwin Litchfield, John Cleveland, Gould, and Bliss—all Litchfield railroad officials—and Hotchkiss, the New Haven Bank's representative. Bliss was named president of the company; David Hoadley, vice president; James Alexander, secretary; and Gould, treasurer—again, all NI officials. Lee, Dwight's appointment as chief engineer, was relieved and replaced by Henry Gardner, a Lee assistant. Edward Keating was the next to go. He was replaced as superintendent by Richard Morgan, Jr., another of Lee's apprentices. For the moment at least, the C&M had become a Litchfield-controlled property.[29]

Though it seemed the company's immediate problems had been solved, the deal began to unravel when Dwight, despite repeated requests, failed to return the $500,000 of inappropriately issued second mortgage bonds. His personal creditors would not accept the deals he offered. Exasperated, Litchfield withdrew the $300,000 loan. When the New England lenders learned of this sudden turn of events, they panicked. Without the Litchfield money, the railroad would surely fail, putting their investment at risk. They pleaded with Dwight to do the right thing. In late February 1854, Dwight relented, somehow found a way to recover the bonds, and turned them over. Only then did Litchfield deposit $150,000—half the promised $300,000—in the company's treasury.[30]

▾▾▾

Though the C&M was armed with authority to lay its own tracks, during the brief period of Litchfield control no move was made to push on to Chicago. Instead, in March 1855 a running agreement with the C&RI with connections at Joliet was announced. Eastbound traffic would be routed over the 45-mile Joliet & Northern (J&N; then nearing completion), its line running almost due east from Joliet to the Michigan Central at Lake Junction, Indiana (later East Gary), at the southern tip of Lake Michigan. At the other end of the line, a running agreement was reached with the newly reorganized Belleville & Illinoistown (B&I) between Alton and Illinoistown.[31]

William Crocker's survey of 1848 had been filled with great promise for the Alton-Springfield route, but he had included an admonition that the absence of a route to Illinoistown was a serious mistake. He recommended that such an extension be added as quickly as possible. Crocker, a well trained engineer but political novice, was oblivious to the ramifications of such a suggestion. What he failed to appreciate was the reason the road was started at Alton in the first place: St. Louis's prominence as a rival city. Alton's leaders had no interest in advancing their competitor's fortunes. They subscribed to a presumed state policy of fostering development of cities within the state and found any project that might be construed as helping places outside the state an anathema. Although Illinoistown was within the state's boundaries, its position directly across the river from St. Louis meant competition.

From the start railroads chartered by the state were vested with rights to benefit only Illinois cities and towns. All of the various state-sponsored lines named in the 1837 Internal Improvements Act, for instance, had terminals specified within Illinois's borders, as did the charters issued for the privately organized companies that emerged a decade later. Even state senator Gridley's amendment for the Bloomington-Chicago extension prohibited the C&M from connecting with railroads approaching from the east.[32]

That understood policy, however, ran counter to the views of Governor Augustus French. Elected in 1846, French, among his roles in other enterprises, was a land speculator in the southeastern part of the state. When he learned in early 1848 that a new railroad, the Ohio & Mississippi (O&M), had been chartered in Indiana with expectations of building east to Cincinnati and west across the state to Illinoistown, he began buying land in the likely path of the new railroad.[33] A year later the O&M petitioned the Illinois General Assembly for a charter. The Madison County delegation, joined by other legislators, immediately rose in opposition.

Governor French realized he had a fight on his hands and called a special session of the General Assembly to formalize the procedure for incorporation of a railroad, which he hoped would put to rest the issue of presumed state policy. The General Assembly passed a bill in November 1849 that formalized steps of incorporation, construction and operation standards, and other formalities. The bill's passage heartened Simeon Ryder, now president of the TH&A, who enthusiastically praised the act in a letter to Crocker. "The call session of our Legislature has been held and we have gained a complete triumph over St. Louis and all other enemies. A General Railroad Law is passed by a large majority providing that all railroads crossing our state shall terminate at our own towns and cities and provides particularly that none shall go to St.

Louis. "This settles the Illinois policy and we shall have no more trouble with St. Louis hereafter."[34] Legislative opposition to an O&M charter persisted until finally in February 1851, with state policy an outmoded concept, the railroad received one. A year later ground was broken at Illinoistown, marking the start of O&M construction in Illinois, the first to establish a terminal there.

A few years later, Alton's domination of railroading was threatened again, this time by the projected Jacksonville & Carrollton. The road's organizers anticipated the same financial support Alton had afforded the two railroads already there, but the organizers became frustrated by Alton's inaction. "The failure of Alton, so far, to take hold of the matter, and cooperate with the friends of the enterprise along the route, is having a most unfortunate influence upon the prospects of the road," the *Carrollton Gazette* editor wrote in 1853. "The feelings of the people, we find, are becoming intense on the subject. They cannot understand why it is, that if Alton really desires the construction of the road, that no stronger interest is manifested by her, than she has given."[35]

After extended silence on the matter, the Alton City Council finally took up the investment issue. This excited the railroad's proponents and quieted their complaints, until, that is, it was realized the proposed resolution included a proviso that gave the city the right to decide the J&C's route and where it would terminate within Alton's boundaries. It was nothing more than another attempt to invoke whatever fading control Alton hoped to have over railroad matters. When the counties to the north objected, the offensive section was dropped, and in September 1852, in a low turnout vote, a stock subscription in the J&C was approved. But by now the bond issues of the counties to the north had passed, and the J&C incorporators wanted nothing further to do with Alton. They informed newly elected mayor Samuel Buckmaster they didn't need Alton's aid and further, Alton would be bypassed altogether in favor of Illinoistown.[36] In its defense of state policy, Alton had suffered another setback.

Alton's grip on railroads was finally broken for good a few years later. In early 1853 Colonel Morrison took control of the moribund B&I and announced his intention to extend his railroad northward into Alton. Again Alton's business leaders were enraged. Though Morrison's plans were perfectly within his rights—his charter provided explicit authority to add an extension, as well as authority to "unite its railroad with any other railroad now constructed"—business leaders, especially those operating boats between Alton and St. Louis, objected. Alton had raised its barricades once again, but, as before, did not have the guns to defend them.[37]

The northern extension of the B&I had reached Wood River, a few miles north of Illinoistown, by early 1854. Both Ryder of the TH&A and Keating, superintendent of the C&M and a director of the J&C, realized the probability of Morrison succeeding and the potential of the line for their roads. The B&I's short mileage would be a critical stretch of railroad and potentially highly profitable for each if they controlled it. Ryder and Keating developed a plan. Ryder's road would complete the remaining mileage between Wood River and Alton for Morrison. Then the TH&A would extend trackage rights from Alton to Illinoistown to the C&M, and both roads would secure B&I trackage rights between Wood River and Illinoistown. In return the C&M would allow the TH&A access to its Alton depot and would share trackage within the city. In February 1855 the C&M's charter was amended, giving authority for the joint depot operation and sharing of track at Alton and the running agreements with the TH&A and the B&I to Illinoistown. Also provided was a change in the company's name, to the Chicago, Alton & St. Louis (CA&St.L)—the road's third and a reflection of its new southern terminal.[38] In November 1856 Morrison agreed to sell his B&I to the TH&A. The renamed Terre Haute Alton & St. Louis (THA&St.L) began operating its own route to Illinoistown thereafter, but two years passed before CA&St.L facilities were completed, and in the interim steamboats continued to perform the railroad's transfers of St. Louis–bound passengers and freight.

▾▾▾

The financial picture President George Bliss portrayed in an 1854 report must have staggered the organizers of the A&S, who had struggled to sell the initial stock of the company. Just a few years earlier, sales of single shares, with only $5 down, was a great achievement when the entire town of Alton could see its way clear to buy only 1,000 shares and incorporators themselves could afford only two or three shares. Bliss now reported that the paid-up stock of the company had a par value of $3.5 million.[39]

Bliss's report was filled with confidence that all was well with the railroad, but Litchfield's next move created a temporary crisis. Soon after the directors' meeting in March 1854, he informed the board that the remaining $150,000 of the $300,000 NI loan would be partially paid with 2,700 tons of surplus rail his road had sitting in Toledo, sufficient to complete the track between Wilmington and Lexington. While the rankling between Litchfield and Dwight went on, tracklaying had been halted. Litchfield estimated the value of the rail to be about the same as the promised cash—a questionable evaluation. He justified the move on the basis the rail the C&M had ordered from England was still on New York docks. To await its delivery, he contended, would further delay completion.[40]

When Dwight received word of Litchfield's action, he became livid. He threatened to sue Litchfield for breech of contract, but the rude response he received from Litchfield was that he "had better come to terms, as a lawsuit would take three years."[41] Consumed by rage, Dwight decided it was time to teach Litchfield a lesson. The proxy Dwight had delivered to Litchfield, which permitted him to vote Dwight's 23,236 shares, was effective as long as Dwight owned the stock. If he were to transfer or sell his interest and rights, however, the proxy granted Litchfield would become null and void. About 18 days before the next scheduled election of directors in June 1854, Dwight sold his stock to Platt.[42] Platt then informed Bliss of the sale and declared he would seek a new board at the upcoming meeting.

When the board met, Dwight and James Wright, president of the Bank of Oswego, New York, to which Dwight personally owed money, were named directors.[43] With Hotchkiss joining them, Dwight once again had control of the board. Hotchkiss's New Haven County Bank held a sizeable number of shares as well as somewhat over 10 percent of the second mortgage bonds.[44] He had been appointed to the board to protect the interests of his and the other New England banks, but it soon became evident, based on the votes he subsequently cast, that Hotchkiss no longer worried about the interests of the banks he was supposed to protect, but only his own. President Bliss and treasurer Gould were not challenged as directors since Dwight now had a majority without them. Dwight wasn't worried about their loyalty to Litchfield. He saw Bliss, a man of integrity, as a welcomed front man to allow him to operate behind the scenes and Gould as a well respected professional in the New York financial community—a personage Dwight desperately needed. A few days after regaining control, Dwight stated to associates that he expected the company's president to resign whenever he decided it was time.[45]

Dwight then named a new associate, Hamilton Spencer, vice president of the company, with offices in Bloomington. Spencer, a native of Utica, New York, had practiced law there before taking his practice to Bloomington. While in upstate New York, Spencer became a principal in a few local enterprises before taking an interest in the Utica & Rochester Railroad, which ultimately became an integral part of the New York Central (NYC). He was also involved in the early formation of the American Express Company.[46]

▾▾▾

The Litchfield-provided rail arrived in spring 1854, and tracklaying resumed. Moving steadily toward one another, crews worked from dawn to dusk. By the end of July, the two sets of rails were joined at a point between Lexington and the Kankakee River.[47] On Monday morning, July 31, 1854, the first train destined all the way to Chicago departed from Alton's depot.[48] The engine, baggage car, coaches, and house car moved steadily north at a brisk 20 mph, making all stops, including those for exchange of engines and for wood and water, through to Joliet. There, a cheering welcoming party met the train to the accompaniment of ceremonial cannon fire. In the early evening hours, the

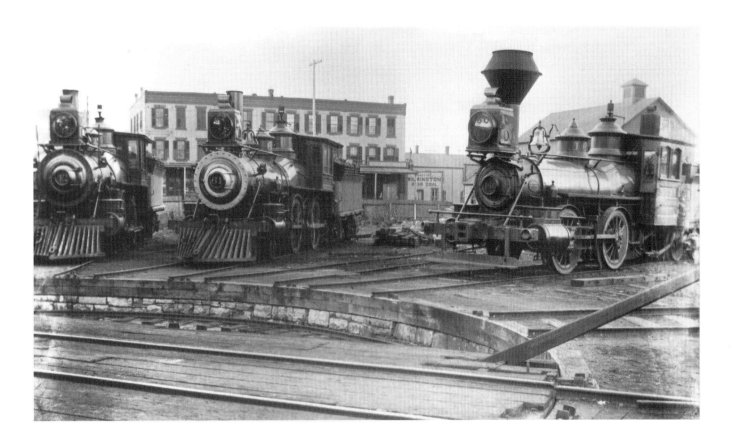

train moved onto the C&RI. The engine's headlight illuminated the right-of-way through open prairie east, then north, to Chicago. Twelve hours after leaving Alton, the train slowly pulled into the Rock Island's Chicago depot. No special ceremony attended the train's arrival. Its consist was just another among the city's more than 100 daily arrivals.

Freight trains, however, at first did not run through to Chicago; they terminated at Joliet. The expected agreement with the C&RI allowing through freight service had not yet been reached. Instead short siding was laid to the I&M canal landing where Chicago-bound traffic was transferred. From there boats took freight upstream to Chicago's elevators and warehouses. Freight destined for the East, as planned, was interchanged with the J&N, the Joliet Cutoff, control of which had passed to the MC.[49]

After the first few months of operation, freight began piling up in Joliet, both at the company's freight house and at the canal's landing. An estimated 1,000 freight cars could have been filled with the awaiting freight. Along with the wheat, corn, and more than

130 other commodities being brought up from the South and from the western parts of the state, freight brought to Joliet by the railroad filled every boat making a run to Chicago.[50]

Just as the opening of the canal a decade earlier had reversed the flow of farm produce from south to north throughout the Illinois River Basin, the opening of the railroad from Alton to Joliet had the same result for farmers in the central part of the state. Their grains, corn, oats, and flax were brought to Chicago markets and purchased by eastern buyers and, increasingly, by agents for European interests, anxious for all the product Illinois farmers could deliver. Chicago slaughter houses too found ready buyers for the best parts of the sheep, cattle, and hogs the railroad brought them. Finished goods, such as farm equipment from McCormick's Reaper Company, became highly evident in southbound trains. So too were carloads of Michigan lumber, headed for Bloomington, Springfield, and other towns along the main line devoid of timber. Through traffic for St. Louis and beyond was initially shared with the Rock Island, which

Three of the C&A's early engine types (4-4-0s nos. 42 and 61 and 0-4-0 switcher no. 160) await assignment opposite the Joliet roundhouse located at Chicago Street between Washington and Lafayette Streets in the 1880s. The sales office of the Wilmington Star Coal Co., one of the early Braidwood Coal Region's producers, is in the background. (Courtesy of Lewis University Canal and Regional History Coll., Bill Molony Coll.)

delivered goods to riverboats, but once that road crossed the Mississippi into Iowa and steamboat frequencies on the Mississippi decreased, C&M St. Louis–bound loads dramatically increased.[51]

Chicago was enjoying amazing growth and prosperity that overshadowed that of any other Illinois municipality or, for that matter, nearly any other American city. More than 2,200 miles of track terminated there, and at least 100 passenger trains and numerous freight movements were arriving or departing daily; not one passed through the city. In just a few years, railroads had captured nearly all of the available traffic save that brought in on the canal. Chicago newspapers stopped reporting tonnage brought in by drayage because so little of it still existed. The city's grain elevators and wharves were bulging with grains and its warehouses with freight. Chicago factories were producing considerable quantities of farm machinery, railroad equipment, finished marble and stone, carriages and wagons, furniture, and items such as shoes and clothing. Lumber was being brought to the city in increased volumes—in 1855 estimated to be more than 306 million board feet. Chicago had no equal as a producer of goods or market for crops throughout the vast area of the western states. The city's commerce was worth $20 million, nearly half the state's $42.3 million. Its population had reached an estimated 50,000.[52]

Through Chicago depots passed passengers headed east, west, north, and south. In April 1855 a 22-car MS train brought in more than 1,000 passengers. MC trains were credited with similar loads.[53] If the newly arrived travelers were continuing their journeys beyond, they would make their weary and somewhat confused trek between stations on foot, usually carrying what they owned in a few hand cases. Sometimes the most treacherous part of their journey was spent fending off the thieves and pickpockets lining the wooden walks between stations, waiting to separate the newcomers from their valuables.

With the arrival of railroads, downstate Illinois communities too began experiencing rapid growth, and new settlements began springing up almost overnight. In 1840 the combined populations of the portion of LaSalle County that later became Grundy County, plus all of Livingston and McLean Counties, totaled just 7,324, with 90 percent of that population located in McLean County, principally in the vicinity of Bloomington. A year after the opening of the railroad, 31,205 were counted in the three counties, with 63 percent living in McLean County but over 4,600 taking up residence in Livingston County and some 7,000 in Grundy County (mostly along the Rock Island at Morris, but in increasing numbers along the C&M). Cayuga, Chenoa, Pontiac, and Odell, all in Livingston County, were platted in 1855, as was Dwight (very close to the Livingston-Grundy county lines).[54] Many new arrivals were drawn to Illinois as the result of the extensive advertising for cheap, fertile farm land the IC placed in East Coast, English, and European newspapers. To be sure, the IC benefited the most from its promotions, but other railroads drew settlers to its territories as well.[55]

Amid the growing population and increased production of the state's farms and growing industries, it seemed improbable that the railroad should be anything other than a thriving company. Lee's estimate two years earlier that revenues, once the railroad was opened to Joliet, should reach $1.5 million had almost been achieved. During the 12-month period of August 1854 to July 1855, revenues totaled over $1 million, but the line's expenses exceeded revenue by $600,000, leaving nothing for interest payments or dividends.[56]

The shortfall in revenues and extraordinary expenses were a result of one of the worst winters in Illinois's recorded history and the start of a serious downturn in the economy. The autumn of 1854 had been extremely dry. In the northern portion of the state, fierce storms arose without warning but brought only damaging winds and hail rather than rain. The last moisture to fall in the southern and central portions of the state came in June, and the corn crop in those areas was a near total failure. Water levels on the Mississippi at Alton were among the lowest remembered in 20 years. These conditions persisted until the middle of January 1855, when snow began falling throughout the Great Lakes area and as far south as St. Louis. Snow continued to fall for several days until accumulations at Chicago measured two feet. Temperatures at night dropped to minus 30 degrees there, and similar low readings were experienced across the state's northern tier. Springfield saw two feet of snow build up, and Carlinville recorded a foot of accumulated snow. Both places noted unusually cold temperatures. For four days the C&M (as well as most of state's other railroads) suffered nearly complete shutdown.[57]

On the fifth day after the storm, the first train in a week reached Alton from Springfield: four engines pulling four coaches that held 300 passengers. More than a week passed, however, before the first train from the north entered the capital.[58] The Joliet-Bloomington segment had become totally blocked by ice and snow. A seven-car Chicago-Alton train had started out on Monday, January 22, yet after two days of effort had only reached a point six miles beyond Dwight before getting stuck in drifts. The train had about 150 passengers aboard, including 30 legislators headed to Springfield for resumption of a session of the General Assembly.[59] The coaches were left abandoned when the engineer decided to move the engine before it ran out of wood and water. Stranded, the passengers and crew grew increasingly worried they may not be rescued. They did not know that the engineer went about eight miles south to tiny Odell before his engine stalled.[60]

In desperation, a courageous man volunteered to leave the train to find help. He trudged through thigh-high snow accumulations northwest for about 20 miles before reaching the Rock Island depot at Morris. The astonished depot agent sat the weary hero next to the station's stove and then sent a telegram to Hickox, the railroad's agent at Springfield, that described the stranded passengers' desperate condition. Meanwhile, aboard the abandoned cars, another passenger left the train using the raised surface of the track's grade as a guide for reaching a town. He plowed nearly 20 miles through heavy, high drifts before reaching Pontiac—alive, but with near-frozen legs.

Railroad officials responded by dispatching an engine north with food and water that brought the first relief to the stranded. Fresh engines, with laborers aboard to dig a path, were sent up from Bloomington. The engines

and crew finally reached the stranded passengers seven days after their train had left Chicago. It took another full day before the train made it to Springfield.[61] This was certainly the most dramatic incident resulting from that winter's fury, but there were other similarly harrowing experiences up and down the line.

The railroad had not recovered from the January storms before new snow and falling temperatures arrived in early February. Again the railroad shut down. The Chicago post office had more than 100 tons of mail stored, destined for Springfield and St. Louis.[62] Freight had built up at all points and hotels, inns, and private homes along the line were filled with stranded travelers. Seventeen engines, nearly half the railroad's roster, and their consists were stuck in drifts between Joliet and Carlinville, three of them five miles north of the capital with another two stalled three miles south of there.[63] The light engines simply could not cope; none had snow plows, which in any case would have been useless in fighting the drifts, given the snow's depth and the engines' limited power.

The crisis did not subside until warmer March temperatures brought a quick melt, but then a new challenge arose as the runoff filled the state's rivers and streams. Water levels on the Mississippi at Alton rose seven feet and strayed from the river's banks. The Wilmington bridge was badly damaged by freshets and floating debris that had built up on the Kankakee River.[64] Eventually, engines and equipment were re-railed and repaired. After months of work on the track, bridges, and culverts, relatively normal operations were resumed, but nearly all of the line from Joliet to Carlinville had suffered severely. More than $200,000 first quarter revenues had been lost, and about the same sum in extraordinary weather-related expenses were incurred. It was a staggering loss that only added to the growing financial woes of the company.[65]

▼▼▼

As a result of the unrelenting storms, few General Assembly members could reach Springfield for the scheduled January start of the 1856 session. It was early February before a quorum was finally mustered. In that session, two bills were passed affecting the company. The first was passage of the amendment allowing the C&M and TH&A joint operations at Alton.

This amendment, in the eyes of J&C president, David Woodson, interfered with his road's progress. Woodson acknowledged the right of the General Assembly to grant the running agreement but once again raised the issue of Alton's earlier opposition to his railroad's appeal for investment. He was convinced Alton's obstructionist stance had undermined his company's ability to raise the capital he needed to start construction. Not a spade of dirt had been turned for his road. In his view, once construction was begun, the funds needed for the extension beyond Alton to Illinoistown could have been quickly raised with the expectation of greater traffic since his road would have been the first to run south of Alton to Illinoistown.[66] Woodson had a point, but more relevant was the tight money situation the nation sustained in 1854–1855 that made it all but impossible for such a modestly ambitious project as his to compete for funds. The J&C had been projected to cost $1.2 million, excluding the Illinoistown extension. By March 1855 $100,000 had been pledged by individuals, and $150,000 by Green, Jersey, and Morgan Counties, but only the first 5 percent, or $11,100, was in the treasury, and $2,500 of that had been consumed by corporation start-up costs.[67] Woodson had bigger obstacles to hurdle than being cut out of an extension beyond Alton.

The other legislative action—naturally opposed since it meant added expenses most railroads could ill afford—required fences to be erected along rights-of-way within six months of the bill's passage—action prompted by the growing outrage of farmers and ranchers whose wandering livestock were being destroyed by trains.[68] The most vexing problem engine crews faced during the earliest days of railroad operations was that of livestock lingering on the track. The light engines usually derailed, often taking a car or two with them, when they hit a farm animal. The killing of wandering livestock became almost a daily occurrence, as did injury or death of railroad crews. For instance, during a period of a few weeks in the fall of 1855, two

cows were struck somewhat south of Lincoln, the engine and baggage car were derailed, both of the engineer's arms were broken as a result of the collision, and the wood handler and fireman were killed; a train from Alton hit a cow north of Carlinville, resulting in the fireman being killed, the wood handler sustaining serious injuries, and the engineer having both his legs broken; a wood train running in reverse to Lick Creek ran into a cow at Chatham, causing the death of one trainman, the injury of several others, and the shattering of four cars filled with wood. One observer suggested the problem was so prevalent that if section men did not bury the destroyed livestock as they passed over their track sections, areas along the tracks would become an "odorous and unmistakable boneyard."[69]

The company was slow to comply with the new fencing legislation. Superintendent Morgan pleaded with nearby farmers for patience, asserting that the railroad didn't have the funds to fence its entire right-of-way, but his claim was challenged by at least one newspaper editor who estimated that fencing 300 miles of right-of-way would equal the cost of constructing 10 miles of track and that the railroad undoubtedly had incurred expenses associated with the accidents far in excess of the cost of erecting the fences.[70] None of these assertions were substantiated but did reflect public perception that the railroad little cared. Wood and wire fences were erected along those sections where livestock was most likely to wander, but it was a token gesture. Lawsuits filed by farmers claiming livestock losses began piling up in the company offices at Bloomington.

By mid-1855 CA&St.L traffic had resumed near-normal levels, and most stations were once again reporting solid business. In just one week, for instance, the railroad delivered at Springfield 125 carloads of lumber; 275 McCormick reapers; and large shipments of lime, coal, and general merchandise. After harvest Springfield-area farmers shipped an estimated 450,000 bushels of wheat and 90,000 bushels of corn over the railroad to Chicago.[71] Similar inbound and outbound figures were recorded at Carlinville, Bloomington, Lincoln, and other farming centers. Business was thriving, but the ultimate goal of reaching Chicago over company rails had not yet been achieved. With an already burdensome debt load, it was impossible for management to consider it, so it was left to others.

A day after the bill allowing the CA&St.L trackage rights to Illinoistown was passed, and on the last day of the Nineteenth General Assembly, February 15, 1855, a charter in the name of the Joliet & Chicago Railroad (J&C) was issued, authorizing an origination at the "Chicago & Mississippi" depot in Joliet, passing through Lockport and continuing on to Chicago.[72] The route along the banks of the canal was the same as what had been considered but rejected as the IC's entry into Chicago after opposition—led by John Wentworth's *Chicago Democrat*—was raised.[73]

The principal town between Joliet and Chicago was Lockport. Until canal construction had started in earnest and Lockport was named headquarters for the canal corporation, the place was merely a collection of a few cabins, known as Runyon Town. As canal headquarters, Lockport became a place of some importance. The town's hotel and hardware and clothing stores enjoyed good business, as did its several taverns. Norton's grist mill, built adjacent to the canal, became the town's principal enterprise.[74]

Joliet was originally settled by Yankees, principally from the Adirondack area of New York State. They opened retail stores and small businesses along Des Plaines Street, on the river's east bank, and with the opening of the C&RI's line between LaSalle and Chicago, the city became the most important town in Will County. An iron foundry was started on Joliet's west side along Bluff Street. It soon attracted other businesses and tradesmen to support it. From the first few hundred who settled there, Joliet's population by 1850 had risen to over 2,600 and was steadily growing. There were almost as many living there as there were at Lockport, where 2,900 resided.[75]

Having seen what railroads were doing for other towns (especially rival Joliet), Lockport's leading citizens decided they too needed a railroad to ensure Lockport's position as a place of growth and importance. During 1853 and 1854, several meetings were held in the canal's office and in the homes of the town's most prominent citizens, where plans were drawn to relieve Lockport's sole dependency on the canal.

Although they had considerable and varied business experience, Lockport's leaders recognized that they knew little about building a railroad and less about running one. They also lacked any particular political skills necessary to guide legislation through the General Assembly. For all three talents, they turned to a man with local roots and statewide power, Illinois's governor, Joel Matteson. They were confident that if he could be persuaded to accept the job, Lockport would get its railroad. Matteson, a native of upstate New York, had moved west during the speculative early 1830s and joined in the wild buying and selling of land in Chicago. In 1836 he wisely sold his real estate holdings at their highly inflated prices—avoiding the fate that befell so many others who lost everything in the collapse of 1837—and moved his family to Will County in the vicinity of a place then named Juliet.

Matteson was quickly recognized as one of the settlement's more enterprising citizens. He became involved in a variety of businesses and civic pursuits. He bid on and won a contract to dig a portion of the canal, then became part owner of a packet, the *Prairie Bird*. When the Rock Island sought contractors for laying tracks east of Joliet, Matteson won a contract and laid a major portion of the line. With the profits from his successes, Matteson opened a water-powered woolen mill on the east side of the river, south of Jefferson Street. Within five years of its founding in 1845, the Matteson & Bradner mill was producing 3,000 yards of cloth a day and had become Joliet's largest industry. He also founded the Merchants and Drovers Bank, Joliet's first. Matteson was a driving force behind the J&N, making Joliet competitive with Chicago for eastbound freight. He joined with Nelson Elwood, a former official of the Rock Island and later mayor of Joliet, in supervising construction of the 45-mile line and presided over its opening in 1855.

But it was politics that soon claimed his interest. He was named president of the public meeting that led to incorporation of Joliet. Later, in 1842, he ran for the state senate to which he was elected as the representative of Du Page, Iroquois, and Will Counties. There he served as chairman of the powerful Senate Finance Committee. After ten years as a senator, Matteson was elected governor, assuming office in January 1853. Though he initiated few programs, he was considered an able and efficient chief executive. He looked after his hometown by ensuring the new state prison was located on a site just north of Joliet. He also continued to expand his private interests while in office. He added banks at Marion, Quincy, Shawneetown, Peoria, and Bloomington to his Merchants and Drovers.[76]

Though the Lockport organizers may well have thought their railroad could be self-sustaining, Matteson knew better. Beyond Lockport there was not another town of any consequence until Bridgeport was reached. He knew the J&C's only hope of success was to serve as the extension the CA&St.L needed to reach Chicago. It was no doubt Matteson who proposed that the company assign its engineering staff to a survey and then build the railroad in return for a guaranteed 8 percent above costs payment. His proposal was quickly accepted. The CA&St.L's chief engineer, Henry Gardner, took personal charge and began a survey in the spring of 1855, finishing his report the following March.

When it was realized that the extension was to be built and eventually to be taken over by the CA&St.L, some downstaters objected. They saw spending of any of the company's resources on expansion as a mistake. They felt all resources should be poured back into the existing line between Alton and Joliet, improving it to enhance profits and provide dividends. The *Chicago Press,* a Democratic paper, came to Matteson's defense, pointing out that the more circuitous routing into the city via the Rock Island was actually costing the company money. The editor suggested that a shorter route would increase profits and lead to dividend payments.[77] No doubt Matteson, a prominent Democrat, had something to do with the article.

In fact, there were limited CA&St.L resources applied to the new venture. The detrimental effects of the horrendous weather of the previous winter were still being felt. While spring and summer business proved strong, expenses were running at a much higher rate than had been anticipated. Short of funds, the right-of-way had been repaired only where needed, not replaced, and operations suffered. The road's equipment and power were taking considerable abuse, requiring frequent repair and replacement, running up higher-than-expected costs. The short, frequent trains that were operated, resulting from inefficient operations, racked up excessive fuel and crew costs.

By the autumn of 1856, the CA&St.L's fortunes were in a desperate state. The situation became so bad that when payments on the bonded debt came due in September, only the $70,000 interest owed on the first mortgage was paid; the interest owed on the second and third mortgages were not addressed. Now workers' wages were being skipped, and supplier bills began to pile up. Though it seemed evident the railroad should make a profit, it did not.[78]

The public began expressing its dissatisfaction with the way the railroad was being managed, and their views began appearing in print. The first newspaper to raise the issue was Springfield's *Illinois State Register.*

> We have repeatedly heard it said that the Chicago, Alton & St. Louis railroad does not pay well. Indeed, some of the original stockholders have never been able to understand how it has been managed. We perfectly comprehend that the company has had great difficulties to surmount; that it is largely in debt; and that the best management is required to carry it through and sustain its credit. All this seems to be perfectly understood. At the same time public opinion is fixed upon these points, that it is one of the best, if not the best, railroad route in the state, and that the road ought to pay well,—that its stocks and its bonds would be as good in market as the best railroad stocks and securities in the Union.[79]

The paper published five more critical reports, in increasingly vitriolic tone. The *St. Louis Republican* jumped in and added its negative views.

> There are no practical western business men having a controlling influence on the road. It seems to be a sort of concern which cousins and nephews and hangers on are sent out west to manage. What is wanted to give confidence to the public and to the business men in regard to this road, is to place in its management prac-

tical business men. A radical reform in the management of this road is demanded by many of the stockholders, and the public feel that such reform would greatly benefit its owners and the community. What is wanted, we repeat, is practical men, to manage the business of the road.[80]

The *Illinois State Register* later flatly stated that "affairs can never be better under the present management" and called for it to be replaced. Singled out for particular criticism was the company's superintendent, Richard Morgan, Jr.[81] Morgan had assumed his duties from Keating the previous summer. Just 26, he was young and really had no management experience and limited railroading experience. Arguably, the road's early management was poor, but so was the hastily built physical plant, which caused slow and unsafe operations, hampering any manager's ability to run an efficient operation. Inexperienced workers under less-than-exacting supervision, poorly built and maintained track, limited power and rolling stock, and inexact dispatching all played a part in bringing about the road's declining situation.

These deficiencies and the neglect of farmers and ranchers to corral their livestock contributed to the continued high instances of accidents. During a six-month period in 1855, there were numerous accidents on the road. Two trains collided at Pontiac, resulting in damage to the engines but luckily resulting in no injuries. Two months later a southbound train hit three cattle at Atlanta. The impact was so great that a rail was loosened and ripped through the floor of one of the coaches. Surprisingly, no one on board was killed. Two weeks later a freight train, three miles south of Joliet, ran over a cow, resulting in a derailed tender and 12 cars. On the same August night, two northbound freights, one 12 miles south and the other 4 miles north of Springfield, derailed. A few nights later, a northbound passenger train hit several cattle at the Sangamon River but proceeded on. Later a southbound freight ran over the carcasses and derailed, resulting in the destruction of two freight cars. Another southbound freight near Sugar Creek ran over several horses. Again several cars were destroyed. In December a dispatcher sent two trains against each other, and when they reached Pontiac,

they had a head-on collision, disrupting schedules for more than ten hours. A day later a passenger train ran off the tracks at Chicago, causing damage to the engine.[82] Few could wonder why the public and newspaper editors were giving Morgan grief.

▾▾▾

Criticism of Morgan's management, though justified, missed the point. It was Henry Dwight who should have been targeted as the cause of the CA&St.L's crisis. It was his fraudulent, reckless wheeling and dealing, more than Morgan's presumed ineptitude, that was the real problem. Morgan, however, was visible; Dwight was not and, because of Dwight, Godfrey's personal finances were a mess. After the Metropolitan Bank took over Dwight's holdings in March, the bank initiated foreclosure proceeding on Godfrey's property. The bank claimed his house, farmlands, and investments, all of which had been pledged as collateral for Dwight's loan. Godfrey's appeals to Dwight to stave off the action got him nowhere. "I believe you admitted the justice of my having the disposal of my own property," he wrote to Dwight. "I cannot consent to have (my) property sold for a paltry sum of a few thousand dollars, at least not until after a settlement has taken place between us, which you know I have been endeavoring to obtain for the last two years."[83]

Dwight could not have cared less about Godfrey's plight and ignored him. He had bigger problems to deal with. He still needed money, and lots of it. He initiated more raids on the company's treasury. Without any authority whatsoever, he offered $24,000 of the company's third mortgage "income bonds" to a personal creditor. A few months later, he converted $30,000 more of the income bonds series for his personal use, again without any board approval. These were the same securities he was charged with holding and disposing of for the benefit of the company as a member of the Executive and Finance Committee. But he wasn't finished. He got the board to pass a resolution making the company liable for payment of his note for the insurance on rail that had been received. This would have been proper had the same payment to the insurance company not already been made the previous March. Dwight also pocketed an insurance payment owed William Swinburne.[84]

With everyone in an official capacity subject to him and having no one to object to his actions, Dwight continued his theft. His brother Edmund had earlier submitted a voucher for a payment that had come due for spikes and tie plates. Dwight now submitted a $9,803 voucher for the identical claim; he pocketed the money. Dwight didn't stop there. He next got the board to approve payment of $11,721 for Dwight's personal promissory notes to nine creditors who had participated in the $800,000 loan.[85] Dwight was robbing the company blind, abetted by his handpicked cronies.

Dwight continued to harass his avowed enemies, the Litchfields. When the notes securing $150,000 of the $300,000 NI loan came due in April 1855, Dwight concocted an excuse to avoid the payment. He charged that the NI had negotiated some of these notes to other parties; thus he wasn't obligated to pay them.[86] Knowing full well that his actions, or those of the board, would compel the Litchfields to seek legal redress, Dwight initiated three preemptive civil actions against NI officials in May and, incredibly, obtained an injunction prohibiting the NI from prosecuting. Dwight claimed fraud and usury were employed to get him to sign his agreement with the Litchfields.[87]

Dwight went public with his charges in a letter published in New York newspapers. Within a few days, his charges were persuasively answered by Elisha Litchfield, so convincingly, in fact, that newly appointed treasurer Samuel Blatchford found it impossible to negotiate for short-term financing.[88] The financial houses could not separate Dwight's personal transactions from the company's and decided they wanted nothing further to do with Dwight or his railroad. By now Dwight's personal creditors realized he was a fraud, and they filed suit to recover what he owed them.

Desperate for cash for the railroad, Blatchford returned to the City Bank and County Bank of Hartford and the Merchants' Bank in New Haven for a short-term loan of $50,000. The banks were willing to invest further but attached two conditions: three of their own had to be appointed to the board, and the board would have to be expanded to nine members. They were no longer willing to tolerate the outrageous moves of Dwight and his cronies. Reluctantly, Dwight acceded to the bankers' demands but hurriedly began another raid of the company's treasury before he lost control.[89] Dwight could have used more time to further steal from the company, but the clock had stopped ticking, at least for the time being.

To accommodate the banks' new appointments, Dwight and Gould (no longer treasurer but still a director and the last of Litchfield's appointments) relinquished their chairs to make room for the banks' representatives. At the annual election of directors, held in Bloomington in June 1855, the board was expanded to nine. Elected were Seabury Brewster, Henry Young, and William Smith to join Hotchkiss as the New Haven banks' choices to look after their interests; Uriah Smith and James Low, independent New York businessmen the New York banks trusted; James Wright of the Oswego Bank; and Spencer and Blatchford as officials of the railroad. From their ranks the board elected Brewster president. Spencer remained vice president; Blatchford, treasurer; and Alexander, secretary. It was the most professional board of directors the company had yet seen.

With the apparent takeover by responsible business people, the New Haven banks were reassured and advanced needed short term money, about $55,000, to ease the CA&St.L's immediate cash crunch. The caliber of men that now made up the board and the exclusion of Dwight from the company's affairs somewhat renewed the confidence of other lenders. In late July Blatchford found more willing to lend short-term capital, and the cash crisis eased.

Spencer, based in Bloomington and having full responsibility for running the railroad, was sending optimistic reports to the new directors. In late August 1855, he stated that the company's revenues would "not fall short of $1.5 million, and would probably reach $1.6 million." He promised the operating ratio (the difference between revenues and expenses) would not exceed 55 percent.[90] Spencer, supported by Hotchkiss and Blatchford, urged the new directors to purchase the company's authorized, but not yet issued, preferred stock.

With the proceeds Blatchford's plan was to pay off the current liabilities and retire a portion of the long-term debt at more favorable rates. Hotchkiss, leading the effort to sell the preferred shares, had some success.

Meanwhile, Morgan saw to the property's repair. Throughout the first nine months of 1855, track undermined by the severe winter's frost; bridge pilings and footings hammered by ice sheets—especially at Wilmington's Kankakee River; and structures whose roofs bore the burden of heavy snow were given first attention. It took several months to finish the work. The chronic car shortages (though new cars were being received almost weekly) left freight waiting at stations all along the line. The engines that had frozen up during the January and February storms were shopped; however, though Swinburne was delivering new motive power on a regular basis, a power shortage persisted. Too many short trains had to be operated. With too few and infrequent sidings, trains often stood idle at stations, sometimes for hours, waiting for clearance. Because of the tight cash situation, paydays for shop workers and train crews were being skipped, and when wages were paid, workers found company scrip in their envelopes instead of cash. What Morgan confronted was not what Spencer was reporting.

Though ostensibly removed from any official company role while the new board was trying to correct the past mistakes and current emergencies, Dwight was engaged in new intrigue. He was relentless in suggesting to the independent board members plans and projects he claimed would bring new strength to the company. He hinted he was in negotiations with John Forbes—a wealthy financier who had interests in both the MC and the Chicago, Burlington & Quincy (CB&Q) and who was a son-in-law of William Astor—and John Phelps, both wealthy New Yorkers.[91] The more responsible members of the board attempted to dissuade Dwight, but he would not listen. When Dwight realized that the company's directors were not his minions but men of conservatism and integrity who would not roll over for him, he decided on a different tack. Hotchkiss and Spencer were still his allies—it was with them that he began holding secret meetings. Neither Hotchkiss nor Spencer disclosed to the others what was discussed or even that meetings occurred.

Dwight decided guerrilla action rather than a frontal assault was needed this time. He would go after the directors, like a sniper, picking them off one by one. His first prey was Young, who, after his election, took an extended holiday in Europe, leaving with Blatchford a signed letter of resignation in the event it was needed in his absence.[92] Dwight learned of the letter through his co-conspirators and somehow persuaded Blatchford to turn it over to him. Then he went after Uriah Smith and persuaded him to give him a letter of resignation. He then approached William Smith and Low and promised them if they would resign, he would see to it that men "of standing and wealth" would replace them. Both agreed.[93] With four resignations and Hotchkiss and Spencer safely in his pocket, Dwight had the majority he needed, remarkably, to take control again.

The next scheduled board meeting took place August 31, in the company's William Street offices with Brewster, Spencer, Hotchkiss, Low, Blatchford, and William Smith attending. As the first order of business, Smith resigned as promised, and Dwight was nominated to replace him. Low then resigned. Hotchkiss nominated a man whose "standing and wealth" was that of "a painter of miniatures," Henry Shumway. Surprising to everyone but Dwight, Hotchkiss, and Spencer, Shumway was just outside the room and immediately took his seat. Dwight then presented Uriah Smith's resignation and nominated another of "standing and wealth," his clerk, Quintard. He too was waiting in the wings and took his seat. Dwight then handed over Young's resignation and nominated his friend, William Platt. He too was seated.[94] Now sitting around the table were five Dwight appointees plus Hotchkiss and two "outsiders," Brewster and Blatchford. Incredibly, all had gone exactly as Dwight had planned. In less than 15 minutes, he was once again in control. He was now poised to launch his most audacious attack on the company's creditors.[95]

Dwight rose and immediately began reading a lease of the railroad he suggested was submitted by Spencer but was actually created by Dwight himself during his secret meetings. When he finished, Brewster vigorously opposed the scheme, but Dwight's appointees, except for Spencer, who had left the room while the lease was presented, voted acceptance. Brewster was the lone dissenter.[96] Only 15 minutes more were spent on the matter, and the meeting was adjourned. It had taken just a half hour for Dwight to regain control of the board and to transfer ownership of the railroad over to Spencer.

What had Dwight presented, and what were the reasons for it? The Spencer Lease, as it became known, turned all the company's assets over to Spencer without a single stipulation protecting the bondholders, stockholders, or creditors. Spencer could terminate the lease whenever he decided to within the 20 next years, but the equity owners had no similar rights. Spencer was to receive all revenues, and he alone could decide their disbursement. The rights of security holders and the claims of creditors, except one, were made subordinate to the Spencer Lease. Hotchkiss, during the secret meetings, secured assurances that his personal investment and that of his County Bank of New Haven would be repaid. There was no similar provisions for the other Connecticut banks whose interests he was supposed to protect.

Spencer was to pay the semiannual interest on the 10 percent income bonds and the semiannual interest on the 7 percent first mortgage bonds coming due in October, plus the past due interest on the first, second, and third mortgage bonds. He also was to pay all future interest on the three bond issues and payment of what had become known as the Illinois Debt (a portion of the current liabilities). Out of net earnings, he was to pay Brown Brothers $223,696 to satisfy its participation in the $800,000 financing. In return the railroad was to receive $100,000 annually for the first three years, $125,000 for the fourth year, $150,000 for the fifth, $175,000 for the sixth, and $200,000 for every year thereafter, up to the 20-year life of the lease.[97]

Of course, the entire transfer was a sham. Spencer did not personally have the funds to make the stipulated payments. Since he could charge almost anything as an operating expense, earnings could be reduced or eliminated altogether, jeopardizing payment of the indebted interest as well as the annual fees for ownership. In truth, the three conspirators—Dwight, Spencer, and Hotchkiss—never intended to see any payments other than to themselves made. The sole reason the lease was initiated was to give Dwight, through Spencer, unchallenged access to the road's treasury.

Within days Dwight went back to Brown Brothers for an advance of $150,000, supported by the lease. It was insufficient collateral for Brown Brothers to accept, so Dwight assigned to the firm the mortgage on his palatial $100,000 Dutchess County, New York, estate.[98] With reluctance and knowing nothing of the lease's legitimacy—but not seeing another way to recover its previous investment—the firm consented to the loan. When word of Dwight's latest ploy reached them, the bondholders, stockholders, and creditors were astounded at Dwight's audacity. The officers of the City and Merchants' Banks of New Haven and the Phoenix Bank of Hartford could not believe that Dwight had actually driven their representatives, except for Hotchkiss, off the board and that Hotchkiss was a knowing and willing accomplice in this latest treachery.

Dwight was confronted at a meeting the bankers requested seeking an explanation of the lease. "You have been all along estimating the future earnings of the road at from 12 to 15 hundred thousand dollars per annum, what becomes of the very large amount of income which will remain undisposed of by the terms of the lease?" Dwight answered: "That is a matter between Mr. Spencer and myself. He was unwilling to take a lease unless it was so left, but he will do with it as I shall direct. He is an honorable man, and will do right." Later Dwight told Gould, quite openly, that he, Dwight, "should not and would not thereafter be in want of money"; that the railroad would "yield enough from which Spencer would receive all the money he should want and at such time as he wanted it"; and that the "entire control of the railroad and its receipts were in Spencer's hands" and he would, in all things relating to the railroad and its affairs, do as Dwight wished.[99]

Back in Illinois there were immediate cries of swindle. Where did Dwight get the right to essentially give away the railroad? Who but Spencer and Dwight would benefit? Locals questioned whether this was just another example of how the eastern capitalists took advantage of the West. From the earliest days of the company's formation, Illinoisans knew the railroad would be finished only with the help of eastern capital. And so it was. But no one imagined how debilitating the process would be.

Dwight began enjoying the spoils of the Spencer Lease almost immediately. Boldly, he confessed to Blatchford that Spencer had paid him the tidy sum of $10,000 although the Bloomington books reflected this payment as having been made to Blatchford (which, of course, was not the case). Another $5,000 payment to Dwight was made a month later, and it can be asserted from other bogus Bloomington entries that Dwight received continued generous payments.[100] Dwight also took care of his friends. He got sizable payments authorized for Platt for his term as president of the company back in 1852–1853 and for Hotchkiss for his two years of service as a director. He further got the board to satisfy Hotchkiss's personal loan to the company, as secretly promised, through transfer to him of title to the company's two steamboats, the *Winchester* and the *Reindeer*.[101]

The plundering continued for several more months before the creditors, led by the New Haven and Hartford banks, who had seen no payments on any of their mortgages since execution of the lease, finally stepped in to void the Spencer Lease. Two justices of the New York Supreme Court were consulted about the lease's validity. Among their findings was the conclusion that the lease was a "gross fraud upon the creditors of the company and also upon the stockholders [who] did not assent to the transaction"; that there was no question that the lessee was "liable to indictment"; and that the "directors of the company as were present and assented to the transaction" were "parties to the conveyance . . . and may be indicted as such." The distinguished jurists also offered the opinion that "the lessee and such of the directors may also be indicted for a conspiracy to defraud creditors and other persons. They conspired together to commit a criminal offence."[102]

When Elisha Litchfield read the opinion, he was eager to see Dwight and his cronies put behind bars. He filed a complaint against Dwight and Spencer in December 1855 for fraud and conspiracy, and an indictment against the two

was issued by a grand jury. Unfortunately for Litchfield, New York state statutes had been changed the year before, giving jurisdiction over such matters to the court of special sessions and not to a grand jury. Thus the district attorney, A. Oakley Hall, was forced to void the complaint. He explained his action in an attachment to the judgment but added that he had voided it "not because I believe the facts are defective."[103] Dwight and Spencer had dodged a bullet.

Neither the grand jury's indictment nor public shame stopped Dwight from continuing his raid on the company. In early January 1856, just 18 days after the indictment had been rendered, Dwight called a meeting of the company's board and boldly confessed that he had taken $54,000 of income mortgage bonds for his own use. His confession was no doubt prompted by Blatchford, the only one besides Brewster who possessed any sense of propriety. Dwight offered as restitution a recall of $24,000 of the bonds, which the board accepted, but whatever came of the matter remained a mystery. After the meeting Blatchford never found the board's resolution in the company records.[104]

While Spencer and Dwight were raiding the treasury, the fury of Illinois's 1856 winter added to the CA&St.L's troubles. The weather became so bad that the railroad was again nearly shut down. For 67 days up to 10 inches of snow was recorded at Chicago with temperatures of minus 20 degrees. Accumulations between Bloomington and Joliet were measured in feet. Despite considerable effort to keep tracks open, weary crews had little success until nearly the end of February. As was the case the previous winter, the engines could not break through the mounting, drifting snow. Shutdowns for periods of from a day up to a week disrupted traffic.[105] Numerous harrowing reports of stranded trains and frozen equipment came into the Bloomington offices, just as they had the winter before. Again the railroad suffered severe losses of income and mounting weather-related expenses. The *Chicago Tribune* reported, "The road has suffered more than any other entering this city."[106]

The winter storms, the strike, and everything going on in New York were too much for Morgan, and in the spring of 1856 he resigned as superintendent. In May, Asa Moore, formerly an assistant superintendent on the MS who had been brought to Bloomington by Bliss in 1854 as assistant superintendent, was appointed Morgan's replacement. Moore was the first superintendent of the CA&St.L to have actual prior railroad management experience but was to be given denial of the resources he needed to keep the railroad running. Moore had little more success than Morgan.

Before long Dwight concocted a final, preposterous scheme intended to liquidate the last remaining asset of the company: its franchise. Hotchkiss presented the obedient directors with a resolution that assigned the entire "corporate property, franchises and effects subject in all respects to the Spencer Lease" to three trustees. The deed of trust provided that if the company did not pay all of its debt in a timely fashion—including debt from the 20 years of the Spencer Lease—the trustees could take possession of the company within 60 days and initiate steps for the company's sale.[107]

Spencer had no intention of fulfilling the payment provisions of the lease. The assignment was clearly devised to blatantly use the company's resources to relieve Dwight of his obligations, including his personal debt of nearly a quarter million dollars owed Brown Brothers and the myriad of other personal and company obligations he had incurred (and those of Hotchkiss)—a sum now totaling some $575,000. If anything was left after the company's sale, those proceeds would be divided among the creditors.[108] It was Dwight's final ploy to defraud those he charmed into loaning him money. On March 1, 1856, the date Spencer was to repay Brown Brothers the $150,000 the firm had loaned him (which was to have paid interest on the first, second, and third mortgage bonds; the Litchfield loan; and part of what Dwight owed Brown Brothers), he defaulted. Brown Brothers wasted no time in foreclosing. With the default the stage was set for the liquidation of the company.

Although their influence had been taken from them by virtue of Dwight's control of the board, both Brewster and Blatchford annoyed Dwight by verbally challenging his every move. Then there were the courts, sympathetic to the charges Litchfield and the New England banks were filing. Dwight decided he

would rid himself of these aggravations by closing the William Street office and transferring the headquarters of the company to Bloomington. There, Dwight figured, the books of the company would be beyond the inspection and meddle of the New York courts and too distant for the two New Yorkers to regularly attend—at least until he finished his thievery. At an early April board meeting, Dwight arranged the resignations of Wright, Hotchkiss, and Quintard and in their places named Alexander, Gardner, and Dr. H. T. Spencer, Hamilton Spencer's brother. He then adjourned the meeting, which was to resume in Bloomington eight days later.[109]

When the board met at Bloomington, the new directors were elected, and a resolution was passed that the company's president had to be a resident of Illinois. This disqualified Brewster as president. Dwight had been in the habit of naming weak and pliable persons as officers and directors of the company, but the man he now selected certainly did not fit that description. Governor Matteson was his pick. Matteson never publicly gave his reasons for taking the presidency, but it's likely at least one of his objectives was to protect the Joliet & Chicago, totally dependent as it would be on the continued operation and success of the CA&St.L. An astute businessman, Matteson also likely saw an opportunity for his personal gain. Whatever his motivations, it was not one of Matteson's wiser decisions.[110]

Dwight may have thought he had escaped the troublesome interferences of his creditors and New York courts by moving the company's offices, but he was mistaken. A month after the move to Bloomington, Elisha Litchfield resumed his legal action in New York and gained an injunction against Dwight, the board of directors, Spencer, Brown Brothers, and the trustees of the assignment that prohibited any of them from any further taking of assets, any further assignments, or the company's liquidation.[111] At least temporarily, Dwight's plunder of the company was stopped. Now in addition to the Brown Brothers foreclosure, Dwight had to deal with the scrutiny of the courts. If he was going to achieve his ultimate goal of the company's liquidation and, with it, the elimination of all his debts, he would first have to satisfy Litchfield and Brown Brothers.

Neither party would have any personal dealings with Dwight and rejected his overtures for a settlement meeting. Faced with imminent arrest and probable incarceration, Dwight ceased suggesting meetings and instead offered as his surrogate Matteson. In June the governor met with Litchfield and representatives of Brown Brothers.[112] The meetings dragged on throughout the summer and early autumn before a settlement was reached. Considering Dwight's personal problems and the strength of his adversaries, the final agreement turned out amazingly in Dwight's favor. Clearly, all Litchfield and Brown Brothers wanted was payment of what was owed them, not the CA&St.L itself. The resilient Dwight wound up largely where he would have been had Litchfield not temporarily interrupted his push toward liquidation.

Agreed to was the buyout, by Litchfield and Matteson, of the odious Spencer Lease. Keeping the lease alive was crucial for Dwight. If it were terminated, the house of cards he had built would tumble. The bondholders would have been able to foreclose and take control, leaving Dwight, Spencer, and the few friends they had left with nothing. As long as the lease was in effect, Dwight's hated creditors were held at bay. Once the lease was transferred, it was agreed sale of the company would proceed, with Spencer the designated buyer. Thereafter, a new company would be formed, capitalized at the same $3.5 million figure. All of the $3 million plus of common stock given Dwight as part of his construction contract and used by him to pay personal debts would become worthless. His personal creditors would be left with valueless paper for the loans they had made him. It was to be the final indignity Dwight's creditors were to suffer and his final victory over them.[113]

The holders of the three mortgages were to be offered a replacement issue of a new series of fourth mortgage bonds, bearing 10 percent interest with a graduated payout schedule and a longer maturity, subject to the acceptance of the creditors. The balance of what was owed Brown Brothers and whatever expenses Litchfield and Matteson would incur in operating the railroad, plus the expenses Spencer might have run up while holder of the lease, were to be paid on a current basis

out of the railroad's revenues. The Litchfield-Matteson ownership was to last three years, starting October 1, 1856.[114]

Dwight no longer needed to be directly involved since he got what he wanted—complete relief from paying his creditors. Spencer too got what he wanted—removal from the lease's obligations. The lease had cost neither man anything; in fact both had profited handsomely. Litchfield was to see total repayment of his railroad's loan. Brown Brothers, the only creditor with the prospect of full repayment, would walk away from the mess unscathed. It was an astounding victory for them all and a disaster for the New England bankers and local creditors and stockholders. The agreement brought Litchfield's consent to drop his injunction, removing all the obstacles to a forced sale of the company under the terms of the assignment trust.

On December 15, 1856, a small group gathered before the Bloomington depot. Litchfield and Matteson were there as well as Hotchkiss, Spencer, and Henry Brown of Brown Brothers. Dwight had asked to be allowed to attend, but because he was under indictment, the courts restricted his travel to the boundaries of New York. The auctioneer began his call and, after a brief period of silence, received the one and only bid of $5,000. It came from Litchfield on behalf of himself and Matteson. The auctioneer called for further bids, but none were offered. His hammer came down, once, twice, and then a third time, finalizing the sale. The rights and interests of nearly all those making up the "floating debt," as well as the stockholders, ended.

A little over a month later and nine days after Matteson's term as governor concluded, on January 21, 1857, the legislature issued a charter for the St. Louis, Alton & Chicago Railroad Company (St.LA&C), the corporate name Matteson and Litchfield would have the railroad operate under for the next three years.[115] The stage was set for one of the state's most prominent political and business leaders to attempt perhaps his greatest achievement: the complete turnaround of a nearly decimated enterprise. Could Matteson succeed in rescuing the railroad from ruin? He was astute, confident, and competent, but he was faced with perhaps the challenge of his life.

The Courts Decide the Future

Scrip such as this $2.50 note was issued in lieu of currency for state obligations. Alleged theft of scrip embarrassed Joel Matteson while he attempted to straighten out the railroad's affairs. (Author's collection)

There was a collective sigh of relief that the worst days were over and a fresh start could be made with the sale of the CA&St.L to Joel Matteson. Calneh Zarley, editor of the *Joliet Signal,* always supportive of the town's most prominent citizen, boldly proclaimed, "Governor Matteson assumes the presidency of the company and of course the management of the road, which is a sufficient guarantee that it will be one of the best managed roads in the west. We know of no man so well adapted to take charge of this important railroad as Governor Matteson."[1] The *New York Times* also took note of the sale.

The concern for sometime past has been one of the ugliest and most involved cases of default in the railway list. There seemed to be less excuse for the embarrassment from the circumstances that the entire mortgage on the property is less than $7,000 a mile, the line completed and equipped, and doing a fair gross traffic through one of the best districts in Illinois. The receipts last year were over $1 million. This year they promise about $1.3 million or a monthly earning of $5,000 a mile. Why or how these earnings have been disposed of, the bondholders, generally have not been able to know, the affairs of the road being mixed up with individual embarrassments, leases, etc.

But we now learn with satisfaction that a different order of things is soon to be brought about; the present lease canceled or transferred and a new administration put in charge of the work, with the concurrence of the heaviest creditors and with every prospect of funding the overages of interest and arranging for the prospective resumption of the cash payments to the bondholders.[2]

Bondholder concurrence to a reorganization plan was precisely what Matteson needed if the railroad's sorry state was to be turned around and the railroad made a viable operating entity. Matteson needed breathing room. The plan he and Litchfield presented clearly outlined the steps they planned to take and the expected results. It also contained a blatant threat to the bondholders if they rejected the plan.[3] Matteson's proposal was a hardball, no nonsense proposition. In effect, he and Litchfield were telling the bondholders to back off and give them the room they needed to put things right.

The second and third mortgage holders were favorable, but the committee representing the first mortgage bonds were not. They objected to anything being paid the second and third mortgage bondholders before their bonds matured. They contended that they had priority over the claims of the other two categories of lien holders and wanted a preference for payment shown them. Further, they wanted their interests protected through election of a board member.

With the first bondholder committee's rejection, Matteson tried another approach. He proposed that the third mortgage bondholders, whose 10 percent bonds were to mature in just two years, accept a replacement income bond series, which would mature in 1870 and would bear 2 percent interest for the first two years and 8 percent thereafter. Once mature, the bonds could then be converted into the railroad's common stock. Ultimately, the third bondholders would receive the same return as with the existing series but over a longer period, which could be far more lucrative at maturity.[4] The offer went out in March 1857. Matteson waited anxiously for the third bondholders' reply. It wasn't long before almost half the third mortgage bonds were surrendered, but with the proviso that they could be repossessed if there was less than a full redemption of them. Though a step in the right direction, the matter was still not resolved. Negotiations with the first and second bondholder committees continued.

Matteson had his hands full trying to restructure the company's debt, but Superintendent Asa Moore was also facing problems. The railroad, devoid of maintenance during Spencer's brief management and not having seen much under Morgan, was in poor shape. The right-of-way had yet to be ballasted. Rails were breaking at their ends, bent where their anchors failed. Decayed ties had not been replaced. The Sanagamon River bridge pilings were already showing signs of rot, some of the timbers being spliced as a stopgap measure.

One estimate claimed as much as $200,000 was needed to rehabilitate the line.[5]

The majority of the freight car fleet (which now numbered about 500) was in reasonable shape, but the oldest equipment was in terrible shape. A profitable railroad would have declared at least some of them bad order and replaced or repaired the worst of them, but Moore could do neither. The passenger car roster was made up of 37 passenger cars, 25 first-class coaches, six second-class or immigrant cars, and six mail and baggage cars, but even when new, the cars were quite utilitarian. The 38 Swinburne 4-4-0s the company had rostered were the backbone of the engine fleet and generally in good shape, but the assorted older engines were mostly bad order. By one assessment there wasn't one that didn't need a new dome and steam chest.

Most of the facilities along the line were in acceptable condition. The complex at Bloomington had been expanded to include machine, carpenter, and blacksmith shops, a small brass and iron foundry, a store room, and a stationary engine room. Close by was a ten-stall roundhouse and a freight house in which offices of the superintendent and other officials were located. What was lacking (and hampering repairs) at the shops was a shortage of replacement parts. An estimated $30,000 was needed to restock depleted inventories. To put in perspective how large a sum this was, one could compare it with the $100,000 cost of building the shops themselves a few years earlier.[6]

Despite the handicaps, Superintendent Moore set out to improve service. Freight trains were called more frequently. Passenger train schedules were adjusted to better serve local markets and to improve connections at Springfield with the Great Western (formerly the S&M); at Bloomington with the IC; at Chenoa with the newly opened Peoria & Oquawka Eastern Extension; at Joliet with the Rock Island; and at Chicago with roads headed east and west. Passenger traffic by far made up the greatest percentage of the road's revenue, and it was continuing to grow, helped appreciably by an ever-increasing number of immigrants.

The railroad had been popular with passengers from the start. As early as 1852, politicians in and out of Springfield; businessmen to and from St. Louis, Alton, and Carlinville;

and farmers and their wives making shopping trips to bigger towns rode the two daily-except-Sunday passenger trains. A few weeks after the Springfield-to-Alton segment was opened, Stephen Douglas used the evening train from Springfield to Alton, where the "Little Giant" delivered a speech to a Democratic gathering. Abraham Lincoln was a faithful user, taking the train to Bloomington for court sessions. He also used the train to make appearances in support of Whig, then later Republican, causes. His travels brought no revenue, however, since, as one of the company's favored attorneys, he had been furnished a pass.[7] Millard Fillmore was the first president to use the railroad during an 1854 appearance at Alton. He was visiting Illinois to see the IC—the road made possible by his signing of the 1850 land-grant bill.[8]

Passengers were usually treated with courtesy and formality, but early on, ugly incidents of abuse arose and soured the traveling public's opinion of the railroad. The sometimes brutish behavior of trainmen forced the company, on more than one occasion, to defend itself in court. One confrontation occurred in 1855 between a conductor on an eastbound evening train running on the Rock Island and a heavily intoxicated man who slept through his stop at Joliet. The conductor later woke him and asked for the added fare to Chicago. When he refused, the conductor roughly pushed him off the train in the dark of night into a deep cut. A few minutes later, after staggering back onto the track, the still-intoxicated traveler was struck and killed by another train following closely behind.[9]

In another crudely handled incident, a boy boarded a train at Lincoln without any money, hoping to ride free to Broadwell, the next station. After confronting him, the conductor had the train stopped in the middle of the Salt Creek trestle and forced the young man off the train. Frightened and unsure of his footing, the youngster tripped and fell into the water below. He probably would have drowned had he not been rescued by some of the passengers and trainmen.[10]

In the most notorious incident, in 1857, Joseph Dalby and his wife presented themselves at the Elkhart depot and requested two tickets to Lincoln. The station agent told

them his supply of printed tickets to that point was depleted but that he would write a note indicating the circumstances, which Dalby was instructed to present to the train's conductor. Once onboard, Dalby produced the note and offered the regular fare of 33 cents. The conductor told Dalby the fare was 44 cents—what a passenger without a ticket was charged. Quite understandably, Dalby refused. The conductor, now backed up by a rather burly brakeman, grabbed Dalby intending to put both him and his wife off the train. Dalby resisted, and as one witness to the incident testified, was "pounded in the face ten or a dozen licks."[11] Dalby filed suit for assault and battery, and the railroad was ordered to pay him damages of the very generous sum of $1,000.

The railroad appealed the case to the Illinois Supreme Court on the grounds that a charge of assault and battery could not apply to a corporation and, further, that it must be presumed to have "authorized its servants to use none but usual means for the purpose of enforcing regulations of the company, and if, instead of using such means, the conductor, or other servant of the company, employed any unusual, unnecessary or unjustifiable measures, then, however culpable the servants of the company may have been, or whatever their liability to the plaintiff, the company was not responsible for the employment of such excess means."[12] The state supreme court rejected the arguments of John Stuart and Cyrus Edwards, the railroad's attorneys, and upheld the plaintiff's position presented by Abraham Lincoln. The case settled the question of the responsibility of a common carrier and its employees and was used as precedent in later cases. Despite Lincoln's defense of Dalby, the company bore no grudge; Lincoln continued to get legal work from the railroad.[13]

▾▾▾

By 1857 more than 2,000 miles of railroad track had been laid throughout the state, a significant leap forward from the 55 miles that existed just seven years earlier. Only the states of New York and Ohio had more railroad mileage. To be sure, there were still areas, such as the southeastern counties along the

Wabash and Ohio Rivers, that had not yet seen a line chartered or surveyed, but nearly all other regions had lines either up and running or close to completion.[14]

One railroad that had not started construction was the Jacksonville & Carrollton. The company was formally brought into existence at a stockholder's meeting held at the Carrollton Courthouse in December 1853 at which five directors were elected and Judge David Woodson of Greene County was chosen the road's first president.[15] Soon thereafter, Joshua Hunt, formerly of the TH&A, was hired to survey a route, a project he and his crew finished in June 1856.

Hunt's survey estimated it would take $1.2 million to complete the project, including power, rolling stock, and structures. Five hundred thousand dollars had been pledged by local interests, but further appeals for more financing had so far proved unsuccessful. Woodson appealed to investors in St. Louis. He thought surely they would recognize his road's importance to them, but few there were persuaded. During 1856 little was added to the company's treasury.[16]

The original five-man board saw its first replacements after a March 1856 stockholder's meeting.[17] There it was announced that the first stock installment payments would be called so that land for a right-of-way could be acquired and contracts for engineering, grading, bridging, and masonry work could be let. It was a cautious start, one that would avoid exceeding the company's limited resources but still provide evidence to those reluctant to invest that the railroad would in fact be built.[18] President Woodson was authorized to solicit bids for completion of the first 40 miles of the J&C starting at Godfrey. He received fifty proposals, but the one he and his board accepted was submitted by two New Yorkers, Edgerton and Sage. They promised completion of the entire railroad, including all structures, and a supply of power and rolling stock: six freight engines, two passenger engines, five mail-baggage cars, eight coaches, 40 flatcars, 75 boxcars, and 25 gravel cars.[19]

The $1.5 million contract called for the J&C to pay the contractors half in cash; 42 percent in 20-year, 7 percent bonds; and the remainder in common stock. The promised cash, however, was $300,000 more than was in the company's treasury. Woodson expected, or at least hoped, he would get that balance from Greene County farmers who hadn't yet invested.[20] In early 1857, grading of the eight miles from Delhi to the south was started, as was bridge masonry work. In May crews began grading near Manchester.[21]

That same month, Judge Woodson surprised the board with his resignation as president, though he planned to remain a director. His colleagues tried to dissuade him because of his excellent leadership, but Woodson was exhausted by his duties both as president of the railroad and as judge of the circuit court. He felt the difficult task of getting the company up and running had been achieved; he was willing for others to see the job completed. Unable to change Woodson's mind, the board reluctantly acquiesced and chose from their number William Shephard of Jerseyville to succeed him.[22]

One of the things that Woodson had done before he left as president was to submit a petition to the General Assembly. After failing to come to agreement with Alton's leaders, Woodson had asked for a change of the J&C's designated southern terminal from Alton to Illinoistown. Passed by the legislature on February 15, 1857, the same bill changed the company's name to the Jacksonville, Alton & St. Louis (JA&St.L), a reflection of its expanded franchise.[23]

The growing fervor for railroads encouraged yet another group to organize a railroad to serve the southwestern portion of the state. The Tonica & Petersburg (T&P) was chartered in 1857 with Richard Yates of Jacksonville heading a group of eight other organizers.[24] Despite its association with Jacksonville interests, the road's roots had been planted in Metamora, a small village 20 miles northeast of Peoria in Woodford County, where in 1856 an association was formed and $17,000 pledged to pay for preparation of a north-south route through Metamora Township, headed for a connection with the IC at Tonica. Later that year representatives of the projected T&P met with those starting the line at Metamora and suggested the two groups pool their efforts. The alliance explains why the charter, when passed, provided for a route from Ottawa south through Tonica, Magnolia, Lyons (south of Varna), Mantua (later Washburn),

Metamora, Tremont, Delavan, with a turn westward to Petersburg and finally termination at Jacksonville.

The new company was also given authority to construct a line from Petersburg south to New Berlin and from Jacksonville through Waverly and Carlinville to an unspecified junction with the IC.[25] Though the rights granted were already extensive, the T&P charter was amended once again a month later in February 1857 with the naming of yet another branch. This one would run off the Magnolia-Ottawa line to Morris (and the coal beds on the Vermillion River). The branch would alter the route between Metamora and Delavan, allowing the line to run through Washington, if citizens there raised $15,000 within 30 days of the amendment's passage and donated a right-of-way and grounds for a depot at the crossing with the (now named) Peoria & Oquawka Eastern. It was a very expansive franchise but one that clearly reflected the time of unbridled enthusiasm for railroads.[26]

It took the T&P organizers only two months to hire contractors for the initial grading, bridging, and masonry work required for the first segment, the 26 miles between Petersburg and Jacksonville. The ceremonial first shovel of soil was turned at Petersburg on May 18, 1857, but crews were already at work at Clary's Grove and Jacksonville. By July, five miles of superstructure were finished east of Jacksonville to about Mauvaisterre Creek and the laying of ties had begun. Another 11 miles had been graded beyond Prentice. By November a grade from Jacksonville to Petersburg had been raised before inclement weather, and the effects of the panic of 1857 forced a cessation of work. Two years passed before work was resumed.[27]

The prosperous economy the nation and Illinois had enjoyed in 1856 had carried over into the first nine months of 1857, but before the year was out a financial panic struck. The unexpected failure of the Ohio Life & Trust shocked New York capitalists, and within days during early October, sudden and forced liquidation of debts caused dozens of eastern banks and trading houses to fail. So sudden and uncontrolled was the loss of confidence that more businesses failed in the brief three-month period before year's end than in the previous five years combined.[28]

As a result of the panic in the East, banks in St. Louis and New Orleans stopped accepting currencies from other places. Trade stagnated. Chicago weathered the storm much better than other cities, though all but two of its banks had failed and some export grain orders had been canceled, causing a drop in prices. Nine million bushels of wheat and 7.5 million bushels of corn were stored in Chicago's elevators, waiting to be sold.[29] The rest of the state felt the panic's impact to a far greater degree, especially those places that traded in St. Louis. By transferring trade to Chicago, most Illinois farmers and merchants managed to survive. Because of the severity of the two previous winters, the corn and wheat yields in some parts of the state, especially the central and southern parts, had wilted or were totally lost, but enormous shipments from the western and northern counties helped stabilize the grain markets, and the reports of a general crop failure that circulated in New York proved false.[30]

▾▾▾

By June 1857 work was under way on all three JA&St.L divisions. Between Jacksonville and White Hall, the Northern Division, about half the grading was finished. Because no stone could be found there, plans for a Howe Truss bridge on stone abutments to span the Big Sandy Creek had to be scrapped. A trestle bridge was installed instead.[31] On the Middle Division, between White Hall and Kane, crews were laboriously digging the deep cuts and building the extensive embankments needed through the hilly country. The foundation and bench walls for a large arch cement culvert over Lick's Creek were completed, and stone was gathered for the bridge itself. Abutment walls for the Macoupin Creek bridge were finished, composed of limestone laid in hydraulic cement. A 150-foot Howe Truss would bridge the creek. Two abutments and six stone piers for another 124-foot stringer bridge were partially finished, but the bridge intended to cross a 124-feet-wide spillway had not yet been started. (Because plentiful ledges of limestone were found in the immediate area, the stones cut and shaped at these nearby sites were easily moved to where the material was needed, such as at Seminary, Apple, and Macoupin

Creeks.) Meanwhile, further south a large force was excavating a several-hundred-feet deep cut. The Southern Division, between Kane and Monticello, required a 50-foot deep cut to the north of the Big Piasa. A series of stone arches, constructed with a crystallized, light gray limestone cut from a quarry not 300 feet from the site, was the most important structure on the division. Under the supervision of subcontractors Park and Robinson, a bridge of near perfection was partially finished. Between the two Piasas, all the culvert work was finished, as was the superstructure. At the Little Piasa, a 60-foot Howe Truss was in place.[32]

The impressive progress slowed appreciably by October, when the effects of the panic and the failure of that year's wheat crop put a strain on the company's limited funding. Without income from crops, the subscribing farmers could not be asked for installment payments. Jersey County fell into arrears on monthly payments, and bond sales had to be suspended to avoid their being sold at deep discounts. Engineering work was cut in half. Purchases of ties and rail were deferred.[33] Because of the board's temperance, however, work was continued, though at a much reduced pace.

The start of construction on the Joliet & Chicago also began in 1857.[34] Matteson had taken responsibility for raising the financing, but it was probably inevitable that his political rivals would somehow complicate his task. And so they did when he attempted to get the cities of Joliet and Chicago to invest in the enterprise. Like a lightning rod, Matteson drew energy from two political rivals. Mayors Firman Mack of Joliet and John Wentworth of Chicago both strenuously argued against either of their cities advancing funds. Despite investments other towns and cities had been making in their railroads, Chicago hadn't spent a dime. The city didn't have to. The railroads would have paid for the privilege to enter the most important market in the West. Wentworth, who had lobbied aggressively for the IC's lakefront routing, was still feuding with Matteson over his promotion of the Joliet Cutoff, which siphoned off traffic from Chicago. Wentworth saw Matteson's latest venture as another threat to his beloved IC, in which he had a substantial financial interest. Earlier in the year, Joliet citizens, led by Mack,

voted 2–1 against funding the projected Joliet & Terre Haute, and Mack now saw no reason to aid a company that would benefit Joliet's rival, Lockport. In any event, neither politician was about to help Matteson add another feather to his cap.

The *Joliet Signal,* as might be expected, professed sarcastic dismay.

> Not withstanding the efforts of the mayor of the city which is to be so greatly benefitted by the completion of this road, to cripple and embarrass the finances of the company, by malignantly and maliciously assaulting Governor Matteson upon whom the progress of the work mainly depends, the road will be built. Most of the grading is done and the track will be laid between this city and Lockport in a few days. It is expected that the entire road will be ready for the cars by the first of January.
>
> The conduct of John Wentworth in connection with this matter is unaccountable and can only be attributed to his inveterate hatred of Governor Matteson. He is willing to inflict a blow upon the road and the interests of his city in order to vent his spite against the man upon whom the success of the enterprise depends. Governor Matteson, with usual characteristic energy and determination is struggling against the hardness of the times and pressure of the money market to finish this road and John Wentworth is trying to prevent him. Well may the people of Chicago feel grateful to their chief magistrate for his munificence.[35]

Matteson never got help from either Joliet or Chicago but did successfully sell the railroad's securities to eastern interests.

The contract to construct the first section, from Joliet to Lockport, was given to C. E. Boyer & Co. of Lockport in June 1857, with hopes that he would finish by November. Grading and tracklaying advanced rapidly across the flat terrain but not without incident. After only a few months, trouble arose as reports circulated that one of Boyer's subcontractors, I. S. Reed, took the $2,000 paid him and "decamped to parts unknown." The money was to pay the wages of the 60 men working for him. "It is hard that these men, who labored faithfully under a burning summer's sun, should be robbed of their pay. $2,000 is not a very large sum to Mr. Boyer or the Joliet & Chicago Railroad company,"

Zarley wrote, "but to the poor men who earned it, the amount does not seem so small."[36] Presumably, neither Boyer nor the railroad felt obliged to replace the workers' lost wages. Despite Reed's greed, by the end of October, the first five miles to Lockport had been completed, and to mark the occasion, a train was assembled and operated.[37]

Seven more miles of track brought the railroad to Lemont, a place originally named Athens, where three houses, a few stores, and a couple of taverns stood. The place owed its existence to the excellent seams of limestone found there during canal construction. Three quarries were already operating before rails reached the place. Lemont Limestone, when exposed to air, turned an attractive pale yellow (some called it buff color), and it quickly became a popular building material, used in numerous structures, many of which still stand throughout Illinois and other states, including the state prison and the Lemont and Lockport depots. Ahead lay the level, forested Des Plaines River Valley, Bridgeport, and Chicago.[38]

▾▾▾

Meanwhile, the bondholders were at each other's throats, fighting among themselves over who deserved priority and who, if anyone, had the right to take control of the company. Charges and countercharges were hurled, increasing the distrust of everyone involved. The situation deteriorated to the point at which no solution could be reached and the whole matter was thrown into the courts.

In May 1858 the *New York Herald* reported:

For several weeks past some of the leading bankers and merchants of this city, aided by eminent counsel, have been probing a terrible charge of fraud in connection with the Chicago, Alton & St. Louis Railroad Company, by which the stockholders, bondholders and creditors generally of that institution, as well as several New England banks and New York merchants, were sufferers to the amount of millions of dollars. A short time since affidavits were made before Judge Russell by Mr. Samuel M. Blatchford, Stewart Brown, Seabury Brewster and Charles Gould, charging Henry Hotchkiss and Hamilton Spencer, directors and chief managers of the rail-

road company, with swindling, embezzlement and sundry other grave offenses. Six warrants were issued against Mr. Dwight, on two separate charges of perjury—one for fraudulent issue of coupons, one for the fraudulent issue of canceled bonds, another for embezzlement, and another for conspiracy. A warrant was issued at the same time for the arrest of Hotchkiss and Spencer on a charge of conspiracy to defraud the creditors of the company.[39]

Mixed in the fray were Godfrey's claims that he too had been defrauded by Dwight, alleging that Dwight had turned over to his creditors Godfrey's land and property, pledged as collateral for the loans of 1851, as Dwight's own property, free of encumbrances, leaving Godfrey faced with the probable loss of his holdings. In such an atmosphere, it was impossible for Litchfield and Matteson to reorganize the company's finances, at least until the creditors' claims and counterclaims were decided.

Amid the confusion the last link was being added to the chain that would anchor the CA&St.L's main line between the Mississippi River and the Great Lakes. After the frost left the ground, work on the J&C between Lemont and Chicago was resumed and advanced rapidly. On March 18, 1858, a nine-car train comprised of CA&St.L equipment left the Joliet depot with a large number of invited guests and two brass bands, Grosh's and the Ancient Order of Hibernians, headed for Chicago for the first time. At Lockport, the train was greeted by cheers and ceremonial cannon fire. The Lockport Band climbed aboard a flatcar upon which the band's beautifully decorated carriage had already been placed. More riders were added, filling the coaches to capacity. According to reports, "all went swimmingly, and the company were enjoying the ride on the rail with much gusto— the greatest mirth and hilarity prevailing, and the various bands discoursing eloquent music alternately until the train arrived at Bridgeport where it was brought to a sudden stand still, and it was announced that the tender was off the track."[40] Track on this part of the road had been laid over low, swampy ground, and the exceedingly wet weather of the previous few days had caused the limited roadbed to be undermined. Superintendent Moore, with the help of several other men, re-railed the tender, but after traveling only a few hundred feet, the tender again derailed.

After considerable delay the tender was re-railed, and the train resumed its journey to Chicago. The J&C had reached agreement with the Pittsburg(h) Fort Wayne & Chicago the previous year for a half interest in the PFt.W&C's bridge over the Chicago River near Archer Road and its track from the bridge along Stewart Street to the line's terminus at Van Buren Street, similar to the arrangements the MC reached with the IC and the MS with the Rock Island. The train reached Chicago, but PFt.W&C had not yet constructed a passenger depot, so where the train terminated is somewhat of a mystery. Two months later plans for a Union Station were announced for a structure at Madison and Canal Streets, two blocks further north. Though the first ceremonial run may have used the west side tracks, it more likely switched over to the Rock Island and ended its run under the train shed of that road's depot at Van Buren and LaSalle Streets.

When regular St. Louis, Alton & Chicago service over its own rails and those leased from J&C rails began, its passenger trains did terminate at the Rock Island depot. After a few months, likely because relations between St.LA&C and Rock Island had deteriorated, St.LA&C's passenger trains began using the IC's lake front depot near the Chicago River, reaching the tracks of that railroad over the St. Charles Air Line. This rather cumbersome and time-consuming arrangement continued until the PFt.W&C and J&C jointly financed a two-block extension north of Van Buren Street to Madison Street where the PFt.W&C opened a modest wood-frame depot in 1863. It was then that trains over the leased J&C tracks found a permanent home on Chicago's west side, bringing to an end the delays the company's trains endured caused by preference given those of the other railroads.

A total of $959,480 had been spent completing the J&C—about $25,500 per mile.[41] It was built to relatively high standards. The Chicago entry also allowed freight to be carried to downtown Chicago. Within weeks of the J&C's opening, transfers of freight at Joliet to canal boats ended. Before long a freight house was built at Chicago and engines were being serviced at a roundhouse

erected at Stewart Avenue, between Wilson and 12th streets.

▾▾▾

Downstate, slow progress toward completion of the JA&St.L continued throughout 1858. The first structures on the Northern Division were completed, grading was nearly finished, and about half the ties needed were stacked along the line. The segment between Jacksonville and Manchester still had some grading to be finished. The soils around the Big Sandy area were particularly ill-suited, and the incessant rains throughout the year had made work there difficult. Between Manchester and White Hall, the superstructure was raised, only awaiting ties and rails. The arches over Lick's Creek were finished, as were culverts at Macoupin Creek on the Middle Division. The Southern Division, where considerable masonry work was required, had progressed to the point where the Big Piasa could be bridged. The Little Piasa abutments were nearly finished, as were most of the culverts.[42]

In contrast, little work was done on the T&P during the year. Weeds and prairie grasses began growing on the raised dirt between Jacksonville and Petersburg. Short of cash, William Greene and Richard Yates had trouble buying rails because New York financiers had lost faith in most railroad bonds, and those the men offered were far down on the list of desirable investments. The New York financial crisis had deflated interest in railroad investing.

Matteson now faced extensive troubles. In January 1859 employees, no longer willing to wait for back pay, walked out. Shop workers at Bloomington, who earlier had gone out on strike twice before, were now joined by operating, maintenance, and clerical workers. Not a wheel turned for the next four weeks before the workers—deciding prospects for getting paid were better if they were working than if they were striking—returned to their jobs.[43] Although sympathetic to the workers' plight, Matteson could do little to relieve their suffering without an infusion of cash. With the railroad shut down and its treasury all but empty, Matteson's only recourse was to initiate negotiations that would release the railroad to its bondholders. On February 16, 1859, the

Illinois legislature quickly pushed through legislation that the bondholders sought for the incorporation of the Alton, Chicago & St. Louis Railroad in order to take possession of the company.[44]

In April 1859 Matteson met the bondholders' attorney, George Davis, in Springfield. Matteson was offered a payment for the employees of $25,000, a small percentage of what was owed, with incremental payments to be made thereafter, but only after the transfer of the railroad was completed. Matteson decided it wasn't enough. He countered with more favorable terms for the workers. Rebuffed, Davis returned to New York empty-handed. Meanwhile, Matteson went to the employees to appeal for their support.

On a Saturday in mid-April, 75 labor delegates from all points on the railroad gathered in Bloomington's Weideman's Hall (the meeting had been scheduled for the day before, but a train from Alton had been canceled, preventing some of the delegates from attending) and heard Matteson at his persuasive best, imploring the men to remain united. He cited how, when reports of the strike reached the New York bondholders, they were shaken; how a takeover by the bondholders had already been attempted which, if successful, would surely not have been in the workers' interests; and how he could borrow no more money himself (he claimed personally endorsing up to $181,000 of loans to date). He promised the men that, if they would stick with him, money would be used to pay them before other bills—aside from actual running expenses—and that regular repayments of past wages would be started immediately. After nine hours of frustrating discussion, the men unanimously agreed to follow Matteson and endorsed the declaration of B. B. Harris, a carpenter foreman at Alton, who declared, "If we can not have confidence in Governor Matteson . . . we can not have confidence in any human being."[45]

The employees' vote of confidence wasn't shared, however, by those who supplied wood for the railroad's engines. They too had gone unpaid and, at about the same time as the Bloomington meeting, took their stand at Brighton, where they blocked passage of a southbound morning train. A United States marshal out of Springfield, with a posse of 20 deputies, arrived the next day, broke up the blockade, and arrested eight of the protesters, charging them with interfering with the mail.[46]

Matteson telegraphed Davis in New York and pleaded for $154,000 to pay employee back wages and woodcutters' invoices. The $25,000 that would still be owed, he suggested, could then be settled when the bondholders finally took over the road. News of the employee meeting must have persuaded the bondholders to review their position, for in May agreement for the higher immediate payout was reached.[47]

As if Matteson didn't have enough trouble, persistent rumors that had been circulating about him for more than a year became formal charges. Jacob Fry, a canal officer, alleged that after assuming the governorship in 1853, Matteson had removed a trunk and shoe box from a Chicago bank vault that held old Canal Board records and several $50 and $100, 90-day scrip, issued in 1839 to contractors (the same type scrip Matteson was paid for his work on the canal and that he previously used to buy the state's rails and the S&M). Matteson, late in his administration as governor, Fry charged, had begun redeeming the scrip for state bonds, using them as surety to prop up bank notes issued by the State Bank of Illinois at Shawneetown, which was one of the six banks Matteson owned or controlled and had came under pressure during the panic. At Senate Revenue Committee hearings, Matteson professed his innocence, but nevertheless, volunteered to repay the state. The investigation dragged on for years, principally at the instigation of Republicans, and new disclosures accusing Matteson of more theft surfaced. Added to his alleged crimes was a charge of forgery, because some of the certificates had been cashed with fictitious names—all determined to be signed in Matteson's hand.[48]

In the face of all that was confronting him, both as president of the railroad and personally, Matteson still found the time to entertain a proposal which not only would benefit the railroad but also would revolutionize the industry for the next 100 years. When the morning train arrived in Bloomington on a spring day in 1859, among those alighting was a smartly dressed young man who took stock of his surroundings, then headed off in the direction of the railroad shops. George Pullman, destined to become one of the country's wealthiest and most powerful men, but now simply a 28-year-old son of a New York family of farmers and carpenters, was set to tackle his latest venture, the building of his first railroad sleeping car.

Pullman had been taught woodworking skills by his father. He had engaged in the house-moving business in his native upstate New York and then in his adopted home of Chicago, when the city decided to literally raise itself out of the mud by elevating its buildings. He bid on several Chicago jobs and successfully elevated the Democratic Building, Jackson Hall, the New York House, and the Tremont House, among others, developing an excellent reputation and a thriving business.[49]

Pullman's long, uncomfortable, and sleepless overnight rail visits home to New York afforded him plenty of time to consider how nocturnal trips could be improved. A close friend and New York neighbor, state senator Benjamin Field, had organized a company that built and operated sleeping cars for the New York Central. While Field's cars improved travel through provision of benches on which travelers could stretch out, they were not the type of accommodation Pullman thought overnight passengers should be afforded. In early 1859, before returning to Chicago to bid on the raising of the five-story Matteson House (considered by some the next best hotel after the Tremont House), Pullman and Field formed a company to build and operate sleepers of an improved design.

Theodore Woodruff, while in the employ of the TH&A, in 1856 conceived and patented the first true sleeping car, which featured seats that were converted into bunks. His design was the first to employ hinges and counterweights that kept the bunks out of the way during the day. The Wason Car Company had built a prototype for Woodruff in 1857 that, when finished, was put on trial runs on several roads, including the TH&A, the MC, and the CA&St.L. By fall 1858 Woodruff had 21 cars in service and would soon add the Philadelphia-Pittsburgh run of the Pennsylvania Central to his list. In the West, Woodruff cars were already operating on the G&CU and the IC. Field had the rights to sell the Woodruff sleeping car to western roads.[50]

Two railroad companies were prospects, the Burlington and the St.L&C. It isn't known whether Pullman ever approached the Burlington or whether Matteson was presented the idea first, but whatever the circumstances, Matteson agreed to provide two cars for conversion at the company's Bloomington Shops. Pullman left his brother Albert in charge of the Chicago-based building-raising business, and headed off for Bloomington.[51] The two coaches the railroad provided Pullman were no. 9 and no. 19. They were among the newest of the 12 coaches on the property. Each measured 44-feet, 1-inch long over end sills and 10-feet, 5-1/2-inches wide at the eaves. The inside dimensions—43 feet, 3/4-inches long; 8-feet, 11-inches wide; and 7-feet high—made them suitable for his plan and as big as any then in use. The cars had nearly flat roofs and 15 diminutive single-sash windows and rode on four-wheel trucks with iron wheels, devoid of springs but cushioned somewhat by rubber bushings. The cars bore link-and-pin couplers and a simple hand brake.[52]

Pullman hired Leonard Seibert, a German immigrant and craftsman in the railroad's Bloomington Shops, who in turn hired a couple of assistants to transform the cars. The railroad's master mechanic, William Cessford, and master car builder, David Shield, supervised construction.[53] Over the next four months, Pullman and Seibert determined details and dimensions as they went along; no blueprints were used. They laid out 10 sections of lower and upper berths, the latter suspended from the ceiling by a somewhat complicated set of ropes and pulleys. The design differed from Woodruff's three-bunk arrangement and did not employ Woodruff's patented mechanical lowering system but that of another, similar to the patented design of Eli Wheeler and C. M. Mann. The bunks were fitted with mattresses and a blanket but were devoid of sheets or pillow cases, a feature introduced a few years later.

Curtains were hung across the berths. A linen locker and a washroom at either end of the car and a marble-topped washstand were installed. Cherry was used throughout the interior, though hickory would have been preferred had it been available. Plush upholstered seats replaced the rudimentary ones with which the cars came equipped. There was no carpeting. Pullman and Field spent about $1,000 on each car. After fresh coats of paint and varnish were applied, the pair were ready to be placed in service.[54]

No. 9's features were demonstrated in a run made for several company officials, a representative of the New York Railroad Bureau, and a group of Chicago newspaper reporters on the afternoon of August 15, 1859. The short consist left the platform at Van Buren Street for Summit, 12 miles southwest of the city, where the group witnessed the changeover from seats to berths. After a champagne toast to mark the occasion, the party returned to Chicago.[55]

A couple of weeks later, on September 1, a night train arrived at Bloomington from Chicago with no. 9 on the train's rear end, outwardly indistinguishable from the rest of the consist except for the words "Sleeping Car" painted above the windows. Most of those on the platform boarded the coaches, prepared to snatch what sleep they could sitting up. A few, however, gravitated to the rear car. Witnessing the event was the man who was destined to take rail travel to a new standard of civility, Pullman. "The people of Bloomington, little reckoning that history was being made in their midst, did not come down to the station to see the Pullman car's first trip," the train's conductor, J. L. Barnes recalled years later. "There was no crowd, and the car, lighted by candles [later replaced with oil lamps], moved away in solitary grandeur, if such it might be called. I remember on that first night I had to request the passengers to take their boots off before they got into the berths. They wanted to keep them on— seemed afraid to take them off."[56]

Though clearly not the first sleeping cars on American rails, the cars were the first Pullman-designed sleepers to operate, one of several firsts the Chicago & Alton throughout its history would rightly claim. A third Pullman and Field sleeper soon joined the roster, and Field, armed with the success of the first three cars, continued building and placing sleepers on various western railroads. Pullman, however, seeing new opportunities in Colorado— where gold had recently been discovered— had no other involvement with Field until 1863 when he returned to Chicago to start his own sleeping car business in earnest.

▾ ▾ ▾

Pullman's sleeping car had been produced during difficult economic times. The effects of the 1857 panic were still felt throughout the country. "Never, in the whole history of railroad enterprises, has there been a time so trying as the past two years. Difficulties of the most embarrassing character have met our [board of directors] at every step." So began President William Shephard's 1859 annual report to JA&St.L stockholders. "Besides disastrous failures in crops, unseasonable weather, nonpassable roads, and unprecedented scarcity of money, there has been an almost universal distrust of all new railroad enterprises in this and in all other states; even railroads in operation, whose credit was high at home and abroad . . reeled and staggered under the financial embarrassments and disasters which have for the past two seasons attended all railroad enterprises in the West."[57]

Shephard's railroad was still not open, but the bridging and grading of the Northern Division and the 24 miles of right-of-way between Jacksonville and White Hall were finished. The junction with the Great Western was in place at Jacksonville, and four miles of track south of town had been laid. The Middle Division, between White Hall and Carrollton, saw no work at all, but track there was to be laid over level prairie, easily accomplished in a few weeks. It was the last segment to be completed. The Southern Division was where the heaviest work remained. One hundred thousand cubic yards of soil were removed from the 150-feet-deep cut at the Big Piasa approach then moved half a mile to create the embankment on the other side of the 60-feet-tall viaduct over the Big Piasa. Its five arches, 40 feet wide, with approaches, made up a truly impressive 300-feet limestone structure. Park and Robinson, the contractors, however, had no end of difficulties in finishing it. Foundation pits repeatedly flooded, temporary bridges washed out, and work was regularly interrupted by the season's flooding. Despite the adversities, the JA&St.L's most impressive structure was finished.[58]

Because of the hard times, neither the company nor Edgerton & Sage could satisfy the provisions of their agreement. In June the two parties agreed to terminate their contract. Charles Noble, chief engineer of the railroad, assisted by Charles Allendorph, took over supervision of the subcontractors, who were thereafter paid directly by the company.

Nine years had passed since the JA&St.L

had been chartered, and in the interim, great railroad systems elsewhere had been completed. The company's reliance solely on local funding slowed progress, but through conservative spending, the defaults of larger systems, like the Erie, the IC, and the neighboring St.LA&C, had been averted.[59]

Work on the T&P resumed in the summer of 1859 once the incessant rains ceased. Before winter's frost ended work for the year, five and one-half miles of track, starting from Jacksonville, had been laid. The road had also been adversely affected by all the circumstances Shephard described but, nonetheless, had managed to stockpile the ties and rail needed for completion of the line at least to Petersburg.[60]

Meanwhile, the attorneys representing the bondholders returned to Springfield in July 1859 to again meet with Matteson to tell him the bondholders had reconciled their differences and were now prepared to assume control of the railroad. They told Matteson the employees and woodcutters would be paid and Matteson's other stipulations would be met. Charles Frost, they informed Matteson, had been appointed chairman of the Bondholder Committee and would arrive soon to sign the transfer papers.[61] But while the negotiations among the bondholder committees were going on in New York, the Northern District of Illinois Court at Chicago was hearing a suit filed by Septimus Crookes, a first mortgage holder. He alleged that the assets of the company were being misappropriated, and he sought relief on behalf of the first and second bondholders through the appointment of a receiver.

Matteson received Frost at his posh Springfield home, heard the proposed details of settlement, and conceded his willingness to relinquish control. But he stated that he no longer had the power to do so, nor did his partner, Litchfield, since the liens awarded Crookes in court had to be satisfied first. Frost was not prepared for this, thinking all issues had been resolved. He returned to New York, seemingly no closer to a resolution than before. Almost six months of negotiations had still not resolved the ownership question.[62]

Benjamin Godfrey's woes related to his disastrous business relationship with Dwight, though not totally satisfied, were partially addressed in a decree handed down in Madison County Circuit Court in October 1859, which settled Thomas Wason's claim against Dwight, the Metropolitan Bank, and Godfrey. As a result of the court's decision, Wason was awarded what he was still owed on the rolling stock delivered nine years earlier plus interest. Dwight was found to owe Godfrey $120,283 and the return of title of Godfrey's property. A claim of A. T. Cowman against Danforth, which Godfrey had inherited after Cowman's bankruptcy, was also settled in Godfrey's favor. Finally, one of the most nefarious and confusing conflicts had concluded.[63] All things considered, Wason did well in receiving full payment for what he was owed. Most creditors of the railroad fared more poorly. Swinburne, for example, wasn't fully paid for the 38 engines he delivered and, as a result, was forced out of business in 1857. Most others suffered near total losses or complete write-offs.[64]

Frost, meanwhile, reported back to the bondholders. He related what Matteson had told him—that if they were to take control of the railroad, the claims of Crookes had to be settled first. This caused yet another uproar. The warring factions were at it once again and could not reach agreement. Finally, with no agreement in sight, the judge in chancery, Thomas Drummond of the United States Northern District Circuit Court of Chicago, acted on Crookes's suit and named a Chicago attorney representing the bondholders, Charles Congdon, and a successful New Orleans businessman, James Robb, as receivers of the company. They took over November 30, 1859.[65]

As convoluted as the railroad's affairs were, as discredited as the preceding managements had been, and as deplorable a condition as the railroad's property was in, it would have been reasonable to assume sorting out a future for the railroad might prove impossible. Instead, one of the most successful turnarounds in American railroad history was about to begin. The dark clouds of excessive debt, fraud, and incompetent management were to pass, replaced by clear skies of expansion, large returns on equity, and heightened prestige for the railroad. A 40-year period of extraordinary success was about to start. The company would soon take its place among the best of the nation's railroads.

5

From Calamity to Prosperity

It was fortuitous for the T&P and the JA&St.L that the city of Jacksonville was named the site of the 1860 Illinois State Fair. Transporting visitors proved an ideal opportunity to demonstrate the value of the newly opened 47-mile Manchester to Jacksonville and 28-mile Petersburg to Jacksonville routes. Neither railroad was finished (no ballast had been applied to either right-of-way, and few depots had yet been erected), but that didn't matter to would-be passengers. The train proved far more comfortable than slow and tiring trips by horseback or wagon would have been. Still, the first trains traversed the countryside so slowly that those wishing to board had

merely to stand at trackside and wave to the engineer to get him to stop.

JA&St.L tracklaying crews had resumed work south of Jacksonville, heading toward Manchester in early March 1860.[1] The incessant rains of the last months of 1859 had made any attempt to elevate a grade and keep cuts in place through the floodplain of the Big Sandy Creek area hopeless. When the rains stopped in December, the soft marshland dried sufficiently so that by the beginning of the new year, work could proceed. By early spring, laborers on the T&P resumed work and, after 30 days of steady progress, had 15 miles of railroad laid from Jacksonville to Ashland. By August Tallula had been reached. The last seven miles to Petersburg were finished in early September. About the same time, JA&St.L crews had reached Manchester.[2]

Once the successful and popular state fair closed, traffic on the two roads diminished. Minimal service was afforded between Petersburg and Manchester by an every-other-day mixed train that took a scheduled five hours southbound and four and one-half hours northbound to reach either end of the line. It was a pattern of service that remained for the next few years. With neither road generating much traffic, it had been wisely decided to save expenses by operating as one, though each road remained an independent corporation. The 75 miles of combined railroad, however, with neither a north nor a south outlet, would serve as little more than a Great Western feeder line for the next eight years.[3]

While operations were getting under way in the Jacksonville area, James Robb and Charles Congdon were preparing the reorganization of the CA&St.L. They had spent the first few months in charge as receivers formulating a strategy that would bring major changes in the way the railroad was organized, financed, and operated. The workers were demoralized. The bondholders were distrustful. The public was dismayed. Robb was a decisive man who wasn't afraid to make unpopular decisions. Within the first months of 1860, he initiated the first of many changes that would transform the company.

Those Bloomington Shop laborers who were still working (many had left, fed up with nonpayment of wages and other indignities) were laid off, and the shops were closed indefinitely to save expenses. Engineers, firemen, and conductors were furloughed. All but two of the general office staff at the Bloomington headquarters were terminated. Robb had decided to move the company's general offices to Chicago. There, he felt, he could find talented and experienced department heads who would take charge of the restoration of the distressed property and set a new course for the railroad.[4]

Robb recruited Roswell Mason to lend his expertise. Mason had begun his career in the engineering department of the Erie Canal Company and later worked on canals in New Jersey and Pennsylvania before taking his skills to the Housatonic Railroad, then the New York & New Haven (NY&NH). In the early 1850s, he was named engineer-in-chief of the IC, where he assembled a staff that eventually numbered almost 100. Overseeing the transportation department was added to Mason's responsibilities before he left to become a director of the Joliet & Chicago. Mason's technical expertise nicely complemented Robb's management skills. Then C. H. Allen was hired as the road's chief engineer and superintendent.[5]

Though Robb himself had no engineering background, he did have experience in both finance and management. A Pennsylvanian, he had moved to New Orleans where he started a banking career, founding the New Orleans Bank. Robb was named president of the New Orleans Gas, Light and Banking Company and two years later, of a subsidiary utility in Havana, Cuba. After the M&O was incorporated, the business leaders of New Orleans realized the potential threat to their city's preeminence as a gulf port. A railroad convention—over which Robb presided—was called, and a year later, in 1852, he was named president of the New Orleans, Jackson & Great Northern Railroad. He was leading that company through its early building phase and first operations when Judge Thomas Drummond appointed him receiver.[6]

The most pressing challenge facing Robb and Mason was the rebuilding of the entire right-of-way. Except for unavoidable repairs, little had been done to the track or roadbed over the previous three years. The men made a couple of inspection trips and concluded that "in fact the whole thing could be fitly [sic] compared to a worn out farm, that had been under rent for several years, the tenant having no object or aim, except to get the most he could from it, without incurring any expense that could possibly be avoided."[7] The single main line, especially the hastily laid Bloomington-Joliet portion, was in wretched condition. Some of it was bogged down in the washed away earth that had been raised as grades. Bridges and culverts were in bad repair, as were lineside structures. Because none of the structures had been painted, considerable wood rot was evident.

When Robb took over, the railroad had 38 locomotives—seven of them judged beyond

repair and 19 others awaiting shopping. That left only 12 serviceable engines on the entire railroad, all 4-4-0s, 10 of them Swinburnes—plus a single Norris, named the *Stephen A. Douglas,* and a lone Rogers, an 1857 replacement for the first Swinburne, no. 1. All seven of the road's original engines were gone. The *Springfield* and *Alton* had been sold as construction engines to the now merged Michigan Southern–Northern Indiana (MS–NI), and the *B. Godfrey, E. Keating, Hickox, Marion,* and *Macoupin* were retired.[8]

Correcting the desperate power situation was made a priority. In February 1860 an order for six state-of-the-art, high-speed, wood-burning passenger engines was given to Norris & Co. of Philadelphia. Along with Baldwin and Rogers, Norris was one of the leading locomotive manufacturers and had already produced more than 1,000 locomotives. A month later another order for 10 more engines, this time with Rogers, was placed. Rogers was one of the most innovative of builders, and its Paterson, New Jersey, plant was one of the largest. Of the second 10 ordered, one was a

wood-burning 4-4-0, but the other nine—made up of two 0-4-0 switchers and seven 4-4-0s—were coal-burning, the first of the type the railroad would own.[9]

To adopt coal as fuel for the road's locomotives was undoubtedly Mason's decision. The IC had experimented with coal as early as 1855 while he was there after a southern Illinois coalfield was unearthed. That road's tests showed that a coal-burning engine could handle an average of five more cars than a wood-burning engine. Since the price of a ton of coal was cheaper than an equivalent supply of wood, the difference in fuel price and impending rapid depletion of a wood supply had been enough to warrant the IC's conversion.[10]

In April the first of the new Rogers engines, named the *Mercury,* arrived at Springfield off the Great Western. During the year 13 more engines were received, three of the Norris passenger engines, plus the rest of the Rogers order. Swinburne-built engine no. 2 was sold to the La Crosse & Milwaukee, and another was scrapped (one of the five judged unfit to be repaired). That same month the Bloomington

Shops were reopened, staffed with rehires and replacements. The first work assigned was the overhaul of nine of the non-serviceable engines and the conversion of one of the Swinburnes to coal. The back shops at Bloomington and the smaller service facilities at Chicago, Joliet, and Alton once again showed activity. The ready tracks outside the ten-stall roundhouse at Bloomington, the eight-stall structures at Joliet and Springfield, the five-stall building at Alton, and the single-stall wooden engine houses at Carlinville and Wilmington once again held serviceable engines. The frequent and disruptive changes of power that had resulted from engine failures over the past couple of years had been brought under control.[11]

The worst sections of track began being replaced with new and re-rolled iron rail over rebuilt roadbeds. These and other track replacements brought immediate improvements to operations. The embarrassingly slow Alton-Chicago passenger schedules that had prevailed for the past few years were reduced by as much as three hours. Schedules of under 12 hours were carded, only slightly slower than schedules from when the line was first opened but faster than any running times in the past three years.[12]

The railroad's transformation from that of a "wornout farm" into one of the most formidable railroads in the region had begun during a period when Illinois's population and commerce were showing phenomenal growth. By 1860 Illinois's population had more than doubled over the start of the previous decade and stood at 1,711,951. Populations of towns and cities had also doubled, and most along the Chicago-Alton route reflected that urbanization. Springfield, the center of the state's government, had an 1860 population of 9,320. Joliet claimed 7,104, a population slightly greater than Bloomington's 7,075. Alton's population had nearly doubled to 6,332; Lincoln claimed 5,700.

The most phenomenal growth and impressive expansion, however, was seen at Chicago. Somewhat more than 6 percent of the state's population lived there, a total of 109,000.[13] In one year, 2,700 new buildings had been erected, many of them warehouses, granaries, banks, and office buildings. Three flour mills were producing in excess of 100,000 barrels annually. Thousands of hogs were being hauled to the various pens throughout the city, commanding twice the price asked at the mid-point of the 1850s. More than 500 million board feet of Michigan and Canadian lumber arrived on lake boats that tied up along the south branch of the Chicago River. Manufactured goods, including iron products, machinery, railroad cars and fixtures, carriages, wagons, and the products of planing mills; sash factories; shingle mills; manufacturers of agricultural implements, shoes, clothing, and millinery; distillers and breweries; bread and cracker bakers; and processors of coffee and spices were generating an estimated $30 million.[14] Railroads were delivering more than 100 times the bushels of wheat previously brought by wagon to the city. Large granaries along the Chicago River stored the bounties of the farms of Illinois and surrounding states. Chicago had already become the largest exporter of grains in the world, each year easily filling the holds of more than 6,000 vessels with over 2 million tons of grains.[15]

▼▼▼

Chicago's reputation as the West's most important city at the start of the 1860s earned it the honor of being named the convention site of the newly formed Republican Party. Eastern party leaders wanted to cement a bond with western voters, feeling that eastern Republicans and former Whigs would easily read the signal the Democrats were sending by holding their convention in Charleston, South Carolina, the center of southern unrest. Five hundred delegates, and the simply curious, began arriving in Chicago in early May. Eventually, thousands made their way to the city. Most arrived by train on special excursion fares the railroads offered. Many from downstate Illinois counties, especially Sangamon, took advantage of the company's low rates to witness what they hoped would be the nomination of their favorite son, Abraham Lincoln.[16]

Although Lincoln himself did not attend, choosing to remain in Springfield—since then it would have been considered unseemly to appear personally—he was well represented by his good friend Judge David Davis, who

The crew of a new and well kept 4-4-0, no. 74, received from Schenectady in 1868, pause at Braidwood to have the moment recorded on film. By the time the engine was delivered, the C&A was a nearly rebuilt railroad. (E. L. DeGolyer, Jr. 5 x 7 Photo. Coll., P727.1147, courtesy of DeGolyer Library, SMU)

ran Lincoln's campaign from the third floor of the Tremont Hotel. He and a handful of trusted lieutenants worked feverishly for Lincoln's victory. Three days into the convention and after three ballots, Lincoln was named the party's nominee. After Hannibal Hamlin of Maine was declared the party's vice presidential candidate, the convention's business was finished. The thousands of visitors and delegates packed homeward-bound trains throughout the weekend and into the early part of the next week.[17] The convention was Chicago's chance to strut its stuff, and from all accounts, the city did that exceedingly well. The spectacle at the Wigwam, the wooden building at Lake and Market Streets built specifically for the convention, was over, but a new chapter in the city's history had been written. Political conventions, Republican, Democrat, as well those of other short-lived but earnest parties, became a nearly every-four-year Chicago event.

When the telegraphed news of Lincoln's election as president of the United States reached Springfield in November, celebrations broke out. Crowds surrounded the statehouse and cheered their hero. It was inconsequential to Lincoln partisans that his opponents had garnered more votes than he had. One of their own had won, and that was all anyone in Springfield needed to know.[18] A few weeks after his election, Lincoln boarded a Chicago-bound train for his first meeting with Hamlin.

At Bloomington he made a two-minute speech to a crowd that had spontaneously gathered when word spread that he was onboard. En route, as cordial and entertaining as ever, Lincoln passed the time spinning the yarns for which he had become famous. Throughout that winter Springfield-bound trains brought thousands of people seeking favors from the president-elect or those just anxious to offer him their good wishes.[19] In early February 1861, Lincoln bid farewell to the people of Springfield from a Great Western car's platform. "I now leave, not knowing when or if ever I may return, with a task before me greater than that which rested on Washington," he told the crowd.[20] He was leaving the state that had embraced him like no other politician of his era and a city he was instrumental in making the state's capital. That the country he was to lead would soon divide was evident to all; how he and the country would cope was yet to be determined.

With Lincoln's departure, Springfield regained a sense of normalcy and the General Assembly resumed its work. In February 1861 the legislators granted a charter for the Chicago and Alton Railroad, the fourth corporate name in the company's history.[21] Though the official founding of the railroad is remembered as February 27, 1847, it is February 14, 1861, that marked the beginning of the most glorious period in the company's history—the last four decades of the nineteenth century. It was then that the railroad forged a powerful presence, achieved its greatest profitability, and earned the admiration of Wall Street and of the leaders of the nation's other railroads. Conservatively managed, the railroad was rebuilt to very high standards, was stocked with new power and equipment, and, as a result, returned steady and generous payouts. But that all lie ahead. The storm clouds of war were rolling in. In April 1861, off the coast of South Carolina, Confederate forces fired the first hostile shots on Ft. Sumter. The Civil War had commenced. Throughout Illinois, men and boys—259,092 of them before the conflict ended—enlisted or were drafted into the army. Eventually, they comprised 10 artillery, 17 cavalry, and 150 infantry regiments and saw action at Shiloh, Vicksburg, and Chickamauga; participated in Sherman's invasion of Georgia; and captured Mobile and Montgomery. Regrettably, nearly 35,000 of them never returned.[22]

Unlike the Baltimore & Ohio (B&O), which ran through both Union and Confederate country and suffered frequent attacks on its bridges and track—disruptions sustained by Missouri railroads and roads elsewhere throughout the South—the C&A was never threatened and incurred no loss to its property through military action. Aside from the shortage of labor, the only inconvenience suffered during the war years was the confiscation by the federal government in 1863 of Swinburne no. 13 and, somewhat later, of 14 assorted freight cars.[23] Production for the war effort only benefited the company through the movement of added carloads of livestock, grain, ammunition, flour, salt pork, blankets, uniforms, gun carriages, tents, camp kits, and other needed military goods. Hundreds of troops were carried to Alton and East St. Louis for embarkation south, but the C&A's share of troop traffic was nothing compared to that of the IC and the roads headed east out of Chicago.[24]

During the war years, Illinois farmers became more mechanized, using such labor-saving implements as the Leper and Kidder riding corn plow, the McCormick reaper, and Bail and John P. Manny mowers to plant and gather the harvests. As a result of the transport of mechanized equipment and added farm production, the company saw 1861 revenues rise to $1.1 million (the first time a million had been reached since 1856) and had a net operating ratio of 58 percent, yielding comfortable earnings of $452,092.[25]

During the first year of the war, 14 locomotives, five passenger coaches, and two mail and express cars—all products of the Bloomington Shops—were added, and another sleeper was leased from Pullman. The freight car fleet was enlarged by 70 cars. Fifteen percent of main-line rail was relaid on 200,000 new ties, and 40 miles of the main line was ballasted for the first time. Covered truss bridges replaced the former hastily built structures over the Kankakee and Sangamon Rivers. Eighty-two other bridges were thoroughly repaired. A 12-car coach house was erected, and the Bloomington roundhouse was enlarged by three stalls. A new roundhouse with adjoining shops was under construction at Alton, replacing the original that had been destroyed by fire in November 1860. Up and down the line, depots and other structures were painted for the first time.[26] Restoration accelerated the next year. Another 130,000 ties were laid. Fifty-four more miles of track were replaced. Cuts were widened, and more fill was dumped through trestle timbers. Seven more engines; eight coaches; four baggage, mail, and express cars; and 88 freight cars were added. There was evidence everywhere that a revitalized transportation artery was emerging.[27]

Throughout the first half of 1862, the New York bondholders moved closer to an agreement spelling out which of them would gain payment priority and how the outstanding claims would be settled. At a July meeting at the Continental Bank in New York, the Brown Brothers claim dating back to the Spencer Lease period was finally settled. To satisfy the liens spelled out in the Crookes suit that forced the company into receivership, the ceiling of $2 million of first mortgage bonds was increased by $750,000, and the proceeds were used to pay claimants.[28] It had taken more than two years to reach a settlement, but at noon, October 15, 1862, seven of the twelve commissioners gathered in the company's Chicago offices and officially accepted ownership of the company from L. H. Meyer and Samuel J. Tilden, trustees of the first and second mortgage holders.[29]

At the same time ownership was being transferred, William Shephard and William Greene, presidents of the JA&St.L and T&P, respectively (Greene succeed Richard Yates who had resigned as president of the T&P to successfully run for governor of Illinois), signed documents of consolidation of their railroads. The two roads had operated as one since their simultaneous openings two years earlier, so the agreement proved a mere formality.[30] On October 27, 1862, the St. Louis, Jacksonville & Chicago Railroad (St.LJ&C) was formed with Shephard as president. A charter was issued the following February (fittingly signed by Governor Yates) with a provision that called for the immediate transfer of the rail and spikes (sufficient for eight miles of track) that sat on the Peoria wharf and in the town of Washington to Manchester and White Hall.[31] This made it clear that Shephard intended to finish the Jacksonville-Godfrey segment before extending the railroad.

On April 1, 1863, the new C&A board of directors met for the first time, a majority of its members made up of residents of Illinois. A week later they elected Robb president and retained C. H. Allen as the road's superintendent (by now Mason had moved on to his other interests).[32] Three weeks later, the board met again. Facing them was the question of what to do about the soon-to-expire annual lease of the J&C. The J&C's president, Timothy Blackstone, earlier had submitted a proposal on behalf of his bondholders to the Bondholders' Committee of Reorganization offering them outright purchase or a perpetual lease of the railroad. The bondholders expressed little interest in taking on additional debt (Blackstone had asked $1.3 million for the railroad), and the offer was rejected. Instead the board authorized continuation of the annual lease. The Connecticut bondholders, however, were anxious to rid themselves of the property, and, once the C&A left the court's supervision, they intensified their pressure. They threatened to sell the property to another railroad, perhaps one less friendly, or to abandon the property altogether once the current lease expired. It would have been unlikely the road would be abandoned, but a sale to another railroad was a real possibility. The great stores of lumber and the slaughterhouses located on the south fork of the Chicago River

the company served were prized generators of traffic that any of the roads at Chicago would have been happy to capture. Interest in the rest of the line to Joliet would have depended on the potential buyer.[33]

The issue became contentious when there was no indication from Robb which way, if any, he would move. In late October, with termination of the annual lease three months away, William Buckingham, governor of Connecticut and agent for the J&C bondholders, tried to hasten a sale with a reduced price of $900,000 but with the caveat that Robb had to accept within 15 days. This was not enough time for Robb to act because the C&A charter stipulated that three quarters of the stockholders had to approve any acquisition or issuance of new securities. Robb could not meet Buckingham's deadline and reluctantly told him he would have to pass on the offer.

It was then that Blackstone stepped in. He told Robb if he could assure him that a perpetual lease would be executed, Blackstone would take an option to purchase the road, giving Robb the time he needed to arrange the lease. Robb readily agreed, and on December 31, 1863, the C&A's executive committee, on behalf of the board, signed papers leasing the J&C, starting January 1, 1864. The deal was the first in which Blackstone played a role in molding the future of the C&A, but it would not be the last. A permanent lease of the Joliet to Chicago trackage brought immediate savings since the perpetual lease cost only $140,000, considerably less than the former $187,122 year-to-year lease,[34] and ended any threat to the C&A's Chicago entry ever again.

Meanwhile, Shephard was struggling to keep the St.LJ&C operating. The few carloads of freight and even fewer passengers turned over to the Great Western at Jacksonville did not provide the returns needed to keep the road's infrequent trains running. He had to find a way of getting the line finished.[35]

It seemed certain since the first discussions of presidents Bliss and Woodson back in the 1850s that the two roads would align. Now, 10 years later, that was less of a certainty given the rights Shephard's road had to build north to the Illinois River coalfields and to a connection with the IC. Were that to have occurred, Shephard's road could have become competition for the C&A if the IC took control of the road. And Shephard now had other options. He could align with John Allen's recently reorganized Peoria, Pekin & Jacksonville—successor to the incomplete Illinois River Railroad—which had started construction at Havana on the Illinois River headed south toward Jacksonville.[36] When Allen took over, he made clear his intention to push north to Peoria and south to Jacksonville as soon as possible (which he accomplished in 1869). At Peoria a connection with the Rock Island's Bureau County would mean Shephards's traffic could move over those railroads to Chicago. Though a link with Allen's road was a less favorable alternative, Shephard still had to consider it. And he had a third, though less likely, alternative. He could apply for authority to extend his own line to Chicago.

It can be assumed Shephard never seriously thought his still unfinished and feeble line could actually reach so distant a place as Chicago. More likely, in getting a charter amendment, passed in February 1863, giving his road rights to "build, construct, and maintain its said railroad from Jacksonville north to the City of Chicago, via Ottawa, or other wise, with a branch road to any point on the Illinois River south of the city of Peru" and to "extend its main line, and to build a branch or branches from such main line to any other railroad or railroads with which it may be able to make a connection," he was making his road more attractive for takeover.[37]

The bill's passage got Robb's attention and led to the eventual alliance of his road with Shephard's. Once again, Blackstone became involved. Though not yet a C&A official, Blackstone had gained Robb's confidence and was employed to negotiate with Shephard. Acting as an independent contractor, Blackstone offered to finish the St.LJ&C railroad from Manchester south to Godfrey and, after that segment's completion, to extend the road northward beyond Petersburg but to extend it to a point on the C&A, likely Bloomington, rather than in the direction of Ottawa. He assured Shephard once that was completed, the C&A would provide rights to East St. Louis and Chicago and a guarantee of a 10 percent override on all traffic his road delivered. In this way Shephard retained ownership and control of his railroad, did not have to incur large construction costs, and would have as a partner a railroad that was quickly advancing to the forefront of Illinois's railroads. He did not spend much time considering Blackstone's proposal. It was the resolution he was looking for. In April 1863 a contract was signed. Nine months later, a joint tariff preventing discriminatory rates from being charged by either road between similarly distanced stations was published. Through the agreement, the threat to the C&A's territorial dominance ended.[38]

In 1863 the C&A was in the second year of a six-year rehabilitation program, but the shortage of supplies the road needed was causing problems. Conflicting demands of the military for weapons and the railroad's need for new rail resulted in skyrocketing iron prices. Due to the shortage of labor to cut them, ties too were in short supply. It became clear that neither would be available for the coming construction season, so the company started re-rolling its own rails (at a facility set up at Chenoa). To ensure a sufficient supply of ties, Robb bought 847 acres of timber along the Illinois River southwest of Wilmington. A sawmill was installed, and carpenters built a few barges to haul ties to the company's tracks at Wilmington. For the next few years, the tract yielded all of the wood the company needed before the useable ash and pine was exhausted and the site was sold.[39]

The road's reconstruction had progressed at a steady pace during the first couple of years of the war, but, as more and more men volunteered or were drafted for service, finding enough laborers became a critical problem. With so many of Illinois's men in uniform, including some of the company's own employees, there were not enough laborers to maintain the fast pace of the past few years. A partial solution was found by hiring state prisoners as laborers. A more permanent solution came after an agent was appointed and sent to England, where he hired 300 permanent laborers.[40]

A milestone was achieved in early 1864 when the first C&A dividends were declared, a 3.5 percent payout on the preferred and 2.5 percent on the common stock. They marked the first of an unbroken string of steadily increased payments that continued uninterrupted for 43 years.[41] The company's size and stature had grown considerably in just a few

years under Robb's leadership, and it became obvious that more managers were needed. Superintendent Allen had performed well during the early stages of rehabilitation, but he was replaced by Robert Hale, who was given the title of general superintendent. He added three assistants, all of whom had long careers with the railroad—S. H. Knight, J. C. McMullin and O. Vaughan. A new chief engineer, Octave Chanute, was appointed, as was a superintendent of machinery, John Jackman, and superintendent of the car department, R. Reniff. Together they formed a long-lasting (with the exception of Chanute who left after a few years) management team.

Meanwhile, there was a modest but strategic extension of the main line. On New Year's Day 1865, the first run of a C&A train from its namesake city to East St. Louis over company-owned tracks was made, ending the less-than-satisfactory seven-year-old trackage agreement with the THA&St.L. That road's single track, bereft of passing tracks, had become a dispatcher's nightmare, particularly for C&A trains, since preference often was given to the track owner's trains. Delays were frequent. Trains from one direction were sent out closely following each other, forcing trains from the opposite direction to hold to await clearance. Almost from the start of the agreement, it was evident there had to be a better way to deliver St. Louis-bound traffic.

Early in his presidency, Robb had approached THA&St.L president W. D. Griswold and suggested the two roads lay a second main line between Wood River and Illinoistown, the most congested section, but Griswold would not agree to share the expense.[42]

Robb was forced to look for an alternative.

One choice Robb had was to acquire the rights of the Alton & St. Louis (A&St.L). It had only a mile of track laid south out of Alton but held valuable rights to extend to Illinoistown. The A&St.L had been chartered in 1859 by William Mitchell and Samuel Buckmaster to take over a moribund Alton–East. St. Louis branch of the Sangamon & Northwest Railroad that had been started four years earlier. Of course, Mitchell and Buckmaster already had close ties with the C&A. Mitchell's Alton Packet Company provided Alton–St. Louis river transfers for the railroad, and Buckmaster had been named an incorporator of the reorganized company. Robb and Mitchell discussed matters sporadically over the course of a few months before it was decided C&A crews would complete the line and then Robb would lease the railroad in perpetuity.[43]

Put in charge of the project was chief engineer Chanute. He designed the line to high standards. Sixty-pound rail was laid on closely spaced ties, and the entire line was ballasted with sand taken from a Mississippi River sand bar at Alton. Culverts of stone and Howe Truss bridges with stone abutments spanned creeks and streams. Pile trestles were erected at Long Lake and East St. Louis, but over the next seven or eight years, they were filled and solid roadbeds were established.[44]

Company facilities at East St. Louis, like those of the other railroads already there, were built on the eastern banks of the Mississippi River on land owned by the Wiggins Ferry Company, which, since 1819, had exclusive rights to provide river transfers. Samuel Wiggins's service performed well handling the limited wagon-load freight delivered to him over the course of the next 30 years. In the early 1850s, when the O&M was making known its intention to reach St. Louis from a terminal across the river at Illinoistown, Samuel's son, William, concluded that that road and the others to follow would need lots of acreage for their facilities. In 1853 he and four partners incorporated and bought 1,200 acres along the Mississippi River and another 300 acres further downriver for coal mining.[45] Over the next 10 years, as railroads established terminals at East St. Louis, Wiggins Ferry Company prospered, selling or leasing land to the railroads, and until 1859—when the St. Louis Transfer Com-

pany was chartered to provide competition—providing an exclusive freight and passenger ferry transfer service.[46]

The C&A at East St. Louis broke ranks and used neither company for its transfers. Its freight and passengers were handled exclusively by a new company, the East St. Louis Transfer Company, formed by Mitchell and two partners, George Miltenberger and Robert Tansey. Until they entered the market, a car's content was unloaded then reloaded onto boats.[47] This was, of course, a costly and time-consuming process. In 1869 Mitchell and Tansey bought the Madison County Ferry Company, which had developed a reasonable business transporting broken freight between its Venice and North St. Louis docks. After takeover, Mitchell had inclines installed at its two portals at Mound Street, on the Missouri side of the river, where a short length of track connected the incline with the St. Louis, Kansas City & Northern, and at Venice where the C&A (and later the Burlington and the Indianapolis & St. Louis, successor to the THA&St.L) delivered cars. For the first time, carload freight between Illinois and Missouri crossed intact. Because the service was more efficient, lower rates (less than those of the other two ferry companies) could be charged. Soon Wiggins Ferry, faced with the competition, started its own carload operation. By the 1870s Madison County Ferry was transporting from 12,000 to 15,000 cars annually. The Wiggins operation moved even more cars.[48]

The C&A leased enough land at East St. Louis for a passenger depot, two freight houses, a six-stall brick roundhouse, engine service facilities, and associated trackage. Along the line, a water station was erected, as was a two-story, wooden depot at the newly named Mitchell Station, located about midway between Alton and East St. Louis. Within a year depots were erected at Venice, Kinder (later Granite City), and Milton.[49] Over seven hundred thousand dollars ($730,932) had been spent building the extension, not including the cost of the four new locomotives and freight cars allocated to the line. It was a sizeable investment, but, after the first full year of operation, the line was already generating $101,000 annually.[50]

Two important figures, neither unexpected, became C&A directors in 1864—John

Timothy Beech Blackstone assumed the presidency of the C&A in 1864 and remained its chief executive for 35 years, the longest continuous tenure of any railroad president. During the Blackstone years, the C&A became one of the most profitable American railroads, but Blackstone's fierce independence eventually led to the C&A's isolation and drift. (Courtesy of Chicago Historical Society)

Mitchell, president of the leased A&St.L, and Blackstone.[51] Both, but especially Blackstone, would be identified with the company for the next 35 years.

President Robb had successfully brought the C&A out from under the court's supervision, and, though not yet finished, the railroad's rebuilding was well along. Satisfied with what he had accomplished and with a likely heir apparent now a director, Robb decided it was time to move on. He had been offered the presidency of the Dubuque & Sioux City Railroad, a fledgling line pushing through the open spaces of Iowa, and, after giving it some thought, he decided to accept. In mid-April 1863 he resigned, though he remained a C&A director until a replacement could be named.[52]

The man Robb saw as his successor was the 35-year-old Timothy Blackstone. Since the age of 18, when he had been hired by Roswell Mason as a rodman for the NY&NH, Blackstone had developed a reputation as a smart, capable, and honest leader. In 1851, when Mason became chief engineer of the IC, he hired Blackstone and 30 others to assist him. At age 22, Blackstone was put in charge of construction of the Bloomington-Dixon seg-

ment of the IC for which he received considerable praise. That task completed, Blackstone waited for another railroading opportunity to arise and, in the meantime, made LaSalle, Illinois, his home. He was elected the town's mayor. The chance to resume his railroading career came when the J&C was looking for a chief engineer. Soon thereafter Blackstone was named the road's president.[53]

The transition from Robb's leadership to Blackstone's was seamless. They both were sound businessmen, careful to attend to detail but trusting of their subordinates. Taking over a road that was emerging as one of the Midwest's most important, Blackstone was elevated to the top ranks among railroad officials and became a leading figure in Chicago's social and cultural affairs. His position also brought him in touch with the industry's suppliers, among them fellow Chicagoan George Pullman. The two forged a friendship and business partnership that would bring fame to Blackstone's railroad and riches to Pullman.

Sleeping car passenger travel had become quite popular by the mid-1860s. By then 23 railroads had scheduled sleeper runs.[54] Each year, improved equipment—whether from a car builder or from a railroad's shops—was added to consists, each more lavishly appointed than its predecessor. Although the C&A was a pioneer among western roads in offering sleepers, its four Field-Pullman cars, though heavily patronized, had become somewhat dated by the early 1860s. Pullman's involvement with the car-building business had been a sideline during the years he spent in Colorado. He had left Field in charge of day-to-day operations. But the prospect of a railroad reaching the Pacific now seemed more probable, and Pullman's interest in the car-building business revived. The Wagner Car Company had clear leadership in supplying sleepers to eastern roads, but Pullman saw a large demand for cars once the soon-to-be-started transcontinental railroad was opened. In 1863 he left Colorado and returned to Chicago to resume an active role in his partnership with Field. They had a contract on the books to provide four more sleepers to the C&A. The first of the new cars they turned out opened a splendid new phase of luxurious passenger travel.[55]

In July 1863 Field and Pullman delivered to the C&A a 58-foot-long car built for them by the Wason Car Company. The car had double-hung windows and doors to provide a barrier to outside noise. The interior was divided into 14 sections, seating four persons per section, with a stateroom at each end, providing a 56-passenger capacity. During daylight travel the car had the appearance of a stately sitting room with sofas extending along the sides. Its conversion into nighttime sleeping quarters was a simple matter of sliding out the sofas, dropping the cushion backs, and extending damask curtains across the sections, leaving a three-foot aisle between. The car was fully ventilated and lighted by six kerosene lamps. The mattresses, pillowcases, and clean sheets provided patrons with the equal of a first-class hotel. The car rode on two double trucks—a total of sixteen wheels—which reduced side sway to almost nothing and provided an exceptionally smooth ride. Field and Pullman initially labeled the car simply the *40*, but as delivered, it bore the name *Springfield*, in honor of the hometown of the car builder.[56] After being displayed at a St. Louis exhibition in competition with the latest products of other manufacturers (most notably those of Woodruff's Central Transportation Company), the *Springfield* was added to the C&A roster.

Pullman was frustrated, however, with the delays Field had incurred from buying cars from others. He realized if his company was to compete in both quality and quantity, he would have to take greater control by building his own cars. Already connected with some of Chicago's leading businessmen, Pullman had little difficulty finding the startup capital he needed to initiate the next stage of his company's development.[57] He hired carpenters and mechanics, bought materials, and rented space in the C&A shop that stood on property now occupied by Chicago's Union Station. It was a small facility in which probably fewer than 20 men worked, but it suited Pullman because it was close to his offices, where he looked after his other businesses. By the autumn of 1864, assisted by his brother, Albert, he began supervising work on a car that would be totally Pullman.[58]

The product they turned out early in 1865 was identified as *Car A* during its construction phase but was soon renamed the more descriptive *Pioneer* when delivered. It was larger overall (a foot wider and two and one-half feet higher) than any Pullman car preceding it and had only 12 large, open sections. The greater space added measurably to passenger comfort. Though its size was remarkable, its lavish interior furnishings distinguished it from its predecessor, the *Springfield*, and set it apart from competitive products.[59] The car was to enter railroad legend.

Pullman's earlier sleeping cars had been modifications of other manufacturers' products, but he built the *Pioneer* from the frame up in the Chicago shops of the C&A. The car was wider and taller than its predecessors, included fewer and more spacious sections, was more luxuriously appointed, and cost four times more than similar cars of the time. (Courtesy of Chicago Historical Society)

▼▼▼

In March 1865 President Lincoln, appearing somber and drawn, took the oath of office for the second time, marking the occasion of his second term as president of the United States with a characteristically poignant speech, which called for "malice toward none; with charity for all; with firmness in the right, as God gives us to see the right, let us now strive on to finish the work we are in; to bind up the nation's wounds; to care for him who shall have borne the battle, and for his widow, and his orphan—to do all which may achieve a just and lasting peace, among ourselves, and with all nations." Citizens could sense the end of the nation's terrible conflict was near.[60]

A month later Jefferson Davis and his cabinet members attended Sunday services in the South's capital of Richmond, then fled the city, bringing to an end government of the confederation of seceded states. Petersburg, then Richmond, fell as Southern troops abandoned their posts. The next day, April 3, there was celebration in Washington. Squads of cavalry spontaneously began parading. Massive rounds of cannon fire resonated throughout the capital. Impromptu citizen-led parades broke out. Flags were posted everywhere. The celebrations went on for days, and, as telegraph reports reached cities, towns, and hamlets throughout the Union, citizens in those places initiated their own celebrations.

At 9 P.M., Palm Sunday evening, Secretary of War Edwin Stanton was delivered a dispatch. "General Lee surrendered the Army of Northern Virginia this afternoon on terms proposed by myself. The accompanying additional correspondence will show the conditions fully." It was signed U. S. Grant, Lieut-General.[61] The next day even greater celebrations broke out. Again cannon fire boomed, and people paraded and gravitated to the White House, where they begged the president to speak. He declined that day, but the next day he addressed the people with words of conciliation and soberly outlined the challenges the postwar nation would face.

On Good Friday, April 14, after spending the day and afternoon in a variety of meetings and conferences, the president and his wife, Mary, accompanied by Major Henry Rathbone and his fiancée, Clara Harris, arrived at Ford's Theatre for a performance of *Our American Cousin.* Seated in his upholstered rocking chair within the flag-festooned presidential box, neither the president nor any of the other occupants heard an intruder's approach. Quietly and cowardly, John Wilkes Booth eased his way within five feet of the president, slowly raised a brass, single-shot derringer pistol, and fired. The half-inch diameter ball entered the left side of the president's head and lodged behind his right eye. At 7:22 the next morning, the 56-year-old president, who had risen from humble origins to ultimate heights, was officially pronounced dead.

As word of his death reached the somber citizens gathered outside William Peterson's house across from Ford's Theatre, where Lincoln had been taken, people bowed their heads, drew handkerchiefs to their tear-filled eyes, and comforted each other. Soon church bells began tolling, first in Washington, then as word spread, in Boston, New York, Chicago, and Springfield. The nation's citizens had quickly come to know the awful truth, and for the rest of their lives could remember where they were and what they were doing when the news first reached them.[62]

For seven days the martyr's remains lay in state in the capitol before his coffin was placed aboard a 48-foot, 4-inch-long open vestibule car, known as the President's Car. The car had been completed in the Military Railroad System shop at Alexandria, Virginia, the year before, but Lincoln had never used it. Six other cars, pulled by a single engine, were added for the officials, friends, and honor guard who would accompany the president's remains on the train's 1,700-mile journey back to Springfield. Among others aboard were four close friends from Illinois: United States Supreme Court Justice David Davis, whom Lincoln had appointed a justice and before whom Lincoln had argued many of his cases as an Illinois lawyer (including those affecting the earliest days of the A&S); Illinois senator Richard Yates, who left the presidency of the T&P to run for governor before heading to Washington; Ninian Edwards, the president's brother-in-law and fellow member of the Illinois legislature who worked with Lincoln on getting a charter passed for a Springfield-Alton railroad; and John Stuart, Lincoln's first law partner and the man who introduced the amendments to the A&S's charter which permitted the northward extension to Bloomington.[63]

For the next 13 days, the president's funeral train traveled a slow and meandering route through 180 cities and towns, stopping at state capitals and major cities, essentially retracing much of the route the president had taken to Washington. The first stop was at Baltimore, then Harrisburg, Philadelphia, and New York City. The train then proceeded up the Hudson River north to Albany, then west to Buffalo, on to Cleveland, Columbus, and Indianapolis—the engine and cars, except for the President's Car and one other carrying the 29-man military guard, were frequently exchanged as the train passed from one railroad to another. At Michigan City, Indiana, some of Chicago's most prominent citizens, including Blackstone, met the train and boarded. Slowly, draped in mourning cloth, the train proceeded westward, entering Chicago over the IC's lakefront trestle, finally pulling to a stop at Park Row (now Grant Park).

There the train was met by a massive, respectful crowd made up of some 50,000 Chicagoans and people from all over the Northwest who had come by train, horseback, and buggies and wagons to pay their last respects as hundreds of thousands had done over the previous two weeks. They formed a procession and escorted the president's horse-drawn hearse to the Cook County Courthouse under dark skies that yielded a steady drizzle. An estimated 125,000 persons passed the flag-draped coffin as it lay in state.[64]

On Tuesday evening, May 2, a 1,000-man torch-lighted escort accompanied the coffin to Union Station where it was once again placed in the President's Car. A train had been assembled, and on the point was no. 57, a Schenectady 4-4-0, one of the road's newest (built in 1862). In the cab were fireman Tom Freeman and engineer James Cotton. The conductor was George Hewitt.[65] By official military order, the train's consist was limited to no more than nine cars.[66] According to the brakeman, William Porter, the train consisted of "One baggage car, several ordinary coaches and the catafalque car, which was the second car from the rear end of the train."[67] Waiting ahead of no. 57 and the funeral train was a pilot engine, no. 40, a mate of no. 57. It would

be dispatched 10 minutes earlier to ensure a safe route. The day prior the track and bridges had been carefully inspected. The brakes of cars on sidings were locked to prevent them from being blown onto the main line. Every telegraph office was kept open, and agents were instructed to ensure that switches at their stations were locked. Guards were posted at road crossings. Any train on the railroad was to take siding 30 minutes before the scheduled arrival of the funeral train. As the engine passed a station, the station's bell would be rung.[68] Every conceivable precaution was taken to ensure there would be no incident causing embarrassment for the railroad.

At 9:20 P.M., no. 40, with Henry Russell at the throttle, gathered speed and proceeded out of the depot. At precisely 9:30 P.M., the funeral train moved forward, crossed the Chicago River, and began its parallel-to-the-canal journey toward Joliet. The train's schedule had been widely publicized, so all along the route sorrowful citizens gathered to watch the train pass on its final leg of its long journey. A bonfire at Bridgeport helped those gathered there to view the train. Crowds stood at Summit, Joy's (Willow Springs), and Lemont. At Lockport an immense bonfire was burning, and people with torches lined the track as the train slowly passed behind the canal's headquarters, a place Lincoln visited regularly while performing legal work for the Canal Commission. The light revealed the mourning cloth on almost every building and the signs of sympathy that were displayed, none more poignant than that which read "Come Home." At Joliet, near midnight in a steady rain, some 12,000 turned out for a silent, torch-lit vigil. Bells tolled, and a band played a funeral dirge. An immense arch spanned the track, decorated with flags and evergreens. A choir sang "There is Rest for Thee in Heaven." At Elwood and Hampton, bonfires lighted the train's path. At Wilmington some 2,000 turned out. At Gardner, hundreds silently stood at the depot. At Dwight, Odell, Cayuga, Pontiac, Chenoa, and Lexington, bells tolled and bands played funeral dirges against a background of shrouded buildings. Though it was 4:30 A.M., hundreds lined the track at Towanda.

At Bloomington the train paused. The engine's tender was replenished with water and fuel, and many who knew or had met Lincoln during his several visits to that city pressed against the President's Car, anxious to be close to him one last time. Some 5,000 turned out. The track was arched and bore the inscription "Go to thy Rest." At Shirley there were large numbers of mourners, as was true at Funk's Grove and McLean. The dawn was breaking when the train arrived at Atlanta. The sound of muffled drums and fifes greeted the train. Some carried portraits of their fallen president. An hour later, the train reached Lincoln. The depot, as was true of all those passed so far, was draped in mourning cloth. Assembled ladies from a local church, dressed in white with black trim, sang a requiem as the train passed under an arch across the track adorned with a portrait of the deceased leader on each column. The words "With Malice to None, With Charity for All" appeared between them. The people of Elkhart too had built an arch, draped in black cloth and adorned with evergreens and the Stars and Stripes. A cross of evergreens rose above the arch, displaying below it, "Ours the Cross, Thine the Crown." At Williamsville an arch also spanned the track with the words, "He Had Fulfilled His Mission."[69]

Lincoln's funeral train had been losing time since departing Joliet. As it approached the outskirts of Springfield, it was running about an hour late. Though many waiting at the Springfield depot grew impatient when the scheduled arrival time passed and no train appeared, they remained reverently silent. Thousands had arrived on trains the day before and filled the depot grounds. Unable to find standing room, hundreds were atop surrounding buildings. Finally, just before 9 A.M., the pilot engine appeared and slowly passed the depot. Then the headlight of no. 57 was seen, and the engine's face grew larger as it made its languid entrance into the city. An image of the president placed on the locomotive's front and the black drape along the boiler confirmed for the assembled that this was the train they had waited to see. With the President's Car spotted at the platform, Lincoln's coffin was removed and placed on a magnificent hearse provided by the citizens of St. Louis, drawn by six splendid black stallions that proceeded east to the Capitol.[70] Nearby was Lincoln's law office, where he had written

letters of support of the railroad and later prepared arguments in defense of it. Somewhat further away was his house—the only one he ever owned. Now he was home. Here he would remain.

Over time, legends surrounding Pullman's *Pioneer* and the composition of the funeral train took life. One story declared that Pullman's then most famous sleeper carried the president's coffin. Government records and published recollections written by those who had been there confirm the President's Car was the only carriage in which his remains were placed throughout the slow, meandering trip. Another myth declared that Mrs. Lincoln rode in the *Pioneer* with her two sons, Tad and Robert. In fact, Mary Lincoln was still in Washington as late as May 22 and only then left the capital; she had not accompanied the president's remains.[71] It is possible that Mrs. Lincoln was afforded use of the car later when she finally returned to Springfield, a fitting accommodation for the bereaved widow, but not as part of the funeral train itself.

So far overlooked in published coverage of the Lincoln funeral train (and thus leading to the erroneous and conflicting reports surrounding the *Pioneer*) was the operation of a special train Superintendent Hale had put together, which operated in advance of the pilot and funeral train. The *Joliet Republican* reported "an elegant sleeping car" was provided for Joliet's mayor and Common Council members, which was used as "a comfortable home during their stay at Springfield. . . ." The *Chicago Tribune* noted a "special train selected by the Chicago Committee [which] left the St. Louis [actually the Union] Depot about an hour before the funeral cortege . . . this arrangement in view of the limited accommodations at Springfield, gave to the Chicago party complete relief from the anxiety and confusion which must otherwise have existed. The train left the depot at eight o'clock on Tuesday evening . . . and arrived at Springfield at seven o'clock on Wednesday morning." Another report in the *Illinois State Journal* stated, "The special train this afternoon on the Chicago, Alton & St. Louis railroad, will leave this city (Springfield) at 6 o'clock P.M. for the north. . . . The special train that goes through to Chicago, will be made up of eleven sleeping cars."[72] Though no record exists, it can be

safely concluded the company's best cars, the *Pioneer* and the *Springfield,* were included in that number—one or the other the "elegant sleeping car" described in the *Joliet Republican* story. It may well have been this train the *Chicago Tribune* writer described as having 10 cars, with the eleventh car added at Joliet.

Because of the *Pioneer's* 10-foot width, it became legend that railroads could not operate the car until restrictive platforms and bridges were rebuilt, and to allow the car to operate over the C&A, crews hastily cut back offending platforms and timbers. In reality, the car's dimensions were not that different from similar luxury cars of the period. The President's Car itself was nine-feet, three-inches wide and made the journey across the country without incident. The C&A was in the midst of its rebuilding program, so it is unlikely anything but the latest railroad clearance practices were employed. There is no evidence, for instance, that the recently rebuilt and covered bridge over the Kankakee River at Wilmington, the most formidable structure to

pose a possible problem between Chicago and Springfield, was altered in any way.[73]

▾▾▾

The loss of the president had momentarily interrupted the normalcy of many lives, but after a period of mourning, activities resumed, including work on the St.LJ&C. By mid-August 1865 enough track was placed to allow trains to run as far as Pinkerton at Apple Creek. A few weeks later, tracks entered Carrollton. A turntable, which might have been an aboveground assembly without a pit, was put in place in early September. To celebrate, railroad officials boarded a train in Jacksonville for the first run through to Carrollton.[74] Tracklaying to Jerseyville up from Godfrey was finished by mid-November.[75]

Blackstone had promised William Shephard he would have a train operating between Jacksonville and East St. Louis by New Year's Day 1866. Given the long struggle thus far to get the railroad built, some must have greeted

Carrollton was an important station on the Jacksonville-Godfrey line and the starting point for construction of the LC&W. The depot, seen here in 1938, had been modified through the years but is typical of depots erected between White Hall and Drake. (William Raia Coll.)

The stations between Bloomington and Jacksonville (such as Minier seen here) did not initially produce the kind of traffic generated on the southern portion of the Jacksonville line. The tower protected the crossing of the Vandalia's Terre Haute–Peoria line. (William Dunbar Coll.)

the pronouncement with skepticism, but on that date, a special, eight- or ten-car train (contemporary reports differed), headed by a Rogers 4-4-0 named the *George Straut,* indeed left Jacksonville at 7:10 A.M. headed for East St. Louis. A pilot engine preceded the train. At East St. Louis, the celebrants walked across the frozen Mississippi River and on to the Lindell Hotel for a New Year's Day meal. They returned the same day. The long-awaited 88-mile railroad between Petersburg and Godfrey was finally opened after 15 years of struggle.[76]

There wasn't much doubt the line would succeed after the first load reports came in. At Carrollton, during the first week, 272 cattle and 450 hogs were shipped and large lots were reported awaiting loading. Another 350 hogs were shipped out of there the second week of operations, with similar counts recorded for the next few months. Wheat and flour began moving in February, and 5,000 feet of lumber from Black's Mill was shipped. In April 3,000 bushels of wheat, 27 barrels of whiskey, more flour, and apples were moved. Inbound lumber tonnage in the first 15 days of the month totaled 148,000 feet.[77] Traffic continued to build.

After survey crews working on the northern extension reached Mason City, towns began vying for inclusion in the route. The town of Lincoln actively promoted itself as the junction for the C&A. There was talk there of offering the railroad sizeable incentives (up to $150,000, according to some re-

ports). But had Blackstone ever considered Lincoln a serious contender, the surveyors would not have taken a northeast course to Mason City instead of a route almost due east directly to Lincoln. It was obvious Blackstone intended to link the roads at Bloomington.[78] That town's leaders were quick to ensure that happened. The city's railroad promoters, Jesse Fell and Ashley Gridley, called a public meeting attended by hundreds of residents of Bloomington and surrounding McLean County at which resolutions were passed for the city and county to offer inducements.[79]

In early 1867 the piles were driven, and the trestle over the Sangamon River east of Petersburg was raised. Grading crews were already working further to the east. By the end of June, a fast construction pace brought tracklayers to Mason City.[80] By mid-August track was laid to Delavan. So was a grade all the way to Bloomington. There the depot was being moved to the west end of Washington Street; the Market Street bridge was being widened to accommodate two tracks; and a switch, where the St.LJ&C would join the main line, had been installed. A month later the connection was made.[81]

Though there was nothing special associated with its departure, the first run of a train between Bloomington and East St. Louis via Jacksonville was made on September 23, 1867. Regular freight and passenger schedules were posted thereafter, and by December the railroad started fulfilling its new mail contract.[82] The almost immediate success of the Jacksonville-Monticello sub-division, however, was not matched on the northern extension. Traffic up from Jacksonville developed more slowly than that from Jacksonville south.

▼▼▼

When the C&A's main line was opened through to Joliet, the only stations north of Dwight were the hamlet of Gardner, the town of Wilmington, and Stewart's Grove, a fuel station where Peter Stewart supplied the railroad with cordwood. Otherwise, there was only an expanse of sandy loam and some low meadows with scattered stands of oak.[83]

In the area, a major new source of revenue was emerging. Until the mid-1860s, Chicago's industries and residences were fueled by coal from Ohio and Pennsylvania anthracite mines, brought to the city by rail and lake boats. In the late 1850s, coal raised in a few southern Illinois counties was shipped over the IC up to Chicago, and the cheaper and more accessible bituminous fuel began to satisfy the city's needs.

In 1858 a couple of aspiring coal miners began digging a hole on Nathan Cotton's land about four miles north of Gardner. Further to the north, around Morris, along the banks of the Illinois River, others already had some success. What the two men found, however, was mostly water, and, short of capital, they soon quit. At least two others tried their hand at finishing the dig before the last found coal and began removing modest tonnage. The shaft became known as the Cotton Mine, and in 1861 Nathan Cotton platted the village of Braceville around it.[84] The same year, a wealthy New Yorker, William Hurry, made a visit to the large tract he had purchased near Stewart's Grove and, before leaving, instructed his agents to begin exploration. By the spring of 1862, light tonnage was brought up from a shaft he financed.[85]

A couple of years later, William Henneberry of Wilmington was commissioned to dig a water well on Thomas Byron's farm located near the tracks just north of what was to become the town of Braidwood. At a depth of about 80 feet, he hit a 15-foot seam of coal. With the help of some others, Henneberry widened the hole and began producing sizeable tonnage.[86] There was enough to make it worthwhile for the railroad to start hauling the product to Chicago. In fact, so much was raised that in the autumn of 1864, solid trains were assembled for runs to Chicago. Before the end of the year, more than 6,000 tons were transported, but four or five times that amount could have been moved if cars and power had been available.

The emergence of coal as a new source of revenue for the company was first noted in General Superintendent Robert Hale's report to the stockholders for 1864.

The coal business, which is an important interest to the road, as well as to the public on our line, as much of the country on, and contiguous to our road, could not be settled for want of other fuel, should be fostered and aided. Coal is now being mined at several points, and would furnish a large and paying business, but want of stock has prevented us from accommodating it, except to a very limited extent. One firm has been compelled to purchase 25 cars, in order to send the products of their mines to market. We do their business, and allow them a small sum for the use of the cars. I think the company should furnish all the cars, as well for this and all other business, and during the fall and winter a coal train should be run, which would be remunerative, and greatly assist in developing the resources of the country.[87]

Henneberry started another shaft 100 feet east of the "Water Well," as his first mine became popularly known, in the spring of 1865. That shaft too immediately started producing. News of Henneberry's find caught the attention of others in the state and more distant places. Within months, mining engineers began arriving, performing tests to determine the area's potential. All reported strong prospects.[88] One of those who heard the news was a 34-year-old Scotsman named James Braidwood. He was the son of a mine operator and was a trained civil engineer who had emigrated to the United States in 1863. After short periods of work in the coal regions around Middlesex, Pennsylvania, he moved first to Belleville then to Danville, Illinois, before moving north in August 1865. He sunk a mine just west of where the Braidwood depot would later be located. His Eagle Mine was soon producing 130–180 tons of coal a day, the largest output of all the area's mines dug to that point. He found a customer, the Bridgeport Rolling Mills on the southwest outskirts of Chicago.[89]

Meanwhile, a few men at Gardner, now a town of about 400, noticed the mining efforts to the north and, to learn if the land surrounding their town also had coal, commissioned soil tests. Buoyed by the positive results, they offered a handsome reward of $2,000 for anyone who would start mining there. James Congdon and William Odell responded. The two leased a portion of the north part of the village during January 1864 and started digging a shaft. When they reached a depth of 60 feet, the shaft's sides caved in, and the project was abandoned. Congdon lost interest and sold out to Odell, who started another shaft almost immediately. Within a few months, he reached a seam of coal.[90] That same year a neighbor of Cotton's, John Augustine, started a shaft but, finding himself short of capital, abandoned the work. He later sold his interests to the Bruce Company, which finished the digging. Eventually coal was found, and the shaft became known as Old No. 1.[91]

The first big operator at Braidwood, organized in 1865, was the Rhodes Coal Company, later renamed the Eureka Coal Company. Over time four Eureka mines, located in the southwestern part of Braidwood, were opened. The company that eventually became Braidwood's largest operator, the Chicago & Wilmington Coal Company, was a well-organized, well-financed operation, backed by Boston money. In 1866 the firm began acquiring existing mines, available property, and mineral rights on land owned by others until 18 mines in and around Braidwood, each identified by a single letter, bore the Chicago & Wilmington name. Eventually nearly 50 mine heads dotted the area, traversed by some 25 miles of track.[92]

Soon mines were opened at East St. Louis, Alton, Brighton, Carlinville, Springfield, Lincoln, Bloomington, Normal, Chenoa, and Pontiac, each contributing small amounts of new tonnage for the railroad, but nothing like what was being produced at Braidwood. Hundreds of resellers located their lots along Chicago's railroads. The ever growing coal tonnage brought up from downstate Illinois mines fed the boilers of the city's thousands of factories, mills, businesses, hotels, and homes. Coal had become as important to Chicago's economy as its already thriving grain storage businesses, lumber traders, and another industry with which Chicago would be associated for more than a century—livestock trading and meatpacking.

Situated at the center of the vast western prairies that provided outstanding grazing land, Chicago seemed predestined to become the trading center for the region's livestock. In 1837, the year Chicago was incorporated, Willard Myrick fenced in some of his southside property to hold the cattle and hogs he butchered. During the 1840s and 1850s, a half dozen other yards, all widely scattered (most as much as two or three miles apart) and lo-

cated outside the city limits, were started. They too had plenty of grazing land around them. Each was served by a railroad. By the end of the Civil War, so much livestock was being brought to Chicago's various pens that the city could rightfully claim title as the world's largest livestock center.[93] But Chicago's borders had expanded and enveloped the yards. Pens such as Bull's Head and Sherman Yards found themselves squeezed by factories and houses that had built up around them. It became increasingly difficult to drive herds through what had been open fields but were now dedicated streets. The yards, once enclaves unto themselves, with drover hotels, saloons, and other essential facilities nearby, had become increasingly obnoxious to residents and businesses that had surrounded them.[94]

It was costly and difficult for the railroads to serve Chicago's several stockyards. Too often livestock had to be held for a day or more in on-line pens until space became available in Chicago. Long delays waiting to unload livestock often led to cars arriving with dead animals. Most railroads provided no dedicated equipment. Instead they modified boxcars by installing a second, ventilated door or by removing roofs.[95] The C&A was an exception. About 15 percent of its freight car roster during the 1860s was comprised of slat-sided stock cars.[96] Unlike corn, grain, lumber, and coal, which required no special handling, livestock shipments were lucrative but also a railroad's nightmare.

What started as the butchering and packing of beef, pork, and lamb only for local consumption grew over time into sizeable enterprises. During the Civil War, Chicago had overtaken Cincinnati as the most important exporter of cut meat. By 1860 there were 30 slaughterhouses butchering 450,000 cattle and hogs annually.[97] That number grew as the government's need for beef and pork to feed the troops led to even greater output. Most of the packers had located along the Chicago River's south branch in Bridgeport. The river was a convenient place to dump the tons of waste and carcasses the plants generated. Before long the waste became a serious health problem. "Might be cut with a knife . . . so thick and so powerful" was how one writer described the stench of rotting meat and the swarming flies attracted by the offal.[98] After a cholera epidemic broke out in 1849, the *Chicago Democrat* editorialized, "The great masses of the deaths . . . in our own city are clearly attributable to butchering within the city limits!"[99] The Chicago City Council responded by establishing a Board of Health and then prohibited erection of any new slaughterhouses or conversion of any existing buildings within the city limits. When a second cholera outbreak hit the city a year later, there was even talk of shutting down the established plants. That didn't happen, but new laws tightened the abandon with which the industry had operated.

As the end of the war neared, the chaotic stockyard situation was addressed. In the autumn of 1864, the Union Stock Yard and Transit Company was organized by nine railroads, eight packers, and a few individuals with a $1 million investment (including $50,000 by the C&A). The new enterprise set out to establish a single yard all of the city's railroads could serve. Named to head the new corporation was Blackstone, a compromise candidate intended to ensure even-handed management since most of the other railroad officials (such as James Joy of both the MC and the Burlington) had either real or perceived conflicts. Blackstone only headed the new company for a year before he saw to it that Peyton Chandler, a Chicago attorney and recently named C&A director, succeeded him.[100]

The site selected for the new yards was on 320 acres of swampy land west of Halsted Street and east of the south fork of the Chicago River in the town of Lake. The site had been selected because all railroads could easily reach it and it was in close proximity to the packers. Four miles southwest of Chicago's limits, there seemed little likelihood the yards would ever be threatened by encroachment from other industry or housing development.

The project was, even for Chicago, a spectacular undertaking. Though well-removed from the city boundaries, the site had the disadvantage of laying two feet below the level of the Chicago River. In the spring, after severe rainstorms, the area filled with standing water and regularly formed contaminated ponds. The best engineering skills would have to be employed to make the land suitable. To

attract that kind of design talent, a competition was held. When the entries were reviewed, the best solution was judged to be that of the C&A's Octave Chanute. In June 1865 the work began.[101]

After just six months, on Christmas Day 1865, the Union Stock Yards of Chicago were officially opened. The next day the Burlington brought in the first livestock train. During the first week, nearly 20,000 animals were penned. During the first full year of operation, 1.5 million animals were corralled, including 42,000 tons of cattle and hogs off the C&A, a level that was generally maintained for the next several years.[102] Within three years it was evident that even so large a complex was already inadequate, and another 1,800 pens covering an additional 40 acres were added. By 1870 three million animals had passed through the yards.[103] The success of Chicago's stockyards led to consolidated operations at Omaha, Kansas City, and St. Louis (the latter located across the river in East St. Louis), but though each handled substantial numbers of livestock, none came close to Chicago's volume. The city's supremacy as "hog butcher to the world" was never eclipsed.

▾▾▾

The increased and heavier traffic experienced during the last years of the war led to an earlier replacement of main line track than had been planned. In 1865, for the first time, 40 miles of main line iron were replaced with steel rails. Most of the replaced rails had been laid just a year or two earlier. Chanute attributed the rapid deterioration problem to the inferior character of the iron used in both English and domestic mills.[104] Though steel was more costly than iron, the road could afford it.

Despite the recently added new power, there were still not enough engines during the years immediately after the war to handle all the business that could have been transported. Nearly twice the number of locomotives could have been rostered, and the fleet would still have been inadequate. Inexplicably, just one engine, turned out by the company's own Bloomington Shops (by all accounts the first home-built engine), was added to the roster in 1866, but a year later, three 4-4-0s from the Hinkley & Williams Works of Boston and three 0-4-0 switchers from Schenectady brought the locomotive roster up to 72. Though an ambitious one-car-a-day building program was started, for the first two years after the war, a car shortage persisted. Besides new boxcars, flatcars, and stock cars for the C&A, the car department was kept busy building equipment for the St.LJ&C, turning out a coach and 135 freight cars.[105]

Even more cars could have been turned out with better facilities, but the rather shabby, hastily built, and inadequate car shops made for inefficient operations. Plans for replacement and enlargement of the complex were on the drawing boards, but work was not to start for another year or two. Master mechanic John Jackman's men, however, had it a little easier now that they worked in a nearly completed roundhouse. Sixteen new stalls had been erected. The new facilities fostered greater efficiency. Six stalls were added to the Alton roundhouse, bringing the total number to 14. Chicago's freight was being handled in a new brick freight house. The Stewart Avenue roundhouse at Chicago and the Springfield engine house got longer replacement turntables. The small depot at Pontiac was moved to Cayuga, and a larger depot was erected. Lawndale got a modest wooden depot, Lincoln and Normal new freight houses. The Bloomington Shops were expanded with the addition of a lumber-drying shop, an extension to the coal shed, a new pattern shop, and a badly needed addition to the car repair shop.[106] The rather primitive rail repair facility at Chenoa was replaced by new ones at Bloomington and Alton.[107] The right-of-way continued to see improvement. One hundred and ten miles of new and re-rolled iron (nearly half the road's main-line mileage) and six miles of sidings were replaced.

Engine watering facilities that had been built thus far were little more than wooden reservoirs, from which water was drawn in buckets, laid by the side of a track. In cold weather an attendant was assigned to keep a boiler fueled to heat the water sufficiently to keep it liquid. In the early 1860s, the C&NW's John Burnham started testing a tower design that effectively eliminated the tank house and boiler. Burnham's patented structure included a tub with an air-tight covering set on pilings with the piping and pumps required to elevate the water enclosed in a vertical box up the center of the grid of supports. A spout fed water by gravity directly into an engine's tender. Quick to recognize the design's greater efficiency, Chanute adopted it for his road. The first two of the many to follow were raised at the Sangamon River and at Pontiac.[108]

The amount of freight moved in 1865 was the greatest thus far in the company's history, and the high level of traffic continued throughout 1866. The only setback to even greater revenues was the reluctance of the public in 1866 to travel because of the outbreaks of cholera in both St. Louis and Chicago. Passenger receipts that year declined 22 percent, but freight revenues were a healthy 25 percent greater.[109] The next year was expected to be equally successful, but it neither started nor ended without major setbacks.

▾▾▾

An unusual warming in late January 1867 led to a rapid snowmelt across the northern reaches of the state. Huge chunks of ice on the Kankakee River were pushed along by the extraordinary volumes of runoff. The combination of the ice's weight and speed of the rushing water brought destruction to anything in its path. One such obstruction was the railroad's covered, wooden bridge at Wilmington, which in mid-February was swept away by a huge freshet described as one of "unparalleled magnitude." With rails dangling over the naked bridge piers, the railroad was severed. For 42 days no carload traffic was transported north or south of Wilmington as improvements and replacements were made.[110] Icebreakers were placed in the river ahead of the bridge upstream to ensure there would be no recurrence. Bridge piers were extended upward six feet, and a 540-foot Post iron truss bridge was installed. When the work was finished, the railroad was reopened but only after a loss of an estimated $150,000 in revenue and a large expense replacing the bridge.

The disaster at Wilmington was disheartening, but that spring there was pride over the handsome Alton Union Station that was opened on Front Street near the river. The two-story, all-brick structure had a mansard

The original Alton depot at 5th and Piasa Streets became the C&A's freight house after Union Depot was opened on Front Street along the Mississippi River in 1867. An addition added to its length but did not change the appearance of the railroad's first depot. (R. E. Collons Coll., Ag82.231:3774, Courtesy of DeGolyer Library, SMU)

roof, a tower at one end, numerous round-headed windows with hooded moldings, quoins, and other details typical of its Italianate style. Some thought the station reminded them of a locomotive, a romantic notion evoked by the elements the architect introduced. The Alton Union Station was the most impressive entrance to a city anywhere along the line. With its opening the original quarry-stone depot four blocks away was converted into the Alton's freight house.[111]

As year-end approached, nature again unleashed its fury. On Friday November 1, at about 10:30 P.M., a fire broke out in the brass foundry of the Bloomington Shops. The last workers had left by 10 P.M. The fire was well along by the time flames were noticed at about 11 P.M. Though firefighters and their equipment were dispatched, high winds, lack of water, and buildings "dry as tinder" conspired against them. The flames quickly spread to the main machine and car shops, lighting the sky. The smoke engulfed the west end of town. Townspeople and many of the 2,000 shop workers returned to help fight the fire and save what they could.[112] At first it was thought the entire shops complex would be lost, but, when the fire had burned itself out, it was discovered that the old and new round-houses and all of the engines within them had escaped. Two locomotives were in the

brass foundry when the fire broke out, but they too were found largely to have escaped destruction.

The next day insurance adjusters surveyed the damage amid the still smoldering ruins and checked off the total losses: the machine shops, car shops, foundry, lumber shed, and dry houses. Also lost were the tools, machinery, and supplies housed within those buildings. The estimated loss was $100,000–$110,000, but the shops complex was fully insured. It was the worst fire Bloomington had yet experienced. It meant lost wages for the workers and a setback for the ambitious building program then under way.[113]

Sensing an opportunity to add an important industry, within a week the cities of Chicago, Joliet, Springfield, and Alton made offers to relocate the shops. Chicago promised the railroad 10 acres of land and $25,000. Joliet proposed a donation of land and $100,000. Springfield's City Council passed a resolution of regret for the company's loss but made no offer of cash. Mayor Broadwell did suggest, however, "should your company take the matter into consideration, and make known a desire to locate your shops here . . . inducements would, doubtless, be offered."[114]

Threatened by the potential loss of their largest industry, Bloomington's Mayor, E. H. Rood; David Davis; Ashley Gridley; and John

McClun called a public meeting at Phoenix Hall, which hundreds attended to rally support. They had no intention of losing the Shops. With the same directness used to get the facilities in the first place, Davis and Fell met with Blackstone and offered 18 acres and $55,000 the city would raise through a sale of bonds. It was enough inducement for Blackstone. The possibility of Bloomington losing its most important industry appeared averted, but the deal almost collapsed when Governor John Palmer vetoed the legislature's approval of the city's bond issue. He considered support of a private company beyond the rights of a municipality, but his veto was overridden, saving Bloomington from the embarrassment of having to renege on its offer.[115]

The rebuilding of the Bloomington Shops began in spring 1868. As many fireproof materials as possible, including stone for foundations and walls and iron for roofs, were employed. Before year's end a foundation was in place for a greatly expanded stores and office building. Much larger paint, car, and planing shops and a stationary engine house were finished. To come were a sizeable machine shop; foundry, tool, and pattern rooms; a blacksmith shop; a boiler room; an iron house; the other half of the roundhouse (which would reach 250 feet in diameter); and an engine transfer table. The complex was so well constructed that most of the buildings remained standing for more than 120 years.[116]

▾▾▾

By the start of 1867, Pullman had formally dissolved his partnership with Field and had formed the Pullman's Palace Car Company, tapping six of his business friends, with whom he had carefully nurtured close relations, for the company's initial capital.[117] Thirty-seven Pullman-built sleepers were now running on six railroads. Pullman had ambitious plans for many more sales, but the space he had leased at Chicago now proved inadequate. He needed more and found it in the Burlington's Aurora, Illinois, shops. There, Pullman launched into building new types of first-class cars to complement his line of sleeping cars.[118]

Daytime travel had been largely limited to utilitarian coaches, but eastern roads had in-troduced the drawing room car, a forerunner of the parlor car, on short daylight runs. Western roads were less inclined to adopt the type, but Pullman did have one of his operating on the MC. On some of the type, his competitors offered light but expensive meals, prepared ahead of time and simply warmed onboard. Pullman, conscious of the style to which his customers were accustomed, thought those paying an extra fare deserved better. He envisioned a car that would offer full meal service, prepared fresh and cooked onboard. Pullman set about designing a true dining car essentially with the same dimensions as his sleepers (60-feet long, 10-feet wide), outfitted with a kitchen and tables that could accommodate 48 at one sitting. The car would be stocked with linens, crystal, silver, and china one associated with the finest eateries in the world. He named his first car the *Delmonico* for the famous restaurant in New York, to denote the style of service and fare to be offered. The car was displayed at a reception held at the C&A's East St. Louis depot, before making a demonstration run over the IC and one or two other roads. Pullman expected the car to be leased by the NYC for Chicago–New York service. That railroad's management, however, could not see how a non-revenue car such as a diner made sense and declined to take it. With two other dining cars, the *Southern* and the *Tremont,* nearing completion, Pullman didn't have a customer for any of them.[119]

It isn't known precisely how it happened that all three dining cars made their first appearances in revenue service running over the C&A during the summer of 1868, but, given Blackstone's and director John Crerar's close friendship with Pullman and the company's investment in Pullman's company stock, it is safe to assume they had come to Pullman's aid. A diner was added to each of the three trains then operating between Chicago and East St. Louis—a daytime run over the main line and two overnight runs, one over the main line, the other via Jacksonville—making them superior to any then running on western railroads. Whether just a move to help Pullman out of a jam or a conscious decision to further distance C&A passenger service from that of competitors, the new service proved instantly popular. Though he continued to build diners, Pull-

man never planned on a sustained dining car operation, which led to the railroad's creation of its own dining car department.

▼▼▼

A permanent linking of the St.LJ&C and the C&A was inevitable from the time Blackstone and Shephard had struck their deal. Physical connections between the roads were in place both at Godfrey and Bloomington, nearly all of the St.LJ&C rolling stock had been built under contract at the C&A's Shops, a common tariff was in place, and operations were fully coordinated. It was only a matter of time before a union would be consummated. Thus, it came as little surprise that the directors, on John Mitchell's motion, appointed a committee in February 1868 with instructions to secure a perpetual lease.[120] Cordial negotiations resulted in George Straut, successor to Shephard as president of the St.LJ&C, and Blackstone signing an agreement on April 13, 1868, giving the C&A control of the 150-mile line.[121] On June 1, 1868, the takeover was made official. The 16 engines, six coaches, five baggage cars, and 183 freight cars that were then carrying St.LJ&C markings, were transferred to the C&A's books and relettered and renumbered into the C&A's system. The 11 acquired passenger cars (plus two other cars completed before the Shops fire) brought the C&A fleet up to 62 cars, not including the three dining cars and the five Pullman sleepers—the *Pioneer, Springfield, Missouri, Illinois,* and *Jacksonville,* formerly the *No. 30*—that the road leased.[122]

Before the Shops fire, the car department had completed 100 flatcars and had planned to start building 300 boxcars. Without facilities in which to build them, the superintendent of the car department, R. Reniff, was forced to turn over plans for each to the Barney & Smith Manufacturing Company of Dayton, Ohio, to fill the order. These 400 cars, along with the 183 acquired St.LJ&C cars, brought the freight car fleet up to 1,938.[123] Five new locomotives were added during the year—all American types—two from Schenectady and three from Hinkley & Williams, increasing the roster to 72.[124]

The frequent number of coal trains originating at Braidwood—added to the mixed freight and passenger runs from downstate stations—made the Bloomington-Wilmington segment the most heavily used portion of the railroad.[125] Fuel-wasting delays and increased labor costs had become unacceptable, so it was decided to double-track the segment. In the spring of 1868, work was started. By year's end 16 1/2 miles of a second main line between Wilmington and Braceville and another 8 miles between Dwight and Odell had been laid.[126]

Structures on the increasingly important segment between Wilmington and Gardner were improved. Braceville got its first depot. Alongside it was built a two-story section house. A wooden, four-stall roundhouse was built, and a turntable was installed to the west of the main line at Braidwood where the assigned switchers were housed and serviced. A coal chute was erected on the east side of the tracks adjacent to the Chicago & Wilmington A Mine, from which coal was fed directly into tenders. A water tank, located south of the depot, was built, supplied by water from the A Mine.

This early view of Bloomington Shops looking west from Poplar and Walnut Streets shows the engine servicing facilities to the left, the smokestack of the power house and car shops at center, with the engine-ready tracks in the foreground. After the fire of 1867 and over the years, both the shops and adjoining freight yard were altered and expanded. (Richard R. Wallin Coll.)

The second Wilmington depot, erected in 1869, was of a unique all-brick design, unlike the mostly wooden stations built elsewhere. It was on the platform of this depot that ownership of the C&A was transferred to the B&O in 1931. (Courtesy of Wilmington Historical Society, Bill Molony Coll.)

At Godfrey a 4,200-foot extension was laid, affording trains off the Jacksonville Line direct access to the C&A's new depot, eliminating the need for trains to stop at the separate depots of the formerly independent railroads, and providing longer approaches, speeding up a crossover from one line to the other. Two other depots, the same size and similar to the one at Braceville (18 x 34), were finished at Ashland and Manchester. A blacksmith shop was erected at Jacksonville. A six-stall stone engine house and a small carpenter shop were completed at Mason City. The care the company was taking of its right-of-way necessitated construction of section houses. Identical, two-story structures were added at Bloomington, Atlanta, Lincoln, Nilwood, Miles, Delhi, and Hopedale, using the plans of the Braceville house. The following year, others were added at Ashland, Chatham, Roodhouse, and Manchester. Five 50,000-gallon tanks were erected at locations along the line in 1868 and five more a year later.[127]

During 1869, at the south fork of the Mazon River, a 250-foot, double-track, wrought-iron truss bridge was erected to accommodate a second main line, replacing the original single-track, wooden trestle. Four miles of the second main line between Braceville and Gardner were finished. Fifty more miles of the

main line track was relaid, leaving but 18 miles of original rails remaining. At Bloomington the foundry, wheel room, blacksmith shop, roundhouse, dry house, and storehouse were finished. A new brick depot replaced the tiny pine shelter at Wilmington that had served since the line's opening.[128]

The locomotive roster had 11 coal-burning engines added. Of the 108 locomotives rostered in 1869, only 24 were still wood burning—the 16 former St.LJ&C engines and eight of the oldest C&A engines—and were assigned to the lightest jobs. The car shops turned out another new mail car for Jacksonville Line service, and two more sleepers, the *Keokuk* and the *Peoria,* were received from Pullman. The added cars expanded each overnight train's sleeper consist to three.[129]

As the next decade approached, the crudest of connectors, link and pin couplers, were still used for both freight and passenger cars. Coupling the links with pins was a hated hazard for brakemen and switchmen. The loss of fingers, hands, and sometimes arms of trainmen was an intolerable injury sustained by too many. On passenger trains especially, sudden stops led to cars telescoping, one car riding up over a preceding one. It was inevitable that someone would invent a method to mitigate the hazardous process. Between 1863 and

1865, a New York civil engineer, Ezra Miller, addressed the passenger car coupling problem. He designed a system (which earned him three patents) that introduced a trussed end platform with draft gear and a fixed coupler that effectively eliminated the problems associated with link and pin couplers, and appreciably improved the added problem of side sway. Miller's modification was so effective that, with the exception of the Pennsylvania Central and a few other conservative railroads, his modification was quickly adopted as the industry's standard.[130]

One of those other conservatively run railroads that elected not to adopt the Miller platform was Blackstone's. Miller earned patent royalties for each car modified or built with his design, which Blackstone figured was an expense he didn't need to pay. Blackstone came up with a design similar to Miller's, which incorporated two large iron-clad beams set under the trucks that projected out from under the platforms, where they mated with corresponding planks of the following car. Couplers were not linked but rather drawn tight with adjustable screws. Performance was not much different than that of Miller's design, but the modification worked, and it became known as the Blackstone Safety Platform and Coupling. During 1869 Bloomington modified 46 of the 73-car passenger fleet to incorporate the new coupling arrangement. Over the next few years, the rest of the fleet was similarly modified.[131]

▾▾▾

The late 1860s had seen considerable expansion of the major railroads as they thrust out to more remote areas of the country, but Blackstone's road was not among them. Unlike other Illinois roads, such as the North Western, Rock Island, and Burlington, the C&A neither branched into new territory nor initiated its authorized extensions of the former St.LJ&C. Though well positioned serving the two most important cities of the West, Chicago and St. Louis, and dominating the territory between, the C&A showed little inclination to stretch out as the others had, especially Joy's Burlington. Between 1868 and 1871, 305 branchline miles were added to the Burlington system, equivalent to three quar-

ters of the C&A's total mileage.[132] The North Western and Rock Island had similarly added track and gained new traffic as both pushed west beyond the Mississippi River.

At the same time, there were others who attempted to start new railroads. One was the Western Air Line. Its organizers had ambitions to provide a bypass of Chicago by laying a line from New Boston, Illinois (on the east bank of the Mississippi about halfway between Muscatine and Burlington, Iowa), to Ft. Wayne, Indiana, where it was to link up with the PFt.W&C. Nothing was done to advance the railroad after its charter was granted in 1853 until a group of Illinois and Indiana politicians and businessmen bought the charter and renamed their enterprise the American Central Railway. Their line too existed only on paper until 1868, when it was announced that their intention was to lay a 585-mile air line between Ft. Wayne and Omaha.[133] It was news those around Lacon welcomed.

In 1859 the citizens of Lacon were energized with the news that the Chicago, Plainfield, Lacon & Warsaw had plans to run a diagonal route from Chicago through Kendall (north of Joliet), through LaSalle and Putnam Counties, across the Illinois River at Lacon, and then southwest to Warsaw (three miles south of Hamilton in Hancock County) and the Mississippi River. Some work had been done on the line to the north in Will County, but Lacon businessmen had not seen surveyors by 1867.[134] That year there was new excitement when it was learned a railroad, the Hamilton, Lacon & Eastern (HL&E), had been chartered with rights to lay a line from Hamilton through Lacon and on to Monee, terminating at the IC. It was to serve as an extension of the Grand Trunk Railroad of Canada, which had reached Grand Haven, Michigan, with plans for continuation westward, like the American Central, bypassing Chicago. But again, nothing was ever done to start construction.

Situated on the east bank of the Illinois River to the south of Peru and Ottawa and to the north of Peoria, Lacon had been bypassed by the Bureau County Railroad, which had laid its Bureau-Peoria line on the west bank through Sparland, just across the river from Lacon. The IC's Dunleith-Cairo main line lay

16 miles to the east at Wenona, but it wasn't the outlet the farmers and businessmen of Lacon sought; they wanted a route to Chicago. The citizens of Marshall, Putnam, and Woodford Counties thought their dreams had come true when an American Central grade was raised over nearly 50 miles of open country west from a point about four miles south of Dwight called Melbourne.[135] But it wasn't long before Judge John Thompson of Chicago, president of the American Central, had to admit defeat when expected French financing failed to materialize. The grades began to wash away, as did the dreams of Lacon's citizens. Realizing outside interests could not be relied upon to build their railroad, Lacon's leaders resolved to build their own.

In August 1868 it was learned that Thompson had sold control of the American Central to the Burlington. Joy's only interest in taking control was to ensure the road was never completed, preserving the Burlington's lock on traffic. A committee from Lacon approached Joy and asked his intentions for the road. They learned he was willing to turn the portion of the former Thompson road east of the Illinois River over to them at no cost. With that assurance, in September 1868, a Lacon delegation traveled to Chicago and met with Superintendent McMullin and asked for the C&A's help.[136]

Given the company's aversion thus far to add branches, especially to Peoria and to other underserved towns downstate, McMullin's willingness to listen to a proposal for such a minimal extension was surprising. To be sure, there would be traffic generated at the recently opened Vermillion Coal Company mine at Streator, but the interest in an extension beyond is less easy to explain. One possible reason is that at the time the Lacon Committee approached McMullin, St.LJ&C engineers were surveying a route up from Hopedale, headed north to Washington and Metamora and possibly to the Vermillion coalfields, a route included in its charter.[137] McMullin might have concluded extending the line beyond Streator to Washington, where the line up from Hopedale could be met, would fashion an alternative East St. Louis–Chicago route via Godfrey and Jacksonville. Whatever his reasoning was remains to be answered.

Phineas Stevens, Washington Cook, and George Barnes, the members of the Lacon delegation, didn't ask McMullin's reasons. They were just happy to leave with his assurance that if they provided a grade, the C&A would lay the rails, build stations, equip the line, and operate it. They set to work. First, they got the dormant HL&E charter, which was then used to take over the donated American Central franchise, transferred to them.[138] Then they raised the needed funding through issuance of bonds, plus contributions from Vermillion Coal to pay the construction costs of the bridge needed to cross the Vermillion River west of Streator. They also got funding from the citizens of Dwight.

The place where the American Central was to cross the C&A, Melbourne, was a few miles south of Dwight. The intent was to avoid passing through Dwight and as many other incorporated places as possible so the railroad could serve as a true air line. What was needed now was a junction point, not a crossing, and that would be at Dwight. Engineers began surveying the Dwight-Streator segment in the spring of 1869. Supplies had been stockpiled there for an early start, but heavy late spring and early summer rains delayed the laying of track until August, when tracklayers, under the direction of William Shephard, began at Dwight and worked westward.

Two years prior to laying the first rails at Dwight, Vermillion Coal had started work on its own line from the mine at Streator to Wenona and a connection there with the IC's north-south main line. In September 1869 the line was opened, operated under contract by the Ottawa, Oswego & Fox River Valley Railroad as an extension of its Ottawa-Streator line. There was little need for that line and another laid by the C&A, so an agreement was reached transferring not just operating rights but ownership of the Streator-Wenona line. In early March 1870, George Straut, on behalf of the St.LJ&C, paid $166,185 for the 12.8 miles of road, $12,983 per mile. By mid-March C&A trains were making through runs from Dwight to Wenona.[139]

Tracklayers who worked on the Dwight-Streator segment were now transferred west of Wenona. By June they were establishing a grade at Crow Creek, where footings for a bridge over it had already been set. Roadbed

at Washburn, Low Point, and Metamora was nearly finished, and rail and ties were being laid at Lacon. By early November a junction was formed for the Lacon branch in open country at Varna and track was in place as far as Metamora. On December 11, 1870, the first scheduled train through from Dwight pulled into Washington and seven days later, into Lacon.[140]

Construction on the next phase, the approximate 35 miles between Washington and Hopedale, should have started as soon as winter passed, but that did not happen. The only hint why is found in the *Lacon Home Journal* which reported, "We understand the I.P.& W.R.R. Co. [sic] (Toledo Peoria & Warsaw) will not let the St.LJ&C R.R. cross their track at Washington."[141] Though the reason has probably been lost to history, it is certain that this minor hinderance alone would not have been the reason. Disputes over crossings arose frequently when one line wanted to cross another but were usually resolved. A more probable reason is that, with Washington and Metamora now provided a rail link—albeit

from the north rather than the south as had been contemplated since T&P days—a southern outlet was no longer deemed necessary.

The Dwight Branch, as the new mileage became known, was laid during a prosperous year for the company. Despite a major corn crop failure, 1869 brought earnings again in excess of $2 million. Passenger income increased nearly 7 percent, the number of passengers, 20 percent. Freight revenue rose nearly 4 percent; tonnage moved 15 percent—helped appreciably by an increase in coal tonnage—to 266,096 tons.[142] As the end of the decade drew near, the C&A had emerged as one of the principal railroads in a state that each year saw its railroad mileage and the number of operating railroads dramatically increase. There were now 20 railroads operating over 4,800 miles within Illinois's borders. Four of those roads crossed the state west to east and had connections with eastern roads at the growing rail centers of Toledo, Indianapolis, and Cincinnati. Because of their longer and more direct routings, the rates those railroads offered were frequently considerably lower,

Once the Dwight Branch was opened, engines such as this American no. 109, a Schenectady product turned out in 1869, proved sufficient to handle assignments. Power was serviced at an enginehouse erected at Dwight. (E. L. DeGolyer, Jr. Photo. Coll., Ag82.232, courtesy of DeGolyer Library, SMU)

The morning train pauses at Metamora in 1908. It was here that the railroad chartered as the T&P first took root. (William Raia Coll.)

making eastbound routings a more cost-effective option than might otherwise have been the case through Chicago. This pressured the traffic departments of roads like the C&A to match or better the cut rates to retain business, which, of course, meant reduced yields. In spite of his road's substantial earnings, Blackstone was becoming increasingly concerned about rate-cutting practices.

It was the beginning of a new era. When the economy was good, as it had been since the end of the war, reduced yields on some traffic was more than offset by overall increased traffic. It was when the inevitable occurred and times got tough that pressures would mount. But all that lay ahead. It had been an enormously successful decade. The company had returned from receivership stronger than ever and was prospering, its stockholders well rewarded. Blackstone had every expectation the company would only build on growing strength.

The Triangle Is Closed

The postwar prosperity of the second half of the 1860s continued into the early 1870s. Illinois's population rose to more than 2.5 million, a phenomenal 48 percent spurt over the prior 10 years. Nearly a quarter of the state's citizens lived in cities, 298,977 of them in Chicago. Places that 20 years earlier had been just collections of crudely constructed cabins and small shops were now transformed into self-sustaining towns and cities.[1] The size of the state's farms had grown too, thanks to mechanization of farm implements that made planting and harvesting easier.

The demand for nearly everything—fostered by the population growth—added fuel to an already hot economy. Though America was still very much an agrarian society, more of the country's needs were being manufactured rather than imported. In the 12-month period between 1870 and 1871, more than 200,000 new American manufacturing businesses were founded. Shoes, clothing, watches, sewing machines, pianos, stoves, and hardware of all sorts that had been handcrafted or imported prior to the war were now being mass-produced in larger mechanized factories.[2]

The nation's railroads obviously benefited from the expansion. Arriving immigrants filled passenger trains, and increased production called for more carloads of freight. By forming alliances and actual consolidations, the industry made it possible to move from the East Coast to Chicago or St. Louis without changing cars or railroads. Clothing, pots and pans, shoes, distilled beverages, machinery parts, carriages, farm implements, and furniture produced in New England factories were now displayed in St. Louis shop windows. What was produced in Peoria, Joliet, and Chicago was found in Detroit, Philadelphia, New York, and Baltimore stores and factories.

No longer solely dependent upon waterways for power and transport, many of the new factories located along railroads. Where that wasn't possible, rails were laid to reach them, including the developing oil patch at remote Titusville, Pennsylvania; cattle ranchers in the Southwest; and, over a myriad of short-lived lines, lumber mills in the forests of Michigan and Wisconsin. The devastated railroads of the South were being repaired and restored, contributing to the reconstruction of the region. Railroads were seemingly emerging everywhere. What lay ahead was the prospect of travel from coast to coast.

A transcontinental railroad had been promoted as early as the 1840s. For the next 10 years, special interests appealed to Congress to get the project started. Asa Whitney, a failed New England trader who knew well how wretched a sea journey around Cape Horn could be, was particularly active in promoting a route to the Northwest, one that would bring the Orient closer. Little was accomplished over the intervening years, but some in Congress promoted the idea and did what they could to move it along. Part of the delay was determining a starting point: Missouri senator Thomas Benton promoted St. Louis; Arkansas senator Solon Bouland pushed for Memphis; and Texas senator Samuel Houston, Galveston. By 1856 a transcontinental railroad had become a national issue, and both Republican and Democrat congressional candidates that year promised passage of a railroad bill, but nothing resulted. A consensus on which of the several routes should be selected could not be reached. The stalemate persisted until the withdrawal from Congress of southern congressmen.[3]

In 1862 President Lincoln had decided on a central route to connect Omaha with Sacramento and had signed legislation creating two companies, the Union Pacific Railroad & Telegraph Company and the Central Pacific Company (CP) of California, to accomplish the task. Subsidy of 20 million acres of government land and $60 million in federally backed loans was promised. Like few other developments so far undertaken, America's transcontinental railroad energized the country. "Like the printing press, the steam engine, and the telegraph, it opens up a new era," the *Chicago Tribune* proclaimed.[4]

Five Missouri River towns were designated as UP terminals: Leavenworth, Kansas; Kansas City and St. Joseph, Missouri; Sioux City, Iowa; and the most important, Omaha, Nebraska. Congress removed Sioux City as a designated terminal in 1864, but St. Joseph was connected with Council Bluffs (across the river from Omaha) by the St. Joseph & Council Bluffs Railroad and with Leavenworth and Kansas City by the UP's takeover of the struggling Leavenworth, Pawnee & Western, soon renamed the Kansas Pacific (KP). In 1868, five years after construction was started at Kansas City, KP rails reached Denver. Through interchange with the UP's Denver Pacific, Kansas City was connected with Cheyenne, Wyoming, and the UP's main line.[5] In May 1869 the unprecedented, monumental task was finished when the rails of the two companies, the CP and UP, were joined in desolate Utah. The arduous, long, and dangerous sailing around Cape Horn, or equally perilous treks across country ended, replaced by the iron horse.[6]

The territory through which the KP was laid was largely barren and absent of inhabitants other than Native Americans, but a few years after passage of the Homestead Act in 1862, tens of thousands of settlers flocked to the vast open spaces, willing to take their chances for the next five years in exchange for 160 acres of free land. During the life of the bill, more than 600 million acres were distributed, but not always in the way Congress intended. Some land granted the states was used to establish agricultural colleges, but 521 million of the best acres wound up in the hands of railroads and speculators. Although primarily intended to attract foreign immigrants, the greatest number of settlers came from Ohio, Indiana, and Illinois. Within a decade the population of Kansas grew to a million. Through perseverance, homesteaders hung on and began producing bountiful crops. Between 1870 and 1880, Kansas wheat production increased by 1,000 percent and corn by 700 percent. In 1880 alone, 23.4 million bushels of wheat and 109 million bushels of corn were harvested.[7] It was a struggle for the sodbusters (as the pioneers were nicknamed), but another group, the cattle ranchers, found quick success with little investment of capital or labor.

The wide-open plains provided excellent grazing land. All ranchers needed was a small stake to buy a few head of cattle. Nature took care of the rest. During the 1870s the number of cattle in Kansas doubled, but the state's livestock population paled in comparison to the millions of head found further south in Texas.[8] As early as the 1830s, Texans had started driving hundreds of head of cattle east to markets. One of the first drives was to New Orleans. In 1842 another drive of some 1,500 head was made to Missouri. Four years later 1,000 Texan longhorns reached Ohio, and in 1856 a comparable number were driven to Chicago. Texas's cattle population in 1860 was estimated at over 4 million, and Texas beef was feeding the nation. A year later, however, the Mississippi River was blockaded by Union forces, and eastern markets were shut off. To survive, Texans drove their herds to the Southwest and beyond to California. With the war's conclusion, eastern markets were once again available. In 1866 an estimated 260,000 head were driven to Sedalia, Missouri, and the Pacific Railroad of Missouri.[9] On that drive the drovers were met by attacks from local ranchers in southeastern Kansas, northern Arkansas, and southern Missouri. They claimed to be fearful of the spread of the dreaded Texas cattle fever, but the Texans contended the ranchers only wanted to steal their herds. The next year cowboys avoided the route and drove their herds north then east to St. Joseph, Missouri, and the Hannibal & St. Joseph Railroad. It was a longer drive, and, after costs were tallied, the Texas cattlemen realized little or no profit.[10]

It was J. G. McCoy and his two brothers, operators of a thriving livestock shipping business at Springfield, Illinois, who had the idea of starting a loading site on the KP, miles closer to Texas. They figured that a remote, unsettled, well-watered spot with excellent grazing grass would serve ranchers well and that, since the railroad was hungry for new traffic, it would welcome the livestock traffic. The McCoys were right. The point they chose was Abilene, 164 miles west of Kansas City. Within two months, pens able to corral herds of 3,000 head of cattle were nailed together on a siding along the main line. The first eastbound shipments were made in 1867. That year 35,000 head were shipped to Chicago. By 1871 700,000 head were loaded at Abilene. It wasn't long before pens were raised at Wichita and Ellsworth and by mid-decade at Dodge City and Ellis. Over the next 15 years, more than 4.2 million cattle were loaded in stock cars headed east, some for packing plants in Kansas City and St. Louis, but the vast number for Chicago's stockyards and slaughterhouses.[11]

The first railroad to reach out to the KP at Kansas City was the Pacific Railroad of Missouri, in 1865. Four years later the first railroad bridge over the Missouri River was completed (designed by Chanute, who had been lured from the C&A to tackle the assignment), giving the Burlington access to Kansas City. The new rails fostered Kansas City's ascension to the ranks of a major rail center, easily outdistancing its up-river rival, Leavenworth.[12]

Timothy Blackstone could not ignore the buildup of traffic that was passing through the new gateway, enriching the roads that served it. Though committed to a reliance on local traffic (still 90% of the C&A's total freight), Blackstone began to question whether the policy still made sense, at least as far as Kansas City was concerned. Blackstone presented his case for extending the railroad to the stockholders: "While your board of directors fully appreciate the fact that the policy of your company in the future should be (as it has been in the past) to foster and encourage local traffic, we have also felt [it necessary] to make such contracts of lease or otherwise as should appear to the board to be expedient to secure a portion of the large and rapidly increasing traffic between Chicago, Missouri, Kansas and the Southwest."[13]

Like every other town on either side of the Mississippi River, Louisiana, Missouri, flourished during the Steamboat Era, but, as railroads advanced and the river was bridged,

Louisiana's fortunes stagnated then declined as freight and passengers that once moved north and south by water headed east and west by rail. Louisiana saw a glimmer of hope for a renewed resurgence when, in the late 1850s, the Toledo, Wabash & Western (TW&W)—the former Great Western—projected its extension into Missouri southwest from Naples to a point opposite Louisiana. Louisiana's city fathers committed to lay a line into central Missouri from the river. In March 1859 the Louisiana & Missouri River Railroad (L&MR) was chartered with rights to build a railroad from Louisiana by way of Bowling Green to "some suitable point on the North Missouri Railroad, intersecting said railroad between the southern limits of the town of Wellsburg, in Montgomery County, and the northern limits of the town of Mexico. . . ."[14] Unfortunately for the lovely town that had seen better days, the TW&W's plans to cross the Mississippi River at Louisiana were killed, and instead the road turned north at Meredosia to Quincy and crossed the river there. Nothing was done during the war years or the three years after to advance the L&MR, but in 1868 the various counties through which the railroad would pass decided to proceed with or without a connecting Illinois railroad. Capital was raised, and contractors were hired for the grubbing and grading between Louisiana and Mexico, Mexico and Cedar City (across the Missouri River from the state capital, Jefferson City), beyond Mexico in the direction of Glasgow, and ultimately to Kansas City.

All this was happening when Blackstone came to call. Like the properties Blackstone had previously leased, the L&MR was in a weak and vulnerable state, not yet completed and facing big hurdles with no guarantees of early completion or success. Its franchise, across the midsection of the state from the Mississippi to the Missouri River, however, was just what Blackstone needed. He met with Henry Block, the L&MR's president, and outlined his plan. He told Block he was going to lay a branch off his leased St.LJ&C line to a point opposite Louisiana on the Illinois side of the river. In return for a lease of his railroad, Blackstone promised Block he would supply and contract for the laying of iron rails; furnish the power, rolling stock, and structures; and operate the road. All Block had

to do, within a year, was provide a grade with ties as far as Mexico and Cedar City and, by 1873, a grade and ties for the line beyond Mexico to Kansas City. To give Block leverage with lenders, Blackstone proposed leasing the L&MR at once. Impressed, Block readily agreed. In January 1870 the two men signed the lease, followed by a construction contract in July. A month later Blackstone and Straut signed a lease for a branch from the St.LJ&C to the Mississippi River.[15] All was ready for the C&A's push westward.

Louisiana, Missouri, was 37 miles almost due west of White Hall, and the town's leaders there were thrilled with the prospect of the town becoming an important railroad junction. To their ultimate surprise, that didn't happen. Instead, a place about four miles north, Roodhouse, was named. In 1866 the principal landowner in the area, John Roodhouse, had platted a village he named for himself and began offering lots. He found few takers. At the time, St.LJ&C trains didn't even stop there. One of Roodhouse's few neighbors, John Rawlins, erected a depot and brick warehouse at his own expense adjacent to the railroad, the only way the hamlet of Roodhouse was added as a station.

That same enterprising spirit came into play again when Rawlins learned the railroad was planning an extension westward and White Hall was to be the junction. Rawlins decided to change the railroad's mind. He sent a letter to Blackstone asking what had to be done to have the Roodhouse settlement named instead. Blackstone's reply held Rawlins off with the excuse that a new survey would have to be completed before he could give him an answer. Meanwhile, White Hall's leaders became aware of Rawlins's initiative. Thinking their town had the junction sewn up, they now realized a contest was brewing. A delegation was named to travel to Chicago to meet with Blackstone to seal a contract before Rawlins made more headway. Rawlins must have been quite a sleuth because he learned of the meeting, and he and another resident, E. M. Husted, took off for Chicago before the White Hall committee. They met Blackstone, who told them if they could secure a right-of-way as far as the Illinois River, plus 10 acres of land for a depot and other facilities at Roodhouse within a week, Blackstone would name their town the new junction. That was all the enterprising Rawlins needed to hear. He and Husted returned home, secured the right-of-way, set aside the required land at Roodhouse, and presented the package to Blackstone. The deal was done.[16] The settlement of Roodhouse now had a future.

The terms of the lease of the LM&R stipulated that Kansas City was to be reached in stages over the course of three years—the 51 miles from Louisiana to Mexico by May 1871, the 56 miles to Glasgow a year later, and the 107 miles from there to Kansas City by May 1873. It was, of course, hoped that Kansas City would be reached sooner, but in the interim and until the full route was opened, C&A trains would operate for a fee over the recently completed North Missouri Railroad from Mexico west. In May 1870 Blackstone and Barton Bates, president of the North Missouri, signed an agreement. Opened just a year earlier, Bates's road had developed only minimal traffic, and he welcomed the added revenue the C&A would bring.

By April 1870 grading of the 37 miles be-

tween Roodhouse and Quincy Junction (as the point opposite Louisiana was named) had progressed far enough for the stockpiled rails at both ends of the line to be laid. Tracklayers started laying rails west from Roodhouse in June. Masons at the Illinois River were close to finishing the limestone abutments and pillars for the bridge to be erected there. Tracklaying progressed rapidly, and by early autumn rails were in place through to Pearl and the Illinois River. The bridge at Pearl was the last obstacle standing in the way of the line's completion. It was designed as a 1,200-foot, wrought iron span with a turning section. On September 6 the pivot span was turned for the first time.[17] At the same time, 32 miles of superstructure from Louisiana westward was near completion. Tracklaying west of the bridge toward Quincy Junction was finished by mid-October. Meanwhile, the L&MR's chief engineer, M. C. Little, declared the Louisiana-Mexico main line opened, and crews were in Callaway County finishing the Cedar City Branch.[18]

No doubt influenced by costs and the urgency to open the line as quickly as possible,

The *J. C. McMullin* provided Mississippi River crossings for only a few years before the river's freezing proved it impractical. Switch engines were assigned to either side of the river for loading and unloading passenger and freight cars. (Courtesy of Douglas A. Shehorn)

Blackstone decided to employ a steamboat for ferry service instead of erecting a bridge over the Mississippi River. John Mitchell's twin-stacked *J. C. McMullin* (named for the C&A's general superintendent) was pulled out of East St. Louis service and sold to the railroad. The boat was capable of transferring 12 freight cars "or an entire passenger train" (between four and six cars) on each trip.[19] Switch engines were assigned at both river banks to handle the loading and unloading. In November 1871 the first trains were run through Chicago to Kansas City, via Roodhouse and Mexico and then over the Northern Missouri.[20]

Elsewhere on the line, improvements were made. In 1869 nine new depots, including most along the Dwight-Washington branch, were erected. Continued increases in rolling stock that year, five new coaches and 218 freight cars, brought the total number of passenger cars operated to 81 and the number of freight cars to 2,256.[21] Good results were recorded in 1870. Another handsome profit of $2 million was earned, despite a general leveling off of revenues caused by a loss of corn traffic, a result of failures of the Illinois harvests for both 1869 and 1870. Those declines were more than offset, however, by increased coal traffic, which in 1870 was nearly 13 percent greater than in 1869.[22] The road's success continued through the first three quarters of 1871, reaching new heights, but not without suffering two severe setbacks.

▾▾▾

Next to flooding rivers, the single most threatening natural phenomena the Midwest periodically endures are tornados. In March 1871, out of the southwest, one started building, finally unleashing its fury in the East St. Louis area. Dark, churning skies and heavy rains signaled the approach of terrible weather. A swirling funnel cloud was spotted. With little warning, the twister skipped across the Missouri side of the river, then with a vengeance, leaped across and attacked East St. Louis. In its path stood the C&A's depot, freight house, and roundhouse. Everything in the tornado's path was destroyed or severely damaged, including the railroad's rolling stock parked there, before the whirling winds

passed into open country beyond. Though cleanup started immediately, railroad operations at the road's southernmost terminal were disrupted for several months.[23] The damage caused by the tornado sustained at East St. Louis proved to be a major loss, but it paled in comparison with what occurred at Chicago in October.

The summer of 1871 had been extremely dry. For three months, only intermittent showers relieved the oppressive heat. Only one and one-half inches of rain fell over Chicago from July to the first week of October.[24] On Saturday night, October 7, fire was spotted in the two-story, brick planing mill of Lull & Holmes near Van Buren and Canal streets on the city's west side. Fed by high winds, flames rapidly consumed the factory, and within 20 minutes, fire spread to John Foster's paper box factory, the Excelsior Vinegar Works, and the Union Wagon Works. Unimpeded, the flames danced across Canal Street, and soon millions of feet of stacked lumber at the John Sheriff and Chapin & Foss yards were ablaze. The adjacent coal yards of B. Holbrook, Lamon & Cornish and W. E. Johnson were soon ignited. Along Clinton Street, the box, blind, and sash factory of Hotslander & Randall caught fire, as did the squalid tenements wedged between the factories. The several fire companies drawn to the multi-block scene were no match for what was now a wall of flame. Within hours the freight houses of both the Adams and United States Express companies, at Canal and Adams Streets, were consumed by flames. It seemed certain the PFt.W&C freight and passenger depots, between Canal Street and the river north of Madison Street, along with the rolling stock spotted there, would soon catch fire, but courageous residents of the neighborhood created a fire wall by tearing down the most exposed portions of sheds to the south and prevented the fire from reaching the facilities.

Within hours, nearly four solid blocks from Van Buren to Adams Streets and from the river to the east side of Clinton Street lay in smoldering ashes. In defiance stood Vincent Nelson & Co.'s National Elevator between Jackson and Adams Streets along the river, one of the few structures that had escaped the fire's wrath.[25] The next evening, winds out of the southwest began to kick up once again, and by nightfall

While Chicago was still ablaze, Bloomington's citizens loaded one of its fire apparatuses on a flat car, and the *Major Nolton*, originally a St.LJ&C engine, made an almost mile-a-minute run to the city in a vain attempt to help save the city. By the time it had arrived, Chicago's wooden water delivery system was already destroyed. (Gulf, Mobile & Ohio RR Historical Society Coll.)

were almost gale-like. Some assumed rain was finally on the way, but instead of rain clouds, the skies became filled with smoke and flames. Around 8:45 P.M., a fire broke out in the O'Leary family's barn at 137 DeKoven Street, about a mile further south of where the previous night's fire had erupted. It was one of many wooden houses, barns, and sheds crowded together in a neighborhood that was littered with piles of lumber and clutter. Within minutes the barn was ablaze.

Richard Riley, a C&A conductor, was standing with his wife on the porch of his house at Twelfth and Canal Streets, waiting for the Canal Street omnibus that would take him to the depot for his overnight run to St. Louis. He looked northwest and immediately told his wife he wouldn't be going to St. Louis that night. He dashed to where he saw the rising flames. By the time he arrived, other barns and sheds nearby had caught fire, then still more buildings were ignited.

The fire watchman on duty in the tower atop the courthouse downtown on Clark Street had not seen the flames as early as had Riley, but when he did, he miscalculated their location and sent a signal to the wrong fire

company. Before he realized his mistake and the correct alarms were sent, several more blocks of tinder-like houses and sheds were in flames. Smoke and sparks from the piles of sawdust alongside the planing mills were ignited. Soon what remained of the lumber district along the river that hadn't been destroyed the night before was ablaze. Within an hour, the fire had spread a mile north along the river's west bank. By 11 o'clock, flames had jumped the river, melted the sides of the grain elevator that had survived the night before, and were running along the wooden Van Buren Street bridge. Before long, the city center became a massive furnace, flames shooting 100 feet into the air. Glass and iron melted, and everything in the fire's path turned to ash.[26]

With communications in the downtown area completely knocked out, the telegraph office at the Stock Yards was used to spread news of the disaster. "Send help" was the message dispatched. Among the first to offer assistance were the people of Bloomington. Sunday night they loaded a fire engine aboard a flatcar. The Alton's no. 97, the *Major Nolton,* originally a St.LJ&C Rogers-built 4-4-0, was attached. At the throttle was Lou Hawks, a tall, swarthy man, and a highly skilled engineer who knew how to get the most out of an engine. Every train between Bloomington and Chicago was ordered to take siding for the special, and Hawks took full advantage for wide-open running. He covered the 10 miles between Chenoa and Pontiac in 10 minutes and the 7 miles between Wilmington and Elwood in a little over 6 minutes. The Bloomington firefighters riding the flatcar and even those in the caboose were holding on the entire trip. Hawks arrived at the depot, having covered the 126 miles in an astounding 150 minutes.[27] The donated fire engine added nothing to the firefighting effort, however, because Chicago's water supply had already been disrupted, but the show of support dramatically demonstrated how many cities and individuals responded to Chicago's need over the next several weeks.

Flames had leapt across the river, and soon the comfortable residential neighborhoods north of the river were burning. It was Tuesday, and with nothing else to consume, the fire finally died out when it reached Fullerton Avenue, then the northern reach of the city. Lying in smoldering ashes in a four-mile-long, mile-wide swatch were more than 17,000 structures. In all, about one-third of Chicago's personal and real property was destroyed, including the more than $1 million in currency and coin at the United States Custom House. Three hundred thousand residents were left homeless.[28]

Left in ruins were the IC's passenger and freight depots, land office, grain elevator, and 26 freight cars along the lakeshore. The North Western's Galena Division depot, general offices, both freight houses, flour warehouse, three grain elevators, and 133 freight cars had been leveled. The Rock Island depot, general offices, freight depot, and considerable rolling stock were destroyed. The MC's facilities were totally wiped out.[29]

The C&A was not spared. Its general offices at 53 and 55 Dearborn Street were left smoldering ruins. All of its records (except one set of director meeting minutes later found in a buried safe) were mere ash. The freight house west of the river between Van Buren and Charles (later Congress) Streets was gone, and all that remained of the 113 boxcars and flat-

cars stored there were their trucks and other metal parts. Fortunately, the round house at Stewart Street was spared. It had not been in the fire's path.[30]

By Wednesday fleeing citizens filled every train out of what was left of Chicago. An estimated 15,000 left that day; nearly the same number departed on Thursday; and more followed as space became available. For weeks thereafter, train loads of food, clothing and other supplies were brought in. The outpouring of aid was unprecedented. "Have courage" was how Chicagoans greeted one another.

Normal railroad operations did not return at Chicago for several months. With nearly all of the city's elevators leveled, what remained of that autumn's grain harvest was diverted to other markets. With all of the stored lumber burned, outbound shipments ceased. There were no manufactured products to ship. The only commerce brought to the city was livestock. Meat and processed byproducts continued to be exported since the Stock Yards and packing plants remained unscathed, located well south of the burned areas.

Nature again brought disruption later that year. The winter of 1871 in the country's midsection arrived earlier than usual and proved unusually cold. As the persistent, abnormally cold temperatures lingered, the Mississippi River froze solid as far south as St. Louis. As a result, the *McMullin* at Louisiana was stuck in the ice.[31] Carloads of freight accumulated on either side of the river, and would-be passengers had to find other routes. Those roads that had bridged the river, of course, faced no similar problems. Blackstone's hopes of demonstrating the new line's potential during its first full year of operation had been denied.

It had been a particularly difficult year, but despite the disruptions at East St. Louis, the disaster at Chicago, and weeks of interruption of Kansas City service, revenues climbed to $5.2 million and profits to $2.2 million in 1871—$130,000 more than in 1870. Amid the setbacks improvements to the property continued. The first of the power needed for the Western Division came in 1871 with a 15-engine order from Schenectady—two 0-4-0 switchers, eight 4-4-0s, and five 4-6-0s—as did Western Division rolling stock—four coaches, 199 freight cars (including 105 combination freight cars, so called because they could be used for either general freight or livestock), and seven Drovers cabooses, used to serve the cowboys accompanying stock trains. To handle the livestock trade, stock pens were built at Louisiana, and existing pens at Normal were enlarged. The following year, another 19 engines, six more coaches, two baggage cars, 486 freight cars, and four Drovers cabooses were added. Work on replacing the devastated properties at Chicago and East St. Louis was started.[32]

Passenger counts in 1872 increased 8 percent and freight tonnage by almost 7 percent, a large portion of it from Kansas City. The best news of the year was the 25 percent rise in coal tonnage carried, to 480,000 tons, nearly all of it forwarded to Chicago to replenish depleted supplies. Since the opening of Braidwood, mines had been opened at about half the main-line stations (and several on branches), but by far, more coal came out of Braidwood than anywhere else.[33]

The Chicago Wilmington & Vermillion Coal Company, a $2 million venture, evolved from consolidation of the Chicago & Wilmington Coal operations at Braidwood and Vermillion Coal at Streator. Four new mines, the F (which proved to be short-lived), G, H, and I (the largest) were opened. Over the years, other mines were added in an expanding radius around Braidwood—the J to the extreme northwest; the K and M located south at Godley; the L to the northeast; the N in Wilmington Township; the O, P, and R just west of what would become Braidwood's city limits; and the Q south and to the east of the railroad's main line. In peak winter months at Braidwood, the Chicago Wilmington & Vermillion employed 700 workers. On an average day, 100–200 cars were switched in and out of its mines. Eureka Mining employed another 400–450, with 75–80 cars shuttled in and out of its four mines each day. A smaller producer, the Star Coal Company sank two mines, No. 1 and No. 2, to the northeast.[34]

An extensive system of tracks was laid to reach the mines. A siding to the east of the main line, behind the depot, served the Star operations. Directly opposite the depot, the tail end of a wye led directly north to the roundhouse and the Wilmington's E mine. Just before reaching the turntable, a spur ran due west, then turned north to the G and H

mines, while another curved south to the shafts of Eureka Coal. To the west was the Five Tracks, a half-mile-long yard. When coal production was at its peak, up to 30 solid coal trains a day were made up there. Later, when Wilmington Coal Mining & Manufacturing operations were started around Diamond (between Braidwood and Coal City), the yard stub was extended northwest about a mile and a half beyond the yard to serve that company's No. 1 shaft. To the southeast a spur off the main line ran to the Braidwood Coal Company shaft. As the radius of mines expanded, miners could no longer conveniently walk to them, so a switcher pulling one or two worn-out coaches each morning and evening would slowly weave its way past the several mines through the area's maze of tracks.[35] By far, the mines at Braidwood had become the largest single source of traffic on the railroad.

▾▾▾

Throughout the 1860s and early 1870s, the railroad industry pricing of transit was a haphazard and too often discriminatory conglomeration of random tariffs. Shippers who had only one railroad to choose from inevitably found themselves paying more than others fortunate enough to have choices. Shippers across the country, but especially farmers, were up in arms over the railroads' practice of charging them higher tariffs for transporting their grain, lumber, and livestock short distances to local markets than those accessed others for much longer hauls. Resentment grew in the late 1860s, and by the early 1870s, organized movements came into existence, demanding state regulation of railroad pricing practices. The individual farmer had no influence whatsoever, but between 1867 and 1874 The Patrons of Husbandry, a secret fraternal order, was formed and, at its peak, counted almost a million members. The movement became known as The Grange. Throughout the Midwest and South, the populist movement gained strength and pressured state governments for relief.

The railroads claimed the differentials they imposed were economic necessities and in Illinois defended themselves by pointing to the liberal charters the state legislatures had

The Ten-Wheeler was the first advance in power over the 4-4-0 the C&A adopted. The type like this example photographed in 1878 at Braidwood first appeared in 1863, but starting in 1871, Schenectady delivered 12 more, then in 1892–1893, 18 others. Baldwin produced the last owned by the C&A in 1901, 10 of them as Vauclain compounds. The last 4-6-0 was retired in 1933. (S. R. Wood Coll., E. L. DeGolyer, Jr. 5 x 7 Photo. Coll., P727.1156, courtesy of DeGolyer Library, SMU)

granted them, by design, to afford railroads greater opportunity to attract capital and develop. But what resulted from the freedom granted railroads was a maze of conflicting prices for similar tonnage over widely differing distances, depending on the level of competition a railroad faced.

In the winter of 1865–1866, farmers confronted sharply lower prices brought on by lessened postwar demand and an abundant harvest at the same time railroads raised their rates. They were left with little, if any, profit. For the rest of the decade, railroad rate differentials became a contentious issue throughout Minnesota and Iowa, and especially in farming centers served by only one railroad, where farmers found they were paying higher rates to ship their grain to Chicago than were shippers more distant. During the same period, Chicago grain storage operators were also angered by the railroads' arrogance. During the war Chicago granaries had overtaken their rivals in St. Louis, and in the years that followed, they offered aggressive pricing to ensure the hinterland harvests were shipped to them rather than to St. Louis. The now higher railroad rates threatened their advantage, and soon the Chicago Board of Trade, the Board of Real Estate Brokers, and the Mercantile Association had joined the protest over high railroad tariffs.[36]

Railroads were being assaulted from all sides. So much agitation for regulation arose that the Illinois legislature could no longer ig-

nore the protests and, in 1871, passed legislation creating the Illinois Railroad and Warehouse Commission (IRWC), the first state agency with regulatory powers over both railroads and grain elevator operators, and the second, after Massachusetts, to regulate railroads. Predictably, the railroads protested, characterizing the commission's creation as an unconstitutional deprivation of corporate rights. Among the most outspoken was Blackstone.

The General Assembly of the State of Illinois, at its last session, passed an Act prescribing rules for the operation of railways, which were designed as remedies for supposed evils relative to railway management, and to enhance and secure the interest of shippers and producers, without, as we think, due regard to your rights. While the Act referred to is manifestly unconstitutional, and will doubtless be so declared by the courts; still we thought that a better understanding might be had relative to proper relations between railways and their patrons, by making, the experiment of a fair trial of the rules prescribed by the Act.

As Blackstone saw it, government regulators could never determine just and proper rates that would satisfy the needs of the shipper as well as provide railroads with a fair return.

The present popular outcry against railways in the West is mainly based upon the erroneous supposition that prices charged for transportation are unreasonably high; not in exceptional cases only, but universally. If it is true that the rates charged do not produce net profits equal to the lawful rate of interest for money loaned, taking as the basis for calculation, actual cost, we presume it will be conceded by all that the charges as a whole, are not too high; and if it be also true that the net profits upon the line producing the best results, do not exceed ten percent, we think it must be admitted that the charges upon that line are not, as a whole, unreasonably high.[37]

In support for his stance, Blackstone quoted the recently started *Poor's Manual,* which reported the average net return for all railroads in the country to be 5 percent; those of New England and the Midwest, 6 percent; and for western roads, 4.5 percent. He further quoted results of the 19 railroads operating within Illinois. Only five paid their stockholders a dividend, in no case more than 10 percent.

When the people of the country learn, as they will ere long, that they have been deceived by political demagogues, they will acknowledge and accept these facts as the basis for proper relations between themselves and the railways, and will no longer attempt by unwise and impractical legislation to deprive the owners of railway property of a reasonable discretion in its management.[38]

The first and defining test of the new law came in what became known as the McLean County case, in which the C&A was accused of charging higher rates on lumber shipped between Chicago and Lexington than it did for similar shipments to Bloomington, a trip 16 miles longer. In defense, the company's attorneys did not dispute the facts but contended that the charter the legislature issued permitted any rate to be set as long as it was "reasonable." The Lexington tariff was reasonable, they suggested, because no competition for the traffic existed there, but so were the lower Bloomington charges because the road faced competition from the IC. As the attorneys saw it, the company had set proper rates based on prevailing conditions. The right to charge lower rates in the face of competition had never been offered as a defense in an American court before. For good measure, the

lawyers contended the legislature's creation of the IRWC was unconstitutional because the power to judge the reasonableness of a rate was a judicial—not legislative—matter. Attorneys representing the IRWC countered with the argument that a railroad was a public entity and therefore subject to laws set by the legislature.[39]

The presiding judge, Thomas Lipton, found for the IRWC. His decision was quickly appealed. In his 1873 decision, Illinois Supreme Court chief justice Charles Lawrence, though expressing some sympathy with the IRWC's position, reversed Judge Lipton's decision on the grounds that the legislature was invoking powers to determine justice and that was the court's prerogative. He pointed out the state's new constitution enacted three years earlier authorized the legislature to outlaw only unjust discrimination while the legislation creating the IRWC outlawed all discrimination, just and unjust.[40]

All railroads operating in the state, but particularly the C&A, appeared vindicated. The issue of rate discrimination, however, did not die. Under pressure from both the Grange, which by now had amassed considerable strength, and the Chicago business community, which had sustained lost business when carloads of goods passed through their city destined for downstate towns, the legislature crafted a bill giving the IRWC greater and better defined powers that met Justice Lawrence's guidelines.[41] With the bill's passage, the era of state railroad regulation was born.

Most of his peers resigned themselves to the new environment, but not Blackstone. As long as he remained in charge, he railed against what he saw as unjust intrusion by government into private business. Other states throughout the Midwest followed Illinois's lead and passed similar regulatory legislation. Before long, the railroads found themselves confronted with different sets of rules in virtually every state in which they operated.

The first significant step the IRWC took, in late 1873, was to create a formula for passenger fares. The railroads were grouped in five categories. In the first rank were the most powerful—the C&A, Burlington, IC, Rock Island, and North Western. Those roads were allowed to charge three cents per mile. Those of the other four groups were allowed to charge from three and one-half cents to four cents per mile. The MC, the Lake Shore & Michigan Southern (LS&MS)—the former MS-NI—and the PFt.W&C, all of which had limited mileage within the state, were permitted rates of only two and one-half cents.[42] The new rate formulas met with the public's approval, but a few months after the passenger rate limits were set, the railroads responded by posting higher freight rates to offset the loss of passenger revenue, and the farmers and other shippers again cried foul. The freight rate increases, though slight, were enough to create some shipper revolts.[43]

Individual shippers had little leverage, but the largest began to extract secret rate cuts and rebates from both strong and weak railroads that wanted to keep the business. Though illegal, the secret agreements remained until they were discovered. Then competitive roads either matched the secret agreements or offered even more attractive deals. It wasn't long before much of the traffic moved either marginally covered the cost of transport or was carried at a loss. Highly principled, Blackstone insisted that his road play by the rules, even if it meant the loss of business. C&A agents did not generally engage in the kind of rate manipulations others did unless absolutely forced to. The C&A lost traffic, but what was carried returned a profit.

Cognizant of the lost business, Blackstone offered his stockholders the reasons, as he saw them.

The reduced amount of traffic is due in some degree to the depression of general business, but mainly to the operation of the present Railway Law of Illinois, which practically prohibits all traffic which might be obtained at rates affording less profit than those resulting from the fixed schedule of charges. At many of our competing points are found railways which extend beyond the limits of Illinois, and are therefore at liberty to make such charges on through freight as they see fit. Under the rules prescribed by the law, the alternative is placed before us of reducing all our rates to the basis of competition, or abandoning business at such points. Such a reduction would very soon lead us to financial difficulties, and it is much better to let our competitors take the traffic until the Courts or the Legislature shall relieve the people and the railways of the injury that results from the present law.

We have been restricted by arbitrary rules at variance with commercial usage and business principles. We have had competition for the past year under circumstances which it would seem could not be more to our disadvantage. We have expended a large amount in returning cars empty that might have been loaded with freight to the mutual benefit of shipper and carrier, had it been within our lawful discretion to make temporarily a slight reduction in rates. We have contended as best we could with competitors who were so desirous of obtaining traffic from points of crossing and intersection with your line that they have reduced their charges in many cases so much below rates affording a reasonable profit, that the result has been to place several such lines in the hands of receivers and to cause serious financial embarrassments to others.

The low rates that have been charged on many of the western railways for transporting the products of the soil for several years past, have caused trouble in many ways. The policy which has been pursued has deprived shareholders, in many cases, of all dividends; and in others, bondholders have failed to receive interest on their bonds. It has led the people—and in some cases, even the courts—into the erroneous belief that such low rates were reasonable, and that higher rates charged on other lines were therefore exorbitant. It has been one of the principal causes of hostile and unwise legislation.[44]

▾▾▾

Because of the formidable investments that had been made in the physical plant over the past 13 years, the company was able to claim an enviable record of safety, especially when compared to the road's earliest days when accidents were almost a daily occurrence. Fencing along the right-of-way was more prevalent, separating wandering livestock and trespassers from trains. Steel rails and better grade ties reduced track failures. Advanced signaling made operations safer and more reliable. Consequently, not a single C&A passenger had been injured or killed between 1863 and 1872, a record of which few, if any, other major railroads could boast. Nevertheless, as long as humans operate trains, accidents—such as the one on the foggy night of August 16, 1873—will happen.[45]

An old-timer, Joseph Mitchey, was assigned to the throttle of no. 122, a 4-6-0, with a northbound extra of 28 cars of coal out of Joliet. His conductor, Edward Beane, had nearly as much time with the railroad. The brakemen, Jacob Claussner and John Metzger, were rookies, hired a few months earlier to replace higher paid employees management thought it could no longer afford. Beane gave Mitchey a highball, and the engineer let out the throttle. His train gained momentum, left the Joliet yard, passed through downtown Joliet, and was soon gliding past the 23-foot-high stone walls of the Joliet State Prison. The train was traveling at about 20 miles per hour through increased patches of fog common in the Des Plaines River Valley on cool summer evenings.

It was somewhat after its scheduled 9 P.M. departure before Henry Russell, conductor of the *Night Express,* gave the highball to engineer Joshua Puffenberger to start moving his engine, no. 143, a year-old 4-4-0, out of the Chicago depot. Puffenberger was new to the railroad, in fact, making his first run. Russell's train comprised a baggage car, an express car, a smoker, two coaches, and a Pullman. The smoking car was filled with a Joliet group, including the prison's warden. Puffenberger was already slightly behind schedule and had orders to pick up a sleeper, the *Mexico,* at Willow Springs, so he was anxious to make up some

time. He arrived at Willow Springs ahead of schedule, but the coupling there did not go smoothly. Russell saw that he would be at least six minutes late leaving. He told the operator to telegraph ahead and have any northbound traffic held at the Lemont siding until he passed.

The Lemont agent dutifully set a stop signal for the coal train. Mitchey's train was now in sight and had slowed to the regulation eight miles an hour for its run through Lemont, but because of the fog, the engineer did not see the stop signal and passed the switch. The agent, standing on the platform, began running after the engine but backed off when he realized he could not catch it and instead paced the caboose trying to attract the attention of the brakeman, Claussner. "Do you have the orders?" the agent shouted up to him. Claussner shrugged his shoulders. He didn't know. The train accelerated and soon faded from sight into the foggy night. By now the passenger train had reached Sag Bridge, and Puffenberger thought he saw a proceed signal through the fog. He was wrong. It was a stop signal. He had fireman Frank Budges pour on more coal as he advanced the throttle.

At Lemont, the agent raced back to the station and screamed at the operator, "Can we signal the coal train somehow?" "No," came the reply. It was a little after 10 P.M. When the two trains met head-on at 10:15 P.M., the coal

Double tracking the line between Chicago and Joliet was already on the drawing boards but did not come soon enough to prevent the tragic head-on collision of a coal extra out of Joliet and the Chicago–St. Louis *Night Express* in 1873 just north of downtown Lemont. The depot, seen here in 1915, was where the agent futilely attempted to prevent the crash. (Courtesy of Lemont Historical Society, Bill Molony Coll.)

train was moving at 28 miles per hour and the *Night Express* at 35 miles per hour. Puffenberger's engine ran up and over the coal train's engine, taking the baggage, express, and smoking car with it. After a few seconds, its boiler exploded and metal flew everywhere. A large piece of boiler plate was later found 100 yards away, buried three feet in the earth. Nineteen bodies were recovered at the scene, and 25 others were seriously injured. Besides the Joliet group in the smoker, the dead included Claussner, Metzger, Mitchey, his fireman, and Budges. Among the seriously injured was Puffenberger.

The collision could be heard for miles. Lemonters rushed to the scene and offered what aid and comfort to the survivors they could. Conductors Russell and Beane compared watches, and Beane found his had stopped. He was incoherent, mumbling over and over that he had forgotten about the southbound train. He wandered off and was not seen again for 16 days until his best friend, Simon Miller of nearby Monee, turned him in to the police for the $1,000 reward that was posted for his capture. Puffenberger, who had run through the red board, and Beane, who had forgotten the meet, were tried and acquitted of criminal responsibility, but their mistakes resulted in the worst accident thus far in the company's history.[46]

▼▼▼

A proud man, Blackstone did not easily admit to mistakes, but he now had to acknowledge, after the Mississippi River froze for the second year in a row during the winter of 1872, that a bridge at Louisiana was needed. "While this brief experience demonstrates the importance of the traffic for which we are seeking in that direction [to and from Kansas City], and leads us to believe that our anticipation as to the value of that line will be ultimately realized, it also demonstrates the importance of a bridge over the Mississippi River to take the place of the ferry," Blackstone reported to the stockholders.[47] Those railroads with bridges (such as the Rock Island and the Burlington) made crossings without regard for seasons. The C&A was operating as a second-class railroad, stuck with a transport mode of another era.

In April 1873 papers were filed for formation of two companies, the Louisiana Bridge and the Mississippi River Bridge Companies in Missouri and Illinois, respectively.[48] In June, under the supervision of E. L. Corthell, construction of a Mississippi River bridge began. The structure was to span the river's 3,900-foot width on 10 spans, including a 446-foot draw span and two 200-foot openings. Railroad publicity was quick to proclaim the draw span as the longest in the world. It took only six months to complete. The short-lived and unreliable two-year experience with boat transfers was over. On Christmas Eve 1873, the first train crossed over the Mississippi River bridge inaugurating uninterrupted runs between Illinois and Missouri.[49]

The bridge's opening came near the end of the year when the nation's economy again collapsed. The panic of 1873 followed a string of boom years. The break came when, in America's financial center, New York, banks started failing, causing the stock market to crash. Soon business and farm failures across the country left the country in despair.[50]

The first full year of all-rail operations to Kansas City proved successful, but the route brought the only traffic increases that year (1874). Overall, tonnage declined 14 percent. Because Illinois farmers could not get credit, only half the usual planting was done, resulting in a 24 percent decline in the amount of corn the railroad carried. For the first time, coal traffic declined—by a whopping 26 percent—a result of a 10-month suspension of work at Joliet Iron and Steel (a large consumer of Braidwood coal) and a three-month miner's strike at Braidwood.[51]

Surprisingly, despite the decline of $450,000 in freight revenue, the company posted increased earnings for 1874 of $215,000, somewhat a result of increased passenger revenue but more significantly of sharply reduced expenses. They were cut by $587,000 from the previous year. To hold down expenses, no new engines or cars were acquired, and most other projects were put on hold. Repairs to the right-of-way, however, were not neglected. Of the road's 649 miles, 183 miles (28 percent) were now relaid with heavier steel rails. Though behind schedule, grade reductions continued on the most troublesome

Extensive and elaborate advertising and promotion was a C&A trademark, most noteworthy during the long tenure of James and George Charlton from the 1870s through the first 20 years of the twentieth century. One example is this poster cleverly employing the road's route map as the reclining chair frame. (Author's Coll.)

segments, the second main line between Dwight and Joliet was nearly completed, and a second track between Chicago and Joliet was finished. Many roads were in the courts seeking protection from creditors, but Blackstone's road continued to invest in the property, paid a dividend, and reported another $2.2 million profit.[52]

As was true of all the nation's railroads by the mid-1870s, freight movements had come to dominate C&A operations. For many roads, passenger service became of secondary importance, but not for the C&A. Safety improvements, including the Blackstone anti-telescoping platforms and the new air brake system designed by George Westinghouse, had been applied to all the equipment, a move not many other roads had adopted. Braking systems were also applied to all of the passenger 4-4-0s, again a practice not all railroads embraced. Overnight train consists included dining cars and Pullman sleepers, a combination that only a few other railroads offered. Three Chicago–St. Louis trains (one daylight, the other two overnight) now ran on 11-hour, 15-minute schedules, a considerable improvement over schedules of the previous decade. These service levels were matched by few other roads and exceeded the one-train-a-day schedules offered by most. The two overnight trains, the *Lightning Express* and *Night Express,* were the featured trains that captured the bulk of the business.

Advertising of passenger service with the placement of small notices in local newspapers started in the 1850s and continued throughout the 1860s but reached new heights during the 1870s as elaborate and colorful folders, brochures, schedules, and promotional items for which the company became famous first emerged. They were the inspiration of James Charlton, an Englishman who started his railway career in 1847 as a junior clerk with the Newcastle & Carlisle Railway. He steadily rose through the ranks to become cashier. Charlton emigrated to Canada in 1857 to join the Great Western Railway of Canada, where he remained for the next 11 years. There he again was promoted and became that road's general passenger agent. Charlton left Canada for the United States to become the general ticket and passenger agent of the North Missouri. It was there in

1871 that Blackstone first met Charlton and offered him the job of heading the passenger department.[53]

Charlton was never shy in portraying the railroad as an important link in the nation's expanding railroad network and as a road that offered exceptional service. The monopoly on St. Louis–Chicago runs had ended in the late 1860s when the St. Louis, Vandalia & Terre Haute—successor to the THA&St.L—linked up with the IC. The roads began running two daily-except-Sunday St. Louis–Chicago trains—one a daylight run, the other an overnight trip—using Effingham, Illinois, as the junction. Both trains ran on only slightly slower schedules over nearly identical mileage as did C&A trains. It was the first passenger competition over the main line the railroad faced, but through Charlton's promotion and with superior equipment, the C&A continued to enjoy the lion's share of St. Louis–Chicago passenger traffic.

When through passenger service between Chicago and Kansas City was inaugurated, Charlton faced entrenched and strong competition from the Burlington, but he widely advertised the service and was rewarded with substantial numbers of passengers, especially immigrants. To enhance the road's reach beyond its own rails, Charlton began promoting connecting service at East St. Louis to Memphis, Vicksburg, and New Orleans over the revitalized M&O. Impressive advertisements in newspapers, city directories, and similar business-oriented publications called attention to the road's Pullman sleeping car service. Passenger service was a priority of the company and, even during the difficult 1870s, was promoted and operated to the highest standards.

▼▼▼

In 1874—a year after Henry Block's L&MR was to have completed the line to Kansas City—the road still reached no further west than Mexico and Cedar City. The capital Block and other backers had raised was spent, and, because of the weak economy, they were unable to generate more. Blackstone had been patient (and had said nothing of the matter to stockholders), but under terms provided in the lease in the event of nonperformance, he stepped in. Claims were submitted to two arbitrators, as prescribed in the lease, to decide penalties. The decision they reached was to relieve the C&A of its obligation to pay rent to the L&MR after November 1. To avoid foreclosure, payments of the interest on the bonds were to be assumed and the payments added to the L&MR's debt. Henceforth, the C&A was only obliged to pay, after taxes, 35 percent of gross earnings. The ruling resolved the immediate difficulties, but beyond Mexico, C&A trains were still operating over a foreign road.

Blackstone realized completion of a Kansas City extension would be up to him. But given the current economic times and his aversion to take on more debt, he was reluctant to commit the C&A to such a sizeable undertaking. After some serious soul searching, he explored his options. One of the road's bankers, the powerful and influential J. Pierpoint Morgan, was approached for his support of a new issuance of $3 million in stock to pay for the extension. Morgan would have none of it. "If the lesson of the last few years [the overbuilding of railroads] is to be disregarded and it is the desire of the Alton stockholders to allow themselves to be saddled with an encumbrance of $3 million more—then I say only let them do it and they will suffer in consequence by the decline of their stock." He further threatened to sell the stock he owned and to retire from any further involvement with the C&A if Blackstone persisted.[54]

Morgan's admonition might better be understood if it was directed at anyone but Blackstone and at any railroad but the C&A. Blackstone had demonstrated over the past decade that he was one of the most conservative of any of his peers in assuming debt and that the railroad he headed was one of the most profitable. A rebuff from Morgan—one of the country's most powerful and astute investors—when found out, would have killed any chance for Blackstone to raise the needed capital anywhere else. As events later showed, Morgan was right, but one has to wonder if Blackstone had been able to raise the capital and complete his line in 1874 whether the fate of the extension that was built might have turned out differently and whether its success might have encouraged Blackstone to expand even further. Would a successful western extension have encouraged him to ex-

pand his road at other points such as St. Louis, Springfield, or Chicago? Would he have continued beyond Kansas City to penetrate the Plains states? Though unanswerable, the questions are intriguing. Rejected, Blackstone retreated and, for the next few years, made no further attempts to reach Kansas City over company-owned rails.

An addition, though not as important or adventurous as an extension to Kansas City, however, was made to the railroad. The Chicago & Illinois River Railroad (C&IR)—organized in 1867 by Charles P. and Charles N. Holden and three other Chicagoans—was intended to run through the rich northwestern sector of the state from Chicago to a point on the Mississippi River opposite Keokuk, Iowa, in direct competition with the Burlington. The Holdens had little success drumming up interest.[55] They spent six years trying to raise capital. The only backer they could attract was a New Yorker, Alexander McDonald. They named him president after he convinced them to abandon the idea of competing with the Burlington and instead to focus their efforts on tapping the rich and rapidly developing Wilmington Coal Field, a far more realistic and potentially lucrative goal. Plans were drawn up for a more modest operation that would run from Joliet through the newly established town of Coal City, where new mines had opened, and then continue on to Streator. Armed with the more modest business plan, the Holdens and McDonald were able to gather some funding just before the economy's failure. In 1873 they formed the wholly-owned Chicago Railway Construction Company to build the line, bought a second-hand Pittsburgh Locomotive Works 0-6-0, and ordered 10 service cars and 120 coal cars. They started work just south of Hickory Creek on the outskirts of Joliet.[56]

Blackstone at first took little note of the upstart company and gave the venture little chance of success. And he was right. After just a single season of work, and after laying only 24 miles of 50-pound iron rail as far as the Mazon River at Coal City, the effort ended. Well short of their ultimate goal of reaching Streator, the Holdens and McDonald decided to exit railroading. They approached Blackstone with an offer of a lease. The value in the short line, beyond the local traffic that would be generated at Coal City, was its potential as a second main line around the busy and congested Braidwood coal district, one with a better profile than the existing main line over Zarley Hill. On March 1, 1875, a lease was executed. The C&IR would take 10 percent of coal and 33 percent of gross earnings of all other traffic generated. To prevent any favoritism for one route over the other, rates for local traffic between Braceville and Joliet and between Coal City and Joliet were to be the same. C&A through trains would be permitted to run over the leased line at no charge.[57] The four miles of track needed to bring about a connection was to be paid for equally by both roads but constructed under C&A supervision. It took only a few weeks for a switch to be installed just east of Coal City, 19.7 miles from Joliet, where the track to the Braidwood spur, past the Diamond mine, was laid. Within a few months, after a connection at Hickory Creek was installed, through operations began. [58]

Interestingly, Blackstone did not acquire the rest of the C&IR's property. The Holdens retained the rights to dispose of the right-of-way beyond the Mazon River to Streator and the rest of their assets as they saw fit. They quickly found a buyer, Francis Hinkley, whose Chicago, Pekin & South-Western (CP&S-W) had tracks in place between Pekin and Streator. Rapid construction brought the line north to the Mazon River. Hinckley secured trackage rights through to Joliet over what was now the C&A's Coal City subdivision.[59] Hinkley continued laying tracks northward to Chicago and, when that was completed in the mid-1880s, laid a line almost parallel to the C&A to fill the Joliet–Mazon River gap.

In the final analysis, Blackstone probably made a critical mistake in ignoring the rest of the C&IR's assets. Hinkley, even before he bought them, had made no secret of his intent to expand south to St. Louis and north to Chicago to become a direct competitor of Blackstone's road. Blackstone could have bought the Mazon River–Streator right-of-way for less than $100,000 (Hinkley paid $91,535). A direct route to Streator over a few miles of flat, open prairie would have added capacity and relief for the busy main line between Dwight and Joliet, affording a shortcut for coal traffic generated at Streator. Hinkley's ambitions may well have been thwarted, leaving his line, like so many others, just a short line with little future. Blackstone's insistence on keeping his railroad reliant on locally generated traffic would seem to have demanded a buyout, but that did not happen. Within 10 years Blackstone's decision would come back to haunt him.

▼▼▼

The most enduring and monumental feats of engineering the country witnessed were often achieved by its railroads. Faced with mountains to climb and rivers to cross, the best engineering skills available were employed to conquer nature's hindrances. Tunnels and bridges—some still in use today—stand as evidence of the genius and tenacity of early railroad builders. Often the engineers who conceived the projects were scorned as dreamers. They were told their ideas defied common sense. Fortunately, they didn't listen.

One such engineering marvel was the spanning of the Mississippi River at St. Louis. A bridge across the Mississippi at St. Louis had been sought long before the advent of railroads, but for lack of funds and the opposition of riverboat operators, no serious effort was raised until 1864. Amid public apathy St. Louis's mercantile and business leaders secured a charter from the Missouri legislature for the St. Louis and Illinois Bridge Company. Similar authority was secured from the Illinois legislature a few months later. Because Missouri was a border state, its economy and its principal city, St. Louis, regressed during the Civil War. Trade relationships with the East were severed. St. Louis's population and wealth preceding the conflict had exceeded that of Chicago by wide margins, but during the years of fighting, Chicago surged ahead in both. Half a decade passed before St. Louis regained the business enjoyed before the war, but levels were below other cities, which had gained strength more quickly. The city's business leaders realized that to maximize St. Louis's potential, they needed to bridge the river.[60]

It took three more years before a corporation was organized and a chief engineer, James Eads, was named. Eads loved the river. He had studied its currents and soil conditions, raised sunken riverboats (claiming the cargos they contained as his profit), and invented the diving bell. During the Civil War, he designed and built ironclad steamboats, which the Union forces used in Mississippi River campaigns. He later designed jetties at the mouth of the Mississippi to reduce the threat of flooding. He knew the river and now was to prove he knew how to bridge it.[61]

In August 1867 construction commenced. By the spring of 1868, a stone abutment for the west approach was finished, but that was all that was accomplished for another year. Eads, plagued by chronic tuberculous, was stricken once again and took a year to recover. Then he returned to his project and finished the second and third piers and east abutment. Andrew Carnegie's Keystone Bridge Company of Pittsburgh won the contract to fabricate three high-strength iron spans (each over 500-feet long). It took three years to finish the components and several months before they were put in place, but on May 23, 1874, the stunning 1,627-foot bridge (4,014 feet including approaches) supporting two tracks on the lower level and a 54-foot wide road above, was finished. Despite past public apathy, opposition of riverboat captains and the Wiggins Ferry Company, Eads's illness, and the havoc wreaked by the 1871 tornado, a truly magnificent testament to man's perseverance and ingenuity was ready. It was neither the first nor last structure to bridge the mighty river, but it stands today as perhaps the most majestic and enduring.

Still the custom to celebrate major engineering feats on Independence Day, a parade of 14 locomotives was staged on July 4, 1874, conclusively demonstrating the soundness of Eads's design (which many of his peers thought improbable). The bridge successfully sustained their combined 700-ton weight. On the upper level, thousands cheered as the engines promenaded from one end to the other.[62]

A new terminal railroad, the Union Railway & Transit was formed to collect freight at the yards of the various roads on either side of the river and drag cars across the bridge. A depot named Relay was erected on the Illinois side. From there, passenger consists were pulled across the bridge, entered a tunnel, and terminated at the newly completed eleven-track St. Louis Union Depot at Poplar Street

between Ninth and Twelfth Streets. The depot was not a particularly attractive structure, incorporating incongruously sized towers at each end of the main building, and they in turn bearing incompatible architectural details. Aesthetics aside, its convenient downtown location and across-the-platform connections were vast improvements for passengers who, until then, were forced to contend with the variety of depots of the five railroads entering St. Louis from the West. The Missouri railroads, and some individual investors, owned the new depot. Eight others, including the C&A, entered it as tenants.[63]

The bridge organizers looked forward to rich returns on their $13 million investment.[64] Instead, they soon faced bankruptcy. Despite their earlier commitments to use the bridge, eastern railroads now claimed they had no authority to operate in Missouri. Within a year, with little traffic, the St. Louis & Illinois Bridge Company fell into receivership. The limited traffic that moved across the bridge was delivered to the St. Louis, Kansas City & Northern (St.LKC&N; formerly the North Missouri), and the Missouri Pacific (MP; previously the Pacific Railroad of Missouri) for westward dispatch at the elevator or freight house situated alongside Union Station between Eighth and Ninth Streets. Broken shipments from East St. Louis were delivered to wharves along the river for the convenience of St. Louis merchants. For the better part of a decade, the mixture of carload and broken shipments, ferries and bridge transfers, created a somewhat complex arrangement for both shippers and railroads.[65]

Though the Eads Bridge had made direct entry from across the river into St. Louis possible, the complexity of companies involved—the bridge, tunnel, and several terminal companies on the East St. Louis side of the river—created a chaotic and expensive mess that snarled traffic and delayed shipments. Adding to the unsatisfactory state of affairs was the nuisance of shippers having to pay an "arbitrary," a toll for using the Eads bridge, which added to the shipping costs. St. Louis interests came to realize they were losing valuable traffic to other places, especially Chicago, where the hindrances did not exist. They decided the solution was a second bridge.

In 1886 the St. Louis Merchants Bridge Company, and a year later, the St. Louis Merchants Bridge Terminal Railway, were organized. The plan was to erect a double-track crossing five miles north of the Eads Bridge to connect railroads—principally the C&A; Wabash; Chicago, Peoria & St. Louis; and the I&St.L—at Madison and Granite City with St. Louis. The plan was to make the route available to any railroad that wished to use it. George Morrison and E. L. Corthell were the bridge's designers, and they came up with a three-span, through truss bridge with 3,100-foot-long elevated deck truss approaches. Instead of using the more costly I beam construction, they employed trussed beams for vertical members and metal rods for diagonals. It was the first bridge placed over the Mississippi that used curved-chord trusses, giving it a graceful, but somewhat fragile, appearance.[66]

The Merchants Bridge opening cried out for order to be brought to the complex of rail service at St. Louis. In 1889 the various bridge and terminal companies, now controlled by Jay Gould, were consolidated into the Terminal Railroad Association of St. Louis (TRRA). This left the Merchants Bridge Company vulnerable as a stand-alone property. After the bridge's completion in June 1890, only one railroad on the Missouri side, the Burlington, had direct connections. Compounding the problem was the absence of access to Union Depot. Only modest traffic (mostly headed for the warehouses and manufacturing plants recently opened on St. Louis's north side), was hauled over the Merchants Bridge. Not surprisingly, after just three years of operations, the company found itself near failure. To save it, the TRRA took it over. Though still far from perfect, the traffic situation at St. Louis did somewhat improve through more coordinated operations.[67]

▾▾▾

Another corn crop failure in 1875 adversely affected C&A results. The railroad carried just 45 percent of the number of bushels usually transported. With prices so low that ranchers and farmers could hardly afford to ship their livestock, the number of cattle and hogs also

declined; so did the bushels of flour. Revenues from most other sources, however, climbed, especially Kansas wheat—by almost one million bushels; oats by a quarter million bushels; coal by 164,907 tons; and lumber by 12 million feet. Their contributions, however, could not overcome the corn and livestock losses. Overall freight revenues declined 8 percent. The soft economy hurt passenger traffic too. The numbers were off 5 percent, reducing revenue by 12 percent, the lowest level of return since 1867. Overall, revenues from all sources declined by 9 percent, a reduction of $455,289. A strong push to contain expenses (reduced more than 6%) was not enough to hold earnings. They fell by more than $225,000, the lowest posted since 1868. Though the results were troubling, because of its sizeable treasury, the company paid all obligations, including dividends, and the road's stability was never threatened.[68]

The next year, 1876, proved to be better. Traffic from the West was starting to pay off. Through passengers showed an increase of 7,491, nearly all derived from Chicago–Kansas City runs. The total number of passengers increased by 11,611, but because of the three-cent-per-mile limit imposed by the IRWC, passenger revenues were reduced 3 percent. Freight tonnage rebounded nicely though, rising 18 percent, and yielded a 12 percent improvement in overall revenues. Through freight tonnage now contributed 15 percent of the total; most of the increase was generated at Kansas City. The number of cattle transported over the line rose by 84,967 as market prices firmed, and, thanks to a bountiful harvest of both, wheat and corn tonnage jumped by 6.4 million bushels (the greatest total moved thus far).[69]

The resurgence in passenger and freight traffic, however, was not repeated in 1877. Overall, earnings dropped 10 percent, nearly $500,000. The passenger counts retreated once again. Corn loads dropped by 2,587,713 bushels, as did Kansas wheat by 500,000, the number of hogs by 62,037, and cattle by 87,882 head. As a result of another strike at Braidwood, coal tonnage declined by 132,198 tons.[70] The *Joliet Weekly Sun* reported, "Ever since coal was mined in Braidwood it cannot be remembered when the work slackened off

so quick as it has done this year."[71] To control costs, the coal companies cut pay rates to less than a living wage, even for already poorly paid miners. When negotiations led nowhere, the men and boys working the mines stopped reporting to work.

In July, with no evidence that the strike would soon end, the Chicago & Wilmington, now the largest operator, erected barn-like dormitories near the shafts to house replacement workers. The 250 scabs brought in to keep the mines open soon became fed up with the low pay and miserable work conditions and either left of their own volition or were run out of town by the strikers. Another 350 were brought in to replace them. The mines remained open through August, but the operators' strategy was already a failure. Production was a fraction of what Braidwood miners raised before the strike. By late September all of the scabs were dismissed. In late October owners resorted to bribes of beer and promises of $10 payments for any miners willing to return to work, but the men and boys held fast.[72]

By November the miners were desperate. They could not wait out the company any longer. Their credit had been cut off at the company store, and the few independent Braidwood merchants could no longer carry them. Their families were hungry. The *Joliet Morning News* summed up the situation this way: "There are two measures used in making unwilling men work: starvation and the bayonet. Starvation has done the work in this case."[73] Defeated, the miners returned to work.

▾▾▾

The continued success of Kansas City service was totally dependent upon maintaining good relations with the St.LKC&N. In 1876 there were signs that good relationship might be deteriorating. Stockholders were apprised of the situation in a message Blackstone signed in the annual report.

We believe that it has been, during the past year, the intention of the managers of the St. Louis, Kansas City & Northern Railway to deal fairly with your company and to accord such privileges in relation to its traffic as from day to day has seemed to them consistent with the interest they represent. But in the nature of the case they are not disinterested judges in matters touching a division of traffic between the two lines, and, as might be expected, our interest is held subordinate to theirs, and we have no remedy so long

Between 1871 and 1878, Schenectady delivered eight larger 0-4-0 switchers, like no. 131 seen here, than the eight already rostered. The bigger, more powerful 0-6-0 type did not start arriving until the mid-1890s. Note the oversized gaslight atop the cab. (David Goodyear Coll. E. L. De-Golyer, Jr. Photo. Coll., Ag82.232, courtesy of DeGolyer Library, SMU) as our access to and from Kansas City is over their line and subject to the conditions imposed.

Our board of directors are strongly impressed with the importance of conservative management, and are unanimously opposed to incurring any obligation of a doubtful character. They are not at present prepared to take steps to ensure the completion of a line to Kansas City, beyond such as are required to obtain full information relating to its cost, and hope that facilities over the line of the St. Louis, Kansas City & Northern Railway will be extended to your company upon such conditions as to render the construction of such a line as unnecessary.

In other words, Blackstone and the board of directors were holding their collective breaths that nothing would happen to disturb the tenuous arrangements.

But lest some apprehension may be entertained in the minds of some shareholders that a contingency may arise in which our company, for the protection of its interests, will be compelled to make an unprofitable investment to procure the completion and use of a line to Kansas City, it may be stated that assurances have been received that, with proper encouragement, a new local company can be organized between Mexico and Kansas City, with the ability to contribute to the cost of construction such an amount as will leave the cost of the line to your company, with steel rails, less than under the original contract (with prices then prevailing) it would have been with iron rails.[74]

The "local company" Blackstone alluded to in his message was already in formation, headed by John Mitchell of St. Louis. Mitchell; Robert Tansey, now president of the L&MR; John Woodson; Mitchell's brother William, president of the Illinois Trust and Savings Bank at Chicago; George Straut; and five Missourians—A. E. Asbury of Dover, H. J. Higgins of Higginsville, Thomas Shackleford of Glasgow, P.H. Rea of Marshall, and John Reid of Kansas City—were the organizers. On April 17, 1877, they filed articles of association with Missouri's secretary of state for formation of the Kansas City, St. Louis & Chicago Railroad (KCSt.L&C).[75]

There were two reasons why the authority found in the L&MR charter was not exercised and why a separate company had to be formed. Though the subsequent agreements between the C&A and L&MR—the lease and the contract to build the line—were explicit in stating the ultimate goal was to extend beyond Mexico to Kansas City, the original 1858 charter contained only rights to connect with the North Missouri at any point between Wellsburg in Montgomery County and Mexico "thence to the Missouri River at the most eligible point. . . ."[76] Both communities and the junction with the North Missouri were well to the east of what would have been the first crossing of the Missouri River, which was ultimately made at Glasgow. The renewed charter of 1868 expanded the territory where the Missouri River could be reached, naming Osage and Cooper Counties, both with their eastern borders along the shores of the Missouri River at mid-state, not along Missouri's western border. When surveyors began their preliminary studies west of what would have to be the first crossing of the Missouri River, attorneys for both the MP and the St.LKC&N filed suit to stop them, alleging the L&MR had no such authority. The courts agreed. Thus, new authority had to be secured. The other reason, given the precarious state of the L&MR at the time, was that Blackstone did not want to risk jeopardizing both it and the C&A (responsible for paying the leased line's bonded debt) if there were a failure, a fate that was befalling many other roads that were finding it difficult to cope. So the KCSt.L&C was formed, its organizers all affiliated with the C&A in one way or another. Five months after the KCSt.L&C's formation, on March 15, 1878, the company was leased by the C&A and mortgaged through director John Stewart's United States Trust Company of New York.[77]

Construction of the road started that spring. Grubbing, grading, and excavation over the 162-mile-long stretch was divided among 16 contractors. Sixty-pound steel rails were laid on closely spaced ties. For the first 20 miles out of Mexico, the right-of-way closely paralleled the St.LKC&N to a place named Larrabee (for the long-serving secretary and treasurer, William Larrabee) just across the Boone and Audrain county lines. At Clark, in Randolph County, the new rails crossed the St.LKC&N. At Higbee the Missouri, Kansas & Texas's (MKT) Hannibal-

Sedalia Division was crossed. The next 20 miles were laid over hilly terrain that dropped 216 feet before reaching Glasgow and the Missouri River.[78]

The formidable task of bridging the river had been planned to consist of five 314-foot Whipple iron spans with 1,140 feet of approach spans and 864 feet of wooden trestle. William Sooy Smith, an accomplished civil engineer, was hired to supervise construction. At the time, he was chairman of the American Society of Civil Engineer's Committee, which for several years had been studying the properties of various metals that might be used in bridge construction. During those meetings Smith learned of a process A. T. Hay of Burlington, Iowa, had perfected, which created a steel alloy superior to iron. Smith became a believer and recommended Hay steel alloy be used. The Carnegie Edgar Thompson Works in Pittsburgh turned out the more than 800 tons of Hay steel used in the bridge. The American Bridge Company gained the contract to erect it.[79]

Iron bridge builders predicted disaster, but Smith was determined. Falsework was erected,

iron approaches were installed, and one by one, the main steel spans were positioned. As the last span was being placed, however, disaster struck. The pressure of a buildup of ice caused the falsework beneath it to shift, and the span dislodged, plunging 70 feet into the river. The 160-ton span lay twisted and bent, but suffered no fractures. Although 60 tons of steel had to be renewed, the span remained together. Inadvertently, the strength and suitability of steel was proved, but it caused the withdrawal of American Bridge, and railroad crews had to finish the job. On April 9, 1879, the first steel alloy railroad bridge was ready to receive traffic.[80]

Workers had begun grading and laying track west of the river before the bridge was completed. They were faced with increasingly hilly terrain through Saline County that required fills and cuts and a number of culverts. Thirteen miles west of Glasgow, at Slater (named for John Slater of Norwich, Connecticut, a member of the C&A's board of directors), a yard was laid out. At Marshall the MP's Jefferson City–Kansas City line was crossed. By the advent of winter, the next 30 miles to

The crowning achievement in pushing west to Kansas City was the erection of this steel bridge over the Missouri River at Glasgow in 1879. The C&A claimed it was the first steel railroad bridge in the country though there is evidence the North Western erected one at Chicago earlier. It was, however, indisputably the longest steel railroad bridge. (Gulf, Mobile & Ohio RR Historical Society Coll.)

The first depot at Braceville in the Braidwood Coal region was lost to fire in 1879. These three retired box cars linked together served as a replacement until a more conventional, permanent single-story structure was built. (Courtesy of Wilmington Historical Society, Bill Molony Coll.)

Higginsville (in Lafayette County) was completed, and it was there that another crossing of the MP, this time its Sedalia–Kansas City line, was made. The last 55 miles through LaFayette and Jackson Counties again found rolling terrain that brought the line into Independence, 10 miles east of Kansas City, and a crossing of the MP once again. At Kansas City the KCSt.L&C's freight terminal and engine servicing facilities were located on 12th Street. From there, traffic was received and turned over to the KP and the Atchison, Topeka & Santa Fe, which had reached Kansas City four years earlier.

Passenger trains terminated at the Union Station but also served the depot at Grand Avenue, used by some of the minor lines serving the city, giving passengers easy transfers to every road. Along the line, day and night stations were established at Centralia, Dolphin, Higbee, Glasgow, Slater, Marshall, Blackburn, Higginsville, Odessa, Oak Grove, Glendale, Independence, and Grand Avenue. Between Roodhouse and Mexico, depots already stood at Pearl, Nebo, Louisiana, Bowling Green, Curryville, Vandalia, Laddonia, and Mexico.

Supplementing them were another 24 stations, 12 day-only depots, and 12 water and fuel stops. The line was opened to traffic on November 1, 1879.[83]

The KCSt.L&C's heavy dependence upon locally generated traffic became better balanced with the through traffic interchanged at Kansas City. Three freight trains out of Chicago were designated Kansas City trains with two returns. Four through freight trains were carded between Bloomington and Kansas City along with locals between Bloomington and Roodhouse, Mexico and Slater, and Slater and Kansas City. St. Louis freight out of Kansas City was routed to Roodhouse and then moved on three local trains to Venice and East St. Louis. The scheduling clearly reflected the importance placed on the traffic from the West.[82]

By the time the railroad had reached the city, Kansas City had grown to become not just a terminus for eastbound traffic but a strong commercial and industrial center in its own right. The stockyards, packing houses, and elevators that had emerged provided more than enough local Kansas City–Chicago traffic for all the roads already serving the city, plus the Rock Island, which reached Kansas City in 1879 through trackage rights over the Burlington from Cameron Junction. It was the traffic brought to the city by the Santa Fe and KP, however, that was the most lucrative and sought after. To ensure relatively even distribution of traffic for all the roads, a pooling arrangement was organized.

Between Kansas City and St. Louis, the C&A became only a minor competitor of the MP and St.LKC&N, since the company did not serve St. Louis directly, but only East St. Louis. Traffic destined beyond St. Louis eastward, however, became important as shippers avoided the delays caused by St. Louis's terminal railroad company. After the first full year of operation over its own line, C&A traffic in and out of Kansas City mushroomed. Freight traffic generated there was already 66 percent of the tonnage moved in and out of East St. Louis and Venice. Passenger traffic flourished

too. It wasn't long before Charlton's advertising showed Kansas City as the best route for tourist and emigrant travel. Places like Colorado, Texas, and California were linked with Chicago, St. Louis, Joliet, and Springfield in the company's advertising. Three daily passenger trains—the overnight *Denver Express*, to and from Chicago; and the *Kansas City Night Express* and *Kansas City Mail*, to and from St. Louis—were furnished with some of the best equipment the railroad owned. Eleven coaches and four postal cars had come out of the Bloomington Shops between 1879 and 1880, and four Pullman sleepers had been added during the same period to equip the three new trains, the first new passenger equipment to be added in almost a decade. Between the line's opening in 1879 and the end of 1881, the number of passengers carried over the line grew by 192,717. Kansas City passenger traffic that year was 43 percent of that recorded at East St. Louis.[83]

Completion of the Kansas City line produced the first emblem incorporating connected links representing the three major terminals of Chicago, St. Louis, and Kansas City. The names of the three cities were soon added within the links and the slogan "The Only Way" placed in the center. The famous "triangle of service" emblem was applied to engines, cars, timetables, and nearly everything else the public would see. (Author's Coll.)

▾▾▾

The C&IR had been under lease for but a few years when it became obvious it was a money-losing proposition. It was decided to skip a bond payment, forcing the line into foreclosure, setting the stage for an outright purchase. A court decree was issued, and on September 3, 1879, George Straut, representing the company, offered the only bid of $400,000, payable in a new issuance of bonds. Thereafter, the Braidwood-to-Joliet line, through Coal City, became the Coal City branch of the Northern Division.

With the folding in of the C&IR and the added Western Division trackage, the C&A comprised 840 miles of main line with 62 miles of second main line. Virtually every station had a depot. The engine roster now included 187 locomotives of five types, all coal-burning, 65 of them equipped with Westinghouse air brakes. The passenger fleet numbered 95 cars, plus 12 leased Pullman sleepers. The freight car fleet totaled 4,112.[84] The condition of the road, its facilities, rolling stock, and power were as good as any railroad its size in the country and better than most larger ones.

Blackstone's railroad had not only survived but had thrived during the difficult and challenging 1870s. He had endured the delays in gaining his own Kansas City line but now had it. He had witnessed disaster strike his facilities at East St. Louis and Chicago but saw improved facilities rise in their place. He had fought the new age of regulation and taxation but somewhat learned to live with it. He had gained increased respect from his peers for operating a first-class property and the envy of New York financiers for his ability to make money. He had social standing and involvement in numerous civic activities in Chicago. Blackstone had been president of the C&A for 14 years as the decade drew to a close and was proud that nearly all of his senior management and most of his directors had been with him for most of those years. His railroad had never been in better shape, poised like few others to capitalize on what looked like even better days ahead.

Defeat at Kansas City, Decline at Braidwood

Until the 1870s most American railroads were largely local operations with independent managements, running comparatively short distances. There was almost no interchange of rolling stock. Freight moving past a road's end point would be unloaded then reloaded aboard the cars of a connecting railroad. Passengers and their luggage were handled similarly, transferring to the next carrier when the end of the line was reached. That changed in

1869 when Cornelius Vanderbilt—fabulously wealthy from profits earned from New York City steamboating—took control of the LS&MS, combined it with his New York Central & Hudson River (itself the product of a merger of four independent lines), and created the first continuous line between New York City and Chicago—the New York Central.

His bold move quickly led others to imitate. J. Edgar Thompson of the Pennsylvania

Central began gobbling up smaller, independent roads through purchase or lease and, by the 1880s, operated 3,773 miles of railroad from the eastern seaboard through to Chicago, Indianapolis, and St. Louis. In the West, the North Western, a road of 119 miles in 1859, expanded rapidly by gobbling up 35 other roads and by 1886 had 3,500 miles under single management.[1] In the West, the North Western, the Burlington, and the Rock Island were the most aggressive in accumulating lines that could feed main-line traffic. "I have long been of the opinion that sooner or later the railroads of the country would group themselves into systems and that each system would be self sustaining," Charles Perkins, president of the Burlington, declared in 1879.[2] His prediction was already being fulfilled. In that year alone, 115 railroads lost their independence. From 1880 to 1888, 425 others were absorbed. By the 1890s there were 1,705 railroads, but fewer than 150 of them were independently owned or operated.[3]

The proliferation of railroads was nowhere more evident than in Illinois. In 1870 the state's railway mileage stood at 4,823. A decade later, the total had mushroomed to 7,918 miles, and by 1890, 62 companies operated over 9,936 miles of track, placing Illinois first among the states in track ownership. By 1893, 85 percent of Illinois's population was within four miles of a railroad. Missouri too saw extraordinary growth in trackage. By 1890, 6,000 miles of track was in place, ranking Missouri tenth among the states. Between 1870 and the turn of the century, railroads attracted the lion's share of investment and became the most dominant industry in the country. By 1891 the Pennsylvania Railroad was the nation's largest single employer, bigger by a third than the federal government.[4] Names like Perkins, Strong, Gould, Scott, Huntington, Villard, Adams, and Morgan appeared regularly in newspaper financial pages as each vied for supremacy over the others. The systems they forged, however, inevitably led to overbuilding and duplication. The massive increase in size, power, and scope of these major systems made it practically impossible for any but the strongest to return anything on invested capital. In 1889, 30 of the 57 Illinois railroads (excluding the five eastern railroads that terminated at Chicago) showed less profit than fixed charges, and six returned even less than their operating costs. Only six paid dividends.[5]

The C&A was among the few that prospered, but it had achieved neither the size nor influence of the leaders. Ranked among the very best of roads, the North Western's business plan might well have been a better one for Blackstone to follow than the one he did: nearly total dependence on locally generated traffic with limited expansion of territory. Through aggressive but prudent consolidation and leasing of lines when it made sense, the North Western's mileage was increased to 4,250, nearly four times that of the C&A. The North Western had plenty of capital and paid generous dividends (similar to the C&A's). It was equally well built and equipped as Blackstone's road, and its traffic was nicely balanced between local and through. The North Western was better able to face adversity when the inevitable economic downturns occured. Through its size and strength, the North Western was more than capable of staving off challenges throughout its five-state territory, an advantage Blackstone was to learn he didn't enjoy.

To be sure, the C&A was a successful carrier of local freight and passenger traffic, but there were limits to how much of that traffic could be generated. Illinois's industrial base had grown substantially, but most of it was in Chicago, not places along the railroad where economies remained agrarian based. The C&A's minimal traffic diversity and absence of significant through traffic (except on the Kansas City line) eventually led to revenue stagnation. Blackstone showed little appetite for competing in a larger arena. Other managements, though equally repulsed by the increased competition and government regulations, found ways to adapt, but Blackstone seemingly preferred to curse the darkness rather than to turn on a light. Throughout the 1880s, he publicly and vehemently denounced the unbridled competition, state regulation of rates, and imposition of taxes on the company's property and income as though somehow his words would change things. He railed against the perceived evils and even called for government takeover of the railroads if the burdens placed upon them were not lifted. What Blackstone failed to recognize was his own inability to grasp the bigger picture.

Blackstone's one flirtation with expansion—the Kansas City extension—apparently convinced him he was ill suited to compete with those emerging as industry leaders. Jay Gould of the MP, Wabash, and Texas & Pacific (T&P); Charles Perkins of the Burlington; and William Strong of the Santa Fe seemed to be more willing to take risks, to better grasp the dynamics of growth, and to understand the necessity of continued expansion. The sheer size and power of the systems these men controlled left the C&A vulnerable. As the industry grew throughout the 1880s and 1890s, it became apparent that Blackstone was content to be a big fish in a small pond. That pond, however, had become overgrown and choked of life-giving oxygen. For the 20 years leading up to the turn of the century, the C&A was an extremely profitable enterprise, but amid the rapidly growing and powerful railroad systems, it was like a boat with its sails at loft in a turbulent sea.

At all three of the C&A's major terminals—Chicago, Kansas City, and St. Louis—as well as at 24 on-line stations where competition prevailed, rate-cutting became so prevalent that some roads would accept freight at rates below the cost of transporting it, while making up the losses on freight taken where less competition was faced. Blackstone would have none of it. He ordered agents to relinquish traffic to the foolhardy rather than carry freight at unprofitable rates.[6] His stance flew in the face of convention but did pay off in steadily increased profits. While others took on enormous debt and moved freight at uneconomic rates, Blackstone increased the company's debt over the course of the 1880s only $1.7 million (from $11.8 million in 1879 to $13.2 million ten years later)—a level easily serviced through steady profits that were never less than $2.8 million and were more typically $3.5 million.[7] His generous payments of dividends became the envy of the industry. Above all else, Blackstone kept his eye on the bottom line but had no vision of the future.

He chose a very conservative course. Maximizing returns seemed the sole criteria by which he hoped to be measured. In 1888 he told his stockholders, "Your company has, for the last 15 years . . . and especially during the last 10 years . . . steadily resisted all inducements to add to its system of lines or increase its obligations for any other purpose," a stance opposite that of any other major road.[8] As other railroad magnates brought competitors into the fold and pushed into new territory, Blackstone did neither. After the push to Kansas City, he added virtually no new mileage. Nor did he add new traffic by taking over weaker, troublesome short lines. He was content to dominate the relatively limited territory he controlled and to leave to others the pursuit of—in his opinion—unwise and unbridled expansion. Blackstone's railroad became increasingly isolated.

Bloomington Shops turned out six ornately decorated chair cars with unique lettering in 1880 for Kansas City service. They featured 40 patented Horton seats that provided a higher level of travel comfort at no additional charge. Some of the cars would later be converted into modified diners, decorated in ethnic motifs, including special china and cutlery for Kansas City coach passengers. (Grahame Hardy Coll., Courtesy of California State Railroad Museum)

▾▾▾

At the start of the 1880s, the passenger fleet dedicated to Kansas City service was expanded and enhanced. Four more sleepers were acquired from Pullman, and the Bloomington Shops were kept busy turning out a mail car and six chair cars. The chair cars were of the same, highly popular type the railroad introduced in 1877. They featured 40 seats designed by a Kansas City doctor named N. N. Horton that offered generous space for the second-class traveler. Horton's chair reclined to a degree, providing coach passengers greater comfort than that of regular coaches of the time. Riders paid no extra fare for their use. The cars' exteriors were handsomely decorated in elaborate, hand-painted floral motifs with letter boards that bore the cars' numbers and the words "Kansas City St. Louis & Chicago."[9] The freight car fleet too was expanded with delivery from the Bloomington Shops of 1,100 boxcars, flatcars, and stock cars. The locomotive roster was enlarged with the addition of 20 American type, Schenectady-built engines.[10]

The country's prosperity was returning, reflected in 1880 C&A earnings, which increased by a third—nearly $1 million over the previous year—to $3.6 million, virtually all of the added revenue derived from the Western Division. The Kansas City extension's $1.7 million profit was already greater than that contributed by the similarly sized but less heavily trafficked Bloomington-Jacksonville-Godfrey line, which earned just under a million dollars.[11]

For the first time in the C&A's history, the number of passengers carried exceeded one million, reaching a total of 1,203,549. Those in and out of Kansas City were about 56 percent of those counted at East St. Louis and 42 percent at Chicago. Freight tonnage stood at three million. Every major category of freight traffic was up, especially coal, wheat, corn, potatoes, lumber, cattle, and hogs. Again the importance of the extension was shown. Kansas City freight was 70 percent of that recorded at Venice and East St. Louis and 32 percent at Chicago.[12] Though the additions made the next year were more modest, the fleets continued to grow. Three more Pullman sleepers were leased in 1881. Bloomington

turned out 660 freight cars. Pittsburgh delivered six 0-4-0 switchers (for switching duties at Mexico, Slater, and Kansas City).[13]

Each year through the 1880s, limited but steady improvement was made to the main lines. In 1881 the company completed a new five-mile stretch starting a mile south of the Coal Branch Junction to Mazon Bridge (renamed Mazonia by 1890), two miles south of Braidwood. The solid stock consists, northbound express freights, and frequent passenger trains that passed through this important portion of the railroad no longer had to contend with delays caused by the switch engines entering and leaving the Braidwood mine area.

Most of the grade reductions started during the 1870s between Joliet and Bloomington were finished, resulting in a lessened ruling grade of 24 feet. Similar reductions were made between Louisiana and Mexico. In 1885 the lines and grades between Clark and Higbee, Armstrong and Steinmetz, and Blue Springs and Grain Valley were altered, improving operations over some difficult terrain. The most challenging mileage found anywhere on the line was the first to have been laid. The steep and twisting route up and out of Alton had been a problem from the start. The severity of the climb regularly required helper engines. Alternatives for the troublesome section had been studied during the 1860s, but it wasn't until the late 1870s that a seven-mile bypass was engineered between Godfrey and Milton Station, running around Alton on higher ground. Since the St.LJ&C already had authority to construct the line, Straut and Blackstone signed a lease in February 1881. Five months later, on July 15, the cutoff was put in service. The new ruling grade became 32 feet to the mile, a vast improvement over the original 90-feet-per-mile grade.[14]

The goal of replacing all main line track with 70-pound steel rail was accomplished in 1881. Branches were still laid with iron rail, as was most secondary main line mileage, but it was generally the best and latest iron removed from the main line. Every year for the rest of the decade, there were annual replacements of from 5,000–7,000 tons of steel rail. And ballast, quarried at the on-line sites of Joliet, Alton, Pearl, and Blue Springs, was added across the system. Solid ballast trains became a fairly common sight. On branches and sec-

ondary lines, cinders—taken from steel mill blast furnaces at Brighton Park and Joliet— were used as ballast.[15]

Passengers at Chicago were afforded a much improved facility with the opening in April 1881 of a new Union Station, located on the east side of Canal Street at the northeast corner of Adams Street. Trains of the PFt.W&C, the Panhandle, the Chicago, Milwaukee & St. Paul (CM&St.P), and the C&A terminated there.[16] A few years later, the Burlington moved its trains in after the IC relocated its Chicago terminal, forcing the Burlington to find a new home. Soon after it opened, Union Station claimed ranking as the city's busiest, based on the number of trains, passengers, and mailbags that moved through it.

Though net earnings were off 6 percent from 1880 to 1881, they were still a very healthy $3.4 million. It was the higher price of goods and services the road had to purchase—not a loss of traffic—that depressed earnings. Prices rose rapidly as demand brought on by the accelerating economy outpaced supply for both materials and labor following the long, depressed period of most of the 1870s. The financial strength of the company was demonstrated by the sale at full face

value of $1.3 million of common stock, largely bought by existing stockholders. Other roads too—many much larger—were issuing stock and bonds but at discounts that reflected their less-than-sterling balance sheets. With the proceeds of the stock sale, in 1882, the J&C bonded debt that had matured was retired on schedule and $1.4 million of other C&A long-term debt was paid off. It was the second consecutive year that the road's debt was reduced, an annual pattern that continued throughout most of the 1880s.[17]

Brought on by the rapid advance toward industrialization, the nation's output was unprecedented. The flow of wheat and livestock from the West and Southwest swelled and constituted 80 percent of farm products the railroad transported.[18] In 1882, 800,000 foreigners arrived in the United States, a total not surpassed again for another 23 years. The thousands carried to Kansas City headed west swelled passenger counts that year to 1.5 million. As a result of the increased through freight and passenger traffic, Kansas City receipts rose to $2 million.[19] More switchers and more road engines were added in 1882, five 0-4-0 Bloomington-built switchers and six 4-4-0s turned out by Schenectady. Though

Before the seven-mile Godfrey-Milton Station bypass of Alton was laid in 1881, all C&A trains ran through Alton streets before attacking the steep and twisting grade up and out onto the higher ground above the bluffs. Train no. 4 is northbound on Piasa Street in 1932. (Roland E. Collons Photo., courtesy of Arthur D. Dubin)

Chicago's first Union Station was located between Adams and Madison Steets along Canal Street. It was opened in 1881 and initially served the PFt.W&C, Panhandle, Chicago & Milwaukee, and C&A. Later, the Burlington began using it when its operations were moved over from the IC's lakefront depot. (Courtesy of Chicago Historical Society)

neither the passenger nor the freight car fleet was expanded during 1882, the following year the Shops turned out six coaches, two baggage and two express cars, and 500 stock cars.[20] Results for 1883 showed another healthy profit of $3.9 million, which was nearly duplicated the following year. In 1884 the formality of folding the St.LJ&C into the company's corporate structure was accomplished through the exchange of a like number of common and preferred shares. This ended lease payments and traffic rebates, further reducing costs.

The nation's economy, however, once more turned soft as a financial crisis in mid-1893 led to fear and uncertainty. By the end of 1894, 3 million were out of work, and businesses—including many railroads—were bankrupt. C&A results declined 8 percent in 1885, 3 percent in passenger revenue and 10 percent in freight, but by cutting expenses—

particularly on maintenance of way and spending for new equipment—there was a decline in profits of only 5 percent, to $3.3 million. The road's performance was remarkable when compared to much of the rest of the industry. More debt was retired, and $1.4 million in dividends was paid out. Almost identical numbers were realized in 1886.[21] So successful was Blackstone in producing steady results that strong earnings, generous dividends, and retirement of debt had come to be expected. There was nothing exciting about the way Blackstone ran his railroad, but no one could deny he knew how to get the most out of it.

Revenues and earnings recovered in 1887, increasing 10 percent and 8 percent, respectively. There was $12 million in cash on hand. A big commitment to the important coal customer was made with the delivery of 200 coal cars. Nearly all of the railroad was now ballasted. Steel rails continued to replace iron at the same steady pace as had been the case over the past few years.[22] The company's fortunes seemed too perfect, and, as results for 1888 revealed, they were. As the year unfolded, it became evident the salad days were over. That year, the excellent and predictable highly profitable results abruptly ended as operating revenues fell 16 percent, and, despite an 11 percent cut in expenses, profits plummeted 23 percent. Unlike previous annual reports that precisely disclosed all reasons for increases or declines, the 1888 annual report included neither. Instead, Blackstone devoted eight of the report's 31 pages to a diatribe once again on the evils of government regulation, particularly as it affected western railroads.

> The net earnings from traffic on your lines last year were less than in any year since 1879, and the earnings on other railroads in the West were reduced in most cases even more than in yours . . . Nearly all the unfavorable conditions attending that result may be directly or indirectly traced to state or congressional legislation relative to constructing and operating railroads . . .

Western railroads are compelled to sell their services at such prices as may be fixed by the people they serve. Slaves in the South served their masters on similar terms. But the law dealt more kindly with the slave. His master was required to support him.

Western Legislatures and Railroad Commissioners have, step by step, reduced the maximum rates which railroads are permitted to charge, until such rates are now lower than are charged on railroads in any other part of the world . . . and this has been done where prices for labor and supplies required to maintain and operate railroads are higher than in any other country.[23]

Blackstone continued for several pages with the same theme but he never addressed the real cause of his anger and the cause of the road's reversal—what had been going on at Kansas City. The 1884 annual report was the last since Kansas City was reached to show a comparison of the volumes of traffic over the Chicago–East St. Louis and Chicago–Kansas City routes. Perhaps it was a coincidence, but it was that year that Western

Aside from a single 4-4-0 turned out in 1869, 12 0-4-0 switchers built between 1882 and 1884, such as no. 2, were the first homebuilt locomotives, produced at Bloomington Shops. They were the last four-driver switchers the C&A purchased. (C. E. Winters Photo., William Raia Coll.)

Division revenues, especially freight, first leveled off, then started a precipitous decline. Revenue increases on the rest of the system could no longer mask the severity of the crisis faced at Kansas City.

The Santa Fe and the KP were still the key feeders of traffic at Kansas City. Under the aggressive leadership of William Strong, the Santa Fe had pushed further west into Colorado and deeper into the Southwest and had brought ever-increasing traffic to the roads running east of the Missouri River. As he concentrated on westward expansion, Strong was content to turn over Chicago-bound traffic to the members of the Southwestern Railway Association, the Kansas City pool. It was only after the Burlington, then the Rock Island, and finally the MP pushed west into Santa Fe territory that Strong decided to retaliate for the transgressions of those roads' incursions by taking his own road into Chicago.

In 1883 Strong quietly ordered a survey of a Kansas City–Chicago route. Conducting the survey was A. A. Robinson—the Santa Fe's chief engineer—and Albert Touzalin—formerly a Burlington vice president who had left to assume similar responsibilities on the Santa Fe. Three years later Touzalin returned to the Burlington and told President Charles Perkins of Strong's intentions. Perkins immediately grasped the implications. He invited Strong to meet with him, and he revealed his plans to build a new line from Kansas City to Keokuk, Iowa, on the Mississippi River, with continuation over existing Burlington trackage to Chicago. He, of course, already knew the route was nearly the same Robinson and Touzalin had proposed. Perkins suggested Strong could avoid a big outlay for his road by sharing a route with the Burlington. As an alternative, Perkins proposed his road would lay a new line from Liberty, Missouri, to Bogard, north of Carrollton, Missouri, or one between Laclede and Ft. Madison, Iowa, with a connection there with Burlington's Illinois trackage to Chicago. Perkins was obviously bending over backward to placate Strong, who listened but made no commitment other than to think the proposals over.[24]

Perkins came away convinced Strong had already dismissed his offers and would move ahead on his own. To dissuade him Perkins decided the best offense was a good defense and decided to outflank Strong. He began thinking of a takeover of the C&A. Integrated with either the Santa Fe or the Burlington, the railroad would become an integral part of a huge and expanding western system. Its status as a profitable but limited local road would be ended and, of course, so would its independence. "I am getting up figures," Perkins informed John Forbes, his principal financier and a director in the road's home office in Boston, "which I think may surprise Strong when he sees them."[25] What Perkins didn't know, however, was that Strong had the same idea for the Santa Fe.

While Perkins was putting his plan together, Strong proposed a buyout to Blackstone. The stubborn Blackstone had no intention of relinquishing control of his company. On the spot, he rejected the proposal by asking an unacceptable high price.[26] Undeterred, but miffed at Blackstone, Strong began his eastward push. His first move was to purchase the struggling Chicago, St. Louis & Western, successor to Hinckley's CP&S-W. He had finished his own line through to Chicago in 1886. Meanwhile, Robinson was out surveying a Kansas City–Ancona, Illinois, route. It was at Ancona (just south of Streator), where the Santa Fe's new construction would join the Chicago-Pekin line. Upgrading of the acquired line was started in the spring of 1887. An agreement with the Kansas City Belt Line, which the Santa Fe partially owned, advanced the Santa Fe eight miles east of Kansas City, at which point construction of 350 miles of new Santa Fe rails began. By April 1888 the air line, including a crossing of the Mississippi River at Ft. Madison (over another bridge designed by Chanute), was finished and the upgrading of the Streator-Chicago right-of-way was completed.[27]

While his Chicago extension was being built—and still bitter over Blackstone's rejection of his buyout proposal—Strong directed that traffic formerly interchanged with the C&A at Kansas City be transferred to other roads. Then, when the Santa Fe's Chicago route was opened, Strong pulled out of the Kansas City pool, rupturing the peace that had previously prevailed. All of the roads east of the river, including the newly arrived CM&St.P, now had to fight each other for the remaining traffic. Predictably, a rate war ensued with all of the roads suffering losses, but none more than Blackstone's.[28]

Despite his aversion to rate cutting, Blackstone did just that, with a vengeance. In 1888 the road announced livestock rates of 22.5 cents per hundred pounds, 5 cents less than the prevailing rate, then further reduced the rate to 18 cents, and finally to 12.5 cents. The other roads serving Kansas City screamed foul, but Blackstone ignored them. At these price levels, it was impossible for livestock trains to make money, but Blackstone was determined. Kansas City traffic arrangements were thrown into turmoil, but so were those set at other gateways.[29] The Burlington and Rock Island Omaha-Chicago routes were similarly distanced as Kansas City–Chicago runs. To prevent diversion of eastbound traffic to Kansas City from Omaha, the roads there matched the Kansas City rates. St. Louis traffic patterns too were threatened. The MP and Wabash were forced to match C&A Kansas City–East St. Louis rates.

Livestock shippers relished the fight, and so did shippers of lumber, when, in 1890, the C&A cut rates on that commodity. Eventually, when no one was making a dime, order was restored, but not before Blackstone's road was irreparably harmed. He had alienated every other railroad with which the C&A competed. Neither freight nor passenger revenues to or from Kansas City ever recovered to levels enjoyed before the Santa Fe pushed its way into the Chicago market. In 1888 overall freight revenues fell to $4.9 million, the lowest level, as Blackstone reported to stockholders, since 1879.[30]

As though the reversals at Kansas City were not enough to contend with, another setback was suffered as coal mining at Braidwood began to ease. Throughout the 1870s the seven Braidwood mining companies produced an average 700,000 tons annually.[31] Even more tonnage was raised when, in 1881, needing a steady supply of coal for its engines and shops, the CM&St.P acquired 3,282 acres around Braceville and three existing shafts, the Cotton, the Augustine, and the Bruce Company's No. 1 Mine, and started three more of its own, the 1, 2, and 3. The railroad's need resulted in nearly 250,000 more tons shipped over the C&A. For the first two years of the 1880s, total tonnage the C&A moved

out of Braidwood topped 1 million.[32]

The Braidwood coal territory was exclusively the C&A's until 1883. That year the Wabash laid a 10-mile branch off its Decatur-Chicago main line at Custer Park to the Braceville area under the corporate name Braidwood Coal Railroad. For the next 10 years, some traffic was siphoned off by the Wabash that otherwise would have been shipped over the C&A. Then, five years later, in the autumn of 1888, serious competition arose when the three-year-old Elgin, Joliet & Eastern (EJ&E), then operating only an 11-mile line between the east side of Joliet and Aurora, formed a new company, the Gardner, Coal City & Northern Railway, and laid a 25-mile branch south from Walker (about a half-mile north of Plainfield) to Braceville and a 28-mile extension north from Walker to Spaulding. There it interchanged with the CM&St.P. Once the EJ&E had penetrated the territory, the 40 cars a day the C&A took out of the CM&St.P. mines, the Braceville Coal's No. 2 and No. 3 mines, and the Chicago, Wilmington & Vermillion's O, P, and R mines were moved out over the EJ&E.

It was during those years—the late 1880s and early 1890s—that Braidwood's operators, facing higher costs for labor than did their competitors in non-organized mines to the south, began slashing prices. "Many believe that this town has seen its best days," a local newspaper reported. Another article questioned, "Can it be possible that Braidwood has reached the limit of its growth, the summit of its prosperity?"[33] A slow but steady production decline began, and when that proved insufficient, the operators began shutting down the area's mines altogether. The first to expire (in 1884) was the CM&St.P's Cotton Mine at Braceville. Three years later, the Chicago, Wilmington & Vermillion's K mine and the four Eureka mines, also at Braceville, were closed. The pace of closures picked up, and by the spring of 1889 with mining activity greatly diminished, miners, faced with another pay reduction, went on strike. That was enough reason for the operators to shut another eight mines. Those still open were worked well below capacities. Coal traffic in 1889 dropped to 1 million tons (from the record level of 1.6 million tons set the year before).[34]

The expansive economy of the late 1880s and early 1890s helped the C&A's ability to produce good revenues and profits, though less than what had been enjoyed before the crisis at Kansas City. Freight moved held to a steady average 3.5 million tons; profits from both passengers and freight hovered around $3 million. In 1891, after it was no longer needed, five miles of track that created the first connection laid between the C&A and the C&IR was taken up at Braidwood. With that reduction there were now 843 miles of first main line, a figure that remained constant for the rest of the decade.

▾▾▾

The early 1890s saw more people traveling, especially businessmen. Serving the three principal commercial centers of the Midwest, the C&A's frequent and popular trains captured most of them. In 1892, for the first time, over 2 million passengers were carried. Some of that number were accommodated in new equipment bought or leased that year—21 high capacity coaches; two sleepers, the *Majestic* and *Teutonic;* and two parlor cars, the *Evelyn* and *Mercedes.* The 70-foot sleepers were the latest vestibuled Pullman offerings. They rode on six-wheel trucks and had gas lamps and all the latest safety features. The cars were configured with a drawing room and only six more-spacious sleeping sections, plus a gentleman's smoking room and toilet. The 64-foot-long parlor cars had 16 revolving chairs and 6 wicker seats. Their interiors were trimmed in bronze with schemes of ivory, light green, rose pink, white mahogany, and light gold accents.[35] The new first-class equipment was added to the company's premier overnight Chicago–St. Louis train, the *Lightning Express,* and received considerable industry attention given their $40,000-per-car price tags. In autumn 1892 four more coaches—60 feet in length, seating 31, and riding on four-wheel trucks—were added to the daytime trains, replacing equipment that dated back to the 1860s. Eleven updated coaches, coach-baggage, and coach-dining cars were turned out for the daylight *Express Mail* train.[36]

The new equipment came just in time to accommodate passengers headed to the Columbian Exposition at Chicago. The fair was to commemorate the supposed discovery of North America by Christopher Columbus 400 years earlier. An array of buildings housing thousands of exhibits, surrounded by glimmering lagoons and a Midway spreading out over 550 acres was opened to the public in May 1893 on the city's south side. Though nearly a year late in opening, by October, when the exhibition closed, over 12 million people had visited. On a single day, one of the C&A's trains arrived up from St. Louis with 1,143 fair-going passengers, and over one four-day period, Pullman reported 700 extra sleeping cars were brought to Chicago in its cars. Before the fair ended, C&A trains brought more than 500,000 visitors to Chicago.[37]

Ironically, such a magnificent event was taking place as the economy was heading into another of its periodic depressions, one that persisted for the next five years. This time the panic was not over the failure of a few New York banks, but over America's indecision whether gold or silver was to serve as backing for the nation's currency. Uncertainty led to a dramatic sell-off of American railroad securities by foreign investors. In February 1892 Wall Street saw its busiest day ever when an incredible 1.5 million shares were traded and over $6 million in bonds were sold. Just a quarter of the currency in circulation was backed by gold, and fears of instability caused massive selling. By May the New York Stock Exchange Index had fallen to an all-time low. What followed was major turmoil. Nationwide, more than 500 banks failed, 15,000 businesses closed, and millions of workers were laid off.[38] By the end of the year, some 30 percent of America's railroads, with an aggregate capitalization of $2.5 billion, were bankrupt. So sudden and numerous were the failings that *Railway Age* started a column devoted to nothing but notices of bankruptcies, a report the editor was compelled to continue until the end of the decade. By August 1894 the nation's deficit, the first since the Civil War, had reached $60 million. The country was saved from total ruin only after J. P. Morgan and the August Belmont Company of New York sold $65 million of government bonds overseas and placed the proceeds in the federal treasury. Confidence was somewhat restored, but much damage had already been done.[39]

Not dependent on heavy borrowing (Blackstone had not borrowed any money over the previous 15 years), the C&A came through the depression somewhat bowed but far from broken. None of the woes associated with the expansion and speculation that afflicted much of the rest of the industry had troubled the C&A. Blackstone's caution had been rewarded during the downturn, but, when the worst had passed and after bankruptcy courts removed much of the industry's debt during reorganizations, the bigger and more powerful systems regained their strength and were in even better positions of domination.

With obvious pride, Blackstone reported to stockholders that "For the last 15 years, your company has not added to the length of its lines, and had no occasion to borrow money." He further boasted that "While it has been said that no American railroad is completed . . . your road may now be considered as nearly completed as any other railroad in this country."[40] The C&A, however—dependent as it was on locally generated traffic—was vulnerable to falloffs in local traffic, and that exposure was evident when 1894 results came in. Profits declined 8 percent, largely a result of a three-month coal strike and, as Blackstone called it, "the unparalleled depression of all kinds of business throughout the entire year."[41] Labor unrest disrupted much of the industry in May when the Eugene Debs–led American Railway Union walked out over a dispute with Pullman. Union members refused to work trains that carried Pullman cars (the C&A operated 25 of them). The walkout ended in July after President Grover Cleveland used federal troops to enforce a court injunction against the strike.[42]

As other railroads continued operating under court protection, Blackstone—having assured himself his railroad was complete—began simplifying the company's structure and continued to reduce its debt. He used internally generated funds to purchase nearly all of the outstanding shares of the L&MR. Three million dollars of first mortgage bonds of the St.LJ&C, which matured that year, were paid off, and more than $523,000 of other debt was paid. There was still enough in the treasury to permit payment of a generous 8 percent dividend. To rebuild the treasury, 24,502 common shares were sold to existing stockholders at a price of $114—a 14 percent premium over par value. In 1895 gross earnings improved 8 percent, and though costs rose 10 percent, with the reductions in fixed charges, 6 percent greater income was posted. This was during a period when three-fourths of American railroads had earned nothing.[43]

▾▾▾

The nation's attention was drawn to St. Louis when on September 1, 1894, 10,000 formally attired guests officially marked the opening of the long-anticipated new St. Louis Union Station, designed by local architect Theodore Link of Link and Cameron, with a gala celebration.[44] The $6.5 million project was located well to the west of St. Louis's center on Market Street, between Eighteenth and Twentieth Streets. Several other sites had been considered before the 22-acre Mill Creek Valley area was selected, but none had been large enough for the massive facility that had been planned.

Among the features incorporated into Link's magnificent Romanesque-styled structure was a majestic, 230-foot-tall clock tower. The 606-foot facade along Market Street incorporated a multitude of large, arched window and door openings, twin turrets, and a graceful *porte cochere*, which led to the main entrance (later removed when Market Street was widened). At the extreme west end, four dormers delineated the Terminal Hotel, which was made an integral part of the structure. Within was a marvel of opulent splendor. The Grand Hall, an 8,500-foot area with a barrel-vault ceiling that rose 65 feet, comprised the second floor of the headhouse, which served as the waiting room. A giant mosaic depicting three great cities—New York, St. Louis, and San Francisco—graced the Market Street wall, under which was a grand staircase leading to the main entrance. Seven plaster relief maidens protruded from the side walls supporting lighted globes, which nicely complemented a giant, 4,500-pound, 20-foot diameter iron chandelier suspended from the ceiling's center. Below the Grand Hall was a 70-foot hall through which travelers passed before reaching a wrought iron fence that guarded access to the 16 train platforms. Above the fence was a giant train board where

The handsome and majestic St. Louis Union Station on Market Street was opened to considerable fanfare in 1894. The trains of the 22 railroads that eventually terminated there entered under what was at the time of its construction the largest train shed in the world, housing 30 tracks. A fine convenience for travelers laying over between trains was the 100-room Terminal Hotel, an integral part of the Romanesque style building. (St. Louis *Globe Democrat* Archives, St. Louis Mercantile Library, University of Missouri-St. Louis)

arrival and departure times were displayed.[45]

The train shed, designed by George Pegram, was the largest in the world at the time. It was 630-feet long and 606-feet wide, covered almost 10 acres, and housed 30 tracks. Its roof was made of five spans—the largest 141-feet wide—and covered three and one-half miles of track. In all there were 19 miles of track with 130 switches controlled by an interlocking plant with 122 levers. The approach was originally designed as a "single throat" but in 1902 was changed to a "double throat" arrangement. St. Louis Union Station quickly became one of the busiest and more captivating railroad terminals built.[46]

The Merchants Bridge's main deficiency had been the absence of access to the former depot. To reach the new Union Station, a two-mile extension of the elevated track on the Missouri side of the river to a point between Twelfth and Fourteenth Streets connected the lead to the bridge with the TRRA and entrance to the depot.[47] C&A passenger trains thereafter used the Merchants Bridge for entry to St. Louis Union Station.

Thanks in large part to through and connecting service at St. Louis, the number of passengers the C&A carried in 1895 again rose above the 2 million level. Pullman tourist sleepers left every Thursday from Chicago for

Los Angeles and San Francisco via St. Louis. This route, labeled "The True Southern Route," was over the St. Louis Iron Mountain & Southern (St.LIM&S), T&P, and Southern Pacific (SP). Other connections were coordinated for service to Little Rock, Hot Springs, Dallas–Ft. Worth, San Antonio, Houston, Austin, Galveston, and Laredo, with connections there to Mexico using trains of the St.LIM&S, MKT, and the St. Louis San Francisco (St.LSF). At Kansas City the C&A and UP linked up with daily through chair car service to Denver.

Other moves were taken to increase passenger business. Completion of the Dwight-Washington branch had brought C&A rails within 12 miles of Peoria, but not into what had become the state's second largest city. The Rock Island monopolized Chicago-Peoria traffic, but after trackage rights over the Toledo, Peoria & Western (TP&W) were secured, on September 29, 1895, C&A trains entered Peoria Union Station for the first time. The route matched the Rock Island's 161 miles, and similar running times were established. Initially, three trains were scheduled—one fewer than the Rock Island offered. During the last three months of 1895, just 4,931 passengers rode C&A Peoria trains, approximately 15 passengers a day, but after schedules were placed in the *Official Guide of the Railways* and James Charlton's agents had a chance to make the public aware of the new service, an annual average 20,000 passengers, about 60 a day, used the service.[48] Stockholders were told the new Peoria service was "experimental," but timetables of the period displayed Peoria schedules as prominently as those providing main line service. Peoria had been added to the Alton map without laying a mile of track.[49] Another entry into Peoria, this time from the south, was made a year later. Trackage rights were secured from the Peoria, Decatur & Evansville from a point where it crossed the C&A main line north of Lincoln, through Delavan to Peoria. Two daily trains originating at Springfield were scheduled. Peorians now had the added option of close connections with Kansas City–bound trains at Delavan.

Reaching Peoria was for Blackstone a major advance, but the year 1897 turned out to be one of retreat. Passenger traffic declined, and another three-month coal miners' strike and a dramatic falloff in farm production all con-

tributed to a 10 percent drop in net earnings. It would have been difficult enough to maintain earnings with reduced revenues, but higher maintenance costs—including $133,881 spent reconstructing the Mississippi River bridge—made it all but impossible to avoid a setback.[50] Though the size and weight of C&A power and equipment had remained constant, bigger cars with foreign markings with higher tonnage ratings were more frequently appearing in consists. Their weight was taxing the bridges, trestles, and culverts built in earlier times. The average C&A freight train still numbered 22 cars, but the average number of tons of freight per car had climbed from 160 to 180. Thus, rebuilding the iron structure was the first replacement step taken. Beginning in 1896 and over the course of the next two years, the bridge was replaced, and some of the other more critical spans were either replaced or upgraded.

Despite the threats of reprisals brought on by their militancy, in the middle of the depression, vocal labor leaders began pushing for higher wages, shorter hours, and better working conditions for the men and boys working America's industries. Chicago had become the epicenter for the labor movement, but the courage shown by the radical leaders there influenced others, including America's coal miners. In October 1897 members of the United Mine Workers of America (UMW) across the country walked off their jobs. So large had the movement become that even miners in downstate Illinois, who until then had rejected organization, joined in. During the last three months of the year and until July 1898 when a national agreement between the UMW and the operators was reached, virtually no coal was mined in Illinois. C&A tonnage dropped to the lowest level since 1879, to just 894,017 tons.

Though a majority of the nation's mine owners grudgingly accepted the national agreement that was reached, southern Illinois mine operators had balked. Along the C&A, 21 owners, including now the largest producer on the railroad, the Chicago-Virden Coal Company at Virden, rejected the national agreement, willing only to accept new pay levels that were 10 cents below national standards. The operators argued that the higher national rates, when added to the already higher shipping costs, would force them out of the Chicago market. With a strong union behind them, the miners refused to negotiate. Angry and frustrated, Thomas Loucks, president of the Chicago-Virden, decided to replace the miners so production could be resumed. Loucks, however, could not find willing replacements locally, so mining company agents were sent to Alabama to recruit workers. The agents found all the willing applicants they needed. Hundreds of African-American share croppers signed on.

Anticipating trouble when the replacements arrived, Loucks hired guards and had a wooden stockade erected around the minehead. Incensed at the provocation, the striking miners awaited the scabs. Tipped off by sympathetic railroad workers, the miners knew when they were arriving. As the day train up from St. Louis approached, the miners, armed with guns and whatever weapons they could muster, were waiting. The train's engineer spotted the mob as he approached the mine and realized what would happen if he stopped. Instead of braking, he opened the engine's throttle and charged past. The miners cheered. The train steamed all the way to Springfield, where union members boarded and threatened to kill any of the scabs that didn't get off and go home. For the moment, it appeared the miners had won.

But a second attempt to bring in replacements came a month later. Once again the miners gathered. This time the engineer was under strict orders to stop the train, which he did, and at once, the miners began firing. Guards returned fire. The wounded engineer released the brakes and headed north a few miles before stopping. At the mine seven miners and four guards lay dead with 30 other miners and five guards seriously wounded. Though none onboard the train were killed, several had been wounded. It was a bloody confrontation that forced Governor John Tanner to call out 100 National Guardsmen to bring a semblance of order. By the middle of November, Loucks, defeated, made no further attempts to bring in scabs, but several more months passed before he and the other owners who supported him relented and the mines were reopened.[51]

The coal strike (which lingered for seven months into 1898) and failures of both the 1897 and 1898 corn crops depressed company results. Net receipts dropped 4 percent. The reduced performance compelled the board of directors to cut the heretofore expected 8 percent dividend to 7.25 percent in 1897 and 7 percent in 1898. This did not go unnoticed by the financial press. The concerns expressed stung Blackstone. In that year's annual report, Blackstone stated:

Much comment has recently been published in the newspapers relative to the reduction of dividends by the company from eight percent to seven and one quarter percent in 1897 and to seven percent in 1898, and unfavorable deduction as to the value of your road appears to have been drawn therefrom [sic].

The dividends paid in cash on the common stock of your company during the last 35 years are equal to an average of eight and a third percent per annum.

The average of dividends of the last 18 years, including seven and one quarter percent paid in 1897, and seven percent in 1898, is a fraction more than eight percent per annum.

A reduction of dividends on Chicago & Alton shares, under similar conditions, occurred about 20 years ago. After paying eight to 10 and one half percent dividends for a period of 12 years, eleven and one half percent was paid in 1877, seven percent in 1878, six percent in 1879 and six and one half percent in 1880. This reduction was followed, with the exception of one year, in which 10 percent was paid, by eight percent dividends for a period of 16 years. After which the rate was reduced for the last two years as before stated.

The capacity of the road to earn such dividends is due to the advantages of having Kansas City, St. Louis, and Chicago as its termini, and to its large local traffic. More than 80 percent of its freight traffic, and more than 90 percent of its passenger traffic is local.[52]

Blackstone made no further comment, convinced no doubt that the facts spoke for themselves. But it was an uncharacteristic, defensive statement. Until now, his long and sometimes tiresome annual report essays attacked the ills afflicting the industry and his solutions of them. It had not been his practice to defend either himself or the management of his railroad. The way America's business was being conducted was changing, and it was not apparent that Blackstone knew it.

There was nothing in all of America as the turn of the century approached to compare with the railroad industry. Its more than 200,000 miles of rails seemingly reached every village, town, city, and port. Thousands of daily trains hauled massive amounts of farm and industrial production. Hundreds of locals and fast, luxurious limiteds carried businessmen, tourists, and immigrants to destinations far and wide. Hundreds of thousands were employed, their wages greater than those paid by any other commercial or governmental entity.

Railroads were also the largest consumers of finished products and raw materials. Constant repair and replacement of power and equipment meant a huge need for steel parts and components. Bridge members, engine boilers and parts, hardware for cars, and rails were just some of the finished products the rapidly growing steel industry produced. And the steel the rest of the economy needed was becoming a growing segment of railroad traffic. The railroads and the steel industry were welded together in a mutually dependent relationship. Railroads brought the raw material to the mills, then moved the finished products out. Steel manufacturers were both customers and suppliers. Railroads and oil refiners were also linked. The lubricants and fuels the country's industries demanded were transported by railroads, and, as with steel products, the railroads were large consumers.

Two men in particular in the 1880s recognized the enormous potential of steel and oil and began to absorb as many small producers as they could until they had formed near monopolies. Andrew Carnegie gained financial control of almost a thousand small mills and brought them together as Carnegie Steel. Similarly, John Rockefeller began gobbling up small, independent producers, forming the Standard Oil Company, eventually controlling 90 percent of all refined product.[53] The consolidation of these two prime industries, both critical to the nation's growth, paralleled the amalgamations of the many short-line railroads into massive railroad systems. The buyouts did not subside before 70 percent of the nation's mileage was under the control of just a few men.[54]

The capital that fostered these giant enterprises came from investment bankers, most of them located in New York City: National City Bank, Kidder Peabody, Drexel, Morgan, Jay Cooke, August Belmont, Winslow & Lanier, and Kuhn, Loeb. The relationships that evolved among the leaders of steel, oil, and railroads, financed by their bankers, led to interlocked business relationships and integrated alliances. The trusts, as they became labeled, brought about efficiencies and huge profits but at the expense of competition.

Blackstone did not embrace the new style of American business. At every turn he rejected overtures to become a player. He managed his railroad as one would a household. Outsized obligations were avoided by limiting his road's capitalization, which comprised primarily stock rather than bonds. He neither entertained nor sought ties with other railroads and was increasingly shut out of arrangements the large systems made. Though prominent in Chicago circles, he was not part of the exclusive New York club. As a result of Blackstone's aversions, the C&A became an increasingly outdated, isolated property. To be sure, Blackstone made money for his stockholders, but anyone with an ounce of vision could see the company, under Blackstone, was ill prepared for doing business in the new environment.

Little had been invested in the property or its equipment for almost a decade. When he declared the C&A "as nearly completed as any other railroad in the country," Blackstone revealed that he did not understand the dynamics of the industry or, for that matter, modern industrial methods. Enterprises that do not grow soon find themselves in decline. The directors and most of his top management had served in their capacities nearly as long as Blackstone himself. John Drake, one of the five originals, had been a director for 31 years before retiring in 1894. John Mitchell had served as a director continuously since 1864. John Stewart, president of the United States Trust Company, joined the board in 1865. Morris Jesup had been a member since 1881. James McMullin, the company's superintendent, then general manager, and finally vice president, held high-level positions for 26 years before retiring in 1894. H. H. Courtright, the road's general freight agent, assumed his position in 1881 and remained until 1895. His predecessor, James Smith, had held the job for 14 years before him. General passenger and ticket agent James Charlton had been with the railroad since 1871. The staid, cautious C&A family under Blackstone had long since settled in with an acceptance of the status quo.

An expert accountant, J. H. McClement, later summed up the state of the company in the late 1890s:

> It [the C&A] had not added one mile of road in 17 years. It had little or no reserve capacity to conduct a larger business. Its costs of operations, per unit of traffic, was very high in comparison with similar roads. Its grades were uneconomical. Its shops and equipment were uneconomical and old. Its settled policy against the expansion of its facilities, because of declining rates, was an absolute bar to the development of the tributary country. While for 25 years it had paid an average dividend of 8.3 percent on its capital stock, the gross earnings for the year 1898 . . . amounting to $6.3 million, were the lowest since 1880, and had been gradually falling since 1887, when they amounted to $8.9 million. In many respects the company was being conducted like a commercial enterprise having in view ultimate liquidation, instead of like a public carrier.[55]

Blackstone was nearing his sixty-ninth birthday in 1898 when John Mitchell, a stockholder and president of the Illinois Trust & Savings Bank of Chicago (having inherited the position from his father, William), began to question the company's future. At 45, he was much younger both in years and attitude than Blackstone. Mitchell was astute in business matters, and he realized the time had come for a change in the way the C&A should be run. The road's aged locomotive and car rosters, the need for replacement of the road's outdated yards, the completion of the second main line, the necessity of new signalling, and the replacement of outdated facilities could not possibly be accomplished on a pay-as-you-go basis as had been Blackstone's practice. Mitchell knew the railroad needed massive new investment if it were to reverse its undeniable downward drift. Someone with greater vision who practiced modern management and one with deep pockets was needed to guide the company into the twentieth century. Mitchell resolved to find that person.

The Harriman Era

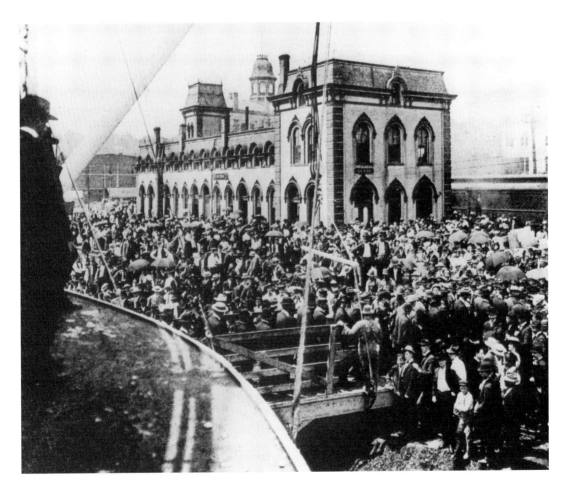

When the 1903 floodwaters crested at Alton, the packets hired to haul passengers and essential freight to St. Louis could dock within six feet of the Alton Union Station platforms. (Alton Telegraph Photo.)

After the devastating collapse of many railroads following the 1893 depression, a stronger industry emerged. Pushed by their bankers, the heads of the larger roads, especially in the East, began stabilizing the chaotic competition that had prevailed by creating "communities of interest," in which the largest roads took financial interests in weaker railroads in their territories. The NYC and the Pennsylvania controlled the actions of the B&O, Chesapeake & Ohio (C&O), Norfolk & Western (N&W), and a number of other smaller coal-hauling roads. The southern roads were brought together into a system where none before existed, led by J. P. Morgan. The Gould Lines—created by Jay Gould and now run by his son, George—included the Wabash, MP, and T&P. In New England there was the New Haven system, another Morgan creation; in the Northwest were James Hill's roads. Edward Harriman controlled the IC and UP.[1]

Timothy Blackstone was one of the mavericks whose road continued to hold its independence. Another was that of a Kansas City real estate broker, Arthur Stilwell, who had recently opened his Kansas City, Pittsburgh & Gulf (KCP&G), a poorly built and lightly patronized 762-mile railroad that meandered north from a new Texas port on the Gulf of Mexico he had immodestly named Port Arthur to Kansas City. Like Blackstone, who had disrupted the peace at Kansas City by savagely cutting rates following Strong's push to Chicago, alienating his competitors in the process, Stilwell, to gain business at any price for his road, had locked his tariffs in the closet, upsetting peaceful operations throughout the Southwest.

In early autumn 1898, reports began circulating that Stilwell was intent on a takeover of the C&A. He needed more traffic, and access to Chicago, he knew, could provide it. Stilwell announced that he held options for a majority of C&A stock, and it sounded like a deal was imminent. Harry Robinson, editor of *Railway Age*, seemed to think so. In November 1898 he wrote, "There can be no doubt that such negotiations have been and are in progress, and our information is that, in spite of difficulties which have arisen, there is every prospect that they will be successfully concluded."[2] A few weeks later, reports appeared declaring that George Gould was negotiating to buy the C&A for his MP.[3] At the time he was attempting to put together a transcontinental railroad system by acquiring control of the Western Maryland and a few short lines to link up with the Wabash to the east; the Denver & Rio Grande (D&RG) to extend his MP from Denver to Salt Lake City to the west; and through control of a new railroad, the Western Pacific (WP), to San Francisco.[4]

These were significant developments, and Blackstone became troubled by the Stilwell and Gould rumors. Stilwell was not a railroader in Blackstone's view, but rather one of the new wheeler-dealers capable of creating havoc. He had little regard for Stilwell. Blackstone and Gould's father had never hit it off, and George Gould and Blackstone made no

effort to improve relationships. They were different in personality, styles, and business practices. Most of the C&A's southwest traffic alliances had been arranged with MP competitors. Blackstone was leery of what—if the reports were true—Gould had in mind. Though Blackstone personally owned a third of the company's stock, no one was talking with him. The reports were coming out of New York, making him wonder if Morris Jesup or John Stewart, or perhaps both, were talking with possible suitors. He doubted that was the case. Both men had been faithful associates. But he still wondered who was negotiating.

John Mitchell, president of Illinois Trust & Savings and a prominent C&A stockholder, also took note of the reports. They confirmed, at least in his mind, that the C&A was about to lose its independence, one way or another. He was a powerful man in Chicago business affairs and decided he would have a hand determining the outcome. What he needed was someone who knew the railroad's affairs well, an insider who could provide him the information he needed to formulate a plan. His uncle John was a longtime director, but the details, rather than high level information the senior John Mitchell was given, had to come from someone absorbed in the daily activities. He found his confederate in Charles Chappell, Blackstone's right-hand man, vice president, general manager, and director.

Chappell had been with the company for 17 years, first serving as assistant general superintendent before being promoted to assistant general manager and, after McMullin's retirement in 1894, to general manager. He was a 40-year career railroader, having served with the Burlington, the UP, the MKT, again with the Burlington, then the St.LIM&S, MP, T&P, and Wabash in successively higher management positions.[5] Mitchell and Chappell together gathered the figures that would convince an investor to step in and take control. The kind of investment that would be needed could only be found in one place— New York City. It was the financial capital of the country, and though Mitchell's own Chicago bank was sizeable, it was low on the list compared to the likes of New York institutions. And it was in New York that a figure who had already proved his skill and savvy as a rehabilitator of railroads had his offices.

That man was Edward Harriman.

Mitchell arranged a meeting with Harriman in his New York office. Mitchell, characteristically, had done his homework well. Harriman listened intently, but his eyes, distorted behind thick, wire-framed glasses, gave Mitchell no clue of his thoughts. Mitchell told him that many stockholders were dissatisfied with the existing management, that in his view the stock might be bought for less than the real value of the property, and that, with sufficient investment, earnings could be greatly increased. Harriman asked few questions, for he had never given any thought to a takeover of the road. He was, however, intrigued and promised to consider the proposal. A methodical thinker, Harriman had a particular talent for quickly sizing up a situation. His two questions were whether the company could be bought for less than its true value and whether he wanted to devote his time to working out a deal.[6] Short, slight, balding and sporting a sizeable walrus moustache, the 50-year-old Harriman's unimposing appearance gave no evidence of the power he possessed. He had made a name for himself by turning around two troubled roads, the IC and the UP, making each a more efficient and stronger property. Though not yet in the same league as some of the other powerful controllers of railroads, he was quickly joining their ranks.

Harriman had started his professional life not as a railroader but as an office boy in a New York securities trading house. He was an observant student and learned the intricacies of the business. In 1870, at the age of 22, he bought a seat on the New York Stock Exchange and opened his own office. Nine years later he married Mary Averell, the daughter of William Averell, primary banker and president of the Ogdensburg & Lake Champlain Railroad. Harriman became intrigued with his father-in-law's railroad and a year later became a director, learning the railroad business in the process. In 1881 he acquired an interest in a poorly managed and unprofitable short line in upstate New York called the Lake Ontario & Southern. Though situated between the NYC and Pennsylvania railroads, neither of those roads had showed an interest in taking it over. Harriman figured if the road was rebuilt, both roads would recognize its poten-

tial and strategic value and pay a handsome price for it. Over the next two years, Harriman reorganized the road under the name Sodus Bay & Southern, bought it, and then proceeded to rebuild it. In its improved shape, both roads bid for control, the Pennsylvania offering the better price.[7] "My experience with this railroad taught me a lesson," Harriman later stated, "with respect to the importance of proper physical condition in a transportation property which I have never forgotten."[8]

In 1883 Harriman was elected a director of the IC, where he applied his theory once again. By 1887 he was made a vice president of the road and competed successfully with Morgan for control of the Dubuque & Sioux City, extending the IC deep into Iowa. In 1897 he was elected a director of the bankrupt and decrepit UP, a railroad Jay Gould had controlled before him, and a year later was named chairman of that road's executive

Edward Henry Harriman started on Wall Street but soon realized his dreams of wealth and success controlling and rehabilitating railroads. He became one of the most clever and powerful of the era's railroad magnates. Though labeled by some as a corporate raider, Harriman was instead a builder, eventually gathering together a massive western network including the C&A. (Union Pacific Historical Coll.)

committee. He applied the same management techniques he used earlier and rebuilt the road with $25 million of new capital. Over the prior six years, less than $1 million had been spent on the railroad. He purchased heavier locomotives and freight cars, reduced the number of trains run, and increased the tonnage each moved. He replaced bridges and track, reduced grades, and removed unnecessary curves. The program of reconstruction proved an unqualified success. In the year following the work's completion, the UP's revenues had increased to $34 million, profits reached $14 million, and the once bankrupt railroad's treasury had a cash surplus of $11.4 million.[9] There were other powerful railroad leaders Mitchell could have approached, but none were more committed to investing in a railroad to maximize earnings than Harriman.

Harriman hired a longtime railroader and trained engineer, Samuel Felton—someone he hardly knew except by reputation—to conduct a study. Four years younger than Harriman at 46, Felton had been railroading for 31 years and had gained respect as an astute appraiser of railroad properties. At the time he was president and receiver of the Queen & Crescent Railroad. Felton had spent only a few weeks on his study when he received a telegram from Harriman. "Wire report on one telegraph page."[10] The always thorough Felton panicked. He had not finished his work and didn't know how he was to convey everything in just a few paragraphs of cryptic comments.[11] Nevertheless, after several failed attempts, Felton sent the demanded telegram and then set about finishing the road's inspection and writing a full report. What he produced cited a need for better management and considerable upgrading of the property that would require an investment of $5.2 million. Once better managers were installed and the property was rebuilt and refurnished, he reported, the road would likely return greater profits of at least $1 million.[12]

Harriman was satisfied. He met with two of New York's most powerful bankers, Jacob Schiff of Kuhn, Loeb and James Stillman, president of the National City Bank, with whom he had formed an alliance in buying the UP. Based on that experience, Stillman and Schiff trusted Harriman. Then Harriman recruited George Gould, someone with whom he wanted to develop stronger ties. Gould had recently become a UP director.[13] By enlisting Gould, Harriman hoped to "eliminat[e] it [the C&A] as a factor, more or less, from the situation as a competitor in the South and Southwestern territory [and to] cement the various roads together. . . ."[14] Harriman figured the previous warfare over rates and territory among the group could be alleviated if not outright eliminated if everyone involved knew firsthand what he was doing with the C&A. The idea of interlocking corporate relationships, such as the one Harriman now proposed, was not original with him; the concept had already been embraced by others who were amassing large industries and personal fortunes.

Harriman sent Mitchell word he was ready to proceed. It was time to confront Blackstone. Mitchell presented the facts. It was now a certainty the C&A would be taken over, he asserted. Whoever the new owner was to be, he was going to have to make a massive investment, an amount far more than could be generated internally. Mitchell told Blackstone he had someone who had already proved he had the expertise and financial backing needed to get the job done. The buyer was willing to offer $175 a share for a majority of the common and $200 for the preferred, sizeable premiums over then current stock prices. As Blackstone was well aware, while shares had sold for just $75.50 in January 1898, shares had climbed rapidly to a high of $167 when rumors of takeover arose. They had dropped to a $150–$153 range—still well below the offered price. Mitchell told Blackstone he already had most of the board members with him, including Marshall Field, Stewart, Jesup, and Chappell, and he was certain most of the other board members would join too. Blackstone asked who the buyer was. Mitchell told him it was Harriman. Blackstone was stunned and wounded. Mitchell, a large stockholder; most of Blackstone's loyal board members; and his senior manager, Chappell, were telling him that they were going to take his railroad from him.

In late 1898 Mitchell, as Harriman's agent, introduced the buyout plan at a special board meeting in Chicago. He stated that Harriman was prepared to purchase all the common and preferred stock and planned to install his own board of directors as soon as convenient. After a brief discussion, a vote was taken, and all but Blackstone and his younger brother, W. N. Blackstone (who joined the board in 1889 as a replacement for the retired John Crerar), voted aye. Blackstone was understandably crushed, but before giving up, he decided to make an appeal to those besides the board members he had enriched, the individual stockholders. He was confident once they knew he did not favor a buyout, they would reject it. After all, it was the honorable thing to do, Blackstone felt, out of loyalty to him. The same day Harriman's tender offer was mailed to stockholders, Blackstone mailed his own letter.

> I know of no reason why anyone owning the shares of the company should wish to sell them. The offer is made by able and sagacious business men, after having employed an expert to examine the accounts and property of the company in detail, and they doubtless believe that the purchase, if made, will be a profitable one for them.
>
> In my opinion the actual value of your property is not only greater than the price offered, but the terms and conditions of the offer are objectionable. However, in view of the interest that has been manifested in this matter by shareholders of the company by reason of the widely advertised intention of the syndicate to make an offer to purchase the shares of your company, I concur with the other members of the board of directors of the company in the opinion that the offer should be submitted to you for such action, if any, as you may decide to be of your best interest.[15]

His contention that the company was worth more than Harriman's offer and should thus result in rejection of the offer carried little weight. Who could possibly ignore an offer that was more than double the price C&A stock traded at just a year earlier? If the company was worth even more than Harriman was prepared to pay, as Blackstone contended, it had not been reflected in share prices.

The tender was mailed in January 1899, signed by Mitchell, as "agent for a syndicate in New York." When the ballots were tallied two months later, 97 percent of the company's capital stock (about 218,000 shares) had been surrendered.[16] Realizing he had been defeated, Blackstone had ultimately sur-

rendered his shares. He was rewarded with a payment of more than $12 million. The 3 percent of holders voting against the offer were given another 30 days to surrender their shares for the same price. The Harriman Syndicate paid $38,815,000 for control of the railroad.[17] Harriman made no immediate moves to remove the directors until he could gather his own men. He did assume the presidency, however, ending Blackstone's 52-year C&A career (though he remained chief executive of the J&C). No one had had a longer continuous affiliation with a railroad.

Though the takeover would have been enough for any man to deal with, Harriman welcomed challenge and had no difficultly dealing with his new property and his other interests simultaneously. His skills in revitalizing the UP had caught the attention of directors of other roads. One was the B&O. Likely Schiff, whose bank was managing the road's reorganization, brought him onboard. Another troubled road that sought his skills and which he joined as a board member was the KCP&G.[18]

By the end of 1898, the solid deal Stilwell thought he had with C&A stockholders had collapsed. The options were canceled in light of Harriman's unexpected takeover. With no other candidate to help bail out his troubled KCP&G, Stilwell was forced to form a reorganization committee in January 1899, which Harriman was invited to join. He welcomed the chance to change the way that road was operated. The KCP&G's weak condition and willingness to cut rates was the opposite of Harriman's approach. He knew the industry had become interdependent and that communities of interest, not disruptive rate wars, was the only successful formula.

Their opposing views of how a railroad should be run soon put Stilwell and Harriman at odds with one another. In a short while, Harriman's forceful presence and arguments drove Stilwell out. Harriman took a financial position in the company and renamed the road the Kansas City Southern (KCS). He installed a board of directors that included Gould, Stillman, Mitchell, and Otto Kuhn, his trusted allies.[19] Speculation that Harriman would align the KCS with the C&A rose immediately, but Harriman knew he first had to deal with the threat posed by William Guy's

St. Louis, Peoria & Northern (St.LP&N).

In April 1898 Guy, a St. Louis businessman, presided over the opening of a 63-mile extension of his St.LP&N from Springfield to Grove. The Peoria Short Line, as Guy's road advertised itself, was put together two years earlier by an amalgamation of three former short lines (with several more predecessor names), which extended for 100 miles from Madison, to Springfield.[20] At Madison connections were established with the TRRA and at Grove with the Peoria & Pekin Union Railway (P&PU), thereby giving Guy's road access to St. Louis's 23 and Peoria's 13 other railroads. Besides the bankrupt railroads he acquired, Guy also took control of coal properties around the Mt. Olive area, the reason for the St.LP&N's existence. Coal, and lots of it, was being consumed at a faster pace and greater scale than at any time in the country's history.

Among the largest coal consumers were the railroads themselves. The increasingly larger locomotives railroads were adding to haul growing tonnage required greater quantities of coal, and the western roads especially were devoid of on-line supplies. Until the post–World War II era and dieselization, railroads were the single largest users of coal.[21] That was one market Guy set out to serve.

Another was a new industry that had emerged in the middle and late 1880s—electric utilities. As technology advanced, small, independent operators—often supplying a single commercial building or factory—were being bought out and collected into unified systems of mass distribution. As electric power generation became centralized, the source to light and power homes and offices, factories, and government buildings became large, centrally located turbines, fueled by coal. Samuel Insull's Chicago Edison Company for one, was absorbing competitors as fast as financing could be raised and was approaching a near monopoly of Chicago-based electric utilities. By 1907 that goal was reached. Insull then began expanding his power grid beyond the city's borders into rural sections of the Midwest while taking control of smaller city utilities at the same time.[22]

In October 1898 Guy revealed his ultimate plan of expansion. He was going to lay about 50 miles of new rails from Marine, Illinois, to Sparta in southern Illinois, allowing the M&O

to bypass the congested East St. Louis area over his St.LP&N. Next would be added an approximate 100-mile extension northwest out of Peoria to East Clinton, Illinois, to feed coal to the North Western, the CM&St.P, and the Rock Island. Then an extension off the Springfield-Grove line would give Guy's road access to Chicago—the most important and threatening extension as far as the C&A was concerned—where his road would tie up with the Chicago Terminal Transfer (CTT), later the Baltimore & Ohio Chicago Terminal (B&OCT), for access to interchange and locally generated traffic. His success seemed assured after he raised $13 million for the project—$5 million from St. Louis interests and $8 million in New York.[23]

The scope of Guy's plans caught the industry by surprise. Extensions, especially in Illinois, were nothing new, but what Guy was proposing was an exceedingly ambitious plan to transform his short line into a major coal hauler and C&A competitor. When finished, the railroad's St. Louis–Chicago route would be but a few miles longer than the C&A's 282-mile route. His projected daily volume of 45 passengers per mile could be disputed, but his estimate of an annual movement of 1.5 million tons of coal could not. With coal rates averaging 50 cents per ton, annual revenues for the railroad of $3 million–$4 million did not seem unrealistic, a level that would indeed make the Peoria Short Line a formidable railroad.[24] What gave Guy's audacious scheme credibility was the support of William Rockefeller, John D. Rockefeller's brother and president of New York Standard Oil, who controlled the unprofitable MKT. He had sought a way to improve the MKT's fortunes, and that logically meant gaining access to Chicago. Guy's road could provide it. Rockefeller had assembled the syndicate, including the CTT, the Deutsche Bank of Berlin, and Henry Bundge of Hallgarten & Co., the source of Guy's New York money.[25]

Consistently supportive of Blackstone and his railroad, the voice of the industry, *Railway Age*, recognized the seeming inevitability of Guy's railroad being completed, but was "strongly opposed to the construction of any line where the business either in existence or in immediate prospect is not in excess of the capacity of existing lines to handle it properly.

It cannot be said that the present lines between Chicago and St. Louis are not abundantly able to take care of the traffic between those points."[26] The editor nevertheless congratulated Guy on his achievement in raising the funds. "The successful financing of the project . . . must be regarded as a great personal achievement on the part of Mr. William E. Guy . . . [and] must be taken as evidence on the part of at least a section of the people of St. Louis of a desire for a new line."[27]

By April 1899 surveys for both extensions were completed. The Chicago section would branch off at New Holland and run east, then run parallel to the C&A's main line north to Chicago. The Clinton extension would be reached using the P&PU through Peoria (to avoid building the railroad's own bridge over the Illinois River), and then follow a northwesterly route to East Clinton. A construction company's crews were at work at Edelstein, Lawn Ridge, Kewanee, and at the Rock River north of Peoria, but by June their work was halted.

Harriman's stated reason for getting involved with the C&A was to bring peace and harmony to the acrimonious relationship among the southwestern railroads. Harriman concluded he could end Guy's venture if he could switch Rockefeller's allegiance. Stillman invited Rockefeller to join the Harriman Syndicate. He was promised a close working relationship for his Katy and the C&A, eliminating the need for an alliance with the Peoria Short Line and any further trouble from the competitive KCS. It was a prime example of how a community of interest was cultivated. Persuaded, Rockefeller withdrew his support of Guy and pledged $5 million to the Harriman Syndicate.[28] That left the way clear for Harriman to buy Guy out. The price would be of little financial consequence compared to the huge deals Harriman and his associates had already consummated. In June 1899 Guy agreed to Harriman's offer.

It was evident to Harriman that the portion of the St.LP&N that lay south of Springfield would be a better fit for the IC. Through a takeover, the IC would gain some valuable coal traffic and, more importantly, long sought direct entry to St. Louis. The Springfield-Grove line would take the C&A into Peoria on its own rails up from the emerging Springfield area coal mines. On December 1, 1899, the Springfield-Madison section and the Springfield-Grove portion were leased by the IC and the C&A, respectively. Three months later, on March 21, 1900, by prearrangement, the Central Trust of New York (which had participated in Guy's financing) foreclosed. A month later, Fred Voorhees, on behalf of the IC, bought the railroad and coal properties south of Springfield, and L. L. Stanton acquired the Springfield-Grove section for the C&A. The 1,862 freight cars—two-thirds of them hoppers, six cabooses, 17 passenger cars, and 16 locomotives—that the Peoria Short Line rostered were divided nearly equally between the two roads.[29]

At the same time, Harriman made another acquisition, this one intended to provide a western outlet for Southern Division coal traffic. In the early 1870s, as railroads were seemingly started everywhere, a plan was hatched for one to run from Litchfield, in the center of the coal region, west to Quincy at the Mississippi River, where the projected railroad was to unite with the Wabash. The Wabash was to build it, but the panic of 1873 killed those plans before construction could be started. It wasn't until 1882 that another group in Carrollton decided to resurrect the idea as the Litchfield, Carrollton & Western (LC&W).[30]

In May 1883 the first rails were laid at Carrollton in the direction of Greenfield—ten miles to the east—which was reached within two months. After more capital was raised, work was started west toward the Illinois River opposite Kampsville. By January 1884 the company had finished laying track. Stations over the western end were designated as Brady's, Hurricane, Palmer (soon changed to Eldred at the postal service's request since there was already a Palmer located east of Girard), and Columbiana (at the river). To get service started, a Baldwin 4-4-0, the *Daniel Morfoot*, was purchased, as was a passenger coach that doubled as the road's caboose.[31]

Over the next two years, the 22-mile railroad generated meager returns. It became obvious that if the road was to survive, the line had to be extended east of Greenfield. Contracts were let in 1886 for the 30 miles of rails needed to reach Barnett Junction and a connection there with the Jacksonville South Eastern (JSE), over which, through trackage rights, trains would cover the final six miles to Litchfield. Intermediate stations at Fayette, Hagaman, and Carlinville were designated, and by December the line was opened.

In early 1887 the JSE took control of the LC&W and thereafter, to hold down costs, operated a single daily-except-Sunday mixed train. Little was done to maintain or improve the property. In 1890 the JSE became the Jacksonville, Louisville & St. Louis (JL&St.L), but a name change was not enough to stave off receivership for it and somewhat later for the Chicago, Peoria & St. Louis, the corporation formed to take over other owned trackage and the LC&W. In November 1893 the LC&W was released to its bondholders.[32]

The inevitable—foreclosure—came a few months later. A receiver was appointed who, along with a successor, none too wisely spent $841,000 in a vain attempt to restore the property to reasonable condition. Physical improvements were made, but no new traffic was developed, and the bondholders finally concluded the matter was hopeless. Though running through a fertile farming region, few carloads of freight and only an occasional rider used the road. From May 1896 to February 1899, the LC&W's total operating revenues were just $130,000. With expenses of $108,300, the payment of $1,200 for a second engine, and $25,600 in maintenance, the line over the three years posted deficits totaling $25,500. Little of its fixed costs were paid.[33]

In August 1898 the receivers asked the court for permission to liquidate. That is when Harriman stepped in. On February 8, 1899, a new corporation, the Quincy, Carrollton & St. Louis Railway (QC&St.L), paid the $140,000 purchase price and another $60,000 of reorganization expenses.[34] Harriman immediately announced his plans for an extension beyond Columbiana north to Quincy. It wasn't long, however, before those plans were abandoned when a better alternative coal route was decided, a cutoff between Springfield and Murrayville. The QC&St.L languished.

On October 1, 1899, the Harriman Syndicate recapitalized the C&A through issuance of $40 million of Three Percent Refunding Fifty-Year Gold Bonds at $1,000 face value through a mortgage arranged with John Mitchell's Illinois Trust and Savings Bank. Fifteen million dollars of the proceeds were placed in trust to retire prior indebtedness as it came due; the remaining $25 million was allocated for improvements and extensions.[35] The managing partners of the syndicate bought $20.8 million of the bonds at $65. Harriman, Stillman, Schiff, and Gould were taking a considerable risk, since the gold bonds, at 3 percent interest, paid about half the return of most securities then circulating. They had no assurance of finding a market for them.[36] Added to the $38.8 million invested in common stock and $3.5 million paid for the St.LP&N, including legal expenses, commissions, and other administrative costs, the syndicate was shouldering $63.1 million of debt.[37] The next steps taken helped reduce their exposure.

Under Blackstone, "betterments"—improvements made to the property—had been expensed rather than shown as additions to assets. Over twelve million dollars ($12,444,177) was entered on the books as improvements. This sum was transferred to a surplus account with a corresponding credit to "construction expenditures uncapitalized." The logic of the move was simple. Investment increased the property's value and was an asset, not an expense. Long after most other roads had changed their accounting practices to reflect improvements as assets, under Blackstone, the C&A had clung to the outdated accounting method. The matter was now corrected.[38] The refinancing and account change greatly enlarged the company's cash position, enough to allow a 30 percent dividend, amounting to $6,669,000, to be declared, paid to the syndicate members.[39] The payout later came under harsh criticism as an alleged scheme to raid the company, but the charges were unwarranted. Harriman was a builder, not a raider. The massive investment that was later made in the property was proof of that.

What happened next was also used as evidence of Harriman's supposed outlandish financing of his holdings. The company's by-laws were extremely restrictive relative to extensions, acquisitions, and financing. They were written nearly 40 years earlier in a different time and had been amended only a few times thereafter. They were purposely tightly written to prevent someone like Henry Dwight from threatening the company's security. For instance, the by-laws required approval of a three-fourths majority, rather than a simple majority, of stockholders for any acquisition. That proviso had caused James Robb difficulty when he was offered the chance to buy the J&C. Additionally, members of the board of directors were initially appointed for life, though that provision was amended within three years when staggered terms were adopted.

The constraints were not suited to Harriman's style of management. When the matter arose, it was addressed by an attorney. Though unwilling to say unequivocally that Harriman would be prevented by the by-laws from consolidating the three Illinois roads he controlled, he advised, "It might be desirable . . . [to] construct a new railroad which need be only a few miles in length, connecting at some point with the Chicago & Alton Railroad which . . . would have the power to take a perpetual lease of the Chicago & Alton Railroad . . . [with] all the powers of consolidation, or making working arrangements with railroads outside of this State, and possess all the powers conferred by the statutes of the State of Illinois, in regard to issuing stock and mortgages, conferred upon any railroad company."[40]

Following that advice, on March 31, 1900, the Chicago & Alton Railway was formed to construct a line "between Murrayville and Woodson . . . to a point in or near Springfield," and to "extend the said railway from a point in or near said Springfield, to a point at or near Grove . . . by the purchase of the railroad . . . heretofore owned by the St. Louis, Peoria & Northern Railway, and sold under foreclosure. . . ." The St.LP&N was purchased by the Railway. It was the formation of the holding company that was later used as an example of how Harriman supposedly "watered" the company's stock, incurring heavy capitalization for only a relatively few miles of railroad.[41]

Though the C&A's total capitalization was greatly increased, it was not beyond the road's expected increased earning potential and thus the road's ability to service the debt. Based on Felton's projections and Harriman's confidence in them, it would take only a few years for this to be manifested. The C&A was capitalized at $40 million, represented by 200,000 shares of common and an equal number of preferred shares earning 4 percent. The syndicate secured a $22 million mortgage, composed of first lien 50-year gold bonds at 3.5 percent, which was arranged through the Farmers' Loan and Trust of New York.[42] While the reorganization was being worked out in New York, excitement was generated on the property with the introduction of a new passenger train that would bring the Alton international recognition.

During the late 1890s, the post office had been seeking faster service from its major terminals of Boston, New York, and Chicago. The railroads met the challenge with fast transcontinental demonstration runs, like those involving the NYC, North Western, and UP, that were so astounding they were given daily, front-page newspaper coverage, filled with exciting details and maps that monitored the trains' daily progress. The C&A too gained at least some regional fame for fast running in May 1898 for what was reputed to be the fastest run of specials on "any of American or English roads."[43] A special train was hired by the *Chicago Tribune* so that copies of the Sunday newspaper carrying news of the events in the Philippines (during the Spanish-American War) could be delivered to the troops bivouacked at Camp Tanner in Springfield, beating any other Chicago or St. Louis newspaper. The train was pulled by engine no. 54, a five-year-old 4-4-0, the second to carry the number, and included a chair car carrying six delivery boys, a business car carrying railroad officials, and a baggage car. The train ran at a remarkable speed, averaging 60.4 miles per hour, only stopping for water at Pontiac and Lincoln. South of Lincoln, the train clicked off two miles at 91 miles per hour before slacking off to 88 miles per hour for most of the rest of the way into Springfield. The stunning, record-setting run covered the 185-mile distance in just three hours. Despite the early hour, an estimated 600 persons gathered at Springfield at five o'clock in the morning to greet the train. The newsboys started hawking the newspapers as soon as the baggage car doors were pushed aside and quickly sold every copy. Within a few hours, *Tribune* copies that originally sold for 10 cents were reportedly being resold for as much as 25 cents. The *Tribune*-sponsored special had been a publicity stunt to be sure but was a portent of things to come.[44]

In 1889, the fastest passenger train on the

Nearing the end of its run to Chicago, the brand new *Alton Limited* pauses at Joliet in 1899. The company's newest passenger engines, 12 Brooks 4-4-0s, including no. 502 seen here, were assigned to the matched six-car deluxe trains. (Bill Molony Coll.)

C&A was the comfortable *Palace Express* that ran on a 10 1/2-hour, nearly all-stop, daylight schedule between Chicago and St. Louis, about 2 hours faster than the same runs were made the decade before. Ten years later the fastest schedules carded were of the *Chicago Limited* and the *St. Louis Limited,* actually the same train comprised of the same equipment making a daily round trip, which made only 16 intermediate stops in just under 8 hours, nearly 2 1/2 hours faster than any previous C&A schedules. The runs were more a result of post office pressures for faster delivery of the mail than for competitive reasons.

Premier trains such as the Rock Island's *Rocky Mountain Limited,* the Sante Fe's *California Limited,* the Pennsylvania's *Pennsylvania Limited,* and trains of other roads had elevated rail travel by 1898 to new standards of luxury. They raised the traveling public's expectations for both comfort and time keeping. The train about to be introduced on the C&A would prove the equal of them all.

Up to this point, the C&A had ordered cars in small lots or as individual cars. In 1899, for the first time, an order was placed with Pullman for two complete trains of six identical cars. When turned out in November 1899, the trains were among the finest products Pullman had yet produced. The cars incorporated Pullman's standard framing, Empire decks, wide vestibules, steel platforms, and anti-telescoping devices. Gas lamps illuminated the head-end equipment, but electric lights were employed in the passenger cars. The postal cars were 66 feet long; the passenger cars were 72 feet, 6 inches in length. The combine had a 39-foot baggage area and a smoker section with 40 seats. The parlor-chair car had 64 revolving and nine stationary seats. A 24-seat cafe-buffet-lounge car (which included a 14-seat smoking section) provided meal service. A luxurious 22-seat parlor car, an observation car with an open deck furnished with settee and easy chairs, and a special ladies' retiring and toilet room provided first-class accommodations.

Though not the first train to adopt a distinctive paint scheme, the C&A finished these cars in a handsome appearance of three

horizontal bands of red with gold striping. The band across the top of the cars was painted a medium red and carried the railroad's name, elegantly centered and displayed in extended letters above the large curved windows. The center band—the area around the window panel—was a lighter red, and the lower band below the windows was painted a high-gloss dark red. The roof was painted gloss black, the underframe and six-wheel trucks olive green. The names of each car were spelled out below the windows—*Chicago* and *St. Louis* for the postal cars, which also bore an intricate design made up of the letters "USM" on one end and "United States Railway Post Office" on the other; *Normal* and *Lincoln* for the combines; *Peoria* and *Pekin* on the parlor-coaches; *Joliet* and *Alton* for the parlor-chair cars; *Springfield* and *Bloomington* on the cafe-buffet-smokers; and *Illinois* and *Missouri* for the observations.[45] "It is claimed that there has never been built in America a train which has received as much attention as to the constructive details as has the '*Alton Limited,*'" the editor of *Railway Age* wrote.[46] He was right, for no detail in producing this premier train, equal to any then operating, had been overlooked.

It has usually been assumed, since the train's name is so descriptive of the runs it made, that the train was always intended to be named the *Alton Limited,* but almost up to the last minute, a selection had not been made. Charles Chappell directed the passenger traffic offices to come up with suggestions. At least 50 were submitted, including "Twentieth Century Limited," "Flying Peacock," "Royal Flush Limited," "Old Glory," "Sunbeam," and "Lightning Lily." Charlton himself favored a name that depicted the type of service the train offered, such as "The Drawing Room Limited" or "The Parlor Car Limited."[47] None of the suggestions prevailed.

The St.LP&N had ordered 12 Brooks Locomotive Works 4-4-0s before Harriman bought the road, but they were received after and thus were delivered to the C&A. Being the newest and heaviest passenger engines on the roster, the type was used to lead the new trains. Their sandbox, domes, and cab were painted the same deep red as applied to the *Alton Limited* equipment. Gold leaf striping trimmed the engine's cab, domes, wheels, and driving rods.

The pilot and driving wheels were painted olive green. The tenders had a 6,000-gallon water and 12-ton coal capacity and were painted the same rich, deep red as the cars, with similar, intricate gold leaf striping.[48]

A few weeks before the train's formal introduction, demonstration runs were made from St. Louis to Alton over the Merchants Bridge and between Chicago and Joliet to familiarize railroad passenger agents and newspaper reporters with the splendor of the equipment. Then, on Thursday, November 9, 1899, the first scheduled train left St. Louis at 8:30 A.M. and Chicago at 11 A.M. on a limited, fast eight-hour schedule.[49] The *Alton Limited* instantly became one of the Midwest's most famous trains and the pride of the railroad. Citizens of the towns through which the trains ran, but didn't stop, soon began referring to the colorful blur passing by as "The Red Train." The *Alton Limited* put distance between the company and its competitors, the Wabash and IC.

The man justifiably credited with creating an outsized image for the railroad, capped now with the *Alton Limited*'s inauguration, was James Charlton. By the end of 1899, he had served as head of the passenger department for 28 years and, at the age of 68, decided it was time to retire. At the start of 1900, his handsome, burly son George took over. He had joined the railroad four years after his father, under whom George had learned well all aspects of selling and promotion. It was George Charlton who coined the slogan "The Only Way" and who labeled the *Alton Limited* "The Handsomest Train in the World." He firmly believed there wasn't a train of greater grandeur running on any railroad.

George Charlton wasn't in his job long before he achieved one of his finest successes. It came from the display of a photograph. Like millions of others, he had visited Chicago's 1893 Columbian Exposition and was impressed with one of the displays, a set of Great Western (of England) passenger cars brought to the fair to give evidence of England's best equipment. Paris was to host the 1900 exhibition, and Charlton saw it as an opportunity to promote his passenger service before the European population that was emigrating to the United States in ever-increasing numbers. Transporting equipment to Paris was out of

To capture an image so large as the entire 1899 *Alton Limited* on film, photographer George Lawrence built this monster camera from scratch. Taken in Brighton Park, the photo created a sensation at the 1900 Paris Exposition (Gulf, Mobile & Ohio RR Historical Society Coll.)

the question, so he decided to send a photograph, not of just individual cars, but of the entire train.

Charlton didn't know how it would be done, but the year before the exposition's opening, he put professional photographer George R. Lawrence in charge of the project. There was no camera yet available that could capture so large an image as the entire side view of a train, so Lawrence had to build one. Over the course of two and a half months, he constructed a camera that rested on four cherry wood beams, about 20 feet long. The bellows were fabricated of heavy rubber stiffened by one-quarter-inch pine frames. The inside of the camera (big enough for a man to stand upright inside) was lined with heavy

black canvas and a thick layer of black opaque material. Over 40 gallons of cement, two bolts of wide rubber cloth, and 500 feet of quarter-inch pine was used in constructing it. Each of four sets of bellows was divided by a supporting frame mounted on small wheels that moved along a steel track. Two Zeiss lenses were installed, one with a focus of five and one-half feet, the other a telescopic lens with a 10-foot focus—the largest camera lens yet made. When finished, Lawrence's camera weighed 900 pounds and the plate holder another 500 pounds.

The camera was tested, loaded onto a flatcar, and moved to Brighton Park. There it was carefully removed and placed in a field parallel to the main line. An engine and six-car set

of equipment was positioned. Fifteen men focused the camera (including one inside the
bellows to move the plates), and when all was
ready, a two and one-half minute exposure on
an 8 x 10-foot negative captured the train in
its entirety. Its colorful appearance was closely
matched through the use of a Cramer isochro-
matic plate.[50] The photo Lawrence produced
was amazing. It accomplished what Charlton
had hoped. Handsomely framed copies were
shipped to Paris. Most of the American exhibits on display there were considered pedes-
trian and lacking flair, but Charlton's train
prints became a hit. One was displayed in the
railway section, another in the photography
area, and the third was given a prominent
place in the United States government's building. The photograph was awarded "Grand
Prize of the World for Excellence in Photography."[51] Charlton had scored a triumph. He
later wasted little time in promoting the camera that had been used in taking the photo.
He sent illustrations of the camera and its
setup to the industry and popular press.
Among other press notices was an extended
story in the prestigious *Scientific American*.
Soon, framed copies of the famous print were
placed in most of the railroad's major depots
and in important off-line offices. They quickly
became prized possessions. A few remain in
collections even today.

▼▼▼

Almost a year had been spent on the refinancing and restructuring of the company before the management was formally changed.
In April 1900 all of the directors except Chappell were replaced with Harriman associates
and four officers of Mitchell's bank. Having
gained Harriman's full confidence, Felton was
named president. All was in place to begin the
job of transforming the railroad.[52]

Blackstone was now spending quiet time
with his wife Isabella in their spacious house
at 252 Michigan Avenue, regularly attending
services at the Second Presbyterian Church,
and taking in the theater or a performance of
Chicago's newly formed symphony orchestra.
Blackstone, 71, had long since overcome his
childhood illnesses and had led a healthy and
vigorous adult life. He made a habit of taking
daily walks, including those to and from his
office mornings and evenings, but during
1900, his health had begun to deteriorate,
and he began using his carriage. After one of
those trips during a cold and wet April, he
contracted pneumonia. He lay bedridden for
two weeks before the strong willed and still
handsome man made what seemed a complete recovery. On Sunday, May 20, 1900,
however, he suffered a relapse, and his condition worsened. By Friday it was clear his end
was near. During the night he slipped into un-
consciousness. Isabella and his doctors were at
his side at 5 A.M. when he took his last,
painful breath.

The *Chicago Tribune*'s editorial that Sunday
described the railroad Blackstone led as "a
monument of his conservative, prudent, and
successful management" and stated further
that with the "qualities which he displayed he
unquestionably would have made a success of
any business, for few men surpassed him in
industry, concentration of purpose, and
knowledge of men and affairs. He was a use-
ful, high minded citizen, simple and unosten-
tatious in all his habits, remarkably genial in
personal intercourse, and open handed towards all benevolent projects. Few men in
Chicago have been held in higher public es-
teem."[53]

Blackstone's leadership of one of the Midwest's most important railroads, his participation in founding the sprawling Union Stock
Yards, and his civic involvement in his
adopted city were later remembered. A south
side Chicago street and a prestigious downtown hotel and theater were named for him.
His devoted wife added to his memory by

George Charlton made
sure the most famous
photographs of the time
got wide circulation by
installing framed copies
in prime C&A ticket and
sales offices and by offering them as gifts to the
road's best customers.
(Courtesy of Chicago
Historical Society)

having built a library in Hyde Park, which she named for him. Much later, his name was applied to a sleeping car that ran millions of miles over his railroad. With his death, an era ended. Although he had adopted Chicago as his home for the past half century, his remains were removed to his wife's ancestral home of Norwich, Connecticut.

The man Harriman now included among his closest associates and placed in charge of the railroad was of a different character than Blackstone. Samuel Felton was seen as autocratic with little regard for the feelings of others. Those who worked under him were quick to point out that he seldom hesitated to harshly dress down employees he felt did not measure up. He had the habit of directly confronting a shop foreman, master mechanic, trainmaster, agent, or any other employee, either verbally or in writing, for what he viewed as an infraction. Walter Chrysler, a former C&A Bloomington Shops employee who became the Chicago Great Western's (CGW) superintendent of motive power, was one man who knew Felton's wrath. After a particularly acrimonious incident over an insignificant matter, Chrysler abruptly quit, went to American Locomotive, and then designed an automobile and founded an enormous corporation.[54] Felton was a railway physician who

correctly prescribed medicine, but he lacked a pleasing bedside manner. Those who remembered the almost fatherly personality of Blackstone soon realized the rules had changed.

Aside from F. A. Wann, the general freight agent, and George Charlton, virtually every other official was replaced. Felton divided the railroad's two-division format—Eastern and Western—into three, adding a Middle Division and a superintendent to look after what was to become the railroad's important coal region.

When Felton took over, the road had a sizeable but largely aged and inefficient fleet of 232 locomotives. Except for the new Brooks 4-4-0s and 12 homebuilt 4-6-0s added in 1893, the rest of the roster had been in service for 20 or more years. Not surprisingly, replacement was made a first priority.[55] During the first two years under Felton, 70 freight engines were purchased. Baldwin delivered 50 heavier and more powerful 2-6-0s. Ten 100-ton Brooks 2-8-0s the St.LP&N had ordered were delivered to the C&A—the first consolidations the company owned—and integrated into the fleet. To add heft to a woefully inadequate roster of switchers, 10 stocky Baldwin 0-6-0s were bought, as were 10 4-6-0s, larger and heavier than those built nine years earlier. The new power dramatically increased

From the late 1870s until arrival of the more powerful Consolidations and Mikados in the early 1900s, the 2-6-0 Mogul type was the mainstay of the C&A's freight roster. No. 332 is an example of a 35-engine order received in 1899. (S. R. Wood Coll., E. L. DeGolyer, Jr. 5 x 7 Photo. Coll., P727.1151, courtesy of DeGolyer Library, SMU)

the average tractive effort from 15,000 to 21,000 pounds and the average weight from 62,000 pounds to 88,000 pounds.[56] The freight car fleet was equally aged and outdated when Felton took over and was quickly upgraded. Added were 1,500 boxcars, 300 stock cars, and 200 furniture cars, all weighing 30 tons, plus 1,000 40-ton and 1,300 50-ton coal hoppers. The massive order nearly doubled the roster's tonnage capacity from 139,720 to 276,090 tons, allowing retirements of worn-out cars, including nearly a third of the no longer needed stock cars.[57] New passenger equipment, 20 coaches, six chair, two cafe-smoking, four coach-baggage, and two coach-mail cars, all with full vestibules, were purchased, and cars already rostered went through a major shopping. Those not already equipped received air brakes, automatic couplers, enclosed vestibules, train signals, and other improvements. As a result, the number of available seats rose from 4,686 to 7,525. With the new and rebuilt cars, every passenger train was upgraded.[58]

Right-of-way maintenance under Blackstone had been accomplished with the barest of dedicated equipment. What was used had been largely homebuilt. Felton bought 89 pieces of service equipment, including three wrecking cars, a derrick, a pile driver, two levelers, and two ditchers, plus five tool cars and six boarding cars.[59] The bridge rebuilding program that was started in the late 1890s was accelerated. The Glasgow bridge over the Missouri River was renovated, 39 other bridges were replaced, and 61 others were renewed, all to higher standards necessary to support the heavier weights of power and equipment.[60]

One of the biggest projects that would take several years to complete, the elevation of the road's trackage through Chicago, was started. In 1899 the Chicago City Council had mandated all railroads be raised above street level. The city's expansion had brought its greatly enlarged street system into conflict with the numerous railroad tracks seemingly running everywhere to reach the city's freight and passenger terminals. Collisions—some resulting in death—with pedestrians, wagons, and carriages, had risen to alarming levels. This was particularly true on the city's south side, where all but two of the railroads serving the city terminated. The railroad had budgeted in

excess of $11 million for the project. It was a challenge to maintain safe and uninterrupted operations through the construction areas, but excellent planning minimized delays, and, miraculously, no death or injury to workers or others resulted.

The Western Division had been laid with very little cutting and filling and closely followed the twisting, hilly terrain. Some work improving the worst sections had previously been done, but of the 264 miles (including the Cedar City Branch) that ran through Missouri, only 24 percent was level (a total 83 miles). Forty-one percent of the road's total 334 curves were in Missouri. The Roodhouse-to-Quincy Junction segment had similar characteristics. Only 35 percent of the 38 miles were level, and 31 percent was curved. Thus it was no surprise that the worst of the trackage—just west of the Missouri River at Gilliam Hill—was attacked first with the removal of 167 degrees of curvature. Elsewhere, tight reverse curves were straightened. In all, 13 miles of main line between Kansas City and Slater were realigned. The eastbound grade between Slater and Roodhouse was reduced to just eight-tenths of one percent, bringing immediate operating improvement.[61]

On the main line, 14 miles of grade between Springfield and Bloomington was reduced to just one-half of one percent. Between Chicago and Bloomington, 12.7 miles of northbound grade was cut to just three-tenths of one percent. Work on a much needed second main line through Springfield was started in anticipation of the increased number of coal trains from the region south of there. Fifty-two thousand tons of 80-pound rail and 620,000 fresh ties were installed, replacing virtually all of the former 70-pound rail from main line mileage. Passing sidings at the most congested places were lengthened. In all, somewhat more than 15 miles of second track were added. Though only a temporary solution until yards could be totally rebuilt, short receiving and dispatching tracks were extended at key terminals.[62] Structures too were repaired or replaced. Four new water tanks and seven standpipes were erected. A new coaling station arose at Mazonia. To solve the brackish water problem at Bloomington, a new water purification plant was put in service. Six new, longer turntables were installed at major terminals.[63]

Pounding the iron south-bound out of Bloomington on a well-maintained roadbed, no. 3, *The Mail,* passes a string of idle stock cars in the early stages of the depression. (R. E. Collons Coll., Ag82.231.3760, Courtesy of DeGolyer Library, SMU)

Harriman was adamant about safe operations. Thus, the first four of 13 interlocking plants were installed in 1900; improved train order semaphore signals were erected at all telegraph offices; and high semaphore switch stands and distant signals to give earlier warning were installed on the main lines. New automatic semaphore block signals were erected between Brighton Park and Joliet. Because communications played a crucial role in safe operations, almost 100 miles of telegraph wire were replaced, and two telephone lines were strung between Chicago and Bloomington, marking the start of a project that would eventually bring the entire railroad into voice communication.[64]

From his office in Chicago's 16-story Monadnock Building, Felton was managing projects that were rapidly and radically changing the railroad's physical plant and the way it was operated. He was matching industry practices. In the last half of the nineteenth century, the railroad industry saw its greatest period of expansion. The 193,346 miles of first track mileage of the nation's railroads had peaked around 1900, but after the turn of the century, nearly as many miles of second, and sometimes third, tracks were laid.[65]

During the first 20 years of the twentieth century, the American railroad system was technologically rebuilt. Most of the inventions that had brought railroads greater safety and efficiency (like the air brake, automatic coupler, and interlocking and improved signalling) had emerged before the turn of the century. It was during the 1900s that these practices were perfected. Iron cars and then all-steel cars—as steel shapes were standardized and became more affordable—were integrated into freight car fleets. By 1914 solid trains of steel freight cars became the norm and outnumbered wooden cars. Engines placed in service between 1900 and 1920, based on designs introduced in the late 1800s, were larger, heavier, faster, and more efficient.

The grade reduction program between Joliet and Bloomington got under way. Until a parallel double main line was in place, the equivalent between Bloomington and Sherman was achieved with southbound trains routed through San Jose, and northbound trains holding the main line. The yards at East St. Louis and Bloomington were enlarged. A freight house, engine house, and power station were erected at Springfield, and a new freight house was built at Joliet. Combination freight and passenger depots were constructed at Granite City, Blackstone, Odessa, Pegram, Williamsville, and Thayer. A depot (built jointly with the Baltimore & Ohio Southwestern) at Ashland was erected at the junction of the two roads, replacing the two former separate facilities.[66] The investments already made and those to come made it obvious management anticipated new and increased traffic. Some of that new revenue came from increased shipments of California perishables off the UP routed through Kansas City. The blocks of reefers required icing en route, so five 8,000-ton capacity plants were built at Kansas City, Slater, Bloomington, Brighton Park, and Alton.[67]

What he had already achieved brought Harriman added recognition, respect, and, in some cases, fear, all of which increased further after he acquired the SP in 1901. He was now seen by the industry and Wall Street as one of the nation's shrewdest and most powerful industrial leaders, a force to be reckoned with and one seemingly powerful enough to get whatever he wanted. Harriman was a personification of the American Dream, a self-made man who achieved his success through ingenuity and hard work. Harriman knew how to take a broken property, rebuild it, and make money from it. His moves were watched closely by fellow railroaders and financiers, anxious to guess his next moves.

Speculation surrounding what Harriman planned for the C&A had been topic A while he was still putting together the syndicate that bought the railroad. After he took control of the KCS, some were sure a merger would follow. By taking over a couple of short lines, they thought, the two lines could be connected with the UP, forging a dominant presence throughout the West, Southwest, and Midwest. A few months after that speculation died down, more arose that the C&A would buy the UP's Kansas City–Denver line, but those reports were soon eclipsed by rumors that instead the UP would absorb the C&A.[68] While the speculation circulated, the job of rebuilding the property continued.

▾▾▾

The fury of America's rivers after unusual periods of snowfalls and rain are legendary. Nowhere is the water's wrath experienced with greater trepidation than along the Missouri and Mississippi Rivers. The two rivers and their tributaries carry the runoff of all the land between the Appalachian and Rocky Mountains. In the winter of 1902–1903, just such a heavy and intense snowfall piled up across the upper plains. Colder-than-normal temperatures that lingered into late spring retarded a normal melt, but rapidly warming temperatures in May brought disaster. The courses of the Missouri and Mississippi Rivers—at first slowly and then with startling speed—spread as enormous volumes of runoff rolled south. Within days, a flood of gigantic proportions developed.

The high watermark at Kansas City was reached at the Twelfth Street Yard and Kansas City Union Depot on May 31. Before the waters receded, the Missouri River reached a depth of 35 feet. Water levels rose a foot an hour, and, despite valiant efforts to move company equipment to higher ground and safety, two C&A engines, 700 freight cars, and 10 passenger cars were trapped. Water rose to the roofs of cars. By midday six feet of water stood on the floor of Union Station, and three feet of water covered the freight house floor. Traffic in and out of Kansas City was suspended for 10 days before the first C&A post-flood train, a local freight from Slater, arrived.[69]

The furious Missouri washed out the roadbed in six places on either side of the recently rebuilt bridge at Glasgow. Though the bridge itself withstood the hydraulic pressures, the approaches and trestle work leading to it were ravaged. For 12 days trains had to be rerouted while repairs were made. At Louisiana, on June 5, the Mississippi's fury was unleashed in spectacular fashion. Eight hundred feet of the levee was washed out by 60-foot-deep rising water. The railroad's right-of-way lay on top of that levee, and to restore operations considerable bridging and piling had to be installed. It took 11 days before the line was reopened. During the disruption, traffic between Kansas City and Roodhouse was rerouted.

The worst was yet to come. Alton, East St. Louis, and St. Louis were all too familiar with flooding and were again inundated and remained so for 12 days. Use of either the Eads Bridge or the Merchants Bridge was suspended.

The company was forced to hire two Eagle Packet Company boats, the *Spread Eagle* and the *Bald Eagle,* to move passengers, baggage, mail, milk, and express between Alton and St. Louis. The waters at Alton had risen so high that gang planks could be laid from the boats within six feet of the depot's platform. Since the C&A was the only road still operating in the area, St. Louis–directed traffic was moved through Alton. Cleanup and repairs to track, structures, and facilities continued throughout the summer and most of the autumn of 1903 before the property was restored.[70]

Natural threats to the property and the company's well-being proved easier to repel than those the company faced with the emergence of a new mode of transport, the electric railway. Before the turn of the century, major electric interurban systems had emerged in Ohio, Indiana, and throughout New England as natural extensions of electrically powered city cars. There was rapid expansion of electric railways once the problem of transmitting voltage over long distances was solved, as it was in 1896. The single cars proved cleaner, faster, and cheaper than steam trains, and their popularity among rural residents grew rapidly.

In 1900 William McKinley, already involved in development of electric utilities and intent on developing an electric railway system in Illinois, took over the Danville Street Railway & Light Company. By 1903 he had extended service to his hometown of Champaign. That same year, McKinley took over and resumed construction of the St. Louis & Springfield (St.L&S), a stalled venture that had started an electric line from Springfield headed for St. Louis.[71] Four years later, McKinley cars were running as far south as Auburn. Work proceeded through to Virden, and then work was pushed toward Carlinville, where the C&A needed to be crossed.

At the same time, another McKinley property, the St. Louis & North Eastern, was laying track north from Granite City to Carlinville in order to connect there with the St.L&S. Felton realized that when that electric line was completed, McKinley's road would provide stiff competition for the C&A, so in an effort to stall such, he forbid electric lines from crossing his road. For 18 months McKinley cars from the north and south terminated at Carlinville on opposite sides of the C&A main

line while McKinley sought relief from Felton's obstruction in the courts. Electric car passengers were forced to walk across the track then board another car for the remainder of their trips. Frustrated by Felton's rebuff (creating the only gap in an otherwise through service between the state's capital and Granite City), McKinley decided to dig an underpass at Carlinville. Nothing at first was done to hinder the work, but when the excavation neared completion, Felton ordered 16 carloads of dirt to be dumped into the cut. The standoff persisted until February 1906, when the matter was finally resolved. Engineers designing the C&A's new air line between Springfield and Murrayville called for a viaduct over McKinley's line at Iles. There was no way McKinley would agree to allow it until the matter at Carlinville was resolved. Before long, electric cars were running regularly between Springfield and Granite City.[72]

Another conflict with an electric line arose when the Chicago & Joliet Electric Railway (C&J), intending to extend a branch at Summit off its main line to Lyons, Illinois, proposed crossing the C&A's big curve there at grade. Based on safety considerations, Felton sensibly demanded and got the electric line to dig a subway in 1904.[73]

By 1907 McKinley had finished a Peoria-to-Bloomington line with a branch at Mackinaw Junction to Lincoln. Within a few more years, McKinley's renamed Illinois Traction System (ITS), crossed the Mississippi River over its own bridge, and St. Louis was reached.

McKinley's electric lines between Carlinville and Lincoln largely paralleled the C&A, as did other electrics: the C&J between Joliet and Chicago; the Bloomington, Pontiac & Joliet between Pontiac and Dwight; the Alton, Granite City & St. Louis between Alton and East St. Louis; and the Alton, Jacksonville & Peoria between Alton, Godfrey, and Jerseyville. The quick clean, and quiet electric cars successfully siphoned off former patrons. To counter the threat, the C&A began experimenting with added local trains south of Springfield, which were advertised as the "InterUrban Service." The addition of a couple of trains, however, could not compete with the hourly service of McKinley's road, and the additional trains were costly to operate. The mechanical department thought it had a solution

when in 1905 a motor car rebuilt from an 1890-era 78-foot wooden day coach was turned out. A motorman's cabin was installed on each end to allow quick turnarounds. The car was powered by a 120-horsepower, four-cylinder motor, which charged batteries that in turn ran four 50-horsepower street railway motors mounted directly on the axles. The car proved short-lived. In 1909, after too many mechanical failures, the experimental car was withdrawn from service and rebuilt once again into a baggage car. Another test of single car operation came from a design of William McKeen, the UP's superintendent of power. His M-4 was a gas car with a mechanical drive but was purely experimental and lasted only a short while in C&A service. For the next 15 years, no other specialized equipment was used to counter the electric railroads.[74] Meanwhile, local passengers, the mainstay of passenger traffic, continued to defect.

The road's advance to fully rebuilt standards continued through 1903. Earnings from all sources climbed once more, to $10 million, and total net income reached $5.2 million—both setting new records—eclipsed in 1904 when revenues rose to $11.4 million and income to $5.6 million, largely due to a 13 percent climb in freight revenue. Livestock, agricultural products (especially flour and other mill products), coal, lumber, machinery, and farm implements, as well as miscellaneous merchandise, all showed substantial increases.

Passenger revenues increased 15 percent (despite losses in short trip passenger counts) and exceeded $3 million for the first time, nearly all of it attributable to low cost fares offered visitors to the Louisiana Purchase Exposition at St. Louis, which opened in April 1904. More than 850,000 passengers were carried to and from St. Louis (320,000 more than were transported to Chicago to attend the World's Columbian Exposition 10 years earlier).[75]

Seventeen engines were added in 1903. Six more Baldwin Moguls and five more 0-6-0 switchers provided added heft for freight hauling and switching. Both types were now numerous enough to replace most of their lighter, less efficient predecessors in road and yard work. Added to the 62 2-6-0s received between 1899 and 1902, these latest six made the Mogul the power of choice for over-the-road movements while the five new switchers and the 18 already working handled most yard chores. But the most impressive locomotive additions were four fast-running Atlantics and two Pacifics, the first of their types on the railroad.

The 4-4-2s were nearly identical to power that was being delivered to Harriman's SP and UP. The Atlantics, introduced in 1896 on the Atlantic City Railroad—thus giving them their name—had large 81-inch drivers, designed for high speed over relatively level track, exactly what was needed for the *Alton Limited*. They were the first of what became

Between 1903 and 1913, the C&A added progressively heavier Pacifics to the passenger engine roster. No. 631, a class I-5A delivered in 1910, was an American Locomotive product. (Gulf, Mobile & Ohio RR Historical Society Coll.)

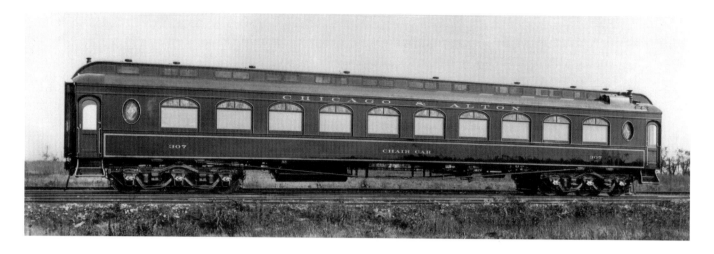

The Harriman period of ownership saw a near-total replacement of C&A equipment and engines. Chair car no. 307, turned out by Pullman in 1901, incorporated all of the latest features. (Pullman Co., E. L. DeGolyer, Jr. Photo. Coll., Ag82.232, courtesy of DeGolyer Library, SMU)

known as Harriman Common Standard engines and began replacing the Brooks Americans.

The Pacifics too were Harriman Common Standard products. The engine type had been introduced on the MP just a year earlier. They too had large driving wheels, 77 inches in diameter, and, though not as quick to accelerate as the Atlantics, were well suited for the demands of the main line and the rolling, twisting Western Division. The Pacific-type engine would eventually become the most widely used in American passenger train service. More than 6,000 of the type were eventually produced, but these two were among the first on any railroad. These new engines, and those previously delivered, increased the road's tractive force 90 percent, from 2.9 million to 5.5 million pounds.[76]

A second very large passenger car order (exclusively from Pullman) came in 1905 and included 30 coaches, eight chair cars, six cafe-smoking cars, five baggage cars, and a coach-baggage car. The coaches replaced the Horton chair cars the railroad had introduced some 25 years earlier. Three of the Horton cars were reconfigured, their interiors modified to include a kitchen and a small eating area with a six-person table. The interiors were refinished in mahogany, each decorated in one of three different motifs—American, English, or German. The cars were stocked with china that carried designs depicting the three ethnic themes. They were added to Chicago–Kansas City trains, supplementing full diners for coach passengers.[77]

The pace and extent of improvement in the right-of-way did not subside. At the end

of 1904, 62 percent of the ties, 59 percent of the rail, and 84 percent of the switches of the railroad had been replaced. All but 59 miles of branchlines had either stone, gravel, cinder, or slag ballast.[78]

Since purchase, the QC&St.L had served no better purpose than it had before Harriman bought it. The line had not been absorbed as had the Springfield-Grove mileage, but in September 1904, the line was folded into the C&A Railway. Harriman probably did not know what else to do with it. Along with the right-of-way and associated structures, the acquisitions brought the company 22 freight cars (mostly boxcars), a caboose, two coaches, a baggage-mail car, and the QC&St.L's two 4-4-0s.[79]

▾▾▾

By 1904 the solid livestock trains of the 1880s and 1890s out of Kansas City—as well as the multi-car cuts of lumber headed for the Plains states—were no longer evident. Kansas City–St. Louis traffic had similarly diminished. The 293-mile Kansas City–St. Louis routing via Roodhouse was only 10 miles longer than the MP's Kansas City–St. Louis route and only 4 miles longer than the Rock Island's. But terminating east of the Mississippi, as the C&A did, made the road dependent upon the TRRA for St. Louis deliveries, a time-consuming process.

Like the C&A's, the Burlington's Kansas City–St. Louis route was less than ideal, but for different reasons. Though the Burlington entered St. Louis directly on the Missouri side of the river, its St. Louis–Kansas City route was a circuitous 348 miles. Trains ran up the west bank of the Mississippi River to Hannibal then west to Cameron Junction before reaching Kansas City. An improvement, an air line that would run from Old Monroe (52 miles north of St. Louis) to Francis (just east of Mexico) was designed. George Harris, president of the Burlington, was prepared to offer Felton access over the air line for his trains in exchange for rights over the C&A's Mexico–Kansas City line. The result would be a 60-mile reduction for Burlington runs, making that road more competitive with both the MP and the Rock Island.

Construction of the Francis Cutoff, as the new route became known, was started in 1903. It was designed as a nearly straight piece of railroad. The latest standards of construction were employed—steel bridges, concrete culverts, and fully stone ballasted 85-pound rail on closely spaced ties. Seven miles of passing track ensured minimal delays. No other railroads would be crossed.[80] C&A rails at Francis were raised to meet the Burlington's, and a second set of tracks, about two miles long, were added between Francis and Mexico. The depot at Mexico was designated a joint station, while the C&A's Mexico yard and the Burlington's Francis yard became joint operations.[81]

To facilitate the change while the cutoff was under construction, Burlington trains ran up its river-hugging line to Louisiana, then diverted west over the C&A to Mexico, before continuing on to Kansas City. In June 1904 the air line was opened with two jointly operated daily passenger trains, the *Daylight Flyer* and the *Night Hawk,* between St. Louis and Kansas City. C&A St. Louis–bound freight was dropped at Francis and then brought directly into St. Louis by the Burlington.[82] Atop the Burlington's St. Louis freight house on the riverfront, a sign proclaimed it had become a joint Burlington/Chicago & Alton facility.

At the beginning of 1904, Harriman's plans for the C&A were finally revealed with the announcement that it would be merged with the KCS, the same plan Stilwell had but with the ownership reversed. C&A preferred shareholders received an invitation from Kuhn, Loeb to deposit their shares. The merger was to be consummated on or before September 30.[83]

The announcement came at a time when the stock market was in turmoil. For the past three years, the New York Stock Exchange had been going through wild gyrations. They started when Northern Pacific (NP) shares rose to as high as $1,000 a share as Morgan and Harriman competed for control. After Harriman called off the fight, NP share prices plummeted and took most of the rest of the stock market down with them, followed by another run up before the market took another plunge. Even the best industrial stocks rode the roller coaster. Morgan's newly formed United States Steel shares, for instance, fell from $50 to less than $10 before another rally led to higher share prices once again.

Amid the tumultuous market swings of 1904, someone began accumulating C&A shares. Inexplicably, Harriman himself held only a quarter of the common and only half the Railway preferred stock. The shares being accumulated were those sold by other syndicate members who had cashed in as prices rose during the market's wild swings. The *Wall Street Journal* was the first to take note, reporting in February that the North Western's Marvin Hughitt was making a play for the C&A. The North Western's recent purchase of over 30,000 acres in the Macoupin County coal region probably led to the reporter's conclusion. Under the name Macoupin County Railway, the North Western had laid 25 miles of track from its mines to Green Ridge, near Girard. The C&A was awarded the contract to move coal to Peoria, where it was picked up and moved over the North Western's recently finished Peoria-Nelson branch to the Chicago-Omaha main line. At Girard, the C&A laid storage tracks and installed a turntable, roundhouse, and related service facilities for the use of both roads. It was a fragile reason for a takeover and was quickly discredited and denied by Hughitt.[84]

It wasn't until mid-September that the guessing ended. Again the *Wall Street Journal* broke the news, reporting that the group that controlled the Rock Island and the St. Louis San Francisco—the "Rock Island Crowd," as Wall Street had dubbed Daniel Reid, W. B. Leeds, and James and William Moore—had accumulated a near majority of the C&A common stock over the previous two years during the down cycles of the market, along with a large percentage of the Railways preferred stock.[85] The Reid-Moore group was not looking at the road purely as an investment. The prize they wanted was the coveted Chicago–Kansas City route for Rock Island traffic and a St. Louis connection for their St.LSF

Harriman had been outmaneuvered. He had fought and lost battles before but always came away with something. This time was different. Only a provision of the company's by-laws fixing staggered year terms for directors prevented the Rock Island Crowd from immediately taking control. At the annual meeting in October, five of the eleven directorships of the C&A and four of the nine of the railroad became Rock Island seats.[86]

The two separate camps now faced the question of how the C&A would be operated. Neither group was accustomed to sharing power. The tenuous accommodation reached was for each faction to manage the railroad for two-year stints, the Harriman team first, through 1906. To prevent either side from wresting control from the other until a final resolution was reached, a trust was created, and the stock of each faction was placed in it.[87] At least for the next two years, Harriman would remain in nominal control of the company, but any plans for merger with the KCS were scrubbed.

An agreement with the Santa Fe in 1905 brought new efficiencies. Though the mileage involved was not great, its strategic worth was. From just south of Joliet to Coal City, the Santa Fe's main line was laid parallel to the Coal City branch. The traffic of both roads had increased dramatically, and both roads needed added capacity over the short but critical distance. An agreement was negotiated for each to use the rails of the other, creating for both roads a virtual double main line between Joliet and Pequot. Some realignment of track and a crossover at Coal City was all that was required to make this happen. At the same time, six miles of a second main line parallel to the Coal City–Mazonia trackage was laid, adding another double main line.

South of Bloomington a two-year $2 million project to add 51 miles of second main line between Bloomington and Sherman was started. Half the sum was to be spent reducing the most troubling six miles of main line be-

tween Atlanta and Lawndale, Atlanta Hill. Since the railroad's earliest days, that elevation had been the ruling grade and worst obstacle for northbound runs. Helper engines were stationed at Lawndale to push trains over the three-mile rise. The planned cut of from 25 to 35 feet would reduce the grade to just three-tenths of one percent. A restrictive curve would be eliminated with the movement of the track about 2,000 feet east. An estimated 1.5 million cubic feet of earth was to be removed from the hill and then transferred to Lawndale where two and one-half miles of a deep cut was to be filled.

Because a few landowners decided to gouge the railroad for the land needed for the track relocation, the Atlanta & Lawndale Railroad was incorporated to gain condemnation rights. The three greedy farmers soon came to terms. In 1915 the Atlanta & Lawndale, which had been nothing more than a paper railroad and no longer served any purpose, was dissolved. Though the Atlanta Hill grade was sharply reduced and the tracks through the section were realigned, the project was never fully completed, but what was accomplished marked the road's biggest grade-reduction project. The Springfield-Grove subdivision was also cut to just three-tenths percent grade, making runs from the Springfield coal district to Peoria as easy as to Chicago.[88]

The ongoing project of installing block signals neared completion; virtually all of the main line between Chicago and East St. Louis was now automatically controlled. About half the Roodhouse–Kansas City line was similarly protected. The erection of more train order signals and high semaphore signals at main line switches continued. Nearly every mile of the main line was laid with 80-pound rail, and 80 percent was supported with stone ballast. New coaling stations, along with water tanks, were erected at Ridgely and Mazonia, replacing the two-year-old tank there that was destroyed by fire. Streator and Steinmetz also got tanks. Glasgow saw a new depot built, replacing the original that had burned.[89] Though freight revenues decreased 7 percent during 1905 (largely caused by reduced shipments of grains and coal), St. Louis World's Fair traffic inflated passenger revenues by 25 percent and more than compensated for the freight losses. Total revenues rose to $11.7

million, and after all expenses were charged, a $6 million profit was earned.[90]

Power was added during the year. In July, 10 large Baldwin Consolidations, with heavier 7,360-pound weights and 2,887 greater tractive effort than the type bought three years earlier, began hauling freights. Twenty more showed up in May the next year. As they arrived, the Mogul types were transferred to yard duties. The parade of new power continued as Baldwin delivered five more Atlantics—with slightly larger cylinders and heavier weights than the previous four—and 10 more 0-6-0 switchers.[91]

By the end of 1906, 10 miles of the Bloomington-Sherman second main line were finished. Two miles of the second main line through Springfield were laid, completing 10 miles of parallel track between Sherman and Iles. Thirty-one miles of grade for the Iles-Murrayville air line were surfaced. At Joliet engineers were planning the elevation of the tracks through the city—a project like that of Chicago's—mandated by the Joliet City Council.

Foundation piers and abutments were in place for the erection of a single leaf bascule bridge over the south fork of the Chicago River at Ashland Avenue, the cost of which was to be borne equally with the two other roads—the IC and the Santa Fe—sharing it. Steel superstructures consisting of nine 64-foot spans were installed on the southbound track over Salt Creek, south of Lincoln, and three 70-foot spans were on the ground at Kickapoo Creek, north of Lawndale, for replacement of the bridge there. The Sangamon River bridge for the northbound track, made up of eight deck plate girder spans placed on concrete abutments and piers, replaced the pile trestle. Two new steel trusses were on the ground at the Mississippi River bridge awaiting installation just eight years after the last upgrading. Four of the original wooden trestles between Sherman and Grove were replaced with concrete arches.

The depot at Springfield received extensive upgrading, and the towns of Mexico and Marshall received new depots, the former to serve as the joint facility with the Burlington, the

The reason the Joliet City Council forced the railroads to raise their tracks above ground is obvious in this view of the junction of the Santa Fe and C&A main lines crossed by the Rock Island. The C&A passenger depot can be seen in the distance to the right of the crossing tower. (Courtesy of Lewis University Canal and Regional History Coll., Bill Molony Coll.)

latter replacing the original structure lost to fire. The banks of the Mississippi River at Louisiana and Quincy Junction and the Missouri River at Glasgow saw revetment work and new dikes, built in an attempt to avoid a recurrence of the damage to both bridges suffered during the floods three years earlier. The perpetual absence of good soft water at Bloomington was again addressed, this time with the drilling of several wells at Normal, where there was better water. Nearly a mile and a half of four-inch wrought iron pipe was laid between the wells and the treatment plant at Bloomington.

▾▾▾

This impressive transformation of the railroad, and indeed of the industry, came at a time of political upheaval in the country. The Spanish-American War had entangled America in a foreign conflict for the first time. When the brief, celebrated war ended, the United States found itself ranked as a world power. With the Gold Standard Act passed in 1900, the economy began a robust expansion. The once totally agrarian-based economy was evolving into one dominated by industrialists, supported by powerful and sophisticated bankers. This occurred during the presidency of William McKinley, an Ohio Republican of quiet, conservative leanings. He took office in 1896, then was reelected for a second term— the first president since Ulysses Grant to be returned to office—but his assassination a few months into his second term brought Vice President Theodore Roosevelt to the White House. Roosevelt was a member of an aristocratic New York family. He was a former New York governor and national hero because of his image as an outdoorsman and his exploits leading a group of volunteers called the Rough Riders in the skirmish in Cuba.

Pledged to carry out the policies of McKinley, Roosevelt nevertheless soon brought a new activism to the White House. He relished the power and prestige afforded a president. Unlike his predecessors whom he considered timid, Roosevelt saw himself as a man of action. In his first message to Congress, Roosevelt made clear his belief that the enormous power of the trusts—steel, oil, and railroads—

had to be reined in by government action. He contended that he was not against their size, but only their abuses of power.

Most members of Congress had little inclination to change the status quo, which left Roosevelt and the executive branch to lead the fight against big business. Roosevelt's first target was Morgan's Northern Securities Company, controller of the Great Northern (GN) and NP. In March 1902 Roosevelt's attorney general, Philander Knox, sued to break up the powerful entity, and to nearly everyone's surprise, the Supreme Court agreed. "When I became President," Roosevelt later stated, "the question of the method by which the United States Government was to control corporations was not yet important. The absolute vital question was whether the Government had power to control them at all."[92] The Northern Securities decision advanced the question.

The unexpected action scared Wall Street. If Roosevelt could get his way with someone as powerful as Morgan, what chance did the other trusts have? Both steel and oil could generate most of the capital needed internally, but railroads could not. They began to see investment dry up. At first it was the more risky projects of weaker roads that were denied, but then even the biggest and most powerful roads saw the spigot tightened.

In addition to the prospect of government regulation and a weaker credit market, railroad presidents found themselves caught in another vise. United States Steel and Standard Oil generated tens of thousands of carloads of freight but—because of their power to designate routings—either demanded rebates and got them or were freely granted them by roads anxious to get their business. Congress attempted to put an end to the practice with passage, in 1903, of the Elkins Act, which imposed penalties for unfair pricing on both the shipper and the railroad. To some degree the practice of rebates ended. But there was still pressure for across-the-board reductions, and the industry was still faced with rising interest rates, higher taxes, and increased labor costs— all factors that contributed to a decline in returns on the traffic that was moved. It was only the ever larger volumes of traffic that prevented the industry from posting lower profits. The C&A mirrored the industry. Between 1899 and 1906, despite increased traffic, lower rates charged reduced the revenue per freight ton mile by nearly 25 percent. For the seven-year period of Harriman control, the company lost more than $10.2 million in net earnings that otherwise would have been enjoyed.

The state regulations that emerged in the 1870s had created a complex and—in the view of railroad management—unfair restraint on the railroads' ability to earn adequate returns. The morass of conflicting rules and regulations of the states led some enlightened railroad presidents (who recognized regulation was something they would have to live with) to support federal, rather than state, regulation. They reasoned that their interests would be better served in Congress, whose members in many cases were indebted to the railroads and other industries for their campaign financing. In 1887, responding to the railroads' wishes, Congress created the Interstate Commerce Commission (ICC), which to management's satisfaction, was given no authority over the setting of rates.

Rate making was left to the railroads, and, over time, two types were devised—commodity rates, which were individual quotes for a specific commodity, and class rates, which established tariffs on the basis of value and a myriad of other factors. Three territories for rate-making purposes—the Official Classification Territory in the East, the Western Territory in the Midwest and Southwest, and the Southern Territory—evolved, and through them, tens of thousands of individual rates were set, with trade association representatives, businessmen, and chambers of commerce (though not the public) included in decisions. The practice had been in place for nearly 30 years.[93]

In 1906, during the early stages of a rejuvenated economy and with inflation gaining momentum, the industry attempted to catch up by setting an across-the-board 10 percent freight rate hike. It caused an immediate uproar. Roosevelt was livid, as were populist members of Congress—mainly senators from Midwest farming states, who for the past two years had sought to give the ICC authority over the rate-making process. There wasn't one railroad president who was prepared for the reaction that resulted. Within weeks of the increase, in June 1906, Congress passed the Hepburn Act, which, for the first time, armed the ICC with rate approval authority. Passage came too late to reverse the 10 percent increase but ushered in a new and unanticipated era of uncertainty for the industry.[94]

Despite passage of the Elkins Act, rebating was not entirely eliminated. Standard Oil had continued to demand and got rebates. The oil company's arrogance and its more sensational abuses had been exposed in 1902 in a series of articles written by a young and tenacious reporter, Ida Tarbell, in a popular periodical of the time, *McClure's Magazine*. Her report created a sensation. Stories of personal and corporate abuse shocked readers, who until then knew little of the secretive Rockefeller or how he used his company to destroy competition and to control prices. Unbowed by the exposé, the oil company's monopolistic practices continued until November 1906, when the federal government sought to break up the company.[95] At the crux of the government's case was a charge of restraint of trade through the seeking of rebates on freight rates from certain railroads, among them the C&A.

Between late September 1903 and March 1905, it was found that the C&A had given Standard Oil of Indiana favorable treatment, and the government sought a judgment against both parties. Though the C&A was also charged, the government's real target was Standard Oil. Before rendering his decision, the federal judge, Kenesaw Landis, had granted railroad officials immunity for their testimony against the oil company. In his decision, Landis (the same judge who ruined the careers and lives of Chicago White Sox ballplayers Buck Weaver and Joe Jackson in the Black Sox scandal) found Standard Oil guilty and accessed an astronomical fine of $29,240,000—$20,000 for each of the 1,462 carloads the C&A moved. An appeals court overturned the absurd ruling on several grounds, but Landis's judgment accurately reflected the government's anger toward Standard Oil.[96]

The timing of what happened next was no coincidence. In the very same month the breakup of Standard Oil was sought, the ICC initiated hearings ostensibly on the matter of "The Consolidation and Combination of Carriers" but which turned out to be a witch hunt to expose the supposed "indefensible financing" of the C&A. Roosevelt; his attorney general, Frank Kellogg; and ICC chairman, Franklin Lane, relished the prospect of publicly humiliating Harriman and, in the process, setting the stage for more railroad regulation.

Ironically, Roosevelt and Harriman had had a cordial relationship as far back as the president's days as governor of New York. After Roosevelt became president, Harriman was a regular visitor to the White House and was consulted frequently. Two weeks before Roosevelt's reelection in 1904, the Republican State Committee of New York found itself $200,000 short of what it needed for the state campaigns for both the president and the New York gubernatorial candidate, Frank Higgins. Since New York was his home state, Roosevelt could not tolerate a defeat. He invited Harriman to Washington to discuss the matter.

The president asked Harriman for the needed $200,000. Harriman agreed but asked a favor in return. He wanted Roosevelt to settle a squabble that had developed within the New York Republican Party. Roosevelt, according to Harriman, consented to intervene. Soon after his reelection, Roosevelt and Harriman again met at the White House. During the course of the visit, Roosevelt told Harriman he could not honor their agreement. Dismayed, but calling the incident a "misunderstanding," Harriman did not push the issue, but the warm friendship between them cooled. Fairly regular correspondence between the two men ceased. In the autumn of 1906, just before the congressional elections, Harriman, remembered by the New York Republican Party for his generosity two years earlier, was approached by the chairman of the Republican Congressional Committee with an appeal for funds. This time Harriman refused. He didn't need to involve himself, he told the committee, since he could buy whichever politician suited him on his own. Harriman's response was reported to the president, who immediately turned on his once close and trusted confidant, supporter, and friend he now labeled an "undesirable citizen."[97] Harri-

man was about to be made the poster child for everything that was wrong with the state of America's railroads.

The Harriman Syndicate's buyout of the C&A was thought by Commissioner Lane to be the perfect example of how unscrupulous men took a "once conservatively financed and extremely prosperous railroad" for their own gain. During the hearings, Lane clearly ignored the fact that it was the stockholders who sought out Harriman to transform the railroad from an old maid into an eligible partner, rather than Harriman grabbing control and then ravaging the company. The massive investment Harriman had made in the property was never addressed. Instead, the commissioners focused on the 30 percent dividend the syndicate paid itself.[98] To be sure, the payment is still the most controversial and perhaps most misunderstood aspect of Harriman's sophisticated capital restructuring of the railroad. The payment was perfectly legal and justified, except in the eyes of those who had an axe to grind.

Though hardly needing their support—Harriman was quite capable of defending his position—legal scholars later came to Harriman's defense. "When the company had used profits for improvements, it may lawfully borrow an equivalent sum of money for the purpose of a dividend, if upon a fair estimate of its assets and liabilities it has assets in excess of its liabilities, and capital stock equal to the amount of the proposed dividend," a contemporary authority on corporation law, W. W. Cook, opined.[99] In fact, the dividend payment was what Blackstone himself was prepared to dispense in his last-ditch attempt to persuade stockholders to reject the Harriman buyout. In his letter to stockholders, Blackstone wrote, "In case a majority of the shares of the company are not sold to the syndicate, I shall advise that you authorize the refunding of the outstanding bonds of the company, and the issue of a stock dividend to represent earnings heretofore invested in permanent improvements."[100]

In truth, the ICC's "investigation" served no other purpose than to allow Roosevelt to embarrass Harriman and to pay him back for his refusal to generate campaign funds. No charges were ever brought against Harriman as a result of the hearings. He was dismayed by the attacks but gave no sign of bending under the barrage. Harriman merely returned to his New York office, undeterred by those less able to understand the way business in the new century was to be conducted.

Although nothing was achieved by grilling Harriman, Roosevelt did not relent in his attacks on railroads specifically and on big business in general. When the nation's economy softened in early 1907, the president placed the blame on his favorite targets. Responsibility for the downturn, he charged, "Lay upon the railway and corporation people—that is, the manipulators of railroad and other corporation stocks—who have been guilty of such scandalous irregularities during the last few years."[101] As stock prices began to fall, he added another group to his list of villains, financiers like Morgan, whom, he declared, had "no moral scruple of any kind whatsoever."[102] Morgan, it is to be remembered, was the same man who helped save the country from total collapse during the panic of 1893. When asked by reporters for his view of the acrimonious relationship and reasons for the current economic problems, Harriman replied, "I would hate to tell you where I think you ought to go for an explanation of all this."[103] He was, of course, pointing a finger at Roosevelt.

Actually, neither railroads nor stock traders had much to do with causing the country's economic downturn. The worsening situation was rather brought on by a capital crunch that victimized Wall Street and the nation's industries as much as the public at large. Capital had dried up, partly a result of the expansion of railroads, but more the result of international events. The costly Russian-Japanese War was draining the world's capital. The rebuilding of the earthquake-devastated city of San Francisco took more investment. A late crop season tied up farmers' cash. There was only so much money available, and with little new capital to invest, stock prices plunged. In one day UP stock dropped 25 points. C&A stock, which three years earlier had traded at $47 a share, in March 1907 was selling at $15. When the mighty UP attempted to float a $75 million bond issue late in the year, only $4 million could be sold.[104]

By October the liquidity problem threatened New York's banks and brokerage houses.

When word of the crisis had leaked out, the public rushed banks to withdraw their money. Soon, news of New York's crisis reached other cities, and even banks with no apparent connection to New York came under depositor attacks. Savings accounts were drained. More New York banks suffered runs. When an outright collapse seemed eminent, J. P. Morgan summoned all the New York City bank presidents to his office, where he told them within 15 minutes they would have to raise $25 million to support the troubled institutions. Through sheer force of his personality, Morgan saw $27 million pledged within five minutes. The man Roosevelt claimed had "no moral scruple of any kind whatsoever" had again come to the country's rescue.[105]

The next day, the *New York Evening Post* ran a headline reading, "Morgan & Company Save Market," but the claim was a bit premature. The city of New York itself was about to go broke, in need of $30 million to pay off short-term bonds. The brokerage house of Moore & Schley faced bankruptcy when Tennessee Coal & Iron stock—placed with the firm as collateral in return for the house's financing, which in turn the brokerage house used as collateral for its own loans—turned out to have no market. Again Morgan intervened. He bought the Tennessee Coal & Iron stock for his United States Steel (which he bought from Carnegie in 1900 for the astronomical sum of $500 million), giving Moore & Schley the funds needed to back their bank loans. There were other flare-ups before the panic subsided, but order was eventually restored, and the fear of economic collapse passed.[106]

Somewhat chastened now that Morgan had again shown his worth to the country, the president sheepishly conceded, "It may well be that the determination of the government to punish certain malefactors of great wealth has been responsible for something of the troubles," but he couldn't resist another swipe at his targets, adding "at least to the extent of having caused these men to bring about as much financial stress as they can in order to discredit the policy of the government."[107]

By year's end, thanks in part to Morgan's intervention, confidence was restored, and the country was again enjoying prosperity, but the bewildered railroad leaders had been left to twist in the wind. Pressure for repayment of vulnerable debt placed some roads in tight cash positions. The more stable roads decided to defer improvements.

Amid all the turmoil, there was widespread speculation over whether Harriman would continue to bother with the C&A. The KCS link had been vetoed by the Reid group, and Harriman's turnover of the KCS to the Dutch investors who held a majority of the stock all but ended any prospect of merger of those two railroads. The Rock Island interests were about to take their turn managing the railroad, and Harriman played second fiddle to no one. His objective of using the C&A to calm the volatile relationships of Midwest and Southwest roads had come to naught. Because of his involvement with the WP, Gould was now a Harriman enemy, posing a threat to Harriman's UP-SP alliance. Further disrupting the peace Harriman sought, Rockefeller had released the Katy to Dutch interests. But if Harriman did pull out, what would the Rock Island Crowd do with the road?

The answers to these questions came in June 1907. The two men, Harriman and Reid, agreed to dissolve the trust they had created. Harriman transferred the stock he owned to the books of the UP and withdrew from any further C&A involvement. The Rock Island group came to realize the combative Roosevelt administration would not stand for consolidation no matter how logical a Rock Island–SLSF–C&A merger might be and would no doubt intervene to block such a move. They began a search for a buyer, and within a few months, they found one, Edwin Hawley.

The Hawley and Union Pacific Takeovers

In a *Saturday Evening Post* interview, Edwin Hawley summed up how he had arrived at his station in life. "I have played a lone hand and stuck to my job. I have simply done two things—I have worked and I have waited."[1] He was not being modest. For the most part he has been forgotten by today's railroad historians as one of the turn-of-the-century railroad titans who rose to prominence (or notoriety), but he was also slighted during his railroad career. He was in his mid-fifties when he quietly started acquiring railroads. Honest, fair, and unassuming, he shunned public attention. By the time he entered the C&A picture, though, he already controlled three railroads. In terms of mileage or strength, his minor collection did not compare with those of Gould, Morgan, Vanderbilt, or Harriman, but he was doing fine picking off turnaround candidates, investing in them, and then getting the greatest return possible from them.

He had been in railroading for 40 years but with little or no operating experience; all of his career had been spent on the clerical and sales side of the business. He started at age 17 as a clerk in the New York City offices of the Erie. After a brief stint as an eastern agent for the Rock Island, in 1874 he was named eastern agent of the California Fast Freight Line, a joint venture of the Rock Island, North Western, and Burlington. In that capacity, he had the good fortune to meet Collis Huntington, the legendary head of the SP. Huntington reputedly told him, "You ought to be working

No. 2999 (originally no. 442) was the last new Consolidation purchased. Built for the B&S, it was taken by the C&A when the B&S could not pay for it. The 192,000-pound engine worked in both road and switching service and was not disposed of until 1950 when it was scrapped. (David Goodyear Coll. E. L. DeGolyer, Jr. Photo. Coll., Ag82.232, courtesy of DeGolyer Library, SMU) for me; you know how to keep your mouth shut."[2] In 1883 Huntington appointed him as the SP's eastern agent. Seven years later he was promoted to general traffic manager, based in New York, and was named a director; he became one of Huntington's closest advisors.

Four years later Hawley made his first tentative step into railroad ownership when he acquired the Minneapolis & St. Louis (M&St.L), a weak, Minnesota-based property he took out of receivership. Five years later he took a much bigger step (though it wasn't seen that way at the time), when, again out of receivership, he took control of the Colorado & Southern (C&S).

Like the M&St.L, the C&S was a north-south line. It reached Orin Junction, Wyoming, and an interchange with both the Burlington and the North Western to the north and the Colorado–New Mexico border to the south, where the Ft. Worth & Denver City (Ft.W&DC) was met, passing through Cheyenne, Denver, Pueblo, and Trinidad. He added a short line or two, then acquired the renamed Ft. Worth & Denver (Ft.W&D), and through that purchase, his C&S reached Galveston, Texas, and the Gulf of Mexico.[3]

In 1900 Hawley acquired another Midwest short line, the Iowa Central, and added it to his M&St.L. Combining the operations of both, he created a 760-mile grain-hauling railroad that reached from Minneapolis–St. Paul to Oskaloosa, Iowa (with connections to the Burlington) and Peoria. Totally dependent on locally generated traffic, the Louie, as his road was affectionately called, was overshadowed by the powerhouses in the territory—the CM&St.P and Burlington—but through aggressive pricing and prompt service, he earned the favor of local shippers. Over time he transformed what had been two struggling, independent lines, into a better property that returned small but steady profits.

That same year Hawley met Harriman for the first time. He had been invited by the aged and weakened Huntington to join him and Harriman in a retreat on an Adirondack Mountain camping trip. Harriman used the two-day getaway to press Huntington to release his Central Pacific to Harriman's UP. That didn't happen, and a month later, in August, Huntington died. His heirs had no interest in his holdings and asked Hawley and Huntington's banker, James Speyer, to dispose of Huntington's railroad properties. Brief negotiations led to Harriman's purchase of the CP and then consolidation with his UP. Because he knew the railroad well, Harriman asked Hawley to remain on the board. He agreed to stay but resigned his railroad position, and—along with Frank Davis, the SP's former assistant treasurer, who also resigned—he set up the New York brokerage house of Hawley & Davis.[4]

Hawley's next encounter with Harriman came soon thereafter. The C&S's most important customer was Colorado Fuel & Steel Company in Pueblo. Hawley had plowed a lot of money into his 2,000-mile C&S, but he made no single greater expenditure than the $600,000 he spent for special equipment to haul the steel company's ore, coal, and coke. Also benefiting from the traffic the steel company produced was Gould's MP, which also served Pueblo. Colorado Fuel was one of the few independent steel producers left after Morgan set up United States Steel. At the time, besides Morgan's oligopoly, there were only a few other companies producing rail. As a cartel, they fixed high prices, preventing Harriman from getting the cheap prices he sought for the rail his railroads needed. Harriman saw Colorado Fuel as his one option and brought Hawley and Gould to his office, where the three decided to go for control of Colorado Fuel & Steel. They succeeded.[5]

In 1902 Hawley acquired another road, the Toledo, St. Louis & Western (TSt.L&W). If anything, it was his weakest property yet. The Clover Leaf Route, as it was nicknamed, had been a sorry excuse of a railroad until 1889. Before then it was narrow gauge, was poorly maintained, and had limited traffic. It was so weak that it was one of the first to fail during the crash of 1893. Seven years passed before it was reorganized, rebuilt as a standard gauge railroad, and extended to an eventual 451 miles between Toledo and East St. Louis. Competing with the better financed, better built Wabash, the TSt.L&W was nearly totally dependent upon what transfers of through eastbound and westbound perishable and livestock merchandise traffic the road could capture. With aggressive selling and more reliable operations—developing Hawley trademarks—freight tonnage and revenues steadily grew. By 1907 traffic had more than doubled again, and, though they were small, the TSt.L&W was earning annual profits.[6]

Hawley's brokerage business and takeover of the Clover Leaf were only a year old when in 1903 he was handed a deal he decided was worth taking. Benjamin Yoakum, chairman of the Rock Island Company, the holding company that controlled the Rock Island and the St.LSF, commissioned Hawley to start buying C&A stock on the open market. Money was no object; Yoakum had wealth behind him. Among his fellow board members were William Moore, a director of First National Bank of New York and United States Steel; F. L. Hine, a director of First National and of Liberty National Insurance; D. G. Reid, a director of United States Steel; James Speyer, Huntington's former banker; and John Mitchell, president of Illinois Trust & Savings, the man who had delivered the C&A to Harriman just four years earlier.

Hawley was surprised that a man as shrewd as Harriman would not have secured a majority interest, but since he had not, he decided that was Harriman's problem. Hawley faced a dilemma, nevertheless, because he knew when Harriman found out he had played a role in the Rock Island's planned takeover, any future business relations between them would end. Harriman would likely add him to his growing list of enemies, but Hawley figured he could deal with that.[7] Hawley started buying and continued accumulating shares until 1906, eventually capturing 48 percent of the C&A's common and preferred stock, just under the 51 percent needed for outright control. The transactions earned his firm sizeable commissions in the process. As the date of changeover from Harriman to Rock Island control approached, Yoakum and Reid concluded that, given the anti-railroad attitude in the White House and at the ICC, they would never be allowed to merge their roads with the C&A. So Yoakum once again approached Hawley, this time to sell the Rock Island's position on the open market. Hawley saw his chance. He offered to buy the stock himself. "I can get the Alton for the Iowa Central," he wrote his M&St.L chief operating officer, L. F. Day. "What's your idea of this?" Day's brief reply was, "Don't think the Iowa Central should buy the Alton."[8] Hawley went ahead anyway.

On August 1, 1907, the day Hawley officially took control, it was the Clover Leaf that got the road, not, perhaps more logically, the M&St.L. To finance the deal, Hawley sold Clover Leaf 4 Percent Collateral Trust Bonds to purchase the C&A preferred and 2 Percent Collateral Trust Bonds for the common stock and made TSt.L&W preferred and common stock subordinate to the new bonds. As would become apparent within a few years, it was a serious mistake. Clover Leaf president Theodore Shonts, a few weeks before the TSt.L&W board formally approved the purchase, summarized Hawley's thinking: "If the Chicago & Alton continues to earn four percent on its preferred stock, as it has done over the past five years . . . the only risk to the Toledo St. Louis & Western will be $100,000 for the first five years and $200,000 for the second five years. This risk seems very light as compared with the benefits to be derived. . . ."[9] The two sums he cited were the annual cost of servicing the bonds issued to cover the purchase of the C&A's common stock over their 10-year life.

There was no physical connection between the two railroads, so to correct the problem, Hawley planned a relatively short stretch of new track from the Clover Leaf at Panama, Illinois, to the C&A at Litchfield. At East St. Louis, operations of the two would be coordinated.

For all practical purposes, Hawley's latest acquisition was a rebuilt railroad. The C&A's yards were still inadequate, and the road still needed more power, but Harriman had spent $22.3 million bringing the road up to higher standards. All but four of the 819.55 miles of main line had been replaced with 80-pound rail. Seventy-two percent of the main line and 40 percent of the branches were ballasted with stone. Much of the rising and falling parts of the railroad had been leveled and straightened. Crossings were interlocked, and practically all of the railroad was automatically signaled. The locomotive fleet's tractive effort had been increased 133 percent since 1898. The worn-out rolling stock had been almost totally replaced. The total capacity of freight equipment had been raised 195 percent, the average capacity per car, 71 percent. Using as a measure the number of freight cars per mile of road operated, the Alton's 10 was four times greater than the IC's and better than the North Western's by 2.5 cars, the Burlington's by 4.4 cars, the Rock Island's by 4.8 cars, and the UP's by 5.7 cars.[10]

The company had been transformed into primarily a coal-hauling road. Fifty-three percent of all freight traffic was now derived from coal. The volume of local farm product was still healthy but had leveled off. Long-haul traffic such as perishable shipments off the UP at Kansas City to the produce market in Chicago and increased blocks of coal and oil from the South and Southwest were still just a small percentage of total traffic.

The road's gross revenues had doubled from 1898 to 1907. Earnings too almost doubled, from $2.7 million to $4.4 million. There was enough revenue to adequately service the fixed debt. Everything earned had been plowed back into the property; during Harriman control, though, no common dividends had been paid. The ratio of interest charges to gross earnings in 1900 was 27.5; in 1907 that ratio had fallen below 20.[11]

By any measure the company was a much bigger and better property than the Clover Leaf. The C&A had almost twice as much mileage, three times the number of locomotives and rolling stock, six times the number of passengers, twice the number of freight tons carried, four times the net operating income, and nearly three times the net earnings, with an operating ratio almost 3 percent lower.[12] For the first time since he had started putting his system together, Hawley had hooked a mountable trophy.

A few months before Hawley took formal control in 1907, the nearly flat, straight, 34-mile Springfield-Murrayville air line was opened. It was a showpiece of modern engineering laid with heavy rail, closely spaced ties over heavy ballast, with six 70-car capacity passing sidings every five miles. With the opening, five-mile reductions on Chicago–Kansas City runs resulted, saving more than 55,000 train miles annually.[13] Westbound coal runs were the first to use the new route when it opened in October 1906. The *Kansas City Limited* out of Chicago started running over the line a month later. An hour was cut off the train's previous time between Bloomington and Murrayville. Over time most Western Division limiteds and through freights used the Iles-Murrayville route, relegating the Bloomington-Murrayville segment to secondary status.

During the last year of Harriman management, the laying of the second track between Lawndale and Sherman was finished, completing a double main line from Chicago to Iles. The drawbridge over the south fork of the Chicago River at Ashland Avenue was replaced with a single-leafed, 150-foot Page bascule bridge. Two new brick depots were erected at Marshall and Centralia.[14] The C&A's growing roster of coal cars that year had been increased with a rather astounding addition of 2,000 50-ton steel flat bottom gondolas with side dump doors, which Standard Steel Car had turned out.[15] By 1909 coal cars comprised 45 percent of the freight car fleet. Also added were 10 heavier 2-8-0s, continuing the program of Mogul replacements for road freight work, and five more Pacifics, the type fast becoming the road's standard for passenger service.[16]

As a fitting windup of the Harriman Era, operating revenues in 1907 reached $12.8 million. Though expenses had risen, operating income of $4.7 million was posted. Even after nearly $3 million in interest, taxes, and preferred dividends were paid, a $1 million surplus was added to the road's treasury.[17] It looked to Hawley like he had gotten quite a catch. The road would cost him nothing as long as traffic continued to grow.

In October 1907 TSt.L&W officials took control of the board. Because of the staggered election structure, three Harriman-era directors remained, Norman Ream, a Chicago investor with a sizeable stake in the railroad; Felton, whom Hawley had asked to remain as president of the road; and Mitchell, though he now was counted as a Rock Island man.[18] Within weeks most of the officials and operating executives were replaced by Clover Leaf men, the most prominent exception being Charlton, who was retained as general passenger and ticket agent. Before long, however, Felton became uncomfortable with the new ownership and, before year's end, resigned to become president of the Mexican Central Railroad.[19] TSt.L&W's president, Shonts, replaced him. Shonts was a New York financier and had limited railroad experience. His first association with railroading came in 1882, when he was named general superintendent and later general manager of the 152-mile Indiana, Illinois & Iowa Railroad. He was hired away by Hawley to run the Clover Leaf. Shonts did not leave New York. Instead, he named P. H. Houlahan, TSt.L&W's general manager and a former transportation official with the Burlington and MKT, to the same position on the C&A to handle day-to-day decisions.

The pleasure Hawley had taken in 1907 fiscal results was not nearly as great 12 months later. After the panic of 1907, the economy worsened, and, with less industrial output, the nation's freight traffic fell by 7 percent. C&A revenues declined in line with the industry, dropping $721,000 from the previous year, the operating profit dropping by $507,234. By cutting expenses, though, the road earned a still substantial $1.3 million profit, from which both the obligatory 4 percent preferred dividends and, for the first time since 1898, a common dividend of 1 percent were paid.[20]

Except for the projects started during the Harriman Era and the replacement of the Ridgley coal tower that had been lost to fire, few new projects were initiated in 1907. Nevertheless, the Mississippi River bridge had two iron spans replaced with steel. Three 1,700-foot-long wooden trestles approaching the Illinois River between Hillview and Pearl were filled. They had been erected to allow the river's sprawl at flood stage to pass through but were no longer needed thanks to work performed by the Corp of Engineers upriver. An attractive brick and plaster-veneer depot was opened at Louisiana and another at Grain Valley, and facilities of both the Alton and the Clover Leaf were enlarged at Front Street in East St. Louis.[21]

A dozen sidings to reach new shippers were laid, and two major shippers located their new facilities adjacent to the railroad's property. In an open field at Argo (about two miles southwest of Summit), Corn Products Manufacturing erected a processing plant, and at Wood River (seven miles south of Alton), Standard Oil opened a new refinery and tank farm.[22] Both would grow and expand and in time would have around-the-clock switching jobs assigned to handle the thousands of annual carloads they generated.

As was evident with both his C&S and M&St.L, Hawley, like Harriman, was a believer in upgrading a property to maximize results. When projects that meant more efficient operations were presented to him, he generally gave the chairman of the board, Thomas Hubbard, approval to proceed with them. Thus, in 1909, the second main line was extended 27 miles south from Iles to Nilwood. Nineteen miles of relatively heavy grades between Bloomington and Atlanta were reduced by as much as 12 feet, bringing major operating improvements. Helpers were still required to push trains up and over Atlanta Hill between Lawndale and Atlanta, but there were plans to further reduce the grade. Slater Yard was reconfigured to include badly needed longer receiving tracks. A new roundhouse, coach yard, and freight yards were started at South Joliet, as the track elevation through Joliet continued. New storage tracks were installed at Auburn for Chicago & Illinois Midland (C&IM) interchange coal traffic from the Pawnee Mine eight miles east and loads from the Auburn & Alton and Solomon Coal mines. Girard and Auburn had become the centers of the new Springfield coal region, as Braidwood had been earlier.

More bridges that had not yet been upgraded were replaced or rebuilt, including those bridging Jackson Creek (six miles south of Joliet) and Perche Creek (between Clark and Higbee), where a 102-foot deck girder span replaced a deck truss type. Two trestles on masonry piers over Sugar Creek at New Holland on the Peoria Branch were replaced with steel girders. New freight houses were finished at Streator and Jacksonville, and a handsome new brick station there was under construction. To service West Coast perishables, a 300-ton icehouse at Mexico was completed, as was a 5,000-ton facility at Roodhouse.[23]

The investment in the property did not adversely affect operating income, which stayed nearly the same as the previous year, but the bottom line was adversely affected by the withdrawal of $1.6 million in dividends. For the first time in almost 50 years, a deficit of $258,620 was posted. Two years of dividend withdrawals had by now all but depleted the road's reserves. Unless new traffic could be attracted and costs better controlled, Hawley was going to be hard-pressed to avoid future

C&A deficits. The withdrawal of C&A surpluses to pay interest on the TSt.L&W bonds had begun to erode the C&A's stability.

The Burlington was in an expansive mood after James Hill took control, and one target was Hawley's C&S. Hawley agreed to sell a 65 percent majority interest for $16.4 million. His outlet to the Gulf had matured and proved successful, its good fortunes directly attributed to the decisions of the man Hawley had put in charge, Frank Trumbull. Both remained on the C&S board after the road's sale to Hill, but they quickly moved to a new venture, acquisition of the C&O, again taking a road out of receivership at bargain-basement prices. Hawley added the Hocking Valley to provide an outlet to the Great Lakes and then the Chicago, Cincinnati & Louisville to reach Chicago. With Trumbull in charge, the once weak, high maintenance C&O, whose purpose had been to tap the rich coal regions of Virginia and West Virginia for hauls to the Atlantic port of Norfolk, Virginia, had been transformed into a coal hauler to both the East Coast and Chicago, just like the mighty B&O. Hawley had no plans to tie the C&O in any way to the Clover Leaf, C&A, or M&St.L. The C&O was operated as a stand-alone property, just as had been the C&S.[24]

Four months after the C&O takeover, Hawley and Trumbull took control of the troubled MKT. As with the C&A, conventional wisdom always assumed the Katy would sooner or later become a part of a much bigger system, but that Hawley would do this was not expected. The *Railroad Age Gazette* commented:

> The gathering of this group of roads under single control, has been a process unlike that which has attended the growth of any other American railway system. Until recently, it was absurd to speak of the Hawley lines as a system at all. The addition of the Missouri, Kansas & Texas to this group has no apparent bearing on the affairs of the C&O end, but fits in admirably with the Clover Leaf and the Alton and, to a lesser extent, with the traffic needs of the [Minneapolis & St. Louis]. Yet it is not apparent that the Hawley system can throw any large amounts of additional traffic over this road [the Katy]. The advantage is apt to work the other way, and the comparatively short line of the Alton appears to be the only direct and important beneficiary.[25]

The Katy's main line ran from Galveston through Texas and Oklahoma to Parsons, Kansas, where it split, one line continuing to Kansas City, the other branching off to Hannibal and St. Louis. Three interchanges with the C&A already existed: at Kansas City, St. Louis, and Higbee. The Katy had been a "weak sister" in a territory dominated by the St.LSF and MP, but Hawley saw new opportunity. Along with its livestock trade, oil out of Oklahoma and Texas needed to be moved to midwestern and eastern cities. Others could not make the MKT pay, but Hawley and Trumbull were confident they had bought a diamond in the rough. It only needed some polishing. Hawley would make no trouble for Yoakum's St.LSF, and he didn't have to worry about Gould raising a fuss, since his empire was crumbling. From all indications, his MP was headed for receivership.

Hawley had pieced together a tenuous though promising system but so far had done nothing to merge the C&A and TSt.L&W. The Panama-Litchfield connection was never started. The only link the two roads ever had came from trackage rights granted by the Cincinnati, Hamilton & Dayton (later the B&O) between Metcalfe, Illinois, and Springfield, over which some high value perishables were more expeditiously moved between Kansas City and eastbound connections.[26] The industry continued to wonder what Hawley planned.

As far as the men working the trains, repairing the engines and equipment, and maintaining the right-of-way were concerned, what management had planned made little difference. There was plenty of work. The increased business the road was seeing meant more cars had to be switched into cuts for more extras, the running of which meant more work for Bloomington Shops. The track projects were keeping track crews busy, and the line and general offices were buzzing. That all of that business was taxing the road's facilities was no one's concern but general manager Houlahan's.

The worst bottleneck on the road was Brighton Park Yard. When built, the facility was perfectly adequate, but as traffic increased, especially the seasonal rushes of stock and coal, delays in making transfers—of sometimes up to a week or more—resulted.

The yard had short tracks, a small engine-house, a relatively light turntable, and engine servicing facilities management labeled "totally inadequate." When built, the yard was well outside the city's boundaries, but the city's westward expansion had brought new residences and industries around it, leaving no room to expand. Besides, the Chicago City Council was pressuring the railroads to cut smoke emissions, not something easily accomplished. In 1907, 296 acres were purchased in unincorporated Cook County a few miles northeast of Summit as the site for a totally new yard. Well beyond Chicago's city's limits—and where the restrictive smoke abatement rules could be ignored—there was plenty of room to expand.

Six stub tracks, running perpendicular to the main line, had been laid earlier, where loaded coal cars were stored for Insull's Commonwealth Edison electric generating plants (such as Fisk Street Station at Pulaski Road). They were retained, and company engineers included them in a plan for a flat switching yard, which, when completed, would hold 3,700 cars on six and a third miles of track. An engine terminal with a 100-foot-deep, 30-stall roundhouse, a 90-foot turntable, two 75-foot inspection pits, two 200-foot cinder pits, a 1,200-ton capacity sand station, and a 250-ton gravity coaling station, all state-of-the-art, were included.[27]

Construction began in 1910 with the laying of six 100-car and four 55-car capacity tracks, providing storage for 820 40-foot cars. In 1912 the second phase of construction was initiated, and the engine facilities were started. The following December what was originally called Summit Terminal but now named Glenn Yard was opened with a set of 24 tracks with a capacity of 1,396 cars to the north, serving as a receiving and dispatching yard for interchange traffic. To the south, 18 tracks, with a capacity of 2,045 cars, served as the receiving yard. The engine terminal was located between the two yards.[28]

The 1910 operating results proved highly successful, thanks to an economy that was picking up and despite a five-month strike of Illinois coal miners that started in April. Revenue from every commodity but coal increased an average 4 percent, and revenues climbed to $13.4 million, another new record.

Even passenger revenues rose by 8 percent. Extra sections had to be employed to handle overflow traffic. Some of the increased passenger traffic resulted from new through car operations at St. Louis and Kansas City.

An agreement with the St.LIM&S led to a through Pullman drawing room car being added to the *Alton Limited*'s consist for travelers to Hot Springs, Arkansas, a health spa marketed as the "world's greatest sanitarium." Though the dedicated through Pullman was short-lived, close connecting schedules continued to be maintained. The *Palace Express* now included a through Pullman sleeper, which the M&O took to its home city. A Pullman tourist car sleeper moved every other day on the *Nighthawk* between St. Louis and Kansas City, where it was turned over to the Santa Fe for continuation on to Los Angeles. Four daily trains, the *Prairie State Express, Alton Limited, Palace Express,* and the *Midnight Special* served the Chicago–St. Louis route, dominating the market. The three Chicago–Kansas City trains, *The Hummer, Nightingale,* and *Night Express,* had a much smaller market share compared to that of either the Santa Fe or Burlington but offered competitive service. Chicago-Peoria traffic via the Dwight Branch and the recently added runs over the TP&W via Chenoa (cars were cut in and out of Chicago–St. Louis trains there) gave travelers between the state's two largest cities an excellent alternative to Rock Island service. Peoria–St. Louis and Peoria–Kansas City schedules had through overnight Pullmans, cut in and out of trains at San Jose. The three St. Louis–Kansas City trains operated jointly with the Burlington over the St. Francis Cutoff; the *Red Flyer, Early Bird,* and *Night Hawk* were supplemented with a daily train through Roodhouse. A cooperative arrangement with the Cleveland, Cincinnati, Chicago & St. Louis (CCC&St.L), the former I&St.L, offered 11 trains between Alton and St. Louis, an attempt by the two roads to meet electric line competition. On nearly every route, dining cars, parlor cars, chair cars, and others with amenities such as libraries or cafe-buffet facilities were offered.[29]

Over the past four years, annual gross freight revenues had increased by 13 percent, but the increased volumes of freight carried (more than half derived from coal) was at rates that had hardly changed since the general rate increase in 1906. During the period, because of inflation and higher labor costs, expenses increased 10 percent, holding operating revenue to only a 6 percent increase. The board of directors could hardly ignore the increasingly tight situation and, while still declaring a common stock dividend, cut the prior year's payout by half. Though less, that payment still caused another deficit. The smaller outlay forced the TSt.L&W to use part of its own limited reserves to pay interest on its collateral bonds. The 1910 C&A dividend was the equivalent of 39 percent of the TSt.L&W's 1910 net earning. Had no common dividends been paid, 73 percent of the Clover Leaf's surplus that year would had to have been used to pay the interest on the bonds.[30]

▾▾▾

There was little question the industry needed another general rate rise to stay ahead of rising costs and increased taxes, and in 1908 one was announced. In Congress a firestorm of outrage arose. The railroad (and big business generally) critics in Congress had not gone away. On the contrary, their strength had increased. They maintained a relentless battle against the trusts. Rockefeller's Standard Oil and Morgan's United States Steel monopolies still prevailed. Each was still free to charge whatever the traffic would bear. But this was not the case with railroads, which some in Congress foolishly considered nearly as evil. The time when railroads could dictate prices had long since passed. The industry's freewheeling expansion had brought competitive rails to most places, holding down rates. Additionally, steel and oil were dictating both the prices the railroads would pay for their products and the rates they would allow railroads to charge them.

Railroads had adjusted rates for thousands of categories of freight, resulting in millions of prices for hundreds of thousands of commodities, but there was so much competition that once one railroad posted a rate, competing roads would quickly meet it. To the industry's critics, this was collusion but, in fact, was merely market forces at work. Where competition existed (which was at most places), if a shipper didn't like a railroad's new rate, he was free to use that of another railroad. This forced the railroad setting the higher rates to either forgo the traffic or to roll back its tariff. The very magnitude of the process precluded the possibility of collusion.

In 1908, an election year, President Roosevelt was determined to ensure that nothing disturbed the strong economy, weakening the chances for election of his chosen successor, William Taft. Using the prestige of his office, Roosevelt demanded the railroads postpone any rate increases until after the election. They meekly complied.

Throughout 1909 and into 1910, cost pressures continued to ruin most railroad balance sheets. Unable to hold off any longer, in April 1910, the 24 railroads that made up the Western Traffic Association filed tariffs for increases on 200 commodities. A few months later, the eastern roads did the same. To Attorney General George Wickersham, it appeared the rate bureaus had filed a single application, and to him that was a violation of the Sherman Antitrust Act. A majority of the members of the ICC—all Roosevelt appointees—saw it the same way. Now in the middle of his first term, so did President Taft. Naively, railroad presidents had thought that by submitting the tariffs collectively, they were making it easier for the ICC to realize the industry's need. Instead, they played directly into the hands of their severest critics.

In Congress, Iowa senator Albert Cummins immediately introduced a bill to give the ICC new and stronger regulatory powers. The result was passage, in 1910, of the Mann-Elkins Act. The waiting period before a rate could become effective was extended from 30 days to six months, and the railroads were obliged to prove that the rate itself, not just the increase, was justified. Never before had the nation's railroads faced such a dilemma. The Mann-Elkins Act did not become effective soon enough for Wickersham and Taft. They charged the railroads with conspiracy to set rates and with violating the Sherman Act. A Missouri judge issued an injunction forbidding the railroads from putting their new rates into effect. No one was prepared for this attack. Though Roosevelt and certain Congressmen had made plenty of anti-railroad noise, this was the first time the full force of the federal government had been brought against the industry's ability to set rates for its services.

During the ICC hearing held in August, railroad spokesmen focused on the need for the rate increase to compensate for the industry's inability to attract outside capital, to offset growing labor costs, to at least keep pace with inflationary prices of supplies, and to have something left over to reward stockholders. Their arguments were completely ignored.

In February 1911 ICC Commissioners Frank Lane and Charles Prouty promulgated a report that rejected any need for a general rate increase. "There is no evidence . . . for higher rates. The probability is that increased rates will not be necessary in the future . . . [but] if actual results should demonstrate that the Commission's forecast of the future is wrong, there might be grounds for asking a further consideration on this subject," Prouty wrote. "This Commission certainly could not permit the charging of rates for the purpose of enabling railroads to pay their laborers extravagant compensation as measured by the general average compensation paid labor in this country as a whole." Lane added: "The railroads may not look to this tribunal to negate or modify the expressed will of the legislature. They have laid before the Commission the facts . . . but to the mind of the Commission their justification has not been convincing." He further contended that the railroad's sole purpose in presenting the new rates was to "discover the mind of the Commission with respect to the policy which the carriers might in future pursue and to secure if possible some commitment on our part as to nationwide policy which would give the carriers loose rein."[31] Their statements left no doubt they were not of a mind to promote the industry, but rather to restrict it. The rate increases were denied.

Across the country railroad presidents were dumbfounded. How could they ever increase a rate if the cost of doing business was not considered justification? How would they ever attract new capital? Wall Street was asking similar questions. How would railroads provide a return for invested capital if they weren't permitted the right to charge a fair and reasonable rate? Why should anyone invest in an industry not permitted to set its own rates? Because of the uncertainty, investment dried up. The industry was facing a bleak future,

seemingly punished for past sins. The denial of rate increases on the federal level was matched by some states, which enacted adverse legislation. In 1907, for instance, the IRWC cut passenger fares to a maximum of two cents per mile.[32] How did the various federal and state agencies justify themselves? They pointed to the increased traffic over the past five years, which was indisputable, but which was a stance giving no consideration to the rising cost of transporting that traffic. The industry was entering a new era, where returning anything to stockholders was going to be tougher than ever before.

▾▾▾

Practically everything possible to update the property between the Springfield-area coalfields and the terminals of Peoria and Chicago had been done. The track, bridges, and signaling had been brought up to the highest standards possible. The sole exception was the short, still restrictive section over Atlanta Hill, which remained an impediment to the transporting of coal, which filled the cars that made up the majority of trains. The hill was the reason three of the largest engines the company ever operated were purchased.

American Locomotive had introduced two engine types over the course of the preceding six years, which their salesmen promised were well suited to the company's needs: the 2-6-6-2 Mallet and the 2-8-2 Mikado. Both types were already working on other roads and gave plenty of evidence that they could help operations and reduce costs. The Mallet was a design that first appeared in the Alpine regions of Europe in the 1880s. It was introduced in the United States on the B&O in 1904. The Mallet's smaller drivers (just 55 inches) were intended for slow, steady dragging or pushing of very heavy tonnage, exactly the type of work the helper engines at Lawndale at the foot of Atlanta Hill had to perform.[33] The Mikado, introduced on the NP also in 1904, was a further development of the Consolidation with a much larger boiler and firebox, which required a trailing truck to support the added weight. The type had gained rapid popularity and was becoming the standard for freight service engines on many of the country's railroads. It would eventually become the

most popular engine (with a trailing truck) produced. Compared to the five-year-old 2-8-0s, the heaviest freight engines the C&A operated, the Mikado could produce 78 percent more tractive effort.[34] The 2-8-2s would tackle the coal runs as well as through freight runs, especially on the Western Division, where trains, because of the irregular track profile, regularly had to be double- and triple-headed. Thus three Mallets and 30 Mikados were ordered. This was an enormous purchase for a road whose balance sheet was looking so anemic. But Hawley was optimistic that the increased traffic he expected could be moved far more cheaply.[35]

The reconstruction and rearrangement of the Bloomington Shops, roundhouse, and yard was started in 1910. A 44-stall roundhouse with a 100-foot turntable, two 200-foot cinder pits, two 100,000-gallon steel water tanks, and a 600-ton coaling dock where engines on four tracks could be serviced simultaneously would bring the shops to a higher level of efficiency. The roundhouse at Brighton Park had three longer stalls added, and an 80-foot turntable replaced the former 65-foot turntable. New 100,000-gallon capacity water tanks were raised on the Western Division at Roodhouse, Slater, Odessa, and

Grain Valley with smaller capacity tanks placed at Pearl and Booth. On the Southern Division, a new coaling station was put up at Miles, and the existing tower at Virden was expanded to provide coaling for trains from either direction.[36] The bigger and heavier cars and engines that now made up most consists were taking their toll on the 80-pound rail, the standard weight for the past 10 years, so a 90-pound standard was adopted, and during the year, 51 miles of the heavier steel was laid in the northbound track between Chicago and Joliet and between Chenoa and Bloomington.[37]

Aside from a half interest taken in the 10-mile Peoria Railway Terminal between Peoria and Pekin to afford easier running of coal deliveries to the Rock Island, there had been no extension of the railroad since the acquisition of the QC&St.L. But in 1910 another 27 miles were tacked on through a lease of the Rutland, Toluca & Northern (RT&N), a corporation created the previous November to take over the bankrupt Toluca, Marquette & Northern (TM&N). The road had been built by Charles Devlin, who had acquired mineral rights under 11,000 acres around Toluca and Rutland and in 1892 had sunk two coal shafts at Toluca along the Santa Fe. In October 1897

Devlin incorporated the Toluca & Eastern Railroad (T&E) and had laid a six-mile extension to Rutland with access there to the IC. In 1899 Devlin extended the line north through Custer, where his railroad crossed the C&A, providing yet another outlet. He got another charter for that construction under the TM&N banner in 1901 and then a year later, combined the extension with the T&E. By then the road had reached McNabb, some 15 miles north of Toluca.

Devlin had several other interests besides railroads, including mining, utilities, retailing, and banking. He attempted to manage each personally, an almost impossible task. Probably as a result of the stress brought on by his responsibilities, in the spring of 1905 Devlin suffered a stroke, followed by a mental breakdown, and finally his death. Receivers took over and resumed laying track north from McNabb to Granville. By 1907 they had a connection with the CM&St.P in place.[38]

Despite its modest ambitions, the RT&N was never successful. From its inception until 1910, the road produced just $7,410 of profit, and, though some interest was paid on the mortgage, $229,163 of overdue payments were outstanding. The road had $1.2 million of long-term debt on the books when the bondholders forced foreclosure in 1910.[39] The road's existence might well have ended then, or—under the best of circumstances—the CM&StP, always in need of coal, might have taken over the Granville-Toluca portion, abandoning the rest of the route to Rutland. Instead, on Hawley's behalf, Shonts stepped in and leased the RT&N for the C&A. The reason undoubtedly was to serve the Milwaukee Road. With trackage rights over the TP&W closing the gap between Peoria and Washington, coal up from the Springfield Region could be hauled north to Custer and up to Granville. Why this never happened is unknown. Perhaps it turned out to be too costly to upgrade the RT&N to handle the heavier power and traffic or too expensive to pay extra crews that would have to be assigned at Peoria; perhaps the TP&W denied trackage rights or the CM&St.P backed out of whatever understanding had been reached. In any event, during the life of the lease, the RT&N limped along as an insignificant local line of limited utility. In 1923 the last mine at Toluca

shut down, leaving little reason for the RT&N's continuance.[40] The bondholders again sought the line's sale. In 1925 papers were filed for abandonment of the entire line. Two years later, local interests tried to revive operations with limited and infrequent operations over the rest of the line (after ripping up the Rutland to Custer trackage in 1930), but in 1937 the last rails were finally lifted.[41]

The C&A's worsening bottom line did not improve in 1911. As Hawley had hoped, freight and passenger revenue continued to grow, up 13 percent and 3 percent, respectively. Overall, revenue climbed somewhat more than 9 percent, to a record $14.5 million, but operating expenses rose even faster, up by 16 percent. Inflationary prices for nearly everything the railroads bought were pressuring the entire industry. The falloff in operating income of somewhat over $900,000 left nothing for common dividends nor enough for the fixed charges to be fully paid. It was the third straight year of growing deficits.[42]

Shonts described the worsening situation: "It is a question how your management shall meet the increased cost of operation due to increased wages and other causes and, at the same time, serve the public in the manner demanded and expected, and, also, maintain the property in the way it should be kept, unless a proportionate advance can be obtained in the rates of transportation to offset the increased cost of operation."[43] He pointed to two sets of statistics to make his point. In 1901 the average C&A rate per ton mile received was 72 cents. In 1911 it was 61 cents. The company's operating ratio was 66 in 1901 but 74 in 1911. Clearly, the higher costs of supplies, labor, and taxes, plus the ICC's denial of a relatively modest rate increase, had placed the company, and the industry, in a precarious position.

To minimize the impact, Frank Morse, who replaced Houlihan two years earlier as general manager, cut 1912 repair spending wherever possible, but despite his best efforts, charges rose an astounding 61 percent, largely the result of higher wages. Improvements were curtailed too, except for projects already started. In October 1912, Joliet Union Station, one of those projects already in progress and a joint effort of the three principal roads serving the

city, was officially opened, adding to the city's prestige and passenger convenience. The depot, paid for equally by all three roads using it—the Alton, the Santa Fe, and the Rock Island—was the culmination of Joliet's track elevation project. It had taken only a year for the rather sizeable building, wedged in on the west side of the Santa Fe and Alton and the north side of the Rock Island tracks, to be erected. Elsewhere, a brick passenger depot was erected at Lincoln, and three others at Fulton, Gilliam, and Cordo were opened. A combination passenger and freight station was put to use at Tallula. A new brick freight station, along with new yard tracks, was opened at Mexico. The Sangamon River bridge's five truss spans, too light to support the heavier train weights, were replaced. A 90-foot turntable was installed at Venice to accommodate the longer dimensions of the new Mikados.[44]

Despite the need to hold down spending, the 10 light Moguls the Bloomington Shops turned out between 1887 and 1889 were replaced by an equal number of larger 2-6-0s delivered by Baldwin specifically for switching service. They were the last Moguls purchased. A canceled Buffalo & Susquehanna (B&S) order left American Locomotive with three unwanted Consolidations, which the builder of-

fered to the C&A at rock-bottom prices. The three were also the last of that type purchased and the only 2-8-0s intended specifically for switching service. Perhaps the offer was made to capture a larger order for 10 Pacifics which were received. These American Locomotive products were different than the earlier models with smaller 77-inch drivers rather than the 80-inch size applied to the previous five.[45]

Up to this point, Hawley had confounded nearly everyone by doing next to nothing to consolidate the roads he controlled. Some questioned whether he knew what to do with his far-flung string of railroads. He had formally merged the Iowa Central into the M&St.L and then had announced plans to lay an extension north from Minneapolis to Canada and south to a connection with the Katy, in the process creating a true north-south transcontinental railroad, but so far he had not given any indication of his plans for his other properties.

The TSt.L&W had become a victim of the same circumstances that increasingly plagued the C&A. Revenues had leveled off during the previous two years, resulting in a falloff in net income of 31 percent. Fixed debt, including taxes, had risen 2 percent. The road's total fixed charges compared to net income was an alarming 94.7 percent. Though Alton revenues had risen 9 percent, increased operating costs now consumed 72 percent of what was brought in. The Alton's fixed charges (as a percent of net earnings) had climbed to a threatening level of 93 percent, practically the same as that of the Clover Leaf.[46]

Hawley might well have been mulling over his dilemma on the evening of February 1, 1912, when he suffered a fatal heart attack. He was found the next day in his New York residence, sprawled out on the floor. Hawley, a bachelor, had no heir. He had planned to gather his many interests into a corporation but never had gotten around to it. His death left disposition of his considerable wealth accumulated during his 45-year railroad career for the courts to decide. Whatever plans Hawley might have had for molding the railroads he controlled into a thriving system went with him to the grave. His untimely death was a sad ending to a rather remarkable career. Though Hawley had never sought or gained the limelight, he had played an impressive supporting role on railroading's stage.

Whether coincidental or a result of Hawley's passing, the loose system he had created began to unravel. A few months before Hawley's death, George Ross resigned as vice president and as director of both the Clover Leaf and the C&A. Hawley's death was followed soon after by the departure of Shonts. No longer feeling an obligation to serve after his mentor's passing, and with most of his attention devoted to heading New York's Interborough-Metropolitan electric transit system, he submitted his resignation in July. The board was left with two openings. Samuel Insull, arguably Chicago's foremost industrialist and head of one of the C&A's most important customers, Commonwealth Edison, replaced Hawley, and B. A. Worthington, a career railroader, replaced Ross. The task of finding a new president began. The directors looked no further than to the end of the table where Worthington sat.

A Californian by birth, Worthington had started railroading with the CP, rose rapidly to positions of increasingly greater responsibility, and ultimately was named the SP's assistant to the general manager. In 1903 he was named assistant director of maintenance and operations of both the SP and UP, a post he held for a year before being named vice president and general manager of the UP's subsidiary, Oregon Railroad & Navigation. After just six months in that post, he left the Harriman Lines to join the Gould system as first vice president and general manager of the Wheeling & Lake Erie (W&LE) and the Wabash lines east of Toledo, Ohio. After the W&LE fell into bankruptcy three years later in 1907, he was named the road's receiver, the post he left upon being named the C&A's president.

Worthington immediately brought changes to the C&A's management, starting with the removal of Morse as general manager. Morse served only three months under Worthington before A. P. Titus was named to replace him. Once Titus got his feet under his desk, he replaced L. J. Ferritor, superintendent of the Northern and Southern Divisions, with two new superintendents, S. P. Henderson for the Northern Division and C.W. Miller for the Southern Division, but retained W. M. Corbett as superintendent of the Western Division. He also removed J. T. McGrath as superintendent of rolling stock and replaced him with J. E. O'Hearne. As superintendent of motive power, O'Hearne was responsible for both power and rolling stock.[47] Obviously, Worthington thought there was a better way to run the railroad.

Though revenues were quite acceptable, the bare bones approach to power and equipment maintenance over the past few years had severely impaired the road's ability to operate efficiently. Even the newest power had seen only running repairs, and the oldest engines were sidelined rather than be repaired. The oldest cars were being cannibalized for hardware replacement. Though some investment in the physical plant had been carried out, that too had been greatly reduced. Evidence of the cutbacks could be seen in the increased number of derailments and injury-causing accidents.

In short order, the departments that had been combined—traffic, accounting, and purchasing—were divided, and the C&A and Clover Leaf were again handling their functions independently. Though the Clover Leaf, through ownership of its stock, was technically still in control of the C&A, from now on, it would be managed independently. The unraveling continued as the looming financial crisis grew worse. Hubbard could read a financial report as well as anyone, and what he contemplated was not good. If the C&A was to avoid default and save the Clover Leaf from failure, a fairly substantial infusion of new investment was needed, and Hubbard knew that would certainly not be raised on the credit rating of either the C&A or the TSt.L&W.

It was also becoming evident to Robert Lovett, chairman of the UP, that his road's $10,343,100 investment in Alton preferred—the transferred Harriman stock—though a relatively small portion of the very large portfolio of railroad securities the UP held, was at risk.[48] Lovett, a tall, thin Texan and Harriman favorite, had taken over after Harriman died in 1909. Some might say Harriman had worked himself to death, but the cause of his demise was actually cancer, found too late to be treated. Lovett had been Harriman's most trusted advisor and now headed his empire. Lovett had had no involvement in Alton affairs, but he was not surprised when Hubbard turned to him to resolve the company's pending crisis. Hubbard had made no secret when he met with Lovett that without a considerable infusion of new capital—which he estimated at $4 million needed immediately and another $8 million to retire debt coming due within the next 12 months—the C&A would fail and would have to seek receivership, a step that would probably wipe out the UP's investment. He was the road's last hope.

The stoic Lovett, perhaps thinking failure of the C&A would become a blot on Harriman's legacy, but certainly feeling he could do something to turn the situation around, agreed to look into the matter. After a couple of months, a staff-prepared study told Lovett what he needed to know. The real need for capital was closer to $15 million. Current accounts payable were a staggering $4.5 million. Needed was an almost equal amount to retire the series A and B Alton–Mobile & Ohio Equipment Trusts, $2.8 million more to retire the 5 percent improvement notes, and $1.4 million to reduce sinking fund debt. Improvements needed over the course of the next three years would take another $3.4 million. The balance, $3.8 million, would be required for ongoing expenses. In all, the investment equalled 23 percent of the road's existing long-term debt. The UP could easily have afforded the total, but Lovett, a trained corporate lawyer, was cautious. He decided to have the UP advance half the needed funds and borrow the other half, and for that he turned to the UP's lead bank, Kuhn, Loeb.[49]

So large an investment had to be protected, and thus UP officers became involved in the C&A's management. Hubbard offered no protest when Lovett made a condition for the loan that he and two other UP officials take board seats. The beleaguered Hubbard willingly agreed, anxious to get out from under a deal that had turned sour. In July 1912, a subordinate $15,330,000 mortgage was added to the C&A's books, representing the UP's and Kuhn, Loeb's investment. The weakened state of the road was reflected in the interest rate, 6 percent, twice that of the rate Harriman had arranged a decade earlier. Lovett; the UP's director of maintenance, Julius Kruttschnitt; and director of traffic L. J. Spence replaced three Clover Leaf men on the C&A board. Lovett assumed the chairmanship.[50] Though the TSt.L&W was still technically its owner, the C&A was effectively once more a member of the Harriman Associated lines.

The effects of the investment and new management could be seen immediately. It was no coincidence that operating revenues and most measures of operating efficiency improved. Over the past three years, freight traffic had steadily increased, coal and products of the land still the dominant categories but manufactured products gaining as well. Total tonnage increased by 5.5 percent. A combination of higher rates and more lucrative cargo brought increased freight revenue of 6.5 percent. What made 1913 different was how much more efficiently that tonnage was moved. Fewer train miles were needed to handle the increased volumes because the average tons per loaded car and the number of loaded cars per train both improved. For years the near solid trains of empties westbound to Kansas City had created an intolerable imbalance. Concentrating on adding loads to Kansas City–bound trains improved matters at once. As a result, though overall freight train miles dropped 4 percent, the average net ton miles increased an impressive 13 percent.[51]

On the passenger front, Charlton was happy to record slightly better numbers, up 2 percent. He extensively advertised new low colonist fares and houseseekers' fares for those planning to stake claims in the expanding West (Oklahoma had become a state six years earlier, causing a land rush among immigrants). He offered reduced round-trips to summer resorts in the East and Canada and promoted popular off-line events with the M&O, such as Mardi Gras. In the face of increased rubber-tired competition, all three traffic measures—revenue passenger train miles, distance traveled, and yield per passenger—increased.[52]

Worthington, who remained in charge as president of the C&A, authorized a staggering 35 percent increase in spending. Engine repair expenditures were increased 61 percent over the annual average spent over the prior six years; passenger car repairs, 67 percent; and freight cars, 55 percent. He had been forced to play catch-up, but the new and safer power and equipment improved efficiency. The company's direct train movement per train mile and cost of fuel per train mile expenses were now better than the averages of 14 other midwestern railroads.[53]

Property improvements in 1913, though minimal, saw six miles of new track added to reach the timber and apple orchards at East Hardin. Elsewhere, the Roodhouse Yard was improved with five miles of new yard tracks, and the coaling station earlier destroyed by fire there was replaced. Longer yard tracks were laid at Mexico and Normal (to relieve pressure at Bloomington). A six-stall roundhouse, machine shop, coaling station, power station, and related facilities were being erected at Bloomington. The freight house at Springfield got a 100-foot extension; the other at Alton was extended 60 feet. Again because of fire, it was necessary to replace three depots at Braceville, Gardner, and Bowling Green.[54]

Because of the investment in maintenance, the operating deficit in 1913 rose to $338,893, but it would have been difficult to continue for another year without the repairs. Accidents had been occurring with greater frequency. In April a truck under a boxcar in the consist of train no. 85 near Macoupin disintegrated, derailed the car, and tied up the main line for several hours, causing three passenger trains, including the *Alton Limited,* to detour. It was the second incident at Macoupin within

weeks. Weakened track in the earlier incident was the suspected cause. In July the engine and express car of the southbound *Prairie State Express* derailed between Atlanta and Lawndale and tore up the track before ramming a new Mikado standing on the helper siding. Both engines were completely turned around by the impact, and the passenger train's engine turned over. Again traffic was disrupted. July was extremely hot, causing rails to buckle. A mile north of Brighton, the two rear coaches on the northbound *Alton Limited* derailed. The same day a filled hopper left the rails two miles further north. A week earlier a boxcar had derailed in Brighton, a result of a loose track joint. Five boxcars were derailed between Plainview and Macoupin in August, forcing the *Prairie State Express* to detour via Roodhouse and causing the *Capital City Flyer* an hour's delay. A month later a major freight wreck occurred at Rinaker, shutting down the district for a full day. In yet another incident, the southbound *Midnight Special* in December was running at about 50 miles per hour through Plainview when spreading rails caused the cars to leave the track. Though no one was killed, 15 persons were injured, two of them seriously.[55] These incidents (and others on the other two divisions) illustrate the seriousness of the problems the maintenance deferrals under TSt.L&W management had caused.

Surprisingly, the company's 1913 annual report was the only one Worthington signed. Just a little over a year and a half after being named president, he resigned. Whether he left of his own accord or was forced out is unclear. Worthington left to become chairman and president of the Cincinnati, Indianapolis & Western. Taking over as president was William Bierd, the former vice president and general manager of the M&St.L. The top job was a culmination of Bierd's career spent in supervisory and executive operating roles with the UP, N&W, Lehigh Valley, Rock Island, Panama Railway & Steamship, and New York, New Haven & Hartford (NYNH&H). The well-traveled, 50-year old Maryland native was the last president of the C&A during its final years of independence.[56]

Unfortunately, Bierd's first year became a baptism of fire. The revenue advances of the past few years were not repeated in 1914. Overall freight tonnage fell an astounding 21 percent. The lost traffic was a direct result of major declines in the road's two most important commodities, farm products and coal. An autumn drought throughout central Illinois and Missouri left crops wasted, resulting in an 8 percent grain tonnage loss. But the major blow came with a 34 percent falloff in coal volume.

For the past 10 years, the North Western business between Girard and Peoria had proved a godsend. It represented 21 percent of total coal volume and nearly 10 percent of coal revenues. Unfortunately, the traffic had been taken for granted, and after some five years of delayed shipments and missed connections, the North Western had had enough. The road laid plans for its own line to tap its southern Illinois mines. It took two years to complete an air line purposely designed to avoid towns to ensure expeditious running between Peoria and Girard. When the North Western's new line opened in September 1913, the C&A contract was canceled and the main reason for the Peoria line to exist nearly ended.[57]

Although passenger miles were up slightly, whatever gain in revenue that might have been expected was wiped out by the Missouri legislature's reduction of passenger rates to two cents, matching those of Illinois. Though a seemingly minor adjustment—just a half a cent per mile—it cost the railroad $156,000.[58] The combined factors of reduced operating revenues (down 25 percent) and increased bond interest (up 49 percent since 1909) resulted in a huge deficit of $5.7 million, a 47 percent leap over 1913.[59] During the year, whatever expense could be avoided was. Fewer trains were operated, and strict fuel economy measures were imposed. Employees were schooled in safety. Immediate improvement in work-related injury claims, which had been steadily growing, were cut by 80 percent. Because of the stepped-up spending on right-of-way maintenance the year before, 1914 spending in that category declined 24 percent. The cost of engine and rolling stock maintenance, which had also been accelerated the year before, was reduced by 12 percent though the amount spent per engine or car was still more than what the Clover Leaf team spent on average annually on either during the six years of its management.[60]

In a highly detailed and perceptive analysis published at the time, *Poor's Manual of Railroads* identified the causes of the road's predicament: a 24 percent increase in total capitalization per mile since 1901; fixed changes that consumed 30 percent of gross earnings when a 19 percent ratio might be considered ideal; a decrease of 48 percent in total net income per mile; a 17 percent increase in maintenance spending as a percentage of total gross overall; a 15 percent increase consumed by fixed charges; and operating and general expense. Though still offering a cautious recommendation for investment in the company's bonds, the analysis carried the caveat, "These conclusions, however [are] based upon the promise that the Union Pacific interests . . . will see that the money is furnished to see it [the C&A] through. . . ."[61]

New engines and rolling stock were acquired, not by the C&A directly, but rather by the UP, which leased the locomotives and cars back to the company. It was a sizeable infusion of new equipment—1,000 50-ton gondolas and boxcars, 500 stock cars, 200 flatcars, and 200 work cars. Two steel diners and postal cars were added to the passenger fleet. Another 475 worn-out coal gondolas, dating from 1900 and already written off, were rebuilt by Haskell & Barker.[62] Ten more 0-6-0 switchers, 20 Mikados from Baldwin, and 10 Pacifics from American Locomotive, all to Harriman Standard design specifications, made up the engine order.[63]

The improvements seen and equipment and rolling stock additions made in 1914 were major, characteristic of the way Harriman-taught railroaders operated. The 14-year Chicago track elevation project was completed. Glenn Yard was officially opened. An imposing new passenger station that also housed Northern and Southern Division offices was finished at Bloomington. New inbound and outbound freight houses were erected at East St. Louis along with a new yard, storage, and team tracks. The coaling stations at Kansas City and Virden, which were destroyed by fire the year before, were replaced with more modern continuous bucket facilities of 108 and 150 tons, respectively. Sixty thousand–gallon tanks were raised at Normal and Carrollton, as were 100,000-gallon tanks at Washington, Wann, and Mason City. Replacement of some com-

Train no. 11, the Chicago–St. Louis all-stop local with Class I-1 Pacific no. 601 on the point, prepares to leave the new Bloomington depot. Also housed here were the division and dispatcher offices. (Ewing Galloway Photo., E. L. DeGolyer, Jr. Photo. Coll., Ag82.232, courtesy of DeGolyer Library, SMU)

ponents of the Illinois River bridge, including a 147-foot truss span, a 297-foot center bearing draw span, and three 118-foot pony truss spans were put in place. The bridge over the Big Snai River east of Louisiana was strengthened. Parts of the Mississippi River bridge were rebuilt, permitting, for the first time, the road's heaviest power to be operated over the entire Western Division. Telephone communication was started between Kansas City and Slater and was extended to Bloomington on the main line.[64]

Carrying the mail had always been an important revenue source, especially on the Chicago–St. Louis main line. The C&A was among the first roads to employ dedicated Railway Post Office cars as early as 1865.[65] Competition for the business between the two important terminals was fierce and brought demands by the postal service for ever faster schedules. This posed a problem for the C&A because several of its intermediate stations had far greater mail volumes than catching it on the fly permitted. Management looked for better ways to handle the time-sensitive traffic.

The Chicago-based Hupp Automatic Mail Exchange Company came up with a radical new system that promised the transfer of a maximum of 12 mail bags from a train moving at 60 miles per hour, all to take place within a distance of 1,080 feet. The operation was started by a worm attached to the middle of an axle of a postal car truck, which was put into gear by a trip located alongside the roadbed, some 390 feet from the station. When the process was set in motion, the car's door was opened, while on the station's platform, arms snapped out toward the advancing train. Unloading mail involved extension of a chute from within the car into which mail bags were pushed. The bags were collected in a wooden, 150-foot-long trough. The chute was then retracted and the postal car doors closed, all automatically.[66] Thirty-three of the ingenious Hupp systems were installed at stations between Chicago and St. Louis in 1914. They may have been unique to the railroad. It isn't known how long the system was used, probably but a few years, but that it was tried showed again that management was eager to hold on to the business it had.

Passengers, mail, and express were now served in a new Kansas City Union Station. The city had been planning a replacement for its three outdated stations since the 1890s. They had long since become inadequate to handle the number of passengers, as well as the baggage, mail, and express passing through the city, but the city's topography had made finding a suitable site difficult. The devastating effects of the 1903 flood convinced the city fathers the present site could not be used. The property selected was between Broadway and Main Streets (opposite 23rd Street), about three miles southeast of the former Union Station at an elevation of about 30 feet above the river's flood stage. To facilitate the reconfiguration of the station's trackage, the company turned over one of its tracks at Rock Creek Junction for a new passenger line, and its tracks were moved north about a mile. A new bridge was built across the river to provide room for the Kansas City

Terminal's new Big Blue freight yard between the Santa Fe tracks and those of the company.

Construction started in 1910. The magnificent edifice in the classical Beaux-Arts style was designed by Chicago architect Jarvis Hunt, the same designer of the more modest Joliet Union Station. The six-story head house—under which 16 through tracks were laid—formed the shape of a "T" and was constructed of steel and faced with Bedford limestone trimmed with Maine granite. The massive, four-story-high interior, with a 92-foot ceiling, covered a 25,000-square-foot grand lobby and an even larger, 27,456-foot waiting room, which led to the 16 gates and the stairways to the platforms below.

On October 30, 1914, the $6 million Kansas City Union Station was opened. At the time it was the third-largest railroad station in the country. More than 260 daily trains either originated or terminated there. Only New York's Grand Central Terminal and Pennsylvania Station (with extensive suburban traffic adding to their counts) were busier. Santa Fe, Burlington, and MP trains were the most prevalent; the C&A had two daily Chicago–Kansas City and two St. Louis–Kansas City trains (operated jointly with the

When Kansas City Union Station opened in 1914, it was the third-largest passenger station in the country. Only New York's two stations saw more activity. Some 260 daily trains passed through or terminated at KCUS. It had cost $6 million to build and had taken four years to complete. (Kansas City Public Library)

Burlington) plus Slater and Louisiana locals.[67]

By now the Clover Leaf was in deep trouble. It didn't have a guardian angel like the wealthy UP. Its flat revenues over the previous three years and rising fixed charges resulted in deficits in both 1911 and 1912 and only a meager profit of $118,306 in 1913. With no dividends derived from its investment in C&A common stock since 1910 and only half the expected interest on the preferred last paid in 1911, interest on the Chicago & Alton Collateral Trust Gold Bonds was skipped. The collateral bondholders immediately sought intervention. In October 1914 the TSt.L&W was declared insolvent. More than $400,000 of floating debt was outstanding.[68] In hindsight, it was a good thing a merger of the two roads never occurred or the C&A would have then been brought down with the TSt.L&W, sooner than that eventually happened, perhaps bringing even worse results. The collapse of the Clover Leaf ended its ill-advised and disastrous affair with the C&A.

War had broken out in Europe in 1914, and though President Woodrow Wilson pledged to keep the United States out of the conflict, he was committed to materiel support of the allies. The C&A benefited from the increased shipments of grains and coal headed for Atlantic ports. Over the course of the next two years, the downward trend in freight, passenger, mail, and switching revenues was reversed. Each year new sidings were laid to reach the growing number of new industries locating facilities along the railroad. In 1916 freight traffic rose an impressive 21 percent, and even passenger revenues, somewhat in decline for the past decade, rose 2 percent. It was not enough to stave off another massive loss, however, which mushroomed to $8 million.[69]

Bierd's solution was to run fewer but longer freights. He also instituted even stricter fuel conservation programs. As a result, operating expenses rose only 5 percent. Few improvements were needed; however, a new freight house was built at Cedar City, the Carrollton passenger station was enlarged and remodeled, and the former Bloomington Shops engine repair shop was converted into a car repair facility for overhauling steel equipment. Though long since concluded, symbolically, the end of shaft mining at Braidwood was marked by the razing of the long-abandoned roundhouse there.[70]

The company continued to attract new industry. Twelve new sidings were laid during 1916, the most important of which were those to serve the Public Service Company of Northern Illinois's new power plant at Plaines, with a daily need of from 10 to 20 cars of coal.[71]

Much needed higher freight rates were finally approved in 1914, the first the ICC allowed since 1910, but they proved too meager to make much of a difference. The industry's percentage of net return that year was the smallest since records had been kept. Specific commodity rates were adjusted upward in 1916 but again proved too little. Another general increase request was filed, a more-than-justified 15 percent, but except for a small increase for coal, the larger increase was rejected.[72]

The denial of higher rates only accelerated the industry's general decline. At the start of 1917, more than 37,000 miles, about one-sixth of the nation's railroad mileage, was in the hands of receivers, among them the Wabash, Rock Island, St.LSF, and New Haven. Thousands of miles of track were up for abandonment, and hundreds more had already been abandoned. On still more, operations were suspended. Without the capital to invest, the nation's car shortage had become critical. American railroads had 20,000 fewer freight cars at the beginning of 1917 than they had in 1914. They also operated fewer locomotives.[73] Over the previous 10 years, maintenance on all roads, to varying degrees, had been deferred, limiting higher speeds and heavier movements. All the while traffic was building.

In April 1917, after anguishing for months over his decision, President Wilson reluctantly signed a declaration of war against Germany. After just a few months, it was evident that all-out mobilization was more than the railroads could handle. By the autumn of 1917, the industry was facing a crisis. The problems became most apparent on the roads serving the Atlantic ports—the B&O, Erie, Pennsylvania, and NYC. Yards of those roads became clogged with excessive tonnage. Freights were stalled on main lines waiting for yard space to open. Because of the blocked tracks, troop trains could not get to dockside.

The situation became intolerable.

The president was armed with congressional authority to take over any transportation system in case of crisis, and he now faced one. He chose the B&O's president, Daniel Willard, to lead the railroads out of the mess. The talented and respected Williard accepted, but before taking direct governmental action, he first wanted to try to convince his fellow railroad presidents to cooperatively resolve the crisis. He called together 50 of them, whose roads represented 90 percent of the nation's railroad mileage, and got them to pledge to operate America's railroads as "a continental railway system," to free up needed passenger equipment by reducing duplicate passenger train miles, to get better utilization of freight cars by maximizing use of capacity, and to relieve car shortages by freely interchanging equipment.[74] He created a five-man committee (the Railroads War Board) with the Southern Railway's chairman, Fairfax Harrison, as president.

Harrison, despite his best efforts, found it impossible to unify the railroads. None of the leaders were willing to give up equipment—in too short a supply on most roads anyway—for a coordinated effort. Congress stepped in and gave the ICC authority to direct rail car movements, but that effort too failed. Each road jealously hoarded traffic they viewed as theirs. Cars were purposely withheld from interchange, and competitors' cars were left standing instead of being returned to ensure a competitor would be shorted cars. After so many years of fierce competition, the railroads simply could not help themselves.

Finally, the ICC, unable to solve the car distribution or any of the other problems, gave up and recommended the president create a new agency to take control of the railroads. Thus, on the day after Christmas 1917, President Wilson announced creation of the United States Railroad Administration (USRA). Put in charge as director-general was secretary of the Treasury, William McAdoo. Most railroad presidents had to admit it was necessary. McAdoo now headed every railroad, water transport, and express company in the country. To compensate the railroads during the government's operation, each would be paid an annual guaranteed sum equal to the average net operating income for the three pre-

ceding years, thus eliminating any windfall profits resulting from the extraordinary wartime traffic. The USRA, with an allocation of $500 million, was to be responsible for maintenance and repair of the confiscated property, which, after return, was to be in "substantially as good repair and in substantially as complete equipment as it was at the beginning of Federal Control."[75]

Creation of the USRA generally proved a popular decision. The military saw it as a way to unsnarl and expedite traffic. Shippers anticipated a hold on rates. Labor saw it as a way to hike wages and finally see implemented the long sought eight-hour rule. For years, union leaders had been lobbying for a reduction in the number of hours their members worked. In 1907 a federal law decreed a man could work only 16 hours in a 24-hour period. The vast majority worked 10-hour days. What the unions wanted was an 8-hour-day rule imposed, for the same pay as a 10-hour day. Management claimed if the rule was implemented, tens of thousands of new workers would have to be employed. Congress stepped in and hastily passed the Adamson Act in September 1916, granting an 8-hour day as the railroad's standard, but the bill failed to lay out a plan of implementation. As McAdoo took over, the issue had still not been decided.

McAdoo first directed that all equipment be pooled as though it were owned by a single company. He decreed the shortest route for all traffic was to be used. He banned shipper routing designations, abolished existing traffic agreements, and called for new rate and wage studies. To reduce congestion at East Coast ports, he implemented rules prohibiting dispatch of trains from distant terminals until it seemed probable that prompt delivery could be made. Lightly trafficked routes became busy as traffic was diverted to them to reduce congestion on the more heavily operated lines. Studies were initiated to determine which railroad facilities might be combined for great efficiency.

McAdoo appointed numerous assistants, including Lovett as director of the Division of Betterments and Additions. Lovett immediately severed his ties with the UP to devote himself exclusively to his new duties, a role that gave him complete control over the industry's planned investments. During Lovett's absence, management of the UP and its properties, including the C&A, was turned over to vice president and controller, C. B. Seger, who served as the Alton's chairman of the board and chairman of the executive committee. Roberts Walker, the bondholder's representative, was named president and member of the executive committee of the corporation while Bierd assumed the title of USRA federal manager, the road's chief operating officer.[76]

The industry's critical car shortage was then addressed. McAdoo ordered 100,000 new freight cars (for $250 million) from 13 manufacturers who were handed standard designs for 50-ton capacity boxcars, hopper cars, and gondola cars. From that supply, the C&A was allocated 500 composite drop-bottom gondolas.[77] Twelve standard locomotive designs for eight-wheel types were produced, and three builders—American, Baldwin, and Lima—divided $60 million for the 1,930-locomotive order.[78] Initially, four of the 575 light Mikados built were designated for the C&A, but that number was increased by six when the need was demonstrated.[79]

To save fuel and free up needed main line trackage, 12 million of the nation's passenger train miles were eliminated in June 1918 through the rationalization of competitive schedules. The 15 runs operated by the four railroads serving Chicago and St. Louis—the C&A, IC, Wabash, and Chicago & Eastern Illinois (C&EI)—were reduced to nine. The *Prairie State Express* became a victim, but it was the only C&A train suspended. The others were the less popular trains of the other three roads. Withdrawal of the *Prairie State Express* resulted in annual reductions of 188,472 passenger train miles and 114,456 tons of coal consumption for the C&A.[80]

In July 1918 the three railroad-owned express companies and the four private express companies—Adams Express, American & National (which had the company's contract), Wells Fargo, and Southern Express—were consolidated into one company called the American Railway Express Company.[81] Under a single management, smoother handling of vital shipments, including government and military documents, resulted. Ownership of Railway Express was later assumed by the railroads after the USRA period ended. The C&A took a half percent position.

McAdoo became sympathetic to management's plight before his taking control after receiving briefings on the industry's past attempts to secure appropriate rates. Now as czar of the industry, he weighted all factors and, in May 1918, decreed a huge 18 percent hike in passenger fares and an even bigger 28 percent increase in freight rates.[82] At first the increases appeared to be a windfall for the railroads, but McAdoo was equally sympathetic to labor. The cost of living had jumped 40 percent between 1915 and 1917, but railroad worker wages had risen only 18 percent. The matter was corrected when McAdoo dictated wage increases from 16 to 43 percent, depending on the craft, retroactive to January 1918. He also implemented the 8-hour rule. The work rule changes, as predicted, forced the railroads to increase employment by 15 percent.[83]

McAdoo removed himself from the USRA in late 1918, turning his responsibilities over to Walker Hines, his assistant director-general. Hines implemented further rate hikes and wage increases and, by 1920, saw the average annual railroad wage climb to $1,820 from $828 five years prior. Railroad employment reached 2 million that year.[84] The exploitation of railroad labor ended. From that point on, a railroad job became very well paid and highly prized.

After months of stalemated trench warfare, the Great War ended with the signing of an armistice on November 11, 1918. One might have expected the war to have been a tonic for the company's ills, but, in fact, the appreciably greater revenues enjoyed during the 26 months of USRA control were almost solely the result of higher rates, not increased traffic. Though greatly reduced, deficits continued to accumulate. Because wartime traffic was largely eastbound and the USRA mandated direct routes, the C&A did not see as much critical traffic as did other roads. Carloads that otherwise would have been taken to Chicago were instead interchanged at Springfield, Bloomington, and Joliet with roads headed to eastern ports, reducing the C&A's share of revenues. As traffic subsided in the early postwar years, gross ton miles and the number of passengers carried both declined by 7 percent in 1918 and ton miles by 9 percent; in 1919 passengers carried declined by 7 percent.[85]

Compounding the problems of less tonnage and fewer passengers carried were the higher labor expense and cost of new government-mandated safety appliances mandated for equipment and power. The company's operating ratio under USRA management rose from 74 percent in 1917 to 85 percent in 1920. The $20.5 million in revenue taken in during 1917 rose to $24.3 million the following year and again to $25.2 million in 1919, but operating expenses rose even faster, from $20.5 million in 1917 to $23.5 million in 1919.[86]

Though hostilities were ended, USRA control continued for another 16 months as the troops and salvageable materiel were brought home. During the postwar years and before USRA control lapsed, the fate of America's railroads was debated. McAdoo was among those who advocated nationalization. Labor leaders had their own ideas and advocated turnover of the railroads to the workers. Only one issue was agreed to by all: the severe restrictions placed on the industry preceding takeover needed to be reexamined if a thriving postwar industry was to result.

This was not a new issue. As early as 1915, President Wilson called for a review of railroad regulations, but though hearings were held over the course of the next two years, the higher priority of buildup for the coming war overshadowed the testimony, and the matter languished. It was only after McAdoo, in December 1918, called for continued government control for the next five years and Glen Plumb—a railroad law specialist and legal counsel for the four railroad operating unions—proposed government purchase of all the lines with management turned over to a board of government officials, labor leaders, and railroad executives that serious attention was paid the matter.

The public was generally against the Plumb proposal; only railroad labor, which had benefited so greatly from USRA management, fully endorsed the idea. Daniel Williard and president of the New Haven, Howard Elliot, became the industry's spokesmen and pushed for full restoration to private ownership with federal regulation taking precedent over the myriad of state regulatory bodies. They advocated legislation that would require the ICC to authorize adequate rates that would attract fresh capital and meet wage and transportation costs. Disputes with labor, they suggested, could be resolved through collective bargaining supervised by a board—comprised of labor, industry, and public representatives—under a new secretary of transportation. President Wilson sided with them.

During 1919 Congress debated a long-term solution. In the House, Congressman John Esch of Wisconsin, and in the Senate, Albert Cummins of Iowa, chairman of the Senate Committee on Interstate Commerce, both introduced comprehensive bills based on the earlier hearings testimony. Anticipating the legislation, Wilson, on December 24, announced that the nation's railroads would be returned to private ownership on March 1, 1920. On February 28, 1920, the day before the railroads were officially returned to their owners, President Wilson signed the bill, which became known as the Transportation Act of 1920, the basis for railroad regulation for the next 60 years.

The more mundane aspects of the bill guaranteed the industry positive operating earnings for a six-month transition period (from March 1 to September 1, 1920). Far more sweeping changes addressed the past prohibitions against railroad consolidation. The act allowed a railroad to acquire another through lease, stock ownership, or merger, provided the ICC found the arrangement in the public interest. Pooling of traffic revenues was legalized, and railroads were made exempt from antitrust legislation to the extent necessary for combinations. The only restriction on a merger was that it had to conform to a plan the bill directed the ICC to create that would group various roads into regional systems, a proviso intended to definitively solve the weak road problem.

The commission was charged with setting both minimum and maximum rates, assuring railroads "a fair rate of return," a total reversal from past practices, based on valuation figures that the ICC had been gathering since 1913. Now instead of acting as an adversary, the ICC was to act as the industry's advocate, affirming a "fair" return to every road honestly and economically managed. Initially, this return was set at 5.5 percent with one-half of any excess earnings recaptured by the government and placed in a reserve fund from which needy roads could apply at 6 percent interest. This was key for the railroads. Daniel Willard especially was pleased, having fostered the idea.[87] The ICC was recognized as the arbitrator over state agencies on issues relevant to interstate commerce matters, something management sought. The commission was also given authority to rule on the appropriateness of the issuance of any railroad security or assumption of any indebtedness related to a lease arrangement, something both Wall Street and the general public applauded.

The workers were not ignored. The Transportation Act of 1920 created the Railroad Labor Board (RLB). If disputes between management and labor arose, they could take the matter to the RLB, which, though having no enforcement power, could rely on public opinion to pressure acceptance. The Labor Board was also charged with establishing just and reasonable wage levels, salaries, and working conditions. The unions were satisfied.

The act was the most sweeping and far reaching transportation legislation yet passed, intended to bring industry and government into a partnership never before seen in the country. It was a constructive piece of legislation that defined the relationship between private enterprise and the nation's government for years to come. It could be argued, as later events would show, that the industry was not always well served, but compared to the contentious relationship that prevailed before the act, it was a master stroke of balanced government involvement in the affairs of industry. There was nothing in the bill intended to do anything but help the railroads flourish, investors regain confidence, and laborers achieve dignity.

The USRA can legitimately be applauded for its near-total success in operating the railroads during a difficult period. It can also be recognized for advancing the case for standardization of rolling stock and power, something Huntington and Harriman had fostered nearly 20 years earlier. But the agency also showed how, when profits and return on investment were left out of the equation, costs could overwhelm results. During the 26 months of USRA control, American railroads collectively lost $1.2 billion.

Because of the shortage of capital, labor, and materials, few improvements to the C&A property beyond what was absolutely neces-

sary were made between 1917 and 1918. Both having fallen to fire in 1917 and 1918, respectively, the depots at Armstrong and Godfrey were replaced—the only significant projects undertaken during those two years. In 1919 the pace of improvements quickened. Though not actually rebuilt, much needed capacity was added at three important yards. Bierd was increased to a 245-car capacity; Venice, to 380 cars; and Slater, to 105. At Kansas City, a larger brick freight house, including division operating offices, was erected. A new freight and passenger depot was finished at Chenoa—a joint facility with the TP&W—and at Wood River, a new freight house—jointly owned with the CCC&St.L—was opened. New, larger water tanks were erected at Griggs, Lawndale, and Blue Springs. And there was the promise of added traffic with the laying of 12 more industrial sidings, the most important being the three-and-a-half-mile branch from Anderson to Schoper to reach a new Standard Oil of Indiana mine.

Standard Oil was emerging as one of the C&A's largest coal customers. Two years earlier the oil company bought the 800-ton-a-day producer, Carlinville Coal, to supply its Kansas City, Wood River, and Whiting, Indiana, refineries. Standard Oil started a second mine about a mile north of Carlinville, which was soon producing about 900 tons a day, and bought a lot of land three miles north and four miles east of Carlinville, where it planned to sink a new mine. Two other railroads in the area, the IC and the CCC&St.L, also sought the traffic, but the C&A won out.

To get the business, the C&A had to make some hefty concessions. It agreed to provide 50-minute miner train shuttle service between Carlinville and the mines. Standard Oil had threatened to build its own interurban electric line unless the railroad agreed. Standard Oil also sought extension of the second main line from its mines to Nilwood for the traffic headed to Argo, where the Whiting traffic would be interchanged with the Indiana Harbor Belt. The railroad was also expected to extend a second main south of Carlinville for runs to Wood River. Kansas City traffic moved over the air line and then on to Kansas City. To ensure enough equipment would be available, the railroad agreed to commit to adding 300 coal cars by January 1, 1921. With fingers crossed, management looked forward to long, heavy trains again. When all three mines were fully operational, 10,000 daily tons of new business, worth $3 million annually, was expected.[88] The new operations were a boon for Carlinville. In 1917 the town had a population of some 3,600. A year later, once Standard Oil finished a new subdivision of 156 two-story miners' cottages, Carlinville's population had ballooned to 4,600.[89]

About three miles north of Carlinville, some existing track was rearranged and extended, two 3,000-foot-long tracks and a half-mile-long drill track were added, and a small yard—exclusively for Standard Oil coal business—emerged. The extension to the Schoper mine came next. Seven miles of second track were added to the main line from Rinaker (south of Carlinville) to Bierd. In 1920 the four miles of second track between Bierd and Nilwood were finished.

The company had made a sizable investment in improvements for Standard Oil, but one promise made that could not be kept was delivering the 500 coal cars. The oil company needed regular, timely deliveries, something the C&A failed to demonstrate it could do for the North Western. To protect its investment, Standard Oil proposed financing the purchases and—to make sure there was power to haul them—five modern Mikados as well. It would be a five-year deal worth $1.7 million including interest. To help the railroad pay them back, an arrangement called for a credit of $8.16 for each carload of Whiting coal that was shipped until the loan was paid off.[90]

The five American Mikados ordered were copies of the 10 USRA locomotives already on the property and the last new steam power of any type the company would receive. Like the other 2-8-2s, they had large engine numbers applied to the tender (a style adopted for all tenders when the first 2-8-2s arrived) but had the wording "Standard Oil Co. Owner" under the cab windows and "Standard Oil Co. (Indiana) Owner" along the tender frame, unique markings not seen on any other equipment in American railroading. The composite coal gondolas, which came in staggered deliveries from February to June 1921, were General American Car products. To cut costs, 344 sets of reclaimed trucks and brake gear off scrapped cars were employed by the builder.[91]

The four-year-old East St. Louis freight house had been destroyed by fire in November 1918 and in 1920 was replaced, as was a depot at Grain Valley, its predecessor also a fire victim. One hundred thousand–gallon water tanks were erected at Glasgow and Mexico. The yearly laying of approximately 75 miles of 90-pound rail continued during the year, and a four-mile second track was laid between Manchester and Roodhouse to relieve congestion there. Extension of the second main line was started between Brighton and Godfrey. The number of new industries locating along the railroad doubled in 1920 over the already impressive 12 in 1919. Superior Alum at South Joliet saw a multi-track installation, and an 80-car storage yard for the Solomon Brothers' Panther Creek Mine at Lefton (located between Springfield and Auburn) was added. Of the total 67,540 daily tons that the 51 mines on all three divisions produced, 93 percent was coming from the 34 mines between Athol and Carlinville. The daily 3,000-ton capacity of Panther Creek Mine ranked it among the largest the C&A served. Only two of the four Peabody mines at Auburn exceeded it, by 1,000 daily tons each. The new traffic was welcomed, but overall, business generated was not nearly enough. Like the industry at large, the C&A saw a steady erosion of traffic during the postwar era.[92]

A *Railway Age* writer described the year 1921 in its annual review of the industry's performance: "There have been bad years in the history of the railways of the United States before. In most respects 1921 was much the worst of all."[93] The industry's net return was 2.75 percent (the narrowest of margins for any year since 1894 except for 1920 when returns were guaranteed), well under the 5.5 percent the government now figured railroads were entitled to earn. Both freight and passenger traffic were off 23 percent, a figure that far exceeded the single-digit declines experienced for most years from 1910 to 1917. The industry's net operating income of $616 million was $24 million less than the $640 million needed to cover debt payments. The situation would have been even worse had a general rate increase early in the year not been approved.

The cause was the inevitable readjustment during the postwar years. The country's economy weakened as farmers and industries readjusted to peacetime needs. Prices for most farm products had dropped sharply, and that factor, combined with increased shipping rates, made it difficult for most farmers to make any profit at all. Postwar reductions in industrial production and the switch from a wartime to a peacetime economy resulted in fewer carloads. Factories used less fuel, and that meant less coal. All roads suffered, but especially those—such as the C&A—that were mainly dependent upon coal and products of the land for traffic.

Along with the challenge of a weaker economy, railroads were increasingly challenged by truckers and bus operators. As the new decade dawned, railroads throughout the East and Midwest faced greater competition. Many states, including Illinois, were aggressively pushing paved road programs. Most of the primary highways were laid parallel to rail lines. Ironically, like gladiators giving treats to the lions, the railroads brought the equipment, gravel, cement, bridge beams, and other needs of the contractors to job sites—and even laid temporary sidings—but once the work was finished, those carloads disappeared. By 1922 there were some 100,000 trucks and buses registered in Illinois and almost 700,000 automobiles.[94] Though Missouri's registered vehicles were fewer in number, the new competition in that state was just as troubling. Locomotive engineers now regularly saw Ford Model Ts, White buses, and Mack and Graham Bros. trucks pacing their trains. Railroads were no longer the only game in town.

The number of miles of new track the industry laid in 1921 was lower than that added in 1920, the industry's previous low point for new mileage. More miles of track were abandoned than ever before. Orders for new locomotives and rolling stock were at record lows. The general malaise of the industry was reflected in a comparison of 1917 and 1921 C&A results. Gross ton miles exceeded 6.5 million in 1917 but declined to 5.9 million in 1921. During the same period, operating expenses almost doubled, from $15 million to $26 million.[95] Interestingly, the C&A's operating costs (as a percentage of revenues) were very similar to those of the mighty NYC and UP, but the much longer runs of those roads and the greater contribution from higher rated manufactured products they carried contrasted sharply with the company's relatively short runs and dependency on lower rated coal, 55 percent of all tonnage moved. Had it not been for a sizeable coal commodity rate increase in August 1920, the situation would have been much worse.

There was little Bierd could do about the loss of business, but he could control transportation costs, and he did. He reduced local freight train miles and secondary passenger service mileage to a minimum. He restricted branchline service to every-other-day runs. He also reduced the labor force. Hundreds of yardmen, roundhouse service workers, and clerical employees were laid off. He saved $2 million as a result, but deficits continued to build.[96]

The pace at which new industries had been added to the territory each of the previous 10 years continued to grow. In 1921, 25 industrial sidings were installed, including coal car storage tracks for the Nason Coal mine at Lefton. At Chicago the new Harrison Street Terminal and General Offices were finished after four years of intermittent work, interrupted by labor and material shortages during the war. "This building . . . is modern in every respect and will meet the Company's requirements as to such facilities for many years to come," Bierd told the stockholders.[97] It was the first phase of a major project to reconfigure the West Side Union Station complex and erect a new terminal and adjoining office building. Though nothing was spent that could not be justified on the basis of bringing in new business, or that was not made necessary by unplanned events—such as the too frequent loss of property to fire—and though every effort was made to reduce transportation costs, the financial well-being of the C&A had become precarious. Only the UP skipping demands for payments on the subordinated mortgage had allowed the company to stay out of the courts since being released from USRA control. How long such a prospect could be held off was soon to be answered.

The Long-Anticipated Receivership Arrives

Chicago Union Station replaced the 44-year-old former depot that was located just a few blocks north along the Chicago River. All tracks were below street level to permit continuation of streets to the city's west side and level passage of trains of both the CA&E and Chicago's elevated trains. CUS was owned by the Pennsylvania, Milwaukee Road, and Burlington. The C&A was only a tenant. (Courtesy of Chicago Historical Society)

It had taken a few years following the end of the war for the nation to adjust and regain momentum before the economy again turned robust. The speculative, high prices of goods and services that prevailed preceding and immediately after the war gave way to reduced wholesale prices as demand for capital goods lessened. Unemployment rose and personal incomes fell. Once America's industry adjusted, sought-after consumer goods—especially automobiles and new appliances for the home such as clothes washers, refrigerators, and radios—helped fuel a resurgence. There was a wave of new residential and commercial building. Farmers, though now fewer in num-

ber, produced increased yields. By 1922 the country was beginning to regain its balance.

The Democrats had lost the presidential election of 1920 as voters rejected Wilson's efforts for sustained world peace and instead voted for a return to the prewar status quo. Now sitting in the White House was Republican Warren Harding, an amiable, handsome Ohioan with an undistinguished political career, who had become his party's compromise candidate. He was anxious to offend no one and was well suited to the mood of the times. The American people had had enough of foreign entanglements and government action; they wanted to get on with their lives. Harding said what the country needed was "normalcy." With less than 10 percent of the world's population, the United States accounted for 25 percent of the world's goods. Somewhat more than 40 percent of everything manufactured in the world came from America's industry.[1] The country was about to enter an era of unprecedented comfortable times.

Unfortunately for the C&A, dependent far more on products of the land than on manufactured goods (industrial products now represented only 9 percent of total traffic carried), the railroad did not enjoy the upsurge in traffic that other roads—especially those in the East—enjoyed during the postwar period. Any hopes for better results in 1922 were dashed in early spring when it became apparent that the nation's coal miners, united as never before, were adamant for higher wages and improved working conditions and planned to strike. On April 1 both anthracite and bituminous coal miners walked off their jobs. For the next five months, little tonnage was produced. Not a ton of coal was raised at any of the 54 mines the railroad served.[2] Since coal tonnage was 49 percent of the road's total freight tonnage, the strike proved devastating. President Bierd anticipated a three-month strike, stockpiled a coal supply, and curtailed all but essential expenditures, but when the strike continued on into the late summer months, it became obvious the road was facing a breaking point.

In the midst of the coal strike, a newspaper report appeared, claiming the company would soon be merging with its longtime dancing partner, the MKT. The 10-year on-again, off-again romance the two supposedly had was being rumored again. Seemingly adding substance to the rumor was the Katy's recent withdrawal from the Kansas City Terminal, which to some observers indicated that the road expected to use its intended partner's membership to enter Kansas City Union Station. The *Chicago Daily Journal of Commerce* in June reported that "negotiations have reached the point where the equipment for the merger is being prepared. The higher officials of both systems are pushing the details in preparation for an early unification."[3] The rumors were intriguing, but neither C. E. Schaff, president of the Katy, nor Bierd ever made a public declaration confirming talks. It is certain that Bierd

was looking for a way out of what increasingly looked like the collapse of his railroad, but no talks leading to a bailout ever reached fruition.

The lingering and debilitating coal strike alone would have been enough to throw the company into receivership, but more trouble came on July 1, 1922, when railroad machinists, blacksmiths, sheet metal workers, boilermakers, electrical workers, car men, and their helpers went on strike to protest the RLB's proposed 10 percent cut in wages, changes in work rules, and abandonment of existing seniority rules. Picket lines immediately formed at company shops of railroads throughout the country. Management hired replacements, further enraging the strikers. Matters quickly turned ugly. Four days into the strike, militant union members seized the shops at Slater, and 25 nonunion replacement workers the company had hired were chased out of town. Missouri National Guardsmen were called in to protect the property. A few days later, strikers at Bloomington staged a peaceful demonstration, but the fear of violence was such that five National Guard units were called in to keep the peace. When 300 replacement workers showed up in mid-July, a large number of the 2,500 striking workers turned violent and began a slugging and shooting incident. No one was killed or seriously injured, but sporadic violence continued to erupt at Bloomington and shops on all three divisions. Operating employees, engineers, firemen, and conductors had not joined the shop workers, but they were sympathetic, so when machine gun nests were positioned around the Bloomington Shops buildings and the patrolling of the property by Guard troops became oppressive, crews refused to report for their runs. Only court injunctions forced the trainmen to capitulate.[4]

In early August 1922, a national agreement between the soft coal mine owners and the mine workers was reached, but Indiana and Illinois members of the UMW refused to ratify the new contract. They wanted even higher wages. On August 22 a local agreement was reached, finally ending the 145-day-old strike. Whistles were sounded throughout southern Illinois once again, signaling resumption of work. The prolonged dispute had cost Illinois mine operators $25 million in lost production; the miners never recovered their lost earnings.[5]

Though the soft coal miner strike was ended (the anthracite miners were still holding out), the shop workers' dispute continued. By early August the federal government had not yet stepped in to settle the strike, and railroad officials began expressing their frustration publicly. "The underlying principle at stake and the principle we are fighting for is that this condition which causes these continuous strikes has gone on long enough and public interest demands this condition be ended," Bierd declared in a letter printed on the front page of the *Wall Street Journal*. "Public interest will be served only if the strike is beaten and railroad strikers are taught a lesson they will never forget."[6]

By mid-August, a hesitant President Warren Harding was prepared to go to Congress to settle the shop workers' strike. Though he did not definitively outline what he would seek, there were reports that he was considering a government takeover of the railroads. Emboldened by the prospect, which he knew the railroads dreaded, Warren Stone, president of the locomotive engineers and chief railway union spokesman, invited De Witt Cuyler, president of the Association of Railway Executives, to negotiate. The talks went on for a week.

On August 22 the executives of most of America's railroads (but not Bierd and others opposed to any settlement granting the unions what they sought) met in New York for an update on what had been accomplished. That night several sticks of dynamite were thrown onto the roof of the Venice roundhouse, causing an explosion that was reported to have shaken buildings three miles away.[7] Four days later negotiations were broken off with the unions and management no closer to a settlement. Once again there were attacks on company property. The roundhouses at Roodhouse and Slater and bridges at Drake and Virden were dynamited.[8] The violence became national news. The next day, President Harding announced that, unless the strike ended, he would indeed ask Congress for power to take over some of the railroads as well as the anthracite mines.

Claiming the railroad was now an unsafe place to work, crews at Roodhouse refused to report. Their action shut down the Western Division. No freight moved, and passenger trains out of Chicago to Kansas City had to be routed through St. Louis. Firemen at Slater now joined those at Roodhouse in refusing to work. A union bulletin was issued. "Effective this date [August 26, 1922], firemen of Slater lodge no. 18, are remaining away from company property until guard stations are changed to our satisfaction and until federal inspectors are on duty and pronounce all engines O.K. on this division and in a safe condition."[9] The next day not a single train moved in or out of Kansas City. The unauthorized strikes on the Western Division prompted Brotherhood of Railroad Trainmen president W. G. Lee to send a telegram warning the members of Lodge 44 at Roodhouse that their action could cause the loss of their charter unless they returned to work. His warning persuaded some, but not all, to return.[10]

Matters got ugly when a union fireman refused to work the mail train, no. 19, after a crew change at Slater. A nonunion shop worker was found willing to fire the train and he, along with the engineer and two deputy U.S. marshals riding in the cab to protect the volunteer fireman, got as far as Marshall, where the train was met by a crowd of strikers from Slater. They had gotten there by automobile ahead of the train and blocked its movement. Management had to work *The Hummer* from Roodhouse to Bloomington. Nearly 100 passengers were aboard the August 26 run. The train arrived in Bloomington 20 hours late, and there were still 200 other would-be passengers left stranded at Roodhouse. Again, not a single train, passenger or freight, moved between Roodhouse and Kansas City for the next three days.[11]

At first the industry's 400,000 maintenance-of-way workers had declined to join the shopmen's strike, but in late August, union president E. F. Grable announced that he would ask the RLB to authorize a minimum wage of 48 cents an hour, the wartime rate, up from the current rate of 23 to 35 cents and, if denied, his men would walk. His threat only added to the contentious confrontation.[12] The *Wall Street Journal* on August 30, 1922, reported:

Chicago & Alton preferred sold off to 11 5/8, while the general rail list was strong. This price compared with Tuesday's high of 14 7/8. Weakness in Alton stocks the past few days has not surprised those who have studied the company's position, though the break of three points Tuesday in the 3 1/2% bonds had the appearance of reflecting definite developments. Some sort of readjustment of Alton's capital has been indicated for years. The company has not paid interest on its $16 million general 6s for five or six years and only the fact that the issue is closely held by Union Pacific and a banking house has prevented the usual result of such a default. The road's troubles with train employees have now been patched up and appear not to be a serious factor in the situation, though they may well have caused some selling.[13]

Bierd read the morning paper as he prepared to participate in perhaps the most disappointing meeting he ever attended. He knew the dire straits of the company better than the reporter. He was in New York to meet with John Mitchell, Robert Lovett, and representatives of Kuhn, Loeb. The previous day a petition for receivership was filed by one of the road's suppliers, the Texas Oil Company, for $33,000 the company owed. Texas Oil was but one of many vendors who could have filed. At this point the company owed an estimated $14 million.[14] The bankers, Lovett, and Bierd had gathered to announce bankruptcy. The news reached traders on Wall Street, and panic selling in the road's already downtrodden securities ensued. Nearly 30,000 shares of common stock were sold with few buyers to stem the downward spiral, dropping the price to 5 7/8. Preferred shares dropped 3 1/8 points, closing at session's end at 9 1/2. The company bonds too were hard hit. The 3 1/2s closed at 42, and the 3s dropped 5 1/4, to 58 1/4.[15]

Judge George Carpenter in the District Court of the United States for the Northern District Eastern Division at Chicago, on August 30, approved Texas Oil's petition, declared the company insolvent, and immediately appointed Bierd and W. W. Wheelock, an Alton director and Chicago attorney, receivers. The night before the receivership was declared, Silas Strawn, the road's counsel, prepared a statement that was released on the nation's news wires following Carpenter's decree:

The Chicago and Alton Railroad has for several years been unable to meet all of the interest on its 6 per cent general mortgage bonds, but the holders of these bonds have permitted the interest to remain unpaid in hope that general railroad conditions ultimately would adjust themselves in such a way as to restore the property to an assured and reasonable prosperity.

The directors, however, have been hopeful that these conditions soon would approach more nearly to normal, or would, in part at least, be met by offsetting factors of a helpful character. But such excessive costs bear particularly heavy on short railroads with expensive terminals, such as the Alton, which operates a little more than 1,000 miles and has terminals in the three great cities of Chicago, St. Louis and Kansas City, with an average freight haul of only 185 miles and an average passenger haul of only 65 miles.

The receivership at the present time, however, was precipitated by the great falling off in earnings due to the coal strike and also to the further long continued and extra expense due to the shopmen's strike. The company's normal coal traffic is heavy, and practically all mines on its line had been closed since April 1, thus entailing heavy loss in revenue, and at the same time it has been compelled to buy much of its fuel coal from southern fields, which, with added freight charges paid foreign lines, cost it two or three times the former price. Through these concurring losses in revenue and unusual expenses the company has fallen behind, exhausted its current resources, and is not able to continue operations without accumulating a large floating debt, which the directors did not feel justified to incur and probably could not have incurred. The board of directors therefore felt that no other course was open to them than to acquiesce in a receivership for the preservation of the property in the interest of creditors and security holders.[16]

An analysis of the railroad's securities in the August 31 *Wall Street Journal* speculated on the prospects for investors after a reorganization. According to the paper's expert, holders of the $45,350,000 worth of 3 percent bonds, due to mature in 1949, stood the best chance of coming out unscathed. The bonds were secured by a first mortgage on most of the property, and in the paper's opinion, "There would be little chance of disturbing this lien. . . . The worst that holders could suffer would be temporary loss of interest or a delay in the payment of coupons." The $22 million of 3 1/2s, due to mature in 1950, were somewhat more vulnerable since only 85 miles of the railroad, the air line, and the former St.LP&N, were pledged as collateral. While there appeared to be sufficient assets to cover their redemption, the reporter found it "questionable whether it is sufficient to save the holders from the necessity of accepting a lesser form of security in a reorganization." As for the $16,834,000 of 6s to mature in 1932 held by the UP and by Kuhn, Loeb, the prospects were poor. "It is not likely that the bonds would fare better in a reorganization than the first lien 3 1/2s, and they are not entitled to fare as well." The holders of either preferred or common shares "could hardly expect anything out of them except what they paid for in the way of an assessment, and this would very likely exceed the present market price of either issue."[17] Such analyses did little to steady the market.

On the second day of bond trading following the road's default, the 3 1/2s opened at 33 1/2, off 8 1/2 points. The 3s fell from 56 1/2 to 51, a break of 4 1/4 points. Security prices of other roads the traders judged vulnerable also suffered. The shares of the CGW, M&St.L, Western Maryland, Katy, Seaboard Air Line, and some others all sustained temporary losses until it was realized they were not as bad off as the C&A.[18]

Within days, two committees made up of insurance company officials holding the 3 and 3 1/2 interest bonds were formed. It took the stockholders a bit longer, but by December they too had petitioned, seeking restitution of $598,912 they alleged was wrongfully appropriated shortly before the road fell into the receivers' hands instead of rightfully to the KCSt.L&C. The estate of William Slater was a principal holder of that road's preferred stock.[19]

Bierd knew there was no prospect of the railroad ever generating enough revenue to cover its heavy debt burden. The local, short-haul passenger traffic that had been a staple of the road's passenger business had continued to migrate to the automobile and bus lines. The decline of short-haul freight and express also continued as the number of commercial truckers increased. Long-haul passenger business was still strong, and there had been a recent upturn in through freight, but neither source of traffic, added to the road's staple commodity of coal, would yield enough to allow the road to return from court jurisdiction as a viable, independent carrier.

On September 1 Attorney General Harry Daugherty got a temporary federal court injunction ending the strike of the industry's 300,000 shopmen and sought a permanent injunction. It was the most sweeping action against labor in the country's history. In his brief Daugherty cited the estimated $1 million cost of the 45,500 marshals and guardsmen that had been called out to maintain order. He stated $75 million worth of California's fruit crop had been spoiled because of lack of freight service, and 45,000 loads of coal had been stalled at Somerset, Kentucky. More than 1,000 mail trains had been annulled during the strike, disrupting service. He estimated that 50 percent of the industry's locomotives had been vandalized. Lastly, he pointed to the C&A's failure as evidence of the strike's harmful effects. What he did not mention, though, was the strikers' loss of $100 million in wages.[20]

Two weeks later headlines in newspapers across the country proclaimed the end of the strike. "Peace on 50 Railway Lines" (there were actually 53 who settled) was splashed across the front page of the *Chicago Daily Tribune*. But there was no settlement on some other of the biggest and most important lines; the UP, SP, Rock Island, Pennsylvania, N&W, NP, GN, and the C&A had not joined their brethren. The presidents of those lines were adamantly opposed to the terms of the agreement, which called for all those who struck to return to their jobs at the same level of pay and with the same seniority they had previously. Bierd and the others wanted retribution. They continued to hold out.[21]

Several weeks passed before those still on strike were no longer able to resist. They returned with a minimal pay raise and no assurance that their seniority would be preserved. Bierd and the others had won a victory, but at a terrible price. "They [the shop workers] went out for more money," Ray Eisenberg, a 54-year career Bloomington

Shop craftsman later recalled. "We got more pay, not too much more, about a nickel more an hour." Ralph Fisher, a 52-year career employee, remembered "I was off for three months and two weeks. We lost the strike and we had to come back to work."[22] Bierd's tough stance and the presence of scabs who stayed on after the strike caused bitterness among the workers that lingered for a long time. The strike of 1922 was the low point in company-labor relations.

The duel disruptions of the miner and shopmen strikes quite naturally adversely affected that year's results. The company racked up a $2.5 million deficit.[23] But despite the turmoil, seven more miles of the second main line between Godfrey and Brighton was completed, as was a little over a mile between Roodhouse and Manchester. A new safety measure the ICC had mandated, installation of automatic train control in high speed corridors (such as between Chicago and Springfield), saw National Safety Appliance equipment installed on 14 miles of main line between Lexington and Normal. A structure repainting program was started, which changed the former chocolate brown and cream scheme to colors described as "steel grey with Irish green trim," the scheme used for the next 50 years.[24] Before year's end, Bierd, as receiver, got court approval to borrow $2 million with the court's guarantee to pay the most pressing bills, the repair of 24 engines and 500 pieces of equipment (including 400 coal hoppers) and the laying of 15 more miles of 90-pound rail.[25]

Perhaps a fitting, symbolic end to an already disastrous year came in late December 1922, just before the Christmas holiday, with the wreck of the *Alton Limited*. On December 20 five of the train's eight cars left the rails within the city limits of Alton alongside the fences of the Illinois Glass Company. An equalizer frame of the second truck of the engine's tender had snapped and was dragged until it tore up a rail that caught the underside of the first car, derailing it and causing the remainder of the train to leave the rails. All of the equipment sustained damage, the diner the most. It took two days for the track to be repaired.[26] The next year had to be better.

And so it was, with gross income and net operating revenue turning out to be the best in the company's history. The year's results, however, were illusionary and proved to be the high point reached during receivership—in no small measure due to the extraordinary coal traffic moved that year to make up for the shortfall in 1922 when only 1.5 million tons of coal were handled. Because of pent-up demand, coal tonnage rose to 5.8 million tons, more than 500,000 tons greater than in 1921, which had seen the previous highest figure. If 1923 results were averaged with those of the abnormal year of 1922, however, neither would have been much different than the declining years that preceded them. Nevertheless, the operating ratio had dropped almost 12 percent to 76 in 1923, and virtually every measure of freight traffic increased by double digits, though the average revenue per ton and ton mile measures declined 5 and 6 cents, respectively. Most passenger measures too were up significantly, except again average revenue per mile, down $1.29.[27]

Four miles from Titus to Reddish Road with a two-mile branch from Bakersfield to East Hardin—a town that until then had been served only by boats—was opened in November 1923. Two years later a two-story freight and passenger depot was erected at East Hardin. The extension, though modest, was expected to produce 1,500 annual carloads of wheat and apples that grew in abundance there. The $217,000 cost of the new construction was divided equally between the railroad and the Nutwood District Improvement Association and the Calhoun Improvement Association, the latter two groups contributing the right-of-way, bridge piling and timber, telegraph poles, and timber for cattle guards, fences, and ties.[28]

During the first year of court protection, an impressive number of industries located or expanded along the C&A, including, ironically, a Texas Company refinery at Lockport and Federal Ice at Mason City. Relief from paying its mortgages also permitted accelerated improvements. At Marshall, a frame freight house and team track were finished. A new brick and stucco freight and passenger station was opened at Mason City, and a brick station at Normal (shared with the IC) and a small joint depot with the NYC at Wood River were under construction. The double track north of Lawndale was moved to a new lower grade.

Springfield's Ridgely Yard, where Peoria and Springfield District coal traffic was classified, had been taxed beyond its limits for years but now got longer classification and storage tracks and upgraded facilities. Enlargement and extension of the Bloomington yard was also started. The main line was changed to run around to the east of the yard tracks, eliminating the slow running of through trains and delays to switching moves. New and longer yard tracks were also laid at Carlinville, Joliet, and Slater.[29]

The government had promised to return the equipment and properties the USRA took over in the same condition they had found them, but some railroads found it otherwise. The USRA deferred maintenance forced Bierd to spend a total of $10.1 million, $3.6 million more than on average spent in any year since 1914, for engine and car repairs. So much work had to be done that neither the Bloomington Shops nor the smaller facilities could handle it all. Bierd was forced to turn to outside contractors. Fifty-three percent of the freight car fleet was repaired and had added ICC-mandated safety appliances such as Cardwell friction draft gear and steel draft arms, ladders, and grab irons. A total of 2,253 cars were rebuilt, and nearly 5,000 others received light to heavy repairs.[30] The passenger fleet got similar attention. One hundred eighty-four of the 212 cars the road owned received heavy or medium repairs. Of the fleet of 340 engines, 80 percent were rebuilt or repaired. Superheaters, the addition of which had started a few years earlier, were added to those road engines that had not yet gotten them. Fifteen of the best remaining Moguls (built in 1899) were converted to simple 0-6-0 switchers.[31]

At the end of 1923, 63 railroads were in receivership, five fewer than the previous year.[32] But one of the roads that emerged from receivership that year was the Clover Leaf. The road had been under court protection for 11 years largely because of the challenges raised by those holding the collateral bonds used to take control of the C&A. When those bonds matured in 1917, liability for them was renounced, but a settlement reached in late 1921 turned them over to the road's bondholders just a few months before the Alton's collapse. Within a year, the TSt.L&W was taken over by the New York, Chicago & St. Louis (NYC&St.L).

Paved highway programs and increased automobile ownership continued to erode local C&A traffic. "In all the territory . . . there has been a very marked increase in public road improvements. This has resulted in a very heavy increase of travel on the highways by automobiles. . . . As a result, much of our short haul . . . passenger business has gone to the public highways and the management because of state regulations and local demands, has not been able to reduce its local train service fully to meet the loss of local traffic," Bierd stated in the 1924 annual report.[33] Cut back in some cases to a single car, local trains were running up big losses. Ridership between Chicago and St. Louis, however, remained healthy despite strong competition. Passenger counts at St. Louis were helped appreciably by connecting business travelers coming up from the oil fields and cotton farms of the Southwest, along with tourists visiting the Alamo at San Antonio. The company's trains enjoyed a 50 percent market share of the Chicago–St. Louis business, thanks largely to the popularity of the finest train operated between the cities, the daylight running *Alton Limited*.[34] The train had been a traveler's favorite since it was introduced in 1899, but the *Limited*'s equipment had become outdated. The cars were wooden, and this was the Steel Age. Though exquisitely appointed, the train's features lacked the passenger comforts now found on more modern equipment. The two original consists (and cars added in 1905) had run up millions of miles of service and, with rebuilding, could knock off many more profitable miles, but competing roads had plans to introduce new equipment on faster schedules, posing a threat to the *Limited*'s dominance. Had the railroad still been on its own and not under court supervision, there would not have been enough capital to replace the obsolete *Limiteds,* and the road's undisputed lead would likely have been overtaken. Instead, in late 1923, the courts granted Bierd a $1 million receiver's certificate to cover the cost of 18 new steel cars.

The cars Pullman produced were remarkable for their beauty and comforts, but especially because of their length, the longest cars the manufacturer had yet turned out. The

A million dollars was spent to reequip the *Alton Limited.* The investment proved worth it, for the 18 cars Pullman delivered were some of the finest yet produced, including the exceptionally long parlor-observation cars *St. Louis* and *Chicago,* shown here. (Kenneth Donnelly Coll.)

mail cars were 66 feet, like those they replaced, but the passenger-carrying cars measured 84 feet over buffers. Each car bore a name but not a number (though numbers were included in internal records). The two Railway Post Office cars, the *Henderson* and *Armstrong,* were named for the second assistant postmaster general and the 1864 originator of the RPO, when Armstrong was assistant postmaster in Chicago. The mail cars, like the other 16 cars in the order, rode on Pullman Standard six-wheel trucks and were heated with a Chicago Vapor system.

The combination baggage and 48-seat smoker cars, the *Illinois* and *Missouri,* were named for the two states the road served. The passenger section seats were cushioned in leather. Sidewalls were finished in wood, like the parlor and chair cars, giving the interiors a warm and inviting appearance. The four 84-seat chair cars, the *Webster Groves, University City, Oak Park,* and *Evanston,* all named for suburbs of St. Louis and Chicago, had non-reversible seats with higher backs than those in the smoker and were upholstered in green mohair. The two 36-seat diners, the *Springfield* and *Bloomington,* had interiors lighted with silver candelabras and deck chandeliers. The cars were equipped with six ceiling paddle fans to increase circulation. The kitchens and pantries were finished in white enamel and were outfitted with an electric exhaust fan and reversible ventilators. The onboard refrigerator had a cigar humidor built in to keep supplies fresh. The silverware and dishes were of a special design.

Especially luxurious were the six 34-seat plus drawing room parlor cars, the *Roosevelt, Wilson, Lincoln, Cleveland, Washington,* and *Jefferson.* Their individual swivel chairs were upholstered in tan plush, striped with braided black. The curtains and carpets were of a harmonious color. The cars were lighted with bronze ceiling lights. The five-person drawing room included a bench-like seat and two individual seats. Separate men's and women's lavatories were placed at either end of the cars. Parlor car seating plus luxurious eating arrangements continued on into the observation cars.

Named the *Chicago* and *St. Louis,* the observation cars were perhaps the finest of the type yet built and offered a unique interior design. At the head end of the car was a women's lavatory (there was no provision for a men's). Next to it was a 12–parlor car seat lounging section reserved exclusively for women. It included a filled bookcase and a writing table. Partitions divided the center of the cars. On the left were located two half moon, three-seat sofas. On the right were two four-seat tables used for tea service provided by kimono-clad Japanese servers. The seats in this area were upholstered in light blue velvet. Next to the tables was a compact buffet for service preparation. The remainder of the car was filled with 14 parlor seats and a writing table that included a telephone (an onboard innovation added to principal trains some 12 years earlier) for use en route. Seating and carpet in this area was done up in green velvet. On the observation deck were four permanent seats with ample room for four to six additional large camp stools.[35]

A handsomely produced, 24-page, colorized booklet that received wide distribution promoted the new *Alton Limited* and the recently opened Chicago Union Station. Included were these interior illustrations to give travelers a hint of the train's magnificent accommodations and services. (Author's Coll.)

Dining Car

Japanese Tea Room

The trains, decorated in the same rich three-tone red with gold striping scheme that had made its predecessor famous, with roofs finished in silver and underframes in black, were examples of the finest accommodations a railroad could offer. They were put on public display at Chicago, Alton, Springfield, and St. Louis in mid-September, then on an unusual and extensive off-line tour over the St. Louis Southwestern throughout Arkansas, Oklahoma, Texas, and Louisiana, drawing thousands of visitors. September 28 had been set as the inaugural date of the first new *Alton Limited* runs, but the IC and Wabash had plans to introduce their new *Daylight* and *Banner Blue* trains, forcing the decision to start runs nearly a week sooner than planned. Thus, on Thursday, September 23, 1924, the new *Alton Limited* made first runs as extras until the new timetables took effect the following Sunday.

Passenger traffic manager Charlton described the *Alton Limited* as "The Handsomest Train in the World" in advertisements and in a rich and fully illustrated brochure that got wide distribution. The trains left Chicago at 11:30 A.M. and St. Louis at 12:05 P.M. on extremely fast, six-and-one-half-hour runs, cutting an hour and a half from previous schedules. On the head end were the speedy class I-6 Pacifics (with rebuilt tenders of greater size for added coal and water to reduce the number of fueling stops). Logically listed as trains 1 and 2 in timetables, the trains' introduction was without a doubt the highlight of an otherwise lackluster year.

With the new *Alton Limited* equipment in service, 10 of the train's former cars were shopped and, over the next six months, received steel underframe and end frames and steel sheathed sides. They had Chicago Vapor heating systems and electric lighting installed. The insides were stripped, and new interiors, closely following the appointments of the new *Alton Limited* equipment, were added. Pullman provided the parlor cars *John A. Logan* and *Stonewall Jackson,* and the former 20-seat observation cars *Illinois* and *Missouri* were renamed the *Ulysses S. Grant* and *Albert Sidney Johnson*.[36]

The rebuilt equipment and Pullmans were assembled and introduced as a new afternoon train, the *Lincoln Limited,* on an equally fast six-and-a-half-hour schedule even though it had seven additional stops plus two setouts en route. At the head end of this fast express train was a class I-6 Pacific. The two *Limiteds* were billed as "Twin Sister Trains." They helped put distance between the company's service and that of competing roads. Within a year the C&A had gained an added 5 percent Chicago–St. Louis market share. The trains were a visible commitment to the best possible passenger service the public could desire.

The first departure of the *Lincoln Limited* out of Chicago came from under the train-shed of the newly opened Chicago Union Station. After 12 years of putting together the 25-acre parcel needed for the new complex, then preparation and reconfiguration of tracks and facilities—all interrupted by the demands of the two war years—the monumental new station was put in service May 16 and formally opened July 23, 1925. The project had cost $75 million.[37] The Pennsylvania held 50 percent ownership, with the Milwaukee Road and Burlington sharing equally the other half. The C&A was a non-owning tenant. In 1925—what turned out to be the station's peak year for operations—the Burlington had the most operations, averaging 95 trains a day (37 percent of operations); the Milwaukee Road, 88 daily trains (35 percent); the Pennsylvania, 48 trains (19 percent); and the C&A, 22 trains (9 percent).

The station's 24 tracks ranked the terminal fifth in size in the country. It was the only double stub station in America. South of the station were the new freight houses of the C&A, Pennsylvania, and Burlington and a new postal terminal, the largest in the world under one roof, through which 45 percent of Chicago's mail passed.[38]

The entrance of the former cramped, Neo-Greco depot was on the east side of Canal Street. The building faced west, with its through tracks wedged in a narrow 134-foot-wide strip of land. The new headhouse now sat between Canal Street and the Chicago River and between Jackson and Adams Streets, positioned so the main entrance faced east, symbolically inviting Chicago's citizens to enter. Across Canal Street was the main waiting room and offices. A passage under Canal Street connected the two structures, which had distinctly different architecture.

Daniel Burnham had been selected to design

the replacement, but he died before construction commenced; the Chicago firm of Graham, Anderson, Probst and White took over. The designers used only one unifying element in the two structures, Roman-Doric columns, two of which graced the main entrance of the headhouse while colonnades lined the exterior walls of the waiting room–office building. Columns were also employed in the massive waiting room, but in the passenger concourse, latticed steel columns supported three broad archways. Bedford stone was used throughout.[39] All of the depot tracks were below street level and covered. It was an arrangement needed to allow city streets to connect the Loop—the downtown core—with the city's west side as well as to allow Chicago, Aurora & Elgin Electric Railway trains access to its Wells Street terminal and the city's west side elevated lines passage.[40]

The project was started in 1914 after long negotiations between the city and the railroads. The Chicago Plan Commission had advocated the depot to be located south of 12th Street (later Roosevelt Road), but the railroads protested that it would be too far from the Loop. Eventually, a compromise was worked out, but a few more years passed before the transfer of the numerous parcels of land could be accomplished. Just to relocate the Alton's freight house and to reconfigure its tracks, for instance, land owned by Commonwealth Edison, Marshall Field, Western Electric, and Anheuser Busch had to be purchased and the buildings on the property demolished or relocated. In turn, 30 percent of Alton property between Van Buren and Polk Streets and a large portion of the Burlington's property south of Harrison Street was sold or swapped. Though there were larger and more impressive stations already opened by American railroads, few of those projects involved more planning and coordination, for while all of the reconfiguration and construction was under way, some 170 through and 115 suburban trains serving 35,000 daily passengers, plus more than 500 tons of mail, still had to be handled.[41] With the opening of Chicago Union Station, C&A trains now terminated at three of the finest examples of railroad stations in America.

The faster schedules and fine appointments of the two new *Limiteds* helped improve long-haul passenger business, but local passengers continued to desert C&A trains. A million local passengers were lost between 1920 and 1925.[42] Though Bierd tried, Illinois regulators would not allow him to eliminate runs that no longer covered operating costs. With no other recourse, he started looking at self-propelled, single operator, low cost cars that a young, self-taught engineer, H. L. Hamilton of Cleveland, Ohio, was struggling to sell to railroads—such as the C&A—that had losing passenger operations. He had founded Electro-Motive Company (EMC) in 1922 and so far had sold just two units, one to the CGW, the other to the NP. The St. Louis Car Company, more closely identified with electric than steam roads, fabricated the car bodies; Winton Engine supplied the 175-horsepower engine; and General Electric supplied the electrical components. Hamilton's company then assembled the parts into finished self-propelled cars.

Demonstrator units were run over the C&A in the summer of 1924 and quickly proved their worth. An order for three cars followed. M-4 was a 44-seat, 57-foot-long car with operator cabs in the engine room ahead of the baggage area on one end and inside an enclosed vestibule on the other end.[43] The M-5 and M-6 differed from the M-4 in most aspects except for their all-steel construction and overall weight. They were two feet shorter and had an operator stand at only the end ahead of the baggage area (the rear end had an open vestibule). They seated only 19 but had baggage-express areas twice the size of the M-4.[44] The cars were initially operated in Mexico–Cedar City service—the lightest passenger revenue producing runs—and on Peoria-Springfield trips, where ITS electric car competition had made inroads. Although trips were short, the loud rumble of the engine and whine of the motors proved a passenger inconvenience, but their faster acceleration and absence of clothes-damaging soot made motorcars preferable to steam-driven trains.

The three EMC gas-electrics proved themselves from the start, raising the question why more were not ordered instead of a turn to homegrown products. For some reason, undoubtedly cost, the next order was for two power kits produced by Railway Motors of De Pere, Wisconsin. At Bloomington, one of the gasoline engines (which drove two 104-horse-

Motor car M-5 with trailer, train no. 51, departs Peoria for its 64-mile early morning run to Springfield. Motor cars were tried as a last ditch attempt to curb local train costs after passengers were lost to electric railways and automobiles. (Gulf, Mobile & Ohio RR Historical Society Coll.)

power Continental six-cylinder motors mounted under the floorboard) was placed in an 1892 52-foot wooden combine. A drive shaft from each motor to a gear assembly mounted on the axle turned the wheels, making the car a gas-mechanical rather than a gas-electric. The car was nearly 12,000 pounds heavier than the EMC models. On the baggage end, a simple single seat for an operator and controls were installed. The M-10 had 32 seats and a 23-foot baggage section.[45] Within a few months, the car got a couple of coats of paint and varnish and new lettering and was placed in service. A year later, the M-11, the second homebuilt, was produced, again using an 1892 vintage car. It was the same as the M-10 mechanically but came out of the shops with a smaller 19-seat passenger compartment and a larger 34-foot baggage area.[46]

The M-10 and M-11 shared one characteristic with the EMCs: they were noisy. But unlike the three EMC cars, they were unreliable. The two cars became the mechanical department's headache. From the start it was realized that their heavier weights limited acceleration and forced their underpowered engines to labor. After only a few months of operation, their greatest flaw was exposed: their driveshafts would snap on sharp curves and through switches as the axles the gear boxes were attached to twisted beyond their design limits.

The M-10 and M-11 were never as cost-effective as the EMC-built equipment—from management's point of view, their greatest failure.

The experiment with motor cars was Bierd's first cautious attempt at reducing the local passenger service losses. The next move he made was truly bold. In February 1926 he unveiled an ambitious and pioneering plan to create a bus subsidiary.[47] His was the first railroad to move so aggressively into highway service, but other roads, especially in the East, quickly followed. Wholly owned, the Alton Transportation Company, under the management of superintendent of Chicago terminals, X. H. Cornell, was to have operations in both Illinois and Missouri, eventually paralleling all but a few miles of the railroad. Bierd recognized that some conventional local service trains would still be needed to transport milk, poultry, and express, but where head-end traffic was not an issue, he was ready to prove buses could adequately serve passengers at lower cost and greater frequency. He expected highway service to be popular, persuading the ICC regulators to authorize dropping money-losing steam trains.

A month after Bierd announced his bus plan, Alton Transportation was given operating rights between Jacksonville and St. Louis.[48] Initial service included two daily round-trips, with short trips between Jacksonville and

Alton and Alton and St. Louis scheduled in between. Three buses purchased from the Versare Corp. of Albany, New York, were employed. They had seats for 33 and could accommodate 37 standees. The huge vehicles were 35 feet, 6 inches in length, much larger than the products of other manufacturers, and rode on two independent four-wheel trucks. Power was supplied by a six-cylinder engine connected to a generator, which in turn was connected to two Westinghouse traction motors mounted on each truck.[49]

The next routes served were between Joliet and Wilmington and Pontiac and Bloomington after independent operators were bought out.[50] Applications for routes paralleling nearly the entire railroad were filed with the ICC and the Missouri Public Service Commission (MPSC). Four separate applications had to be filed for routes between Joliet and Bloomington, Bloomington and Springfield, Springfield and Carlinville, and Carlinville and Mitchell. Other filings included Dwight-Lacon, Peoria-Springfield, and Peoria-Chenoa (to replace the discontinued passenger service

of the TP&W). In late 1927 Jacksonville-Carrollton service was started, and applications were filed with the MPSC for routes between Mexico and Jefferson City, Mexico and Roodhouse, and St. Louis and Kansas City over new Highway 40.[51]

In July 1928 Chicago–St. Louis rights were granted, but to three separate operators. Alton Transportation received Joliet-Carlinville authority, but the Carlinville–St. Louis route was given to the ITS and a Chicago-Joliet certificate to Chicago & Joliet Transportation.[52] The ICC expected the three companies to work out an operating arrangement themselves. Negotiations among the three led to Alton Transportation being designated the operating company. In return for gaining the full franchise, the railroad agreed to sell the stock of the bus subsidiary to its two new partners, with an option to buy it back within two years. Getting authority in Missouri was not nearly as easy or successful. It was not until January 1930 that rights to operate between Louisiana and Mexico and Mexico and Jefferson City were granted. The application for a

The Versare Corp. of Albany, New York, supplied five large and very difficult-to-operate buses for the short-lived Alton Transportation Co. Because of regulatory delay and restrictions, the innovative bus subsidiary soon failed. (Kenneth Donnelly Coll.)

St. Louis–Kansas City route, however, was denied, and a petition for Mexico–Kansas City rights had not yet been heard. Limited service (the only Alton Transportation runs ever made in Missouri) was started between Louisiana and Jefferson City.[53]

The regulatory delays and predictable opposition of independent operators frustrated Cornell from putting a true bus system in place. Instead of the more than 1,000-mile system planned, Alton Transportation buses were operating 200 miles of disjointed routes. The bus line's full potential could not be tested with so limited an operation. Thus in May 1930, with far more important matters facing him, Bierd suspended operations. The Jacksonville–East St. Louis franchise was sold. The other Illinois routes were taken over by other operators. The MPSC objected over the suspensions in Missouri and filed a $20,000 suit against Alton Transportation for suspending service without authority. The MPSC gave the company 60 days to restore service. Two of the five buses Alton Transportation eventually owned were sent to Missouri, where they operated until May 1933 when the Louisiana–Jefferson City rights were sold to the Mark Twain Bus Company of Columbia, Missouri, bringing to a close the road's venturesome but brief experiment with bus operations.[54] It had been a noble effort but, in the end, a failed one.

▾▾▾

The second main line extension program continued. Eleven miles between Brighton and Plainview were finished in 1924. Six miles of a second main line between Manchester and Murrayville were added to the six miles laid between Roodhouse and Manchester, completing a double main line between the end of the air line and Roodhouse. This minimal improvement eliminated train delays and overtime expense for freight trains in and out of Roodhouse. The cost of the 10 miles of new track was more than offset by the savings that resulted.[55] But by far the most ambitious projects initiated that year were the start of the reconfiguration of the Bloomington and Ridgely yards.

Over the prior 40 years, Bloomington Yard had pretty much remained as originally planned without a well-defined layout of switching leads and with the main lines running through the middle of the classification tracks. None of the receiving tracks could take the growing train lengths that built up during the first 20 years of the 1900s. Around 1905 in Normal, three tracks were added for overflow storage, but as traffic grew, more tracks were added and extended, and Normal became an auxiliary yard by default. Trains would start at Bloomington, then move to Normal Yard, where cars were added or completely reclassified a second time. Straightening of existing Bloomington classification tracks, the addition of another four 72-car capacity tracks, and creation of proper drill tracks resulted in a far more efficient facility.[56] The changes made an enormous difference at Bloomington.

At Ridgely five new 70-car tracks, extensions to 65-car capacities of four existing classification tracks, and the relocation of the main line tracks around the yard brought relief for an outmoded facility. A new engine terminal, including a 16-stall roundhouse and associated facilities, was put into service, replacing the costly and time-consuming five-mile runs back and forth to the outmoded downtown Springfield terminal and its inadequate three-stall house. The small and inefficient freight car repair shop at Springfield, which included a blacksmith shop and woodworking mill, was also transferred to Ridgely.[57]

The downward traffic drift and deficit operations continued throughout 1926 and 1927. There were a few bright spots in an otherwise gloomy picture. In 1926 the passenger department announced a direct connection of train 5 with the M&O's new *Gulf Coast Special* for through Chicago–Mobile, Alabama, service. Though the arrival and departure time of both trains was 10:30 P.M., the M&O agreed to hold its train to make the connection for southbound travelers beyond St. Louis to Mobile and points in between. Also inaugurated was year-round operation of the MP's through sleeper to Hot Springs, Arkansas. In spring 1927 luxurious all-bedroom sleepers with only six rooms were added to the Kansas City–St. Louis *Night Hawk* and the Chicago–St. Louis *Midnight Special* consists. Pullman had earlier introduced the cars on eastern roads. They immediately became the accommodation of choice for those on expense accounts

Bloomington was the heart of the railroad, where both locomotives and cars were serviced, repaired, and rebuilt and freight reclassified. The locomotive backshop is in the upper left, behind the 44-stall roundhouse. The car shops are in the lower right. The reconfigured yard is to the far right. (*Bloomington Pantagraph* Photo., Gulf, Mobile & Ohio RR Historical Society Archives, J. W. Barriger III National RR Library, St. Louis Mercantile Library, UM-St. Louis)

and persons of wealth who could afford the extra fare for the safety and privacy the rooms afforded. Each bedroom had an actual bed and its own washstand and toilet, in and of itself worth the added fare to avoid the single facilities at the end of the corridor associated with the conventional sleepers of the day.[58]

Interchange of head-end and sleeper traffic, though modest by most roads' standards, had become an increasingly important part of passenger operations. It was never enough to offset losses sustained in local service, but the added head-end revenue helped. Foreign equipment became a regular part of consists. A CM&St.P express car out of Milwaukee and four Katy express cars to San Antonio were in the consist of train 7, the *Midnight Special*. The Milwaukee Road car returned on train 78, an overnight mail train. The four Katy express cars returned on train 12. Three MP mail storage cars for Texarkana were in the consists of trains 8 and 79. A CI&W express car was added to *The Hummer* at Springfield for runs

to Kansas City. Its return was over the Wabash. Two MP sleepers left St. Louis for Chicago on train 8 each night, one from Houston, the other from Hot Springs. They returned on *The Mail,* train 79. Trains 9 and 10 had a St.LSF 10-section sleeper-observation tacked on to the rear end. It provided through Oklahoma City service.[59]

A year after the 1922 strike, coal-mining production in Illinois reached an all-time high and looked to be an industry in total recovery. Freight traffic manager J. A. Behrle had predicted the road could expect annual tonnage to reach 6 million tons.[60] In 1923 tonnage fell just 128,000 tons short of that target, but thereafter nothing like the predicted levels were again reached. The following year's total tonnage dropped an alarming 1 million tons and continued a precipitous downward slide each year thereafter. Over time, the least productive shaft mines in the Springfield District and along the Western Division closed.[61]

Irreparable harm was caused in 1927 when Illinois coal miners struck once again, this time for six months. For several years, the Rock Island had contracted for delivery of 650,000 to 700,000 tons of Springfield region coal to Peoria. The strike forced the Rock Island to cancel its contract, and thereafter the CRI&P got its coal from its own mines around Peoria. The loss of the business was a major blow. Though revenues from all categories of freight declined, the suspension of mining resulted in coal tonnage dropping to just 38.5 percent of freight traffic.[62] By the end of the 1920s, total coal tonnage transported was averaging 2 million tons, a figure other roads with better traffic mixes would have been happy with, but a level that only meant more red ink for the C&A.

Trucks were increasingly eating into the once important transport of live animals. Just 679,110 tons of livestock were carried in 1927, down from the more than 1 million tons transported in 1920, and the lowest total ever. The only bright spot in an otherwise dismal traffic report was an increase in Texas and Oklahoma petroleum product shipments,

which reached 1.2 million tons for both 1926 and 1927, new record levels.[63] Gross 1927 revenues were the smallest since 1922 and the deficit, nearly $4 million, the largest thus far recorded. No interest had been paid on the first and second mortgage since 1923 and 1917, respectively. Neither had interest been paid since 1910 and 1911 on the two preferred stock issues. Reflecting the road's sorry state was the trading price of its common stock, between $4.50 and $10.67.[64]

▼▼▼

Although freight train derailments were a fairly common occurrence every year, accidents involving passenger trains were not. A rare but deadly accident on January 23, 1927, brought unwanted attention to the railroad. The incident involved *The Hummer* and the second section of eastbound freight no. 84. A baggageman and 13 passengers were killed, and two other trainmen were seriously injured in the mishap. The eastbound freight was on the siding at Clark and had been given clearance to proceed through the manual

Foreign road head-end traffic became an important contributor to passenger department revenues. One such car, a Milwaukee Road express car, is seen here on a southbound train at Dwight. (Paul Slager Photo., William Raia Coll.)

block territory after passenger trains 25 and 9 had passed. The wait was long, and given the early morning hour (5 A.M.) and their fatigue, the entire crew fell asleep. When train 25 passed, the locomotive crew awoke, and when someone shouted "Let's go" the brakeman threw the switch, and the freight train lumbered out onto the main line. Coming at it was *The Hummer*. Each engineer saw the headlights of the other's train, but as they later testified, both thought the other was standing still at sidings at Larrabee or Clark. It wasn't until each train crested a hill that they realized they were headed on a collision course. All of the crew members were experienced railroad men, but the freight crew had slept only about two and one-half hours before being called for the run because, as an investigator stated in his report, "They had not anticipated being called back on duty as soon as actually was the case." Besides the tragic loss of life, the two locomotives were damaged and a baggage car destroyed.[65] Safety was improved in 1927 when 28 color light signals, the first the road employed, were installed between South Joliet and Mazonia, replacing the semaphores that had been used.[66]

That year also saw the deaths of three board members, Festus Wade, L. B. Patterson, and John Mitchell. Mitchell and his wife were killed in a tragic auto accident on a rural road outside Chicago. He was 72.[67] Wade, a St. Louis businessman, had been a board member for four years; Patterson, a Chicago lawyer, had joined just a year earlier; but Mitchell had been a director since Harriman took over. His uncle of the same name had been a director before him, from 1864 until the younger Mitchell orchestrated the road's takeover. William Mitchell's Alton Packet Company provided river transfers between Alton and St. Louis. William and his brother, John, had offered their uncompleted railroad, giving the C&A its entry into East St. Louis. The senior John Mitchell and his partners furnished the road's ferry service at East St. Louis and Venice (and later at Louisiana) and then organized and arranged the financing for the KCSt.L&C. After the younger John Mitchell's father, William, moved his family to Chicago in 1873 to take over the Illinois Trust & Savings Bank, John, at the age of 26, was named president and, over the course of the next 20 years, saw

its assets grow from $1 million to $69 million. After merger with three other financial institutions, the Continental Bank emerged to become the state's second largest. It was John Mitchell who approached Harriman and became a participant in the syndicate that bought the railroad and removed Blackstone.[68] The Mitchells and the company had been linked since the road's earliest days. The family's relationship with the C&A and predecessors was one of the longest any family had had with an American railroad.

End-of-year results continued with recurring themes: lost traffic, revenue declines, and increased losses. In 1928, for the first time, interchange traffic exceeded local traffic and was now 51 percent of freight tonnage, an indication of how locally generated traffic, especially coal, had declined rather than how through traffic had increased. The only significant improvements made in the property in 1928 was erection of the College Avenue depot on the Alton Bypass at Upper Alton—forced upon the company to satisfy a judgment brought against it by the city of Alton challenging the road's right to bypass the city. Also erected was a joint depot with the IC at Delavan.[69]

The homebuilt motor cars M-10 and M-11 had proved a failure, so the company returned to EMC in 1928 for four more motor cars with larger, 275-horsepower engines. These were the last motor cars purchased new. The M-15 and M-16 had mail compartments, enlarged baggage areas (complete with milk can and fish racks), and seats for 12 persons. The M-17 and M-18 were similarly configured but had enlarged 24-seat areas.[70] The cars replaced more local runs.

Each year over the course of the past five or six, at least 10 new industrial sidings were laid to serve new industries, among them Joliet Gravel at Millsdale, Inland Stone at Plaines, and Cuneo Press in Chicago. But the six miles of track laid in the Wilmington Coal Field for the Northern Illinois Coal Corp. became some of the most important because they marked the resumption of mining in the Braidwood area, this time employing the less labor-intensive strip-mining method. By the end of 1928, production at Mine No. 10 was already totaling 2,500 tons per day and growing.[71] Eventually, most of an 11-square-mile area around Coal City was stripped until 1949, when operations were shifted to the west of the main line where the Essex and Northern Illinois mines were started. Extraction continued until the early 1970s when the Clean Air and Water Act made Illinois's high-sulfur content product unmarketable. During the 21 years of strip-mining operations at Coal City and Braidwood, 30 million tons of coal were removed, not enough to replace all of the lost tonnage from mines further to the south, but helping nevertheless to stabilize revenues from the once pervasive commodity.

With the death in 1928 of George Charlton—one of the company's most valued officials—the company again started a year with sadness. Charlton had been the last of the pre-Harriman officials still with the railroad. His immense accomplishments were legendary. His death brought to a close more than a half century when the name Charlton was irrevocably linked to Chicago & Alton passenger service. His replacement was a 41-year veteran of the railroad, William Abel. He had previously served as agent at several locations including Denver, Dallas, Kansas City, and St. Louis before being brought to the Chicago headquarters as general passenger agent before his latest promotion.

A few weeks preceding Charlton's death, A. P. Titus, chief operating officer, resigned to become vice president of the ITS. Titus had been with the C&A since 1913 and had provided faithful service under the most trying of circumstances. Replacing him was Stroad Henderson, the former general superintendent at Bloomington and an 18-year veteran. Assuming the general superintendent's position was Clarence Bearden, who over the course of 26 years worked his way up from dispatcher to chief dispatcher, trainmaster, and assistant superintendent.

The company had been in receivership for somewhat more than six years, and there had been no improvement in its fortunes, nor was it likely that there would be in the future. The holders of the 3 1/2 and 6 bonds had run out of patience waiting for a restructuring plan and filed for foreclosure. The court appointed master in chancery Harbert Lundahl to determine if a reorganization could be accomplished, and he quickly concluded one could not. The company had done nothing but de-

cline during receivership and now, as the final days seemed to be approaching, would expire unless someone came along and breathed new life into it. On July 6 federal judge George Carpenter ordered the sale of the railroad. He found that its reduced assets were inadequate to satisfy any but the first mortgage bondholders, leaving all others out in the cold. Holders of the 6s, the second mortgage, immediately appealed his ruling. Since the outcome of the appeal could not be predicted, the judge set no specific date for the sale until a ruling was rendered.[72]

Unlike the circumstance nearly 75 years earlier, the pending liquidation had not been brought on by fraud. Rather, following Harriman's ownership, it was the result of too frequent changes of management, too many missed consolidation opportunities, and in the final analysis too little revenue-generating traffic to support the heavy capitalization incurred over a 30-year period.

Even today, some argue that it was Harriman who caused the road's failure by overcapitalizing the road. But calculating the rate of return during and following the periods preceding Harriman's control—as Lloyd Mercer did in *E. H. Harriman: Master Railroader*—shows this not to be the case. Under Blackstone, from 1892 to 1899, the rate of return on invested capital was 4.8; under Reid and Moore, Hawley, and then Lovett, from 1908 to 1918, the rate was 6.4. Neither figure came close to the 15.3 number under Harriman from 1900 to 1907. Admittedly, the economic environment during the years of Harriman control were more favorable than either the years preceding or following his tenure, but it is undeniable that Harriman's sophisticated refinancing of the railroad when interest rates were low, plus excellent management, helped produced far superior results.

It is purely speculative to assume how Harriman, and then his successors after his death in 1909, would have dealt with the challenges that faced the road and the industry had he not lost control, but comparing the success of Lovett's roads with the ultimate falls into receivership of the Rock Island, St.LSF, and TSt.L&W gives strong indications that the outcome might have been quite different. The company's failure came only after control was wrested from Harriman. Bonded indebtedness in 1907 was close to $74 million, but by 1918 that figure had risen to $92 million, nearly a 25 percent increase.

If blame is to be found, it surely would be with Reid and the Rock Island Crowd—who got cold feet and cast the road aside rather than attempting to consolidate it with their roads—and with Hawley, who drained scarce surpluses to finance his buyout at a time when the road could least afford it and then seemingly dithered in bringing about any meaningful consolidation. The men Hawley had running his railroads were hard-pressed by worsening economic conditions but also seemingly lacked the vision and talents to perpetuate what Harriman had started. Hawley was handed a solid, profitable railroad. By the time Lovett stepped in, it was already too late to arrest the road's problems: too little mileage with too great a dependence on low value traffic that mandated too large an investment. Could the C&A have escaped receivership? Possibly. Consolidation with any of the southwestern roads would surely have brought the much needed longer hauls and greater traffic volumes that the road desperately needed. Every potential partner—KCS, MP, and MKT—either terminated at St. Louis or Kansas City, making a merger with any of them an end-to-end proposition with no duplication of trackage whatsoever. Of the actual opportunities that existed for consolidation, the best arrangement might have been inclusion in the Rock Island system. That a consolidation never happened makes one wonder if the later failures of that system, as well as the C&A, might have been averted, given the greater strength through a consolidation that would have resulted.

In fairness, the company's substantial debt load would have been a challenge for any other road to absorb. In 1907 the company's capitalization per mile amounted to $114,480 compared with, for instance, the Rock Island System's $52,268; its net earnings on net capitalization were 3.7 percent versus the Rock Island's 4.2 percent. But its fixed charges on total net income were 73 percent while the Rock Island's was 83 percent, and its gross earnings per mile, $11,944, were far superior to the Rock Island's $7,098.[73] Had the Rock Island Crowd stayed the course, Hawley's ill-advised takeover would not have happened. By the time the difficulties the industry faced after 1910 arose, the C&A would have been integrated into a larger system, and the benefits of greater feed of longer haul traffic might well have staved off the trouble both the C&A and the Rock Island system ultimately endured. Clearly, the alignment with the eastern-oriented TSt.L&W had not been the answer, as another attempt by an eastern-oriented railroad would prove not to be either.

▾▾▾

The Western Division had been the bane of the road—though not the reason for the railroad's failure—since the Blackstone Era. Because it was never straightened and leveled as the main line had been, nor double-tracked, operations between Slater and Kansas City particularly were the most difficult on the railroad, especially at Independence Hill. There 85,000 pounds of tractive effort was required to move 45 to 60 cars.[74] Though a vast improvement over the Moguls and Consolidations they replaced, even the new Mikados had to be double-headed. Drivers slipped climbing hills and lost traction rounding the numerous curves. If trains had to take a siding, which occurred frequently, they struggled to restart. The division's restrictive 35 miles per hour speed limit was seldom achieved. More often, freights moved at around 10 mph.[75] It was an expensive and time-consuming process moving freight east or west on the Western Division, and despite the company's desperate state, an attempt was made to address the problem.

C. M. House, the newly named superintendent of motive power, realized the division was not going to be rebuilt anytime soon, so he rented a Wabash dynamometer car, then borrowed two Santa Fe 2-8-4s with trailer boosters, one a Baldwin and the other an American Locomotive product, both producing 85,000 pounds of tractive effort. In August 1929 he conducted 11 test runs between Kansas City and Slater, measuring the results of the engines hauling varying tonnage to see what improvements might result. The results were mixed. House found heavier trains pulled by the Berkshires still had problems. Those pulling consists of 25 to 35 cars did very well, but that was not the major leap forward he was looking for. Mechanical engineer C. W. Esch, however, was sufficiently satisfied with the overall results to recommend that, if any new power was ever acquired, it should be superheater-equipped Berkshires.[76] That never happened. After the stock market collapsed a few months after the tests and the worst depression in the country's history set in, any plans there might have been to acquire any larger power were scuttled. The reduced tonnage of trains for the next decade made them unnecessary.

By the end of December 1929, when the ICC finally produced its Consolidation Plan, there was no prospect of the C&A emerging from its hopeless state. Mandated by Congress in 1920, the plan was to give direction toward the rearrangement of America's railroads into logical regional systems that would lead to amalgamation of the weakest with the strongest. The report, perhaps not unexpectedly, left the C&A little more than a footnote, as though its still vital link among the Midwest's three largest rail terminals was of little or no consequence. A first draft in 1921 was reviewed and generally reviled. That version recommended the 986 miles of the railroad be tacked on to a system built around the Pennsylvania, a mighty road to be sure, but one with which the C&A had little in common.[77] President Rea of the Pennsylvania was ambivalent. In replies to the ICC, he seemed to indicate indifference as to whether the Alton was or was not included in a package with the other mostly eastern lines the Pennsylvania was expected to take over.

In the years that followed, various modifications to the plan were proposed, including bringing the C&A into the Wabash's tent. The merging of the two might have made a strong alliance, since, by combining them, some competition would be eliminated in some of Illinois and parts of Missouri. Both served the same three key midwestern cities.

In the midst of the sorting out process, influential ICC commissioner Joseph Eastman spoke for several of his fellow members in saying, "No consolidation for which it [the plan] provides can be accomplished until we have found, after full hearing, that the public interest will be promoted thereby. The plan is very little more than a procedural step. There is nothing compulsory about it, nor even any

assurance that authority will be sought to carry out the consolidations which it proposes."[78] It probably would have been impossible to satisfy all the interests of the core railroads. As Eastman understood, the ICC needed to leave the door open for modifications if it could be shown a better plan would result.

A few changes to the plan were submitted as the debate over how the systems would be formulated went on. Some wondered midway through the process if a final version could ever be issued. The commissioners nearly admitted defeat and at one point asked Congress to rescind the requirement of coming up with a report, but to no avail. After much delay, a final plan a divided ICC approved was adopted. It called for 21 regional systems with the biggest and most prosperous railroads (that were already systems in their own right) taking over the lesser roads. What was identified as System 5, anchored by the B&O, called for the takeover of 62 mostly eastern coal-hauling roads and, surprisingly, the C&A. Aside from the tiny 26-mile Kansas & Sidell, which operated in Edgar County in the southeastern portion of Illinois, no other road operating in Illinois or Missouri was included in System 5.[79] It was System 6, built around the now powerful C&O and the NYC&St.L, that included most of the other Illinois roads—the C&IM, Jacksonville & Havana, Chicago Springfield & St. Louis, and Alton & Eastern. System 7, built around a combined Wabash and Seaboard, included the only other independent Illinois road, the TP&W.

While the B&O did serve Chicago, Springfield, and St. Louis, even President Willard, during the course of debate, argued the C&A should be made part of the Wabash-Seaboard alliance since the C&A and the Wabash were direct competitors and since both already served Kansas City, new territory for his road that was deep in foreign territory. Surprising, however, was that the even more logical linkup for the C&A with a western or southwestern road was never proposed.[80] Willard had been a longtime proponent of consolidation. Even before the final plan was disclosed, he had been proactive, making moves on roads that could strengthen his already strong system. In February 1929 Willard sought to acquire the Reading, the Central Railroad of

New Jersey, the Buffalo, Rochester & Pittsburgh (BR&P), the B&S, and even the Wabash "for the purpose of strengthening the western end of the system." No hearings on Willard's application were held, and the petition was withdrawn at the direction of the ICC a year later. Willard did gain financial control of the BR&P and the B&S in February and May 1930, and later of the Reading, but not of the Wabash and—until the Consolidation Plan was produced—had made no overture to Bierd. Thus, his very quick move to take the C&A out of the courts is a bit surprising. Willard, though never seeking it, did not fight the C&A's inclusion in a B&O-centered system. He possibly saw a show of cooperation relative to the C&A as a way to clear the way for the ICC's quick approval of his taking control of the roads he really wanted. No other major road president was moving so quickly into the consolidation arena.

From what Willard knew of the C&A's foreclosure decision Judge Carpenter had rendered, stockholders' claims were given no weight, so he realized control would not come through a simple stock purchase, as had been employed in previous acquisitions. He put staff members to work to figure out how it could be done.[81] In light of the court's ruling, his lieutenants advised him he would have to settle with the holders of the defaulted 3 1/2s. It was concluded that acquisition of the railroad could only be justified, "provided it could be done with a total capitalization of, roundly, $75 million." With the $38,834,000 of 3 1/2s paid off, the $45,350,000 of the 6s due to mature in 1949 would constitute the capitalization of the reorganized company, reducing servicing charges to just $1.3 million a year.[82]

Through the spring and early summer of 1930, the B&O's senior vice president, George Shriver, carried out negotiations with representatives of the 3 1/2 bondholder protective committee. In July all parties involved accepted an offer of purchase of their bonds at 80 percent of face value, a total payout of $23 million.[83] With the 3 1/2 bondholders satisfied and those holding 6s now removed from their subordinate role, the path seemed clear to approach the courts. But it wasn't long before the C&A stockholder protective committees filed suit for redress of what they felt were

injustices in Judge Carpenter's decision protecting only the interests of the bondholders. Once again, however, their claims were found to have no merit, and the judge quickly dismissed their case.[84]

On December 11, 1930, Wheelock, Bierd, Morton, and a few others representing the C&A, George Shriver and H. B. Voorhees of the B&O, and Douglas Moffett and Colin Ives of the Maryland Trust, gathered on the Wilmington depot platform to witness the sale of the once proud and fiercely independent Chicago & Alton. Precisely at 2 o'clock, Harbert Lundaul began reading the notice of sale, taking 50 minutes to finish. Then bids were solicited. Moffett and Ives offered $23 million, the only bid submitted. Lundaul declared them the successful bidders. The entire proceedings, including the reading of the notice of sale, took but 90 minutes.[85] On January 8, 1931, Judge Carpenter affirmed the sale and assigned the road to the Alton Railway Company, which Moffat and Ives had incorporated two days earlier. The five men named as incorporators were all officers of banks in Chicago, New York, and Baltimore. A few weeks later, as soon as the necessary papers were drawn up and filed, the B&O applied to acquire the Alton Railway.

Hearings on the application began on April 13 before O. E. Sweet, director of the ICC's Bureau of Finance. They lasted two days. Once again the C&A stockholders petitioned to intervene in the case. They charged that B&O and Kuhn, Loeb officials abandoned plans for a reorganization of the company that would have included the stockholders' interests. In court, Willard and Shriver denied direct knowledge of any such plans (though Shriver admitted he had understood some such discussions involving others did take place). Though their protest was made part of the record, the stockholders' charges played no part in the remainder of the hearings.

Willard testified that he sought the railroad to gain simple control and had no plans for a reorganization of the company. He stated that under his road's control, the Alton would remain a separate corporation, though not independent. "It is not the intention to abandon any of the important services or facilities of the Alton, but it is our hope rather to improve and expand them in the interest of both companies." He suggested two steps might be taken immediately to reduce costs: consolidation of adjoining freight facilities at East St. Louis and the transfer of Alton passenger trains into Chicago's Grand Central Station (saving the $500,000 annual charges the Alton paid as a tenant in Chicago Union Station). As examples of how the Alton would benefit under B&O control, he suggested a surplus of more powerful locomotives, perhaps 40–50, might be transferred to the Alton, as might needed freight cars—all without new or additional financing. Willard saw the present difficulties of the adopted road as temporary and "Although there may be some doubt as to the ability of the railroad . . . to 'stand on its own two feet' as an independent carrier, I am confident . . . it will not only continue to serve the public effectively, but its opportunities will be enlarged and it will be an additional source of business to the Baltimore & Ohio and will justify the Baltimore & Ohio's investment."[86] Aside from the stockholders, the owners of the Kansas & Sidell and two of its subsidiaries, the Casey & Sidell and the Yale Short Line—which petitioned for inclusion—and the TP&W—which wanted its 1895 trackage rights agreement between Washington and Peoria annulled—were the only other parties to intervene.

In surprisingly quick action, on July 17, the full commission approved the takeover of the Alton and its leased lines. The new corporation was to be called simply the Alton Railroad. The B&O parent would assume liability for the payment of dividends, interest payments on the bonds, equipment trusts, and receiver notes. The B&O purchased the Kansas & Sidell and its two subsidiaries and added those properties to the B&O's books. The TP&W got what it wanted. As for C&A stockholders, they wound up empty-handed. "They have nothing left for us to protect," the commissioners concluded.[87]

Would Willard succeed where Hawley had failed? There were plenty of railroad officials who scoffed at Willard's optimism. There was then only one other family of roads, the Van Sweringen lines, which extended from New York to the Missouri River and beyond, comprising the Erie, the Nickel Plate, and the MP. The industry had nothing but respect for Willard as a person and a railroad man, but questioned the wisdom of his extending the eastern-based B&O into the Western Traffic District.

The B&O and the War Years

The operator at St. Louis Union Station Tower One looks over the Alton-Burlington *General Pershing Zephyr,* the joint Kansas City–St. Louis dieselized, lightweight train started in 1936. In the last years of operation, heavyweight cars were sometimes pressed into service. (*St. Louis Globe Democrat* Archives, St. Louis Mercantile Library, University of Missouri-St. Louis)

The New York Stock Exchange crash in late October 1929 did more than just break a few windows on Wall Street. The market lost $40 billion in value—utilities, industrials, and railroads were especially hard hit.[1] Since much of the frenzied buying preceding the crash had been on credit, or margin, banks started failing, taking their customers with them. Before long, factory orders dried up, first for industrial products, then, as workers were laid off, for consumer goods. As factories closed, management too was out on the street. With their customers out of work, shopkeepers on Main Streets across the country began hanging "going out of business" signs in their windows. Reduced production of nearly everything led to lower demand for coal to fuel the nation's plants, shops, schools, hospitals, and homes. Farmers could not get enough for their crops to pay their loans. Soon, the nation's economy was in a free fall.

At first, President Herbert Hoover, a moderate Republican, was confident that market forces would right the ship of state. He appealed to the nation's industrial leaders to maintain production and avoid cutting wages. A cooperative Federal Reserve relaxed its lending rules to encourage borrowing. Unions withdrew demands for pay and benefit increases. Though Hoover's remedies were right, they were quickly undermined when the industrialists reneged on their promises. Between April and November 1930, 4 million factory workers lost their jobs.[2] Those still working received smaller paychecks. In December Congress passed the Smoot-Hawley bill, thought by the sponsors as a way to shore up the nation's economy by putting higher tariffs on exports, especially farm products and raw materials. The increase the bill called for was only about 5 percent, but by 1932, with falling prices, export tariffs had grown from 40 to 60 percent of a product's value.[3] Exports dried up. In retaliation for higher priced American goods, more than 50 other nations placed restrictions on American imports. International trade collapsed, and soon the rest of the world too was thrown into depression.

By 1931 the nation's unemployed doubled to 8 million. In May of that year, 91 banks failed. By October the number had swelled to 522. Mortgage foreclosures and tax sales of property escalated. Though those working for wages suffered; farmers got hit the hardest. Between 1929 and 1932, farm prices dropped by two-thirds.[4] The unemployed and their families were going hungry while farmers saw their production lay wasted for lack of demand. Some farmers found it more economical to heat their homes with their harvested corn than to ship it to market.

In the winter of 1931, Hoover realized his earlier efforts at persuasion had failed, and he now proposed the most sweeping government intervention in the nation's economy the country had ever seen. The Federal Reserve relaxed its rules further, Congress appropriated money for public works projects to create jobs, farmers were given new supports, a mortgage rescue plan for homeowners was created, and a new agency with initial lending power of $500 million and a reserve of another $1.5 billion—the Reconstruction Finance Corporation (RFC)—was established. It was to guarantee government loans so industries could restart production. Within a year the RFC dispensed loans to more than 5,000 banks, building and loan associations, insurance companies, and railroads in a desperate attempt to stimulate the economy.[5]

Hoover's intervention temporarily stalled the economy's decline. In August 1932 something of a rally began to build a head of steam, but it was short-lived. America—and the rest of the world—soon resumed its plunge into the deepest economic depression the world had known. American industrial production stood at half of what it was in 1929. Profits fell from $11 billion to $2 billion. New investment almost totally disappeared as the figure fell from $10 billion in 1929 to just $1 billion in 1932. Imports and exports fell from $10 billion to $3 billion. By 1932, 2,294 banks had closed. Unemployment had reached 15 million, about one of every three eligible workers. The average weekly pay of those still working had fallen from $28 to $17. Personal income dropped from $82 billion in 1929 to $48 billion. Farm income plunged 70 percent.[6]

At the start of the economy's decline, Willard was one who agreed with Hoover that a correction would quickly come, and he fulfilled his pledge to continue spending. He poured $14 million into the B&O in 1930.[7] But within a year, the reality of the situation was evident to him, and he too was forced to curtail spending. For the rest of the decade, little more than 30 percent of the road's spending during the previous decades was maintained. Far more power and equipment was retired than purchased.[8]

It was the same on the newly acquired and already depleted Alton. H. B. Voorhees, vice president of the parent road and president of the subsidiary B&OCT, had been put in charge. He replaced the retired Bierd, whose 18 years with the Alton had been filled with nothing but headaches. Voorhees wasn't given an easy task. The railroad he would supervise saw its revenues decline from $28.7 million in 1929 to $14 million in 1932, leaving next to nothing for improvements. Over $3 million ($3.4 million) had been spent at the start of the depression on maintenance of way and $6.3 million on repairing engines and rolling stock, but in 1932 only $1.6 million was spent in each category. With traffic drying up, and despite every effort to control expenses, net operating income in 1932 plunged from $3.3 million to $486,783.[9]

The depression-induced decline in traffic required fewer trains to be called. Incredibly, half the Alton's freight tonnage now came from interchange through Kansas City and St. Louis, not from local farms, mines, and industries. Local traffic, especially the two staples, corn and coal, had plunged to the lowest levels of production in memory. The once lush, abundant, crop-filled acreage of Illinois and Missouri was now only dusty fields of dead, unharvested crops thick with weeds. In the two years since the depression started, more than half the 58 mines the Alton still served had been shut down, including the two mines at Corder and one at Higginsville, the last on the Western Division. None of the 25 still producing were operating at anything close to maximum production. The Northern Illinois's no. 10 strip mine at Wilmington; the two Standard Oil operations in the Carlinville area; three of the Peabody mines around Springfield; the four Lincoln Coal mines around Girard; the Chicago, Wilmington and Franklin mine at Thayer; and the Prairie State mine at Granville were the prime sources of loads.[10]

The crisis was real and prospects for a turnaround anytime soon remote. During the hearings leading up to the Alton acquisition, Willard offered few specifics and only modest goals for the Alton under B&O management. He testified that he planned to operate the Alton as a separate railroad, "But in harmony with the Baltimore & Ohio System. Generally speaking it is not the intention to abandon any of the important services or facilities of the Alton, but it is our hope rather to improve and expand them in the interest of both companies." His words were soon forgotten. Compelled by forces beyond anyone's—including the president's and Congress's—control, Alton operations, especially on the Western Division, were cut significantly. After 1932 only a single through Kansas City–Bloomington freight was carded. The historically light, local passenger business on the Division was next to nothing, being easily accommodated in a motor car put on to replace the conventional, all-stop local of a few years prior. Two local pas-

senger runs on the main line between Chicago and St. Louis were dropped, and Peoria-Chicago service over the Dwight Branch was reduced to mixed train service. System wide, the average number of passengers per train mile stood at just 38; the number of passenger cars, excluding head-end and nonrevenue equipment operated per train, just four.[11]

Willard had also testified that his road had an "excess of locomotives of higher capacity than many now being operated on the Alton, and I believe if forty or fifty of the engines . . . were transferred to the Alton the results would be beneficial not only to both of the companies involved, but also to the public served by the Alton company."[12] That too never happened. Soon after takeover, the Alton fleet of engines were renumbered into the B&O system. A large number of them, though not needed, were overhauled to keep shop forces busy, but a year after the renumbering, numerous gaps appeared in the list. In 1933 a massive scrapping of former C&A power was ordered, many of them fresh out of the shops but never run. Of the 320 C&A engines rostered in 1929, only 181 Alton engines remained active—a 56 percent reduction in number representing 3.9 million pound reduction in tractive effort.[13] Long lines of dead engines filled tracks no longer needed to classify freight cars at Bloomington, Kansas City, Venice, Roodhouse, Mexico, Slater, Alton, and Ridgely. All that remained were 15 0-6-0 switchers, five Moguls, 53 Consolidations, 70 Mikados, 34 Pacifics, two Ten-Wheelers, and two Mallets. A year later the Ten-Wheelers were retired; four years later, so were the Mallets. Aside from some surplus switchers the B&OCT provided during the 1940s and an occasional road steam engine to help out, the "higher capacity" engines Willard talked about didn't make their way over to the Alton.

The once numerous freight car fleet, which numbered 13,547 in 1929, was cut by 36 percent three years later. In 1932 there were 4,850 cars bearing either C&A or Alton reporting marks, comprised of automobile cars, boxcars, flatcars, flat bottom and drop bottom gondolas, and stock cars. The road no longer rostered refrigerator cars. Despite the 36 percent reduction in number, the average capacity slipped only 2 tons, to 45 tons, an indication of how dated the Alton equipment had become.[14]

Much of the fleet had to be kept on-line because cars did not meet interchange rules. The newest cars, the coal gondolas, were of USRA vintage; the oldest, the three series of wooden boxcars, were Harriman Standard vintage. Thirty-nine percent of the fleet was either flat bottom or drop bottom coal gondolas.[15] The passenger fleet in 1932 numbered just 86 cars, including the 7 motor cars. Again the oldest cars with least utility were either dismantled or added to the maintenance-of-way fleet. The number of passenger cars operated were a far cry from the 231 C&A cars rostered in 1929. Not counting the motor cars, 45 percent of the remaining fleet was head-end equipment.[16] Besides eliminating insurance and other incidental costs, the equipment reductions resulted in big savings on car maintenance. Before the takeover, an average $6 million was spent keeping the passenger fleet running; in 1932 just $1.7 million was spent.[17]

Equally worn-out were the Alton's 171 cabooses. Most had been built in the late 1890s and early 1900s and lacked steel reinforcement and underframes, except for a dozen Western Steel Car & Foundry cars delivered sometime before 1914. In the late 1920s, the B&O had rebuilt many of its cabooses, upgrading them with steel components. In the early 1930s, 73 of them in five classes were transferred to the Alton, replacing almost all of the C&A's fleet. Seven more were added between 1942 and 1943.[18]

The first track reductions came in 1932. In February the 38 miles of the former QC&St.L between Barnett Junction and Carrollton were abandoned. The mileage from Womac to Barnett Junction had not been used for several years. Service from Carlinville to Womac was put on an as-needed service basis. An every-other-day mixed train was operated between Carlinville and East Hardin. Two years later, in 1934, the Cedar City Branch was cut back 25 miles to Fulton.[19]

Passenger service between Chicago and St. Louis, however, continued at the highest levels. The comfort of travelers was greatly enhanced with introduction of air conditioning on the *Alton Limited* in June 1932, another first for the railroad, at least on the highly competitive St. Louis–Chicago route.[20] Those cars not yet converted were cooled using a system that forced cold air through a train before passengers boarded at either terminal. Within weeks of the Alton's introduction of air conditioning, the Wabash's *Banner Blue,* the C&EI's *LaSalle,* and the IC's *Daylight Special* also received air conditioning equipment to keep competitive.

The RFC was in operation only a few months before a $2.5 million loan was extended to the Alton. The proceeds were to pay off $1.5 million in receivers' certificates, $200,000 in taxes, and $800,000 in equipment trust obligations.[21] Forty percent of the road's fixed charges had been eliminated with

Yards were all but empty and weeds were growing between rails of all but the main line during the depths of the depression. This is Glenn Yard in the early 1930s. (R. E. Collons Photo., Ag82.231.4068, courtesy of DeGolyer Library, SMU)

The *Abraham Lincoln,*
with the *Lord Baltimore* in
charge, backs into St.
Louis Union Station as it
ends its five-and-one-half-
hour, limited-stop run
from Chicago. (Gulf,
Mobile & Ohio RR Histor-
ical Society Archive, J. W.
Barriger III National RR
Library, St. Louis Mercantile Library, University of
Missouri-St. Louis)

the Alton's purchase, but the road was still not generating enough cash to service even its greatly reduced debt, nor would it ever under B&O ownership. At the depths of the depression, in 1935, the road incurred a deficit of $2.1 million. Weeds were beginning to show through the ties of not only yard trackage but also secondary main lines. Work forces, especially maintenance-of-way workers and shopmen, were laid off for extended periods then recalled. Those men working were appreciative of having any job at all.

As a cost-saving measure, the industry considered facility consolidation where it made sense, an idea first promoted by the USRA. The Alton and Santa Fe yards at Joliet were considered candidates, but nothing came of it. Transferring Alton motive power repairs to the EJ&E at Joliet was proposed, but that never happened either. A major review of the Bloomington Shops to determine their suitability to serve other roads was started, but aside from the occasional emergency repair of another road's power and the Springfield-based B&O power, only Alton engines were shopped. Moves to integrate power and equipment servicing brought B&O engines to the Alton's Venice and Ridgley engine facilities and Alton passenger equipment to the B&O's Lincoln Coach Yard at 14th Street in Chicago, though whatever plans there might

have been to move Alton trains from Union Station to Grand Central Station that Willard had suggested never materialized.

The lion's share of Chicago–St. Louis passenger traffic was still claimed by the Alton, but the total market had shrunk. Voorhees, in an attempt to cut costs for the Alton as well as its competitors, approached the Wabash and IC with a proposal for each to drop a train. Since the C&EI had already removed an afternoon train in 1931, nothing further was asked of it. An agreement resulted in a six-daily train schedule for the Alton, three each for the Wabash and the IC, and two for the C&EI.[22]

In the middle of the depression, the Boston & Maine, Burlington, and UP—in an attempt to attract more traffic—began experimenting with faster, diesel-powered, lightweight, articulated trains and equally lightweight passenger cars. The already heavy, traditional all-steel cars had become even heavier as air conditioning and other appliances were added. Weightier trains meant higher operating costs, and cost reductions, as much as passenger comfort, was the reason the more progressive American railroads started experimenting with lighter construction materials. The cross-country tours of the first of the new trains quickly captured the public's attention. The Burlington's extremely fast run of its *Zephyr* from Denver to Chicago's Century of Progress fair in 1933 marked the beginning of the streamliner era of railroading.

The B&O, like other roads, was suffering huge passenger losses. The road was locked in a competitive fight with the Pennsylvania for traffic over the highly trafficked New York–Washington corridor. Both ran a premier, limited train on the route—the *Royal Blue* and the *Congressional*. Not surprisingly, the B&O—far more progressive than the tradition-bound Pennsylvania—announced in 1934 that it had placed an order with American Car & Foundry (ACF) for two experimental lightweight, air-conditioned streamlined sets of eight cars. Each was to test the relative merits of two material types, aluminum alloy and Cor-Ten steel, a cheaper, corrosion-resistant, high-tensile material.[23] The cars would have the latest appointments, including air conditioning. They would ride lower to the rails and have full width diaphragms to reduce wind resistance (a calculation recently introduced in equipment design as the demand for lower operating costs and higher speeds increased). Unlike the lightweight trains turned out earlier for the Burlington, the ordered equipment would be conventionally coupled rather than articulated.[24]

Two different engine types, like the passenger equipment, were selected for direct comparison purposes. They were rebuilt at the B&O's Mount Clare Shops. The first was a 4-4-4 type, named the *Lady Baltimore,* the road's no. 1. The second was a 4-6-4, named the *Lord Baltimore,* its no. 2. The Class J-1 4-4-4 had 17x28 cylinders and 84-inch drivers, weighed 217,800

pounds, and could develop a tractive force of 35,000 pounds with a high-speed booster added. The engine bore a single-drum, 146-tube water-tube firebox, Walschaerts vale gear, superheater, stoker, power reverse, and train control. The tender carried 14 tons of coal and 8,000 gallons of water and was fitted with a full width diaphragm to present a seamless appearance with the cars. The Class V-2 4-6-4 carried larger cylinders, measuring 19x28 inches; weighed 294,000 pounds; and with a booster, developed even more tractive effort—41,000 pounds. Its tender carried two tons more coal and 2,000 gallons more water. The *Lord Baltimore* was almost 9 feet longer—at 42 feet, 10 inches—than the *Lady Baltimore.*[25]

Both engines were to have a shroud over the length of the boiler, reminiscent of British locomotives, but when President Willard saw the *Lady Baltimore* for the first time, he ordered the shroud removed. Chief of motive power and equipment George Emerson must have persuaded him to keep the streamlining on no. 2, to test its effect on wind resistance, because that engine emerged with an English-style smokebox front, smooth sides, and a long, pointed pilot with a retractable coupler.

Work was under way on both the cars and engines when a more startling order for a single passenger diesel unit was announced. What made the order surprising was Willard's (a former locomotive engineer) love of steam power. Earlier, the Pennsylvania and the New Haven had started electrification of their eastern seaboard routes, but Willard was not tempted to follow. The B&O already had diesels on the property, but they were switchers, bought 10

The first diesel the Alton operated was parent B&O's no. 50. As delivered, the unit had a flat nose but was modified in 1937 to give crews an added measure of grade-crossing safety. (William Raia Coll.)

years earlier to comply with New York City's smoke abatement mandate. Undoubtedly it was Emerson who convinced Willard to try a diesel for a direct comparison with the experimental *Lord* and *Lady*.[26]

The newly acquired Electro-Motive Division of General Motors (Hamilton's Electro Motive Corp.), flush with the success of the articulated trains it had turned out, had two 1,800-horsepower box cab demonstrators. The units had been manufactured for the company by General Electric at its Erie, Pennsylvania, plant since Hamilton, president of the General Motors subsidiary, did not yet have a production facility of his own. He was as pleased as he could be when the B&O order was handed to him. Two 900-horsepower Winton engines housed in a 66-foot-long box rode on two sets of four-wheel trucks. Its plain, squared appearance was in sharp contrast to that of the sleek lines of the earlier articulated units.[27]

In December 1934 the IC joined the fray and placed an order with Pullman for a diesel-electric streamlined train for its Chicago–St. Louis service to challenge the Alton's market supremacy. The development brought concern in Baltimore because the Alton could ill afford any loss of traffic, as the IC's train was sure to cause. It would be almost a year before the IC received its train, so a quick decision was made to assign one of the B&O train sets and an engine to the Alton to get the jump on the IC.[28]

That fast running was possible was proved in the spring of 1935. Test runs of a mail-baggage car, three reclining seat coaches, one combination lunch counter-diner, two parlor cars, and a parlor observation—with the *Lord Baltimore* on the point—were conducted over the Alton. In one run the train knocked off the 284 miles between terminals in 4 hours, 34 minutes—an average speed of 62 miles per hour. Another 124-mile run was made at the rate of 80 miles per hour. It was obvious that only track conditions would dictate how fast the train could be operated. During one of those tests, the Alton's chief engineer, Armstrong Chinn, President Willard, and a few other B&O executives, including a member of Willard's engineering department, Belin Bodie, were on board. The Alton's road foreman of engines, J. J. Siegfried, was at the controls. Siegfried was told to watch his speed and provide "a nice easy ride." When the

train took the sharp curve at Lemont, Willard was thrown back in his chair, and the others clung to the arms of their chairs to avoid being thrown to the floor. After the train returned to straight track, a not-too-happy Willard looked at Chinn with a menacing glare and said, "Your curves need working over." Chinn responded with a smart "Yes sir." Willard then asked, "How many men will it take to rework all of your curves?" Chinn thought for only a moment before he replied, "Oh, a thousand men." He thought he might as well have asked for 10,000, but Willard responded, "You've got 'em. Now go fix those curves!" Thereafter the curve at Lemont was known as the "1,000 Man Curve."[29]

On May 15, 1935, the new train was introduced with much fanfare at the Springfield depot. Governor Henry Horner broke a bottle filled with water taken from the Sangamon and Mississippi Rivers and Lake Michigan over the engine's pilot to the cheers of thousands who had gathered to witness the event. The Columbia Broadcasting System transmitted the ceremony live to its millions of radio listeners across America in a 15-minute broadcast. Popular singer Kate Smith in New York and the B&O Glee Club in Washington started the broadcast with song, followed by the governor's dedication and speech. Then the radio listeners and those standing trackside heard two long and two short whistles from the locomotive, marking the end of the celebration. It was a public relations coup that the Charltons would have appreciated.

A high-speed demonstration run to Chicago had been planned, but that was scuttled, and instead a series of public inspections was scheduled. The train was left on display for the remainder of the day and part of the next at Springfield before moving on to Lincoln, Bloomington, Pontiac, Dwight, and Joliet for brief walk throughs, and on to Chicago, where the engine and train was placed on public display for two days. Throughout May and into early June, thousands walked through the train at Detroit; towns in Indiana and Ohio; Louisville, Kentucky; Wheeling, West Virginia; cities in Pennsylvania, Delaware, and New Jersey; Baltimore; and finally Washington, D.C.[30] On June 24, the train made its first revenue run as the *Royal Blue*.

Meanwhile, the Cor-Ten steel set of equipment was delivered to the Alton. On July 1, 1935, lightweight passenger equipment made its debut in Alton passenger service. Named the *Abraham Lincoln,* the train's schedule, at five and one-half hours, was an hour shorter than any previous Alton train. At 8:58 A.M., the large drivers of the *Lady Baltimore* began rotating, and the blue-sided, gray-roofed consist, with Baltimore & Ohio spelled out across the letterboard, pulled out of St. Louis Union Station, headed for Chicago with stops only at College Avenue, Springfield, and Bloomington before nosing into Chicago's Union Station at 2:28 P.M. There, switching, cleaning, and commissary crews had only a little more than an hour to turn, clean, and stock the train before its scheduled 4:15 P.M. return. The train's introduction was another first in the road's storied passenger service history. It quickly began turning in the highest passenger revenue per mile returns of any long-haul passenger train.[31] Even the beloved *Alton Limited* was overshadowed by the appearance and performance of the *Abraham Lincoln,* which quickly earned the nickname the "Blue Train."

Similarly, Kansas City–St. Louis passengers were introduced to a sleek and fast new train with the inauguration of one of the Burlington's newly arrived four-car, EMD-powered,

Budd-built articulated diesel trains. The *Ozark State Zephyr* was inaugurated on December 20, 1936, on five-and-one-half-hour runs over the 279 miles between Missouri's two most important cities. Convenient 8:00 A.M. departures out of St. Louis and late afternoon returns at 4:00 P.M. soon made the train a popular choice.[32] The Burlington added the *General Pershing Zephyr* as a midday run, which filled out a three-daily train schedule with the conventionally equipped *Night Hawk* running overnight.

The *Abraham Lincoln's* inaugural beat that of the IC's new streamlined *Green Diamond,* but when the IC's streamliner was introduced in May 1936, it was put on an even faster schedule—just 4 hours and 55 minutes. Though the *Lady Baltimore* was a fast runner, it required a fuel and water stop, something that no. 50—the box cab the B&O put at the head end of the *Royal Blue* the previous August—didn't require. Baltimore decided to transfer no. 50 (the first non-articulated road diesel placed in main line service) to the Alton. It took up its chores on the head end of the road's increasingly popular *Abraham Lincoln* in April 1936, a month before the IC's fast runs started. The colorful race of lightweight thoroughbreds was on.

Eight months later the aluminum set of cars

Just a few minutes out of CUS, no. 3 begins picking up speed for its daily 284-mile run to St. Louis. EMC produced no. 50 as an experimental demonstrator, but it continued to be used into the 1950s. (J.W. Barriger III National RR Library, St. Louis Mercantile Library, University of Missouri-St. Louis) and the *Lord Baltimore* were withdrawn from *Royal Blue* service and sent to the Alton. At the Bloomington Shops, one of the reclining seat coaches was reconfigured as a 38-seat buffet lounge car, and the two 30-foot mail-baggage cars were converted into a straight baggage, 44-seat coach and a 36-seat coach. A Cor-Ten steel coach was rebuilt as a buffet lounge at the B&O's Mt. Clare Shops. Another 64-seat Cor-Ten steel coach was ordered from ACF.

The original and reconfigured equipment was to be used as a companion train for the *Abraham Lincoln*. The train was given the name *Ann Rutledge* (for Lincoln's sweetheart during his New Salem days). On July 26, 1937, train no. 18, headed by the *Lord Baltimore*, left Chicago Union Station at 8 A.M. for its maiden run. Though it made seven scheduled stops en route, the *Ann Rutledge* pulled into St. Louis Union Station in 5 hours, 20 minutes. The train was quickly turned and serviced, and at 4:30 P.M., it emerged from under the great shed for its return. Northbound it had only two scheduled stops, so it easily

made its 9:25 P.M. arrival in Chicago in just 4 hours, 55 minutes.[33]

All of the positive public attention paid the pair of streamliners was welcomed but could not disguise the Alton's otherwise desperate state. By 1937 the Burlington found it increasingly difficult to coordinate schedules with the Alton and stopped running its freight trains between Francis and Kansas City (though joint passenger operations continued). The Alton's revenue loss was small, but any dissipation of income was a hit the struggling road could ill afford.

The persistent depression actually got worse in 1938 after showing earlier signs of improvement, all but eliminating any hope of an Alton recovery. The $3.3 million average annual loss during the first four years of B&O control had more than doubled in 1936 to $6.8 million. In 1937 it climbed to $7.7 million despite slightly higher revenues. When the $2.5 million RFC loan came due in 1935, the Alton could not pay it. Baltimore had to step in and turned over $415,000 worth of

The robust consist of main line passenger trains had faded from memory during the 1930s. Here train no. 11 at Bloomington in 1938 carries only a smoker combine and single coach, mail storage car, and RPO. (Paul Stringham Photo., William Raia Coll.)

Monongahela Railroad stock the road held as partial repayment. A five-year extension for repayment of the balance was requested, but only three years were given. When that deadline arrived, an extension was again requested, and once again the parent road had to intervene, guaranteeing repayment.[34]

Between 1931 and 1938, the freight car fleet continued to see reductions. The fleet now numbered just 2,890 cars. With less demand, 68 percent of the coal gondolas were scrapped in 1938, leaving just 398 in service. Only seven mines directly served by the Alton were still active. The once large fleet of stock cars had been reduced to just 234, most of the livestock trade having disappeared. There were now 97 flatcars. The rest of the freight roster comprised rebuilt wooden boxcars that had steel ends and underframes added—2,119 of them.[35] That year 11 engines, including a switcher, three Consolidations, the two Mallets, and five of the oldest Pacifics were retired. With no. 50 heading the *Abraham Lincoln,* the *Lady Baltimore* was returned to the B&O for reassignment.[36]

Thanks to the popularity of the twin lightweight trains, the Alton's share of the Chicago–St. Louis passenger market grew, though the total market was far smaller. And the number of passengers on local runs were now often fewer than the members of the crew. The year's total passenger count was a paltry 707,418, though the average trip length had risen to 169 miles, a reflection of the popularity of the *Abe* and *Annie.*[37] The automobile (there were now 1.6 million automobiles registered in Illinois) had captured 85 percent of all intercity trips. More than 13,300 miles of paved highway now crisscrossed the state, including the mother of all roads—U.S. 66—which paralleled the Alton's main line nearly the entire distance between Chicago and St. Louis and extended all the way to California. Chicago–Kansas City passenger service, after the Santa Fe added new lightweight equipment and diesels on speedier schedules, was all but lost. Though *The Hummer* was still running, only a single 10-section, dinette lounge car and chair cars made up its consist. A daily mixed train served the Mexico-Fulton mileage. The Illinois branches—except the Dwight branch, where a three-day-a-week mixed worked—

had no passenger service whatsoever.[38]

To achieve economy and greater efficiency, between 1935 and 1938 three of the Class P-16 Pacifics, now almost 30 years old, were modernized with the addition of Standard Stokers and Hudson Tuyere type grates. The tenders were lengthened by five feet to increase their water capacity to 13,650 gallons and the coal capacity to 19 tons. The modernized Pacifics produced sizeable savings to passenger train operations.[39]

▼▼▼

Daniel Willard had been at the helm of the B&O and its affiliated companies for 31 years when he celebrated his eightieth birthday in January 1941 and decided to call it a career. He relinquished the presidency in May to Roy White, a career railroader who had worked his way up to the top through the operating department. An unsentimental, no-nonsense man of different skills and accomplishments would now be running the railroad. In July, following a six-week illness, Willard died.[40]

It was the middle of the day in the Midwest on Sunday, December 7, 1941, when radio broadcasts were interrupted with a special news bulletin that the Japanese had attacked the U.S. naval base at Pearl Harbor and in the Philippines. People turned to one another and asked, "Where's Pearl Harbor?" Newspapers had published daily reports concerning the war in Europe since September 1939 after German forces invaded Poland and before that when Hitler's troops invaded Austria and Czechoslovakia, but Japan's aggression in the Pacific had gotten far less attention. The attack at Hawaii shocked the country. President Franklin Roosevelt had been repeatedly on the radio with "fireside chats" to calm the fears of many Americans who felt that he was anxious for war. At the same time, he pushed to increase production of needed materiel and deliver supplies to a beleaguered England in its lonely stand against a vicious enemy. The attack on the naval port far out in the Pacific removed all doubts why buildup was necessary. Japan had sucked a reluctant United States into the Second World War.

Until that attack there had been little improvement in the nation's economy. In 1939 the nation's factories were still underutilized

THE CHICAGO & ALTON RAILROAD

During World War II, even secondary trains like the *Prairie State Express*, seen here approaching Joliet Union Station, were running at full capacity. Only the availability of power and equipment limited the size of trains. (Gulf, Mobile & Ohio RR Historical Society Archive, Robert Collons Photo. Coll., Ag82.231:3272, courtesy of DeGolyer Library, SMU)

and 9.5 million Americans were still unemployed—17 percent of the total work force.[41] Within days of the attack, young men lined up outside recruiting offices, and others received draft notices. The government issued industrialists instructions to forget about producing refrigerators, tractors, and automobiles. From now until the conflict was concluded, almost everything produced would be painted olive drab and bear the marking of the army, navy, and marines. Factories were reactivated and once again were approaching full production.

The buildup forced the railroad industry to face the challenge of transforming itself into a wartime transportation system. It was only slightly better prepared this time. American railroads had 31 percent fewer engines, 24 percent fewer freight cars, and 35 percent fewer passenger cars than at the start of the country's involvement in 1917, but the freight cars averaged nearly 10 tons greater capacity and the industry's motive power produced much greater tractive effort.[42] The greatest deficiency the industry faced was in the number and capacity of passenger cars. All

roads engaged in wholesale scrapping of outdated equipment during the depression as passenger losses mounted. Now with American railroads about to engage in the most massive movement of military personnel in the country's history, they had an inadequate passenger roster to do it.

Every railroad had deferred maintenance during the depression. Nevertheless, the industry's physical plant was in remarkably good shape. Multiple track main lines and sophisticated signaling installed over the previous 25 years had made the roads better prepared to handle what was to come. The clogged main lines of World War I were not going to be an issue this time.

In May 1940 Roosevelt established the Advisory Commission to the Council of National Defense, made up of six members of his cabinet and an advisory council of leaders of the nation's important industries. Ralph Budd, president of the Burlington, was named to the council as commissioner of transportation and, in that role, had the responsibility of transforming all forms of transport into an efficient machine that had just one goal: keeping the traffic moving.[43] Budd implored the railroads to repair bad order equipment, which they did, reducing the figure in 1941 to 4 percent, the lowest ratio in memory. He recommended stockpiling coal during the summer months to even out traffic peaks. He promoted discontinuance of the least productive passenger runs. He ordered traffic studies to find the most strategic routes to insure no one line would become overwhelmed. He also brought attention to the need for better access roads to defense plants to reduce bottlenecks for trucks and buses and got the icebreaking season on the Great Lakes extended so shipping could continue later into what normally would be the off-season. Through his efforts the transportation industry was put on a solid footing, better prepared for the coming onslaught of new traffic.

By the end of 1942, Alton freight revenue train miles and average revenue freight train load in tons had jumped 21 percent.[44] Though passenger train miles increased only 2 percent, passengers carried swelled by 28 percent. Trains were again numerous, long, and heavy.

▾▾▾

After the several acquisitions during the late 1920s and early 1930s, the B&O corporate structure had become somewhat complex, comprising of 107 separate entities. During the early 1940s, that number was reduced to 70. Streamlining the corporation was White's objective. He had been president for little more than a year but was already making his mark. It was in 1942 that the question of what to do with the Alton arose. It had been kept separate from the B&O System, never having been placed on the parent's books, and White decided it was time to cut all ties. The savvy team of executives carrying out the restructuring put together a report that concluded the Alton's improved performance brought on by the windfall of wartime traffic would not be sustained after the end of the conflict. After the war, the losses so far sustained (deficits had been posted every year of B&O control) would only increase. A postwar marginal existence would undoubtedly require periodic B&O financial intervention, an uninviting prospect. White had no interest in keeping a

property that drained company resources.[45]

Thus, on November 25, 1942, a reorganization petition under chapter 77 of the Bankruptcy Act was filed in federal court in Chicago. Included was the assertion that the Alton was unable to meet its accrued indebtedness and could not obtain funds to do so. According to testimony, efforts to get the principal debtors to accept a readjustment of scheduled payments had gone nowhere. The bondholders' only counter was for White to lend the Alton more money. He did not see that as a solution. The aggregate outstanding claims plus interest on December 31, 1942, was $48.4 million.[46]

Federal judge John Barnes named a Chicago attorney, Henry Gardner, as the road's receiver. He took over officially January 22, 1943. Early in July Gardner submitted a reorganization plan that made no provision for the capital stock, all held by the B&O. All of the assets, including the leases of the J&C, L&MR, and KCSt.L&C, would be conveyed to a new company. When that happened, all the debt comprised of the company's bonds, notes, and other debts, as well as the stocks of the leased lines, would be canceled and the leased lines would be dissolved. Total capitalization of the new company would be $57.7 million, fixed interest $206,780, and contingency interest $968,222.[47] Bondholders of the KCSt.L&C particularly objected to a reorganization of that road. Persuaded, Gardner amended his plan, dropping that part of the petition. Though Gardner had planned for the reorganization to be consummated in early 1943, Judge Barnes did not act on the petition as quickly as hoped but finally set February 29, 1944, as the date to hear arguments.

Meanwhile, the hard-pressed Alton operating officials struggled to match too little power and too few cars with the demands for both being asked of them. In 1937 Electro-Motive received a sizeable B&O order of 12 diesel units, six cabs, and six boosters. Like the no. 50, these units had tandem 900-horsepower Winton V-12 engines, but they generated 800 more horsepower. Unlike the 50, these units were housed in streamline carbodies with sloping front ends that provided a greater measure of crew safety as well as a more attractive design. Since production of the first experimental units, numerous internal improvements had been introduced, and the units rode on A1A six-wheel trucks instead of the four-wheel B types used on no. 50.[48]

The sleek, new power in blue-and-gray dress—designated EMD's EA model—began arriving in 1938. EMD added more physical and electrical changes to the product over the course of the next two years and, by 1940, was offering an even better model, designated its E6. The B&O bought seven A and B unit sets. The 28-unit diesel fleet was naturally assigned to the road's best trains, the *Capitol Limited, Royal Blue, Columbian,* and the newly streamlined Jersy City–St. Louis *National Limited.* The schedule of that train involved a 19-hour layover in St. Louis, a prolonged period of downtime that was quickly realized as sufficient to protect a round-trip over the Alton. This became the practice on a somewhat intermittent basis until 1940, when B&O EA no. 52 was leased. It ran north at the head end of the *Ann Rutledge,* no. 18, returning south on no. 7, *The Fast Mail.*

In late 1941 the Alton directors approved the purchase of an A-B set of diesels for passenger service. After it was placed in service, 61 percent of all through St. Louis–Chicago service would be dieselized. The addition of just that one diesel set would retire eight Pacifics of three classes and bring considerable fuel and labor savings.[49] A month after the board's action, White authorized Voorhees to proceed with the $340,000 purchase.[50] Then

in January 1942, White asked Voorhees to determine what was required to dieselize all Alton main line passenger trains. It was determined that two more sets would accomplish the goal: eliminating half the Pacific fleet (13 engines, most double-heading) and the running of second sections (including the second parlor car section of the *Alton Limited*).[51] White agreed and gave Voorhees's direction to proceed. But during the brief two weeks it took for White to get back to him, Voorhees's mind was changed by House on the road's requirements. Voorhees went back to White and asked him to approve a change for all A units, instead of half cab and half booster units, to eliminate the need to turn pairs at either terminal.[52] He did, and the contacts with EMD were modified. House looked forward to delivery of the first units later that year.

Within weeks of placing the orders, however, EMD informed Voorhees they could not deliver as promised. A few months before the attack on Pearl Harbor, Roosevelt had given official status to the Advisory Commission headed by Budd by creating the Office of Defense Transportation (ODT). Budd returned to the Burlington, and the president named ICC member Joseph Eastman to head the ODT. But like Budd, Eastman was only partially successful, and in 1942 Roosevelt gave sweeping power over the nation's economy to yet another new agency, the War Production Board (WPB), headed by Donald Nelson of Sears, Roebuck. It was the country's first

The Alton had only two diesel units to power the swollen passenger train consists during the war, and neither alone could handle the expanded trains. The solution was to remove the slanted nose of the original no. 50 to mate the engine with no. 52. In winter, a Pacific was added to provide the steam needed to heat the cars. (Walter A. Peters Photo., Richard R. Wallin Coll.)

The first 1,000-horsepower switcher Alco-GE delivered in 1944 was no. 10. Fifteen Class DS switchers were delivered during 1944–1945, allowing twice that number of steam switchers to be retired. (William Raia Coll.)

attempt at central planning. Everything produced, including critical manufacturing of railroad supplies and equipment, came under Nelson's authority. One of the first WPB actions taken was to restrict locomotive manufacturers from duplicating efforts. Production of EMD's passenger units was suspended.[53] In April EMD told Voorhees the bad news and offered the option of canceling the orders, "in view of the present uncertainties."[54] Wisely, Voorhees decided to leave the orders alone and hope for the best. EMD officials suggested the regulations might be lifted within 12 months but could make no promises.

As a result of the suspended orders, the assignment of steam and the diesel pair remained as it was for the war's duration. There was enormous pressure to maximize utilization of the locomotives available. The no. 50 had a sloping false front applied in 1937 to add to crew safety, and it continued heading the *Abraham Lincoln*. But as wartime consists lengthened, more horsepower than the no. 50 alone could produce necessitated the false front's removal and the box cab's status reduced to that of a booster unit, paired with no. 52 as a 3,600-horsepower set. To avoid paying claims for double-heading, no. 52 was renumbered 50 too.[55] The modified P-16 Pacifics were once more on the point of the *Ann Rutledge*.

Even with 3,600 horses, the diesel pair assigned to the *Abraham Lincoln* had to be operated wide-open on the number eight notch, resulting in frequent traction motor failures, an intolerable situation. Orders were issued to limit train consists to 13 cars when the two units operated in tandem and to seven cars when either operated alone. When the units were out of service or loads were particularly heavy, Pacifics were employed in expensive double-header service.

As a stopgap measure, starting in 1943 and continuing into 1944, seven more of the latest Pacifics were improved in the same manner as the prior three. The new efficiency brought on by the modernization proved to be worth the equivalent of almost two additional locomotives.[56] Nearly $100,000 in annual fuel savings and most of the expensive and inefficient double-heading was eliminated, proving the worth of the program. Every effort was made to reduce running expenses. Coping was added to switcher tenders (and part of the 2-8-2 fleet, now known as the McArthur type since Mikado was too closely associated with the enemy) to reduce the number of coaling stops. Superheaters were applied to power still lacking them.

There were only nine 0-6-0 switchers and five 2-6-0s rostered in 1943 and even leased B&OCT switchers and the transfer of 2-8-0s and 2-8-2s to switching duties were not enough to handle Alton marshaling chores. By now Voorhees and House were fully committed to dieselization as quickly as possible. The road's experience with the two EMD passenger units and Baltimore's obvious preference for the builder made House an EMD fan. But because the WPB restricted EMD from producing its 600-horsepower and 1000-horsepower models—which had both been introduced in 1939—the choice was between Baldwin and Alco-GE products. House was leery of reports of repetitive problems roads that had bought Alco-GE units were experiencing, but a number of roads, including the Gulf, Mobile & Ohio (GM&O), had placed large orders for the products turned out and seemed to be able to deal with the associated teething problems. Thus, in late 1943, four 660-horsepower and five 1,000-horsepower Alco units were ordered.[57]

The Alco salesman was happy to take the order but told House it might be a year or two before the 10 could be delivered since Alco's order books were already full, largely owing to the 20-unit GM&O consignment. Since House's need was immediate, he contacted the GM&O's general superintendent of motive power, B. H. Gray, and asked if his road would allow the Alton to take part of the order. Gray, after consulting with vice president and general manager Glen Brock, agreed to help House out. Thus, between February and June 1944, 10 Alco S2 models—painted in two-tone red and bearing the name Alton, the Alton insignia, and the numbers 10–19—were assigned to Alton yards. They replaced 19 steam engines at Venice and Bloomington Yards, which were reassigned to Glenn Yard. Those engines in turn allowed the release of an equal number of rented B&O and B&OCT switchers, saving a substantial annual cost of $100,000.[58]

There was still a need for more switchers, and in 1945 five more Alco S2s were ordered. Numbered 20–24, they first saw service at South Joliet. Two of the original 10 were transferred from Bloomington to Joliet, releasing 11 steam engines there, including seven 2-8-0s and four 2-8-2s, which were returned to road service. One of the Consolidations released was sent to the Lincoln Street Coach Yard to equalize service hours. Another replaced no. 2661, which had been assigned to

Dwight for Washington Branch service to replace an engine destroyed in an enginehouse fire. Two others were sent to Bloomington to replace the diesels sent to Joliet and another to Twelfth Street Yard at Kansas City.[59]

In 1943 the first orders of critically needed freight equipment—the first new rolling stock in 20 years—were placed. Included were the first all-steel cars the road ever purchased—600 50-ton steel boxcars from ACF and another 500 from Pullman Standard. The same two manufacturers also turned out 150 50-ton steel offset side hoppers and 850 composite hoppers. Bloomington Shops began rebuilding most of the remaining flatcars, gondolas, and boxcars that had been in service for more than 30 years. By the end of 1944, most of the new equipment had been added. In the spring of 1945, 10 aluminum-alloy boxcars—laid over a steel underframe and produced by Mt. Vernon Car Manufacturing Company—appeared, part of a 30-car order shared with the Rock Island and M&St.L. They were equipped with steam and signal lines and weighed some 10,000 pounds less than a conventional steel 40-foot boxcar, important since they were to be used as head-end cars for mail storage in passenger trains. Gardner also leased 300 double-deck stock cars from the Mather Stock Car Company.[60]

During the early months of the war, civilians and the first men in uniform could find a seat or a section on most Alton trains, but the massive upsurge in military and government traffic changed all that. Soldiers, sailors, and airmen in and out of Camp Lincoln at Springfield, the Great Lakes Naval Training Center and Ft. Sheridan at Chicago, Jefferson Barracks and Ft. Leonard Wood at St. Louis, and the two airfields—Richards Field and Marshall Field (as well as Ft. Riley) at Kansas City—now filled almost every seat on every train. But as more camps, forts, and airfields were activated throughout the country, members of the military were handing multi-part tickets to conductors and trainmen to far more remote destinations. As equipment could be marshaled, solid troop trains were operated. The increased traffic was massive. In 1940, before the buildup, the Alton moved 740,054 passengers. In 1942, the first full year of mobilization, 1.4 million passengers were boarded, but by the war's

conclusion in 1945, 2.2 million passengers were transported—numbers not seen since before the advent of the automobile.[61]

To supplement its limited and taxed fleet, the Alton leased 37 surplus B&O passenger cars, one postal car, a single combine, and 35 coaches. Passenger equipment was getting so much use that regular maintenance had to be deferred. The already dated equipment (and even the lightweight equipment) had never looked so bad. The leased B&O coaches were in even worse shape. Assistant passenger traffic manager Roy Pearce complained, and House knew he was right, but House was reluctant to return the leased B&O cars to Mt. Clare for class repairs for fear they might not be returned.[62] Letters and packages with APO addresses nearly overwhelmed the capacity of mail storage cars. A train made up of nothing but boxcars began running as a second section of no. 7, *The Mail*.[63] In May 1943, Chinn—recently elevated to the general manager's position under Voorhees—and IC representatives agreed to coordinate sleeping car service between Chicago and Springfield to free up two badly needed sleepers for military

movements. Thereafter, each road operated Springfield sleepers in alternate months.[64]

The increases in freight moved matched the increased passenger volumes. In 1940, 7.2 million tons of freight was transported; in 1942, 12.6 million tons; and in 1945, 13.2 million tons.[65] War material and coal, as was to be expected, accounted for the greatest increases (32 percent and 53 percent, respectively). The tonnage was almost evenly divided between traffic originating on-line and that picked up from other roads. The amount of freight, especially boxcars full of ammunition and bombs out of the newly opened arsenal at Elwood; tank cars of petroleum from both on-line producers at Lockport and Wood River and refineries in Texas, Louisiana, and Oklahoma; and flatcars filled with half tracks, tanks, and Jeeps produced at Peoria's Caterpillar and Springfield's Allis Chambers plants was staggering. Yards that were virtually empty during the depression were now full of cars waiting to be moved to other roads and ports on both coasts.

The right-of-way was taking a beating from the extraordinary weight of trains. The 1940

Double heading became the norm as the number of cars that had to be added to accommodate wartime travel proved too much for the elderly fleet of Pacifics. This is the *Ann Rutledge* at Bloomington in 1942. (Paul Stringham Photo., William Raia Coll.)

figure of $2.5 million spent on maintenance of way was fairly typical, but by 1943 that total had nearly doubled and continued at high levels for the duration of the war. Every dollar possible was put into replacement of ballast, rail, switch frogs, and ties. Selective abandonments of under utilized trackage were attempted. A petition to abandon the almost useless 19-mile Carrollton–East Hardin Branch was denied based on a protest of the War Food Administration despite acknowledgement that "It is true that much of the agricultural produce . . . has been handled to the markets by truck in preference to the railroad. . . ."[66]

It was a struggle to get the most out of a worn-out and depleted property. But despite the numerous shortcomings faced, revenues increased dramatically during the war years. Income nearly doubled from $16.4 million to $31.7 million from 1942 to 1943 and peaked in 1944 at $38.2 million. The deficit of $1.7 million in 1940 was turned into a $2.1 million profit in 1942, a level that was similarly maintained for the duration of the war.[67] WPB restrictions on EMD production were finally lifted in 1945. The diesel builder's designers and engineers during the intervening months had continued to refine the E unit product, and in March a new 2,000-horsepower E7 model, an evolution of the previously offered E6, was unveiled. The Alton and the B&O, because the 1942 orders had not been canceled,

were at the head of the line to receive them. In May the first two off the line appeared in the classic two-tone red paint scheme that left no doubt where they were headed. The pair were the first to operate on any road.[68]

No longer a part of the B&O, the original double digit numbers that had been planned (to fit the B&O's numbering system) were dropped, and instead the E7s appeared with numbers 101 and 101A. The next two units, of an eventual 18, went to the B&O, but the four after that left the new LaGrange, Illinois, EMD plant as the Alton's 102, 102A, 103, and 103A. After a few break-in runs, the six units were assigned to four of the Alton's featured trains, the *Abraham Lincoln, Ann Rutledge, Alton Limited,* and *Fast Mail.*

In mid-1945 a seventh and last E7 was ordered to replace the much-traveled box cab. Hamilton had built the box cab for experimental purposes and, at the time, expected to use it for engineering tests for perhaps three years and then scrap it. To his and everyone else's surprise, no. 50 was still operating in regular, high-speed service and, over the past nine years, had racked up nearly 2 million miles of service. But major repairs to the unit had become more frequent, and it was costing the railroad about 40 cents a mile to maintain it. When a seventh E7 (no. 100) arrived in December 1945, the EA (no. 52) was repainted in the Alton scheme, was numbered 100A, and was placed in service as the 100's mate. The box cab was shopped, had train control added, was renumbered 1200, and was placed in service hauling passenger trains 14 and 15 (the locals between Chicago and Bloomington), freights 98–99 between Bloomington and Roodhouse, and extra freights between Bloomington and Joliet. House obviously did not want the 1200 to stray too far from the Bloomington Shops.[69]

The seven E units released 13 Pacifics from main-line passenger service. The 4-6-2s served as freight service substitutions when no other power was available for a period but then were prepared for storage. When an unexpected call for trains carrying returning troops to Kansas City in late 1945 arose, they were pressed back into passenger service. After the war, they continued to be used on specials for a few years but then were stored again. In September 1950 the last Pacific was scrapped after several months of service in stationary boiler service.[70]

▼▼▼

The February 1944 hearings date set for the Alton's reorganization came and went as Henry Gardner persistently sought a negotiated agreement with the dissatisfied bondholders. They claimed the road was worth more than Gardner was proposing and, to prove it, commissioned Coverdale & Colpitts, well known and respected evaluators of railroad properties, to come up with an independent assessment. On the basis of that study, in January 1945 Gardner filed a revised reorganization plan that called for a higher capitalization and greater payments for each of the various creditors. He was now proposing a capitalization of $74.3 million—$4.4 million in equipment trusts; $15 million of 50-year, 4 percent bonds; and 75-year, 4.5 percent bonds totaling $20 million. The remainder would be $34.9 million of stock. The result would be reduced annual fixed charges of $100,000 on equipment obligations, $600,000 on the first mortgage, and $900,000 of contingency charges. Instead of continuing to recommend release of the three leased lines, Gardner capitulated and recommended their absorption, with holders of their securities scheduled to receive a combination of bonds and stock in the reorganized company. The $173,166 claim for unpaid dividends by KCSt.L&C securities holders would be paid in cash.[71] The plan was filed, but no hearing date was set.

Not surprisingly, given the road's sorry history for the past 37 years and its unlikely prospect of success, not one railroad expressed an interest in the Alton following the B&O's release—that is, until Issac Tigrett, the

The seven EMD E7s appeared in 1945-1946, too late to help relieve wartime needs but sufficient to dieselize the Alton's main line passenger trains, including no. 1 seen here at Joliet in 1946. (James Scribbins Photo., William Raia Coll.)

The leased B&O no. 52 was eventually acquired, repainted, and numbered 50, then 100A. In 1952 the EA was rebuilt by EMD and emerged as the GM&O's only E8. (David Goodyear Coll., E. L. DeGolyer, Jr. Photo. Coll., Ag82.232, courtesy of DeGolyer Library, SMU)

unassuming, conservative president of the 1,948-mile Gulf, Mobile & Ohio (GM&O), began to take an interest. His road had successfully welded together—from a collection of worn-out, struggling lines—a scrappy, regional line that, after absorbing the Southern Railway's castoff M&O in 1940, had connected the gulf ports at New Orleans and Mobile with St. Louis.

Tigrett, a Tennessee banker, was drawn into railroading to help out a friend. In 1911 he became treasurer of the 49-mile Birmingham & Northwestern (B&NW). A year later he became the road's president. In 1920 he became president of the Gulf, Mobile & Northern (GM&N), a line he became acquainted with when the road needed financing to extend its trackage into Tigrett's hometown. Though it did manage to make marginal profits, the GM&N was never a big moneymaker. He combined the B&NW with the GM&N and added strength to both. His road had trackage rights

to Paducah, Kentucky, and friendly connections there with the Burlington. As the country emerged from the depths of the depression and the Southern decided to rid itself of its insolvent M&O, Tigrett saw another opportunity. In 1940 he merged the M&O with his GM&N, creating the GM&O.[72]

Though the road had a physical plant no one would call first-class, Tigrett and his loyal associates were innovative. They introduced the South's first diesel-powered, streamlined passenger train (featuring trained nurses as onboard hostesses), started bus and trucking subsidiaries, and became one of the first roads anywhere to agressively move toward full dieselization. But Tigrett's road throughout its territory was overshadowed by the bigger and more powerful IC. While that road moved traffic from the Gulf through to Chicago over its own line, Tigrett's railroad terminated at East St. Louis.

Just three years after the GM&O was formed, one of his directors suggested Tigrett look at the Alton as an extension that would take the road to Chicago, creating the second—along with the IC—true north-south railroad. The reorganized Alton could probably be bought cheaply, Tigrett was told, but he demurred. "No, we have enough railroad now," he replied.[73] Somewhat later at a meeting in St. Louis, the idea was discussed again by Tigrett and three of his officers. Again Tigrett rejected the idea. "No. The Alton has an east-west line and we are a north-south road. We don't want to operate east-west," Tigrett declared, ending the discussion.[74] It was only when a close friend and business associate, Ralph Budd of the Burlington, again brought up the prospects of an Alton takeover that Tigrett somewhat relented. What changed his mind was Budd's suggestion that if Tigrett took over the Alton, Budd would lease the Kansas City–Francis portion of the Western Division, relieving Tigrett of most of the unwanted east-west mileage.[75]

Budd's proposal proved pivotal. Tigrett decided to pursue the matter. He put his staff to work estimating traffic, sent officials out for on-site studies, had his officers interview their Alton counterparts, and personally visited bankers. He received positive reports from virtually everyone. The Alton's physical plant was in reasonably good shape (better than Tigrett's road), and if the Western Division question could be resolved as Budd proposed, only the cost of reequipping the Alton remained to be answered. Gardner had used receiver certificates for $6 million of new equipment, but the Coverdale and Colpitts study indicated another $17.9 million of equipment investment was needed. The GM&O was already committed to heavy spending. Could the combined roads generate the revenues needed to pay for both? It was concluded they could.

Tigrett's next step was to see if the bondholders were willing to sell. A Dow-Jones ticker report in early 1945 disclosed Tigrett's interest in the Alton. In the interview Tigrett stated traffic studies had been made that concluded a merger of the roads would be mutually beneficial, but he questioned whether a buyout could be accomplished. He understood, he told the reporter, that Alton bonds were widely scattered among many holders

and there didn't seem to be anyone representing them, so it wasn't likely a deal could be made. The bondholder representative he was looking for was Louis Boehm of the Alton Bondholders Protective Committee. Learning of the news report, Boehm immediately telephoned Tigrett and told him he and the bondholders he represented wanted to talk and were anxious to sell. Boehm did not want to miss his only chance.

Tigrett and a team of advisors went to New York and met with Boehm and Patrick McGinnis, another bondholder committee member. Talks were continued in Chicago, where an agreement was reached. In late April 1945, Tigrett announced publicly that he would purchase the Alton. What Tigrett proposed was a wipeout of the Alton's debt and a merger—not just a purchase—of its assets with those of the GM&O. Each holder of a 3 percent Alton bond would receive a $500 4 percent income bond and seven and one-quarter shares of GM&O common stock. The receiver's equipment obligations and the leases of the J&C and the L&MR would be assumed though the lease of the KCSt.L&C would not. Instead, Tigrett suggested leaving open the possibility of others taking it over.[76]

Tigrett could have shut out the B&O entirely since its $15 million in claims and the $25 million of Alton common stock it owned had already been written off, but Tigrett wanted no possible opposition to his takeover, and he made White an offer. Four hundred thousand dollars would be paid for the B&O's unsecured claims and its Alton common stock, plus $790,925 for the collateral pledged for the RFC loan. It was the equivalent of two cents on the dollar. White, not expecting anything, readily accepted. He had a motive for accepting such a minimal payment. The write-off of the Alton's value from B&O books was being investigated by the Internal Revenue Service. With so meager a payment, the claimed tax deduction already taken could be easily justified.[77]

In June 1945 ICC examiners opened hearings on Finance Dockets 14931 and 14932. The hearings proved to be some of easiest any road faced. Executive vice president Frank Hicks and assistant vice president in charge of traffic E. B. DeVilliers were the two GM&O executives who testified. They were

By the end of World War II, the Alton's local Roodhouse-Bloomington turn was protected by a single motor car like no. 6002 (formerly the C&A's M4) seen here approaching Minier to pick up the few headed for Bloomington and a day of shopping on a beautiful summer day in 1947. (Paul Stringham Photo., William Raia Coll.)

well prepared. No opposition was raised once officials of the IC, Wabash, and C&EI were assured that existing interchange agreements with the GM&O would continue as before. Embarrassed by its misadventure into foreign land, no objection was raised by representatives of the B&O. White was glad to be rid of the Alton problem child. His road had violated the unwritten rule of no eastern road entering western territory and vice versa. The ill-advised, 14-year experience was about to end.

On September 19, 1945, in one of the quickest decisions in ICC history, the examiner's findings were approved.[78] On February 19, 1946, the merger plan was submitted to the Federal District Court in Chicago, and on May 28, 1946, Judge Barnes signed off. With the B&O officially removed from Alton affairs, in October Voorhees was replaced as the Alton's chief executive officer. Chinn, the road's general manager since 1943, was named president. Department heads of both roads, House and Gray especially, were working closely together even before formal takeover. Dieselization had been made a priority for Gray's road and a necessity for the Alton. The 15 Alco switchers working in Alton yards had eased the switching crisis, but still more were needed. House figured another 10 could re-

place all steam switchers. Since the first 10 switches were bought, Alco had introduced a similarly powered unit but one that afforded greater flexibility, including road service (made possible because of the more stable AAR-designed trucks the units rode on)—later catalogued as its RS1, a type introduced on the Rock Island. Gray had already ordered the type for straight switching and light road service for the GM&O, and three were in service (with another eight expected) when the Alton was ready to place its order. It was Gray who persuaded House to order RS1s.

During October and November 1945, after the most challenging six-year period in American railroading came to a close with the end of World War II, the first Alton RS1 road switchers were put in service. On an elongated frame, a short hood was added behind the cab, housing an optional toilet and boiler to generate steam heat. Three of the RS1s arrived so equipped and were assigned to Brighton Park and Harrison Street in Chicago for passenger work. The other seven conventional RS1s were assigned to the principal yards—three at Glenn Yard, two at Bloomington, and one each at Springfield and Venice. The 25 diesel switchers the Alton had acquired permanently replaced 47 steam switchers.[79] The RS1s came decorated and lettered in the Alton's two-tone red scheme.

Until the formal merger date was reached, whenever the GM&O could supply surplus equipment to the Alton, it did. Even before ICC examiner hearings began, the two roads considered swapping worn-out Alton gondolas for south end log loading in return for still useable coal gondolas the GM&O no longer needed since so much of the road's power was now diesel. But after Gray visited Bloomington to look over the cars, the plan was dropped. The Alton equipment (which Gray described as "not too rosy") was unfit for use. Without receiving any equipment in return, in June 1945, Gray transferred 46 hoppers and 25 boxcars to the Alton.[80]

The Alton's aged passenger fleet badly needed replacement. At the time of the merger, only 112 Alton passenger cars (including nine motor cars and trailers) were rostered. Excluding the 17 lightweight cars, there were eight coaches, five diners, five diner-parlors, six straight parlors, five baggage-coaches, two mail-smoker cars, and two observation cars. The other 53 cars were either mail, baggage-mail, or straight baggage cars. Some (the 1924 *Alton Limited* equipment and two diners)

were all steel, but most of the rest of the non-lightweight cars were rebuilt wooden cars with steel underframes and steel sheathing. It was decided that 25 coaches would be needed for postwar Alton territory trains.

The GM&O had surplus heavyweight equipment that, through rebuilding, could see several more years of service, so it was decided in June 1945 that 10 of its coaches would be shopped and rebuilt.[81] The work was to be performed at the Bloomington Shops, but when it was realized the shops were fully committed to refurbishment of the *Annie* and *Abe* sets, the work was assigned to ACF at its St. Charles, Missouri, plant. Upon their delivery, the Alton saved $225,000 in annual lease payments after a similar number of B&O coaches were returned. A mail-baggage car, no. 29, was sent north to replace a leased B&O mail-baggage car, again saving costs since the GM&O charged 75 percent of the standard rate while the B&O assessed full charges.[82]

In July 1945 the first new passenger equipment since the lightweight train sets were received ten years earlier was ordered. ACF, the longtime supplier to Tigrett's roads (the three Alco-powered articulated trains of 1935 and

Ten, 1,000-horsepower Alco-GE road switchers replaced nearly all steam from switching and local service. Class DSa unit no. 58 is at Washington on the Dwight Branch. (William Raia Coll.)

In July 1945, 15 light-weight coaches were ordered from ACF as replacements for the Alton's worn-out fleet. The order was soon modified to include four parlor cars, such as the *Springfield,* replacing a similar number of coaches. By the time the order was delivered, the GM&O takeover was a certainty, so the cars were delivered with the new road's name. (ACF Photo., courtesy of Arthur D. Dubin)

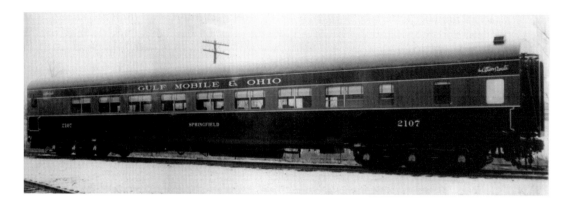

1937 and a number of inherited M&O cars came from the manufacturer), was to deliver 15 smooth-sided, lightweight, 68-seat, 85-foot-long coaches. A year passed, however, before construction of even the first car was started. Shortages of steel, fabric, glass, and fabricated parts caused by the postwar rush to produce consumer and industrial goods prevented the car builder from delivering the equipment as promised. As it turned out, the delivery delay was a blessing in disguise.

By 1946 passenger traffic on both the GM&O and Alton had reverted to prewar levels. With gasoline restrictions lifted, many had resumed their love affair with the automobile for business trips, shopping excursions, and holiday ventures. It was realized the downward trend would continue, lessening the need for so many coach seats. Overnight travel was still in demand, however, so it was planned to change the ACF order to include four sleepers for the same number of coaches. The Alton leased Pullmans, but the economy-minded GM&O operated their own sleepers. ACF representatives talked officials in Mobile out of the idea of modifying the coach order this way. Instead, in 1946, vice president of purchasing and stores, H. E. Warren, sent bid requests to Pullman Standard, Budd, and ACF for a separate order for four, duplex roomette cars with 22 or 24 spaces. Despite the competition, ACF submitted the winning bid and got the order in December 1946.

Parlor car service on the *Alton Limited, Abraham Lincoln,* and *Ann Rutledge* had been popular for some time but had gained new popularity after the war, especially between Chicago and Springfield, and was actually showing gains in an otherwise declining post-war passenger market. Politicians and others having state government business at Springfield favored the first-class service. The need for new cars again was addressed with an alteration of the coach order.

In September 1947 ACF agreed to turn out 11 coaches and four parlor cars from the same plans on the condition that the GM&O would purchase the coach seats that ACF already had on hand to equip the four coaches the builder anticipated building. The first coaches started arriving in November and December 1947 in time for the holiday rush. They were immediately put in service, releasing 12 leased cars (at least five of which were Florida East Coast equipment). On Christmas Eve 1947, the first of the four parlor cars were received, and they too were immediately pressed into service. Over the next three weeks, the other three appeared.[83]

Still to come were the sleepers. Six months after deciding on roomette cars, management had second thoughts. A through sleeper was to be introduced between Chicago and Mobile on the *Abraham Lincoln* and *Gulf Coast Rebel,* and it was felt as many different spaces as possible needed to be offered, so a configuration of four bedrooms, eight roomettes, and, somewhat surprisingly, four sections was selected. All three manufacturers had order books filled with a variety of sleeper types, but cars with open section space had become a rarity though the IC had similarly configured cars (six sections, six roomettes, four double bedrooms) running on its *Panama Limited* between Chicago and New Orleans. The reason sections were included (over the protest of the passenger department) was to provide the train's dining car steward and train hostess space on overnight *Gulf Coast Rebel* trips.[84]

The sleepers finally appeared in the summer of 1950, almost four years after they had been ordered. Traditionally, sleepers bore names, but how they would be identified without duplicating others already used by Pullman became a problem. Glen Brock asked passenger traffic manager Pearce to generate suggestions, and he came up with "I. B. Tigrett," "MacArthur," "Eisenhower," and "Lincoln," but suggested if Tigrett objected to use of his name, "Patton" might be substituted. A quick check showed that Pullman already had a *MacArthur,* so Pearce gave up on famous names of generals and recommended "Laurel," "Tuscaloosa," "Bogalusa," and "Joliet." It was found that Pullman already had a *Tuscaloosa.* Vice president of traffic L. A. Tibor then suggested state names "Illinois," "Missouri," "Mississippi," and "Alabama," but again, Pullman already had used the latter two. Tibor then substituted "Louisiana" and "Florida," but the naming game went on until a set of names exclusively identified with the GM&O and its predecessors (probably selected by Tigrett himself) was decided: the *Culver White,* for the GM&O's late finance vice president; *Judge Milton Brown,* the president of the M&O during the Civil War; *Samuel King Tigrett,* Issac Tigrett's father; and *Timothy B. Blackstone.*[85] They were some of the most distinctive names ever applied to railroad equipment.

While an official date of merger was awaited, the high-cost operations and physical weakness of the unwanted Western Division came under scrutiny. Electro-Motive salesmen were promising significant savings in operating costs with new freight road diesels. Elimination of the time-consuming and labor-intensive stops for water and fuel were obvious, as were the savings on maintenance and removal from the tax roles of such lineside facilities. A string of units pulling longer trains with less manpower was EMD's answer to the problem. In 1945, just before relinquishing his role as chief operating officer, Voorhees had been set to place an order. The B&O had already acquired a fleet of EMD's FTs with more to come. Good reports of their reliability and excellent performance plus the fact that EMD was a B&OCT customer (a Glenn Yard job serviced EMD's LaGrange plant through trackage rights at Argo) gave Voorhees more than

enough reason to select EMD. If a problem were to develop, the Alton could expect a quick response, something Gray knew was important, given the early problems with Alco the GM&O had endured.

During meetings of officials of both roads, when purchase of the new passenger equipment, diesel switchers, and 40 steel cabooses (which ACF delivered in February 1946) was being considered, Voorhees raised the question of the purchase of freight diesels for the Kansas City line. He told GM&O executive vice president Hicks that he planned to buy 10 1,350-horsepower FT freight units. Voorhees had been quoted a price of $2,325,000. Hicks knew 10 Alcos could be had for $1,170,000—a savings of $1,155,000—and asked Voorhees to wait, offering instead some of the 1,500-horsepower Alco FAs his road could make available. In a spirit of cooperation with the owners to be, Voorhees complied. Thus, for several months, 10 FAs worked the west end out of Venice, and no FT unit was ever purchased.[86] The delay Hicks asked for was fortuitous, because within months EMD introduced a new 1,500-horsepower unit, their F3. It had the same 16-cylinder, 567 engine of the FT but also had improved electrical wiring and other improvements and generated 150 additional horsepower. It was this model that EMD next offered the Alton. In July 1945 the builder submitted a proposal for 20 units to replace all Alton road steam engines. Over the next few months, various modifications requested by the Alton were considered, and by March 1946 the final list was decided. Among other features common to all units (large classification number boxes, type E couplers, a third cab seat, back-up lights, relocation of the controller, brake valve, and engineer's seat with a window armrest to facilitate switching operations), eight units were to be equipped with a steam boiler for passenger service. Other additions—such as hand holds and rungs applied to the nose to facilitate windshield cleaning, footboards on each unit's front end, front and rear push pole sockets, and battery-charging receptacles, which House had asked EMD to provide—were instead applied at Bloomington after delivery.[87]

One of the more curious aspects of the merger still had to be addressed. Despite both

The EMD F3 cab and booster units the Alton ordered, like 801B shown here, never wore Alton dress since it was evident the GM&O would soon take over. Instead, they came lettered for the successor but bore the slogan "The Alton Route." (Gulf, Mobile & Ohio RR Historical Society Coll.)

roads having East St. Louis facilities, the two roads had no physical connection. The Alton terminated at a point on Front Street north of the Eads Bridge; the GM&O terminated south of the bridge. The Alton had four yards in the vicinity: Lower Yard near Front Street, Middle Yard just north of Bridge Junction, Brooklyn Yard north of the Middle Yard, and Venice Yard north of Brooklyn Yard. Tolson Yard was the GM&O's only St. Louis area facility, adjacent to Trendley Avenue. Alton cars for the GM&O were delivered to the TRRA's no. 2 Yard. Transfer runs took the cars to Tolson. GM&O cars for the Alton were moved from Tolson to the TRRA's no. 2 Yard and then to the Alton's Middle Yard. Needless to say, this arrangement caused considerable lost time. Cars could be on the TRRA from 2 hours to as many as 31 hours; the average, traffic studies showed, was 8 hours and 20 minutes.[88] The arrangement was hardly suitable for a successful combined railroad operation.

Negotiations in late 1945 led to the TRRA agreeing to allow both roads to use its Front Street track for a connection; however, a snag developed when the TRRA objected to the track's use before formal merger occurred. Only the threat of laying its own Front Street track brought Terminal officials around. A revised agreement was reached in July 1946, and thereafter the two roads used the TRRAs Front Street track as the lone physical connection of the two roads.[89]

Before it was taken over, the M&O termi-

nated passenger trains at St. Louis Union Station, but after 1940, to avoid terminal costs, the *Gulf Coast Rebel* finished runs on the Illinois side of the river at Trendley Avenue. Passengers transferred to Greyhound buses or Yellow Cab Company taxis either at downtown St. Louis or Trendley Avenue for the river crossing. Since there were plans to run a through sleeper between Chicago and Mobile, arrangements were made to return to St. Louis Union Station.

Since 1942 Alton and B&O passenger diesels had been serviced at a three-track service area adjacent to the station's train shed the TRRA built and then leased to the Alton. It was a spartan, open facility, which needed upgrading to service the Alcos and Baldwins that would come up from the South. A 25 x 158-foot corrugated steel canopy was erected to allow the Alcos' cylinder heads (which had to be lifted through the car body roof) to be removed and protected from the elements. An inspection pit and multi level inspection platforms were installed, as was a 60-ton hoist used when trucks needed replacement. Though compact, after it was completed in 1947, the new facility proved extremely efficient. A set of diesels could be inspected and serviced in 45 minutes and returned to service.[90]

During the first few months of 1947, the process of dotting the i's and crossing the t's on the various ICC-required documents that had been going on since autumn 1946 continued. Meanwhile, to the extent permitted, departments of both roads were merged. The

Alton's Chicago headquarters was shut down in stages, its functions transferred to Mobile. Everything necessary for a smooth alliance had been put in place by late April 1947, when Tigrett was informed that his road could proceed with the formal takeover of the Alton. General manager Glen Brock issued a memo to employees: "As a matter of information, and consistent with our policy to keep you advised, we now expect the GM&O-Alton merger to be legally consummated as of 11:59 P.M., May 31, 1947."[91]

It was comfortably warm (in the high 70s) that Saturday in all three Alton terminal cities, though light rain fell intermittently in St. Louis. The second place Cubs beat the Phillies 7–1 at Wrigley Field; the Kansas City Blues slugged it out with the Milwaukee Brewers for an 18–10 win in their minor league home park; but neither the Browns, Cardinals, nor White Sox played that day. John L. Lewis, president of the UMW, made headlines by threatening another coal strike if his demands were not met. President Harry Truman signed a bill to provide $350 million in aid for relief of the war-devastated countries of Europe, the start of the Marshall Plan. Robert Todd Lincoln, the slain president's son, made a gift to the Library of Congress of some 12,000–16,000 of his father's documents. In Chicago, United Air Lines announced the start the next day of the first nonstop flight between Chicago and San Francisco. It would take only six hours. And at Chicago's Soldier Field, General Motors employees were dismantling a display of its Train of Tomorrow that had been on public view.[92]

Since the two roads had been running as practically the same company for the better part of the past two years, when May 31 rolled around, there was little evidence that a once proud and heralded 100-year-old railroad—which had started as a means of connecting a river town with a distant state capital and had grown into an iron highway that tied together three great American cities—would be passing out of corporate existence. It was destined to serve an even bigger role, connecting the Great Lakes with the Gulf of Mexico. The names Godfrey, Blackstone, and Harriman had long since passed from memory, their legacies left for others to write about in years to come. What they fashioned had seen better days but—perhaps unexpectedly—was still there as a reminder of persistence, enterprise, and skill.

No ceremony marked the joining of the railroads. There was no ribbon cutting or speeches. The next day, some Sunday editions of newspapers in the new territory carried an advertisement with the headline "Announcing America's Newest Major Railroad System," brief copy signed by Tigrett, and an illustration with a map highlighting the cities of Chicago, Kansas City, St. Louis, Memphis, Birmingham, Montgomery, New Orleans, and Mobile.[93]

Few shippers and even fewer of the traveling public in the former Alton territory knew of the GM&O. Thus for at least five years after formal merger, road diesels running between Chicago, Kansas City, and St. Louis bore the slogan "The Alton Route" on their flanks to help establish the transition to new ownership. Over time the slogans on the diesel sides and the reporting marks and Alton emblems of the few remaining Alton freight cars were painted over, removing nearly every public reminder of the road that once billed itself as "The Only Way."

An Alton RS1 and a former B&O caboose with new GM&O markings are at work in Peoria, symbolizing the creation of a 2,700-mile system from the Gulf of Mexico to the Great Lakes that would last for another 25 years. (William Raia Coll.)

Epilogue

The ink on the documents formalizing the merger had hardly dried before Tigrett became involved in yet another move to enlarge his road. In August 1947 *Railway Age* noted that Clark Hungerford, president of the St.LSF, and Tigrett had agreed to a study possibly leading to a merger of their two roads. A brief mention on the front page of the house organ, the *GM&O News,* informed the employees.[1] The combined 4,925-mile Frisco and 2,900-mile GM&O would have created an 11-state system with great possibilities. Frisco, like the former Alton, was a popular passenger road, and its oil and petrochemical traffic was growing steadily. It was a formidable competitor of the MP and MKT. Talk of the combination, however, ended as quickly as it had begun.

Though no public statement was made by either Hungerford or Tigrett to confirm the reasons, it was likely Tigrett who backed away. His business plan thus far was to grow through takeover of other roads. This was not going to result from a merger with the St.LSF. The prize for that road was the St. Louis–Chicago corridor. The rest of the mileage would have helped solidify its presence in Tennessee, Mississippi, and Alabama. Most, if not all, GM&O management would likely have been relegated to a subordinate role, running the south end, with Frisco people in overall charge—not what Tigrett had in mind. Besides, he had more immediate concerns.

In December the ICC approved acquisition of the two leased lines remaining, the J&C and the L&MR, through purchase of their stock, nearly all of which the B&O owned. To acquire the J&C common and the L&MR preferred shares still outstanding, $2.7 million of

GM&O bonds were issued. That left only the unwanted KCSt.L&C to deal with.

Between the time Budd and Tigrett first discussed the sale of the west end to the Burlington, Budd had come up with a far more intriguing plan. He had sought a way to reduce his road's mileage between St. Louis and Kansas City (69 miles longer over his own rails since 1937 when the Burlington-Alton agreement was dissolved), but he also wanted a more direct route from Kansas City to Chicago. The Santa Fe's main line from Bucklin, Missouri, to Kansas City was 22 miles shorter than the Burlington's. He knew that Fred Gurley of the Santa Fe for years had coveted an entry into St. Louis. Budd decided that in return for trackage rights over the Santa Fe's Chicago line, he would let Gurley share in purchase of the Alton's Kansas City–Mexico trackage and afford trackage rights to St. Louis over his Francis–St. Louis air line, giving Gurley's road the desired St. Louis entry.[2]

In June 1946 a joint Burlington–Santa Fe application was filed to purchase the preferred and common KCSt.L&C stock for $24,000, plus assumption of its 4.5 percent, 75-year first mortgage bonds of $2,093,890. Once the purchase was approved, the two roads would assume the lease. In support of their case, Budd and Gurley promised to invest within five years at least $5 million rebuilding the line. Trackage rights would be granted the GM&O from Mexico westward.[3]

The proposal was a stunning development that generated considerable public and industry press coverage because it had the potential to alter, in a big way, Kansas City–St. Louis traffic patterns. The approval of the purchase would have resulted in the two giant railroad systems redrawing the eastern gateway map—at least as far as St. Louis was concerned—and, in the process, causing harm to the roads already operating there, possibly destroying the chances of recovery from bankruptcy of at least four of them. Opening St. Louis to the Santa Fe would likely lead to cancellation of traffic agreements at Kansas City with the roads already serving St. Louis. The Santa Fe would be in a position to capture the lion's share of interchange traffic to the East as well as to the South, leaving little for the others. Budd and Gurley knew there would be a fuss and prepared a strong case, but neither anticipated the ferocious opposition that arose.

Examiner hearings got under way on November 12 at St. Louis's Coronado Hotel. Budd and Gurley were the first to testify. Both made clear that all aspects of their petition were "interrelated and indivisible in character, [with] consummation of any part of the plan depend[ent] upon approval of the plan in its entirety."[4] Throughout all the prehearing discussion, little attention was paid to that part that included Burlington rights over the Santa Fe. Gurley stated he would establish St. Louis sections of his road's extra-fare *El Capitan* and *Super Chief* with shorter running times than those between the West Coast and Chicago. He suggested his road's handling of freight would be improved because interchanges at Kansas City would be eliminated. Budd offered that, after the sale was approved, the two roads would spend nearly $11 million—$9 million on the line from Mexico to Kansas City and the remainder on his line east of Francis. Centralized Traffic Control would be installed between Mexico and Rock Creek Junction, and the existing 100-pound rail would be replaced and upgraded.[5]

Expert witnesses during five days of testimony made clear they favored the Burlington–Santa Fe petition, but then the opposition was given its chance. The most outspoken was Paul Neff, president of the MP. He asserted that his road stood to lose $15 million annually if the application was granted. He testified that his road over the past 20 years had spent more than $49 million on its St. Louis–Kansas City line, in his view already furnishing the superior line Gurley and Budd were proposing. Neff suggested the plan would turn a "healthy competitive transportation situation between competing lines to one of wasteful transportation between St. Louis and Kansas City." He further claimed the proposal would cause irreparable injury to the MP, the Frisco, the St. Louis Southwestern, and the Rock Island (which had traffic agreements with the Santa Fe)—the four lines that opposed the Santa Fe's St. Louis entry. Neff also said the Katy and the Wabash (neither of which filed formal objections) would also be injured. He refuted Gurley's claims that freight would move more quickly through Kansas City. He stated that his own passenger service, in conjunction with the Rock Island, T&P, and the proposed service with the Denver & Rio Grande Western and WP, would equal what the Santa Fe was proposing for St. Louis.[6]

Neff's forceful and persuasive arguments were followed by those of F. W. Green, chief operating officer of the St. Louis Southwestern, who estimated the injury to his road would come close to $8 million annually—perhaps 20 percent of its revenues. J. Russel Coulter, chief traffic officer of the Frisco, testified that his line would lose $6.5 million annually. John Farrington, president of the Rock Island, after spelling out the harm that would come to his road, suggested Santa Fe's entry to St. Louis might cause his road to completely abandon its St. Louis–Kansas City line. Three more days of testimony by various traffic officers added more damaging testimony.[7]

Some shippers too opposed the plan, suggesting that St. Louis traffic would be impaired rather than enhanced by the scheme. Then state officials entered the fray. An Arkansas Public Service Commissioner testified his state would lose taxes and that the proposal might cause abandonment of the Missouri & Arkansas, which was largely dependent upon Santa Fe interchange traffic at Joplin, Missouri. Illinois's assistant attorney general intervened in opposition based on his assumption that the plan would threaten the continued existence of the lines between Mexico and Roodhouse and, somehow, 40 other Illinois towns. He also claimed diversion of traffic off the MP between East St. Louis and Thebes, Illinois, would hurt that part of the state's economy.[8]

Figuratively bloodied and battered, Gurley and Budd returned to their offices wondering why they ever had proposed the plan. They could see that they had failed. Examiner A. G. Nye took little time in rendering his negative recommendation. On November 22, he found, "There is no lack of transportation facilities or of competition," and any new arrangement would be "wasteful and unwarranted."[9] He saw a $10 million–12 million diversion of traffic from carriers already in the market and questioned whether any new passenger service could be made profitable.

In July 1948 at the full ICC hearings— though three members vigorously supported the petition—the application was rejected in its entirety by a majority on the grounds that there was no pressing need for additional St. Louis–Kansas City service. Would the outcome have been different had Budd not introduced the Santa Fe into the picture? Possibly. But the efficiencies of better track utilization between Kansas City and Chicago as well as the development of a near–super railroad between Kansas City and St. Louis would definitely have advanced railroading in the strategic corridors.

As a result of the defeat, Tigrett was left with the part of the Alton he never wanted. In July 1949 the ICC allowed him to dissolve the KCSt.L&C and to permit the Burlington to once again operate from Mexico through to Kansas City. In consideration of the rights, Budd agreed to pay 50 percent of the interest on the $2 million of KCSt.L&C bonds, 2 percent annually on the cost of the line's improvements, 50 percent of the taxes, and a minimum of 30 percent of the annual costs of maintenance.[10] Tigrett would have preferred a total release of the line to the Burlington, but it was not to be. It was his only setback in an otherwise nearly perfect plan.

Through tight cost controls and conservative operations, the expanded GM&O turned out to be a profitable operation and regularly paid dividends throughout its 25-year existence. It was the first Class I road in the country to fully dieselize its roster. New freight cars were periodically ordered specifically to handle on-line shipper requirements. Though slow to implement it, some piggyback service

was introduced. Passenger service south of St. Louis ended in 1958 and main line locals to the north were removed, but the last sleeper between St. Louis and Chicago continued until 1968, long after most roads had removed theirs. Right to the end of the railroad's operation of passenger trains, parlor car service, especially between Springfield and Chicago, was offered and remained popular.

In 1971, long after it was apparent the industry could not make money transporting passengers, Congress created the National Railroad Passenger Corporation, relieving railroads of the costly and burdensome passenger service. Amtrak selected the GM&O's Chicago–St. Louis route as part of its nationwide system. A year later, in August 1972, arch rival IC absorbed the GM&O, resulting in the Illinois Central Gulf (ICG). The new management wasted little time abandoning redundant former Alton lines, first the Dwight-Washington Branch, next the Sherman-Grove line, and then the Bloomington-Murrayville Jack Line.

In 1987 the ICG sold the 631 miles from Joliet to Kansas City and East St. Louis to a start-up company called the Chicago Missouri & Western (CM&W). The CM&W lasted only a little more than a year before it failed and filed for Chapter 11 protection. It took two years for the SP to be enticed to acquire the badly deteriorated East St. Louis to Joliet mileage with considerable help from the State of Illinois. Another start-up company, the Gateway Western, purchased the 461-mile Kansas City–East St. Louis line via Roodhouse with haulage rights via Springfield to Chicago. In 1996 the UP bought the SP and with it the East St. Louis–Joliet main line. A year later, the KCS bought the Gateway Western.

It is one of those ironic aspects of history that, as the next century was approaching, the consolidation Harriman had advocated nearly 100 years earlier had been realized, though perhaps not exactly as he had envisioned. One can assume that, were they alive to witness what happened to the railroad they had once controlled, Blackstone would have been aghast, but Harriman very pleased.

Railroads and Abbreviations

Alton

Alton & Eastern

Alton, Granite City & St. Louis

Alton, Jacksonville & Peoria

Alton & St. Louis (A&St.L)

Alton & Sangamon (A&S)

Alton & Shelbyville

Alton, Chicago & St. Louis

American Central

Atchison, Topeka & Santa Fe (Santa Fe)

Atlanta & Lawndale

Atlantic City

Baltimore & Ohio (B&O)

Baltimore & Ohio Chicago Terminal (B&OCT)

Baltimore & Ohio Southwestern

Belleville & Illinoistown (B&I)

Birmingham & Northwestern (B&NW)

Bloomington, Pontiac & Joliet

Boston & Maine

Braidwood Coal

Buffalo, Rochester & Pittsburgh (BR&P)

Buffalo & Susquehanna (B&S)

Burlington & Missouri River

Bureau County

Casey & Sidell

Central Pacific Co. of California (Central Pacific; CP)

Central Railroad

Central Railroad of New Jersey

Chesapeake & Ohio (C&O)

Chicago & Alton (C&A)

Chicago, Alton & St. Louis (CA&St.L)

Chicago, Aurora & Elgin

Chicago, Burlington & Quincy (Burlington; CB&Q)

Chicago, Cincinnati & Louisville

Chicago & Eastern Illinois (C&EI)

Chicago Great Western (CGW)

Chicago & Illinois Midland (C&IM)

Chicago & Illinois River (C&IR)

Chicago & Joliet Electric (C&J)

Chicago, Plainfield, Lacon & Warsaw

Chicago, Milwaukee & St. Paul (CM&St.P)

Chicago, Missouri & Western (CM&W)

Chicago & Mississippi (C&M)

Chicago & North Western (North Western; C&NW)

Chicago, Pekin & South-Western (CP&S-W)

Chicago, Peoria & St. Louis

Chicago & Rock Island (C&RI)

Chicago, Rock Island & Pacific (Rock Island; CRI&P)

Chicago, St. Louis & Western (CSt.L&W)

Chicago, Springfield & St. Louis

Chicago Terminal Transfer (CTT)

Chicago & Vincennes

Cincinnati, Hamilton & Dayton

Cincinnati, Indianapolis & Western (CI&W)

Cleveland, Cincinnati, Chicago & St. Louis (CCC&St.L)

Colorado & Southern (C&S)

Danville Street Railway & Light Co.

Danville, Urbana, Bloomington & Pekin

Denver Pacific

Denver & Rio Grande (D&RG)

Denver & Rio Grande Western

Dubuque & Sioux City

Elgin, Joliet & Eastern (EJ&E)

Erie

Florida East Coast

Fort Worth & Denver (Ft.W&D)

Fort Worth & Denver City (Ft.W&DC)

Galena & Chicago Union (G&CU)

Gardner, Coal City & Northern

Gateway Western

Grand Trunk Railroad of Canada

Great Northern (GN)

Great Western [of England]

Great Western Railway of Canada

Gulf, Mobile & Northern (GM&N)

Gulf, Mobile & Ohio (GM&O)

Hamilton, Lacon & Eastern (HL&E)

Hannibal & St. Joseph

Harlem River

Hocking Valley

Housatonic

Hudson River

Illinois Central (IC)

Illinois Central Gulf (ICG)

Illinois River

Illinois Traction System (ITS)

Indiana Harbor Belt

Indiana, Illinois & Iowa

Indianapolis & St. Louis (I&St.L)

Interborough-Metropolitan

Iowa Central

Jacksonville, Alton & St. Louis (JA&St.L)

Jacksonville & Carrollton (J&C)

Jacksonville & Havana

Jacksonville, Louisville & St. Louis (JL&St.L)

Jacksonville & Meredosia

Jacksonville & St. Louis

Jacksonville South Eastern (JSE)

Joliet & Chicago (J&C)

Joliet & Northern (Joliet Cutoff; J&N)

Joliet & Terre Haute

Kansas City Belt Line

Kansas City, Pittsburgh & Gulf (KCP&G)

Kansas City, St. Louis & Chicago (KCSt.L&C)

Kansas City Southern (KCS)

Kansas Pacific (KP)

Kansas & Sidell

La Crosse & Milwaukee

Lafayette, Bloomington & Mississippi

Lake Ontario & Southern

Lake Shore & Michigan Southern (LS&MS)

Leavenworth, Pawnee & Western

Lehigh Valley

Litchfield, Carrollton & Western (LC&W)

Liverpool, Canton & Knoxville

Louisiana & Missouri River (L&MR)

Macoupin County

Mexican Central

Michigan Central (MC)

Michigan Southern (MS)

Michigan Southern-Northern Indiana (MS-NI)

Minneapolis & St. Louis (Louie; M&St.L)

Missouri & Arkansas

Missouri, Kansas & Texas (Katy; MKT)

Missouri Pacific (MP)

Mobile & Ohio (M&O)

Mt. Carmel & Alton

Nauvoo & Warsaw

New Orleans, Jackson & Great Northern

New York Central (NYC)

New York Central & Hudson River

New York, Chicago & St. Louis (Nickle Plate Road; NYC&St.L)

New York & Erie

New York & Harlem

New York & New Haven (NY&NH)

New York, New Haven & Hartford (New Haven; NYNH&H)

Newcastle & Carlisle

Norfolk & Western

North Missouri

Northern Cross

Northern Indiana (NI)

Northern Pacific (NP)

Ogdensburg & Lake Champlain

Ohio & Mississippi (O&M)

Oregon Railroad & Navigation

Ottawa, Oswego & Fox River Valley

Pacific Railroad of Missouri

Panama Railway & Steamship

Panhandle

Pennsylvania Central

Peoria, Decatur & Evansville

Peoria & Oquawka Eastern

Peoria & Oquawka Eastern Extension

Peoria, Pekin & Jacksonville

Peoria & Pekin Union Railway (P&PU)

Pittsburgh, Fort Wayne & Chicago (Fort Wayne; PFt.W&C)

Queen & Crescent

Quincy, Carrollton & St. Louis (QC&St.L)

Reading

Rock Island & LaSalle

Rutland, Toluca & Northern (RT&N)

St. Joseph & Council Bluffs

St. Louis, Alton & Chicago

St. Louis, Iron Mountain & Southern (St.LIM&S)

St. Louis, Jacksonville & Chicago (Jacksonville; St.LJ&C)

St. Louis, Kansas City & Northern (St.LKC&N)

St. Louis Merchants Bridge Terminal

St. Louis & North Eastern

St. Louis, Peoria & Northern (St.LP&N)

St. Louis San Francisco (Frisco; St.LSF)

St. Louis Southwestern

St. Louis & Springfield (St.L&S)

St. Louis, Vandalia & Terre Haute

Sangamon & Morgan (S&M)

Sangamon & Northwest

Springfield & Alton Turnpike

Sodus Bay & Southern

Southern

Southern Cross

Southern Pacific (SP)

Terre Haute & Alton (TH&A)

Terre Haute, Alton & St. Louis (Terre Haute; THA&St.L)

Terminal Railroad Association of St. Louis (TRRA)

Texas & Pacific (T&P)

Toledo, Peoria & Warsaw

Toledo, Peoria & Western (TP&W)

Toledo, St. Louis & Western (Clover Leaf;
    Clover Leaf Route; TSt.L&W)

Toledo, Wabash & Western (Wabash; TW&W)

Toluca & Eastern (T&E)

Toluca, Marquette & Northern (TM&N)

Tonica & Petersburg (T&P)

Union Pacific (UP)

Union Pacific Railroad & Telegraph Co.

Union Railway & Transit

Utica & Rochester

Wabash

Western Air Line

Western Maryland

Western Pacific (WP)

Wheeling & Lake Erie (W&LE)

Yale Short Line

Notes

Chapter 1: The State Sets Its Course

1. For comprehensive narratives of Illinois's primitive period and subsequent development, see William Cronon, chap. 1 in *Nature's Metropolis* (New York: W. W. Norton, 1991); Edgar Lee Masters, chaps. 4–5 in *The Tale of Chicago* (New York: G. P. Putnam's Sons, 1933); Paul M. Angle, chaps. 3 and 5 in *Here I Have Lived: A History of Lincoln's Springfield, 1821–1865* (Springfield, Ill.: Abraham Lincoln Association, 1935); and Theodore Calvin Pease, chap. 6 in *The Story of Illinois* (Chicago: University of Chicago Press, 1949).

2. Angle, *Here I Have Lived,* 150; Carlton J. Corliss, *Main Line of Mid-America: The Story of the Illinois Central* (New York: Creative Age Press, 1950), 2.

3. H. Roger Grant, *The North Western: A History of the Chicago & North Western Railway System* (DeKalb: Northern Illinois University Press, 1996), 7.

4. H. J. Stratton, "The Northern Cross Railroad," *Journal of the Illinois State Historical Society* 28, no. 2 (1977): 46; Donald J. Heimburger, *Wabash* (Forest Park, Ill.: Heimburger House, 1984), 14.

5. John Clayton, *The Illinois Fact Book and Almanac: 1673–1968* (Carbondale: Southern Illinois University Press, 1970), 331–32; John H. Krenkel, *Illinois Internal Improvements: 1818–1848* (Cedar Rapids, Iowa: Torch Press, 1958), 26–46.

6. Corliss, *Main Line,* 3.

7. Ibid., 4–5.

8. Krenkel, *Illinois Internal Improvements,* 56; *Laws of the State of Illinois,* 1835–1836, 3, 8, 12, 16, 21, 24, 36, 46, 51, 54, 64, 76, 81, 129, 214.

9. Krenkel, *Illinois Internal Improvements,* 60–61.

10. Ibid., 61.

11. *Chicago Democrat,* October 28, 1835.

12. Krenkel, *Illinois Internal Improvements,* 65–72.

13. Alexander Davidson and Bernard Stuve, *A Complete History of Illinois From 1673 to 1873* (Springfield, Ill.: H. W. Rooker, 1884), 433–35, is particularly scathing in criticizing what the authors viewed as the delegates' recklessness. Krenkel in *Illinois Internal Improvements,* on the other hand, takes a more moderate view, though acknowledging the hasty process that brought passage.

14. Dumas Malone and Basil Rauch, *The Republic Comes of Age, 1789–1841* (New York: Appleton-Century-Crofts, 1960), 216–17.

15. *Laws of the State of Illinois,* 1837, 36, 47, 84, 138, 148, 156, 168, 175,189, 204, 214, 245, 255, 262, 273, 279, 292, 312, 321, 326, 431.

16. The legend that Lincoln and his fellow Sangamon legislators traded their internal improvement votes in return for naming Springfield the new capital is persuasively dis-puted in Paul Simon's definitive study of Lincoln's legislative career, *Lincoln's Preparation for Greatness* (Norman: University of Oklahoma Press, 1965), 6–105. Krenkel adds insight; see *Illinois Internal Improvements,* 72–74.

17. Krenkel, *Illinois Internal Improvements,* 99–102.

18. Clayton, *The Illinois Fact Book,* 202–9; Robert P. Howard, *Mostly Good and Competent Men* (Springfield: Illinois Historical Society, 1988), 81–82.

19. Howard, *Mostly Good and Competent Men,* 82.

20. Ibid., 83–84.

21. A. T. Andreas, *History of Cook County* (Chicago: A. T. Andreas, 1884), 150–53; Donald J. Miller, *City of the Century* (New York: Simon & Schuster, 1996), 71; Krenkel, *Illinois Internal Improvements,* 110–13.

22. Cronon, *Nature's Metropolis,* 64–65; Brian Dukes, "Reaching the Goal," *Illinois History* 34, no. 3 (1980): 61.

23. Davidson and Struve, *A Complete History of Illinois,* 135.

24. *Laws of the State of Illinois,* 1847, 118, 135, 144.

Chapter 2: A Railroad Emerges from the Prairie

1. Sangamon County was then much larger and included the areas that later became Christian, Logan, and Menard Counties.

2. Angle, *Here I Have Lived,* 35–36, 48, 87.

3. Krenkel, *Illinois Internal Improvements,* 53.

4. *Sangamon Journal,* January 5, 1832.

5. *Sangamo Journal,* November 14, 1834.

6. Ibid., November 14, 1834, April 4, 1835.

7. Krenkel, *Illinois Internal Improvements,* 54–55; *Sangamo Journal,* May 9, June 27, 1835.

8. *Sangamo Journal,* October 3, 1835.

9. Ibid., April 11, 1835.

10. *Alton Telegraph,* February 16, 1835.

11. "The Story of Alton's First Railroad Station," pamphlet by Jean Floss Paul (Alton Area Landmarks Association, December 1970); Dennis E. Suttles, *Godfrey Papers Collection,* Illinois Historical State Library, 1989.

12. Krenkel, *Illinois Internal Improvements,* 27; Angle, *Here I Have Lived,* 145–46.

13. *Alton Telegraph,* December 8, 1838.

14. Ibid., April 10, 1841; *Laws of the State of Illinois,* 1841, 150.

15. *Illinois State Register,* February 19, 1841.

16. *Laws of the State of Illinois,* 1841, 353–55. The commissioners of the Springfield & Alton Turnpike Company were John W. Buffum, Cyrus Edwards, B. K. Hart, Jonathan Hudson, Thomas Hawley, F. A. Olds, S. B. Opdycke, M. Tinsley, and J. A. Townsend—all Springfield merchants, businessmen, or political figures.

17. *Alton Telegraph and Democratic Review,* April 10, 1841.

18. Stratton, "The Northern Cross Railroad," 44–48.

19. Harry C. Pratt, *Lincoln 1840–1846* (Springfield, Ill.: Abraham Lincoln Association, 1939), 307; *Illinois State Register,* November 15, 1845. Supreme court judge Samuel Treat of Springfield presided. State auditor Levi Davis of Alton served as secretary. Among the 13-man Sangamon delegation were Illinois House members Abraham Lincoln and Stephen Logan, former House member John Calhoun, and state senator Ninah Edwards. Morgan County's four-man delegation included former state representative John Hardin, and former attorney general Josiah Lamborn. Madison County sent men of similar rank and reputation.

20. *Laws of the State of Illinois,* 1847, 144, 150. Named as incorporators of the Alton & Sangamon were Benjamin Godfrey, Thomas Clifford, Robert Dunlap, Robert Ferguson, William Martin, and Simeon Ryder. All were prominent business or political leaders of Madison County.

21. Stratton, "The Northern Cross Railroad," 49–50.

22. *Alton Telegraph and Democratic Review,* May 21, 1847; John W. Starr, Jr., *Lincoln and the Railroads* (New York: Dodd, Mead & Co., 1927), 84–85.

23. *Carrollton Gazette,* October 15, 1847.

24. *Sangamo Journal,* July 6, 1847.

25. Ibid., August 5, 1847.

26. Masters, *The Tale of Chicago,* 101–2; Andreas, *History of Chicago* (Chicago: A. T. Andreas, 1884), 161–65; Dumas Malone and Basil Rauch, *Crisis of the Union, 1841–1877* (New York: Appleton-Century-Crofts, 1960), 18.

27. *Alton Telegraph and Democratic Review,* February 4, 1848.

28. *Report of Survey, Alton & Sangamon R.R., From Alton to City of Springfield,* August 18, 1848.

29. Ibid.; Crocker estimated the completed cost of the railroad, including equipment, at $978,520. Annual revenues were estimated at $315,790. Allowing $76,800 for expenses, net receipts of $238,990 were envisioned, a nearly 44 percent return; *Alton Telegraph,* March 30, April 20, August 20, September 28, 1849.

30. *Alton Telegraph and Democratic Review,* October 12, 1849.

31. Elizabeth Pearson White, "Captain Benjamin Godfrey and the Alton and Sangamon Railroad," *Illinois Historical Society Journal* 67, no. 5 (1974): 470.

32. Ryder to Crocker, November 8, 1849, *Godfrey Papers;* White, "Captain Benjamin Godfrey," 470.

33. *Alton Telegraph and Democratic Review,* February 15, 1850.

34. Stratton, "The Northern Cross Railroad," 50–51.

35. *Alton Telegraph and Democratic Review,* September 20, 1850; White, "Captain Benjamin Godfrey," 473.

36. *Alton Telegraph and Democratic Review,* October 4, 1850.

37. Ibid., November 22, 1850.

38. White, "Captain Benjamin Godfrey," 475–76.

39. Ibid., 474.

40. John F. Stover, *History of the Illinois Central Railroad* (New York: Macmillan, 1975), 16–21; Corliss, *Main Line,* 15–20.

41. Frederick Gerhard, *Illinois as It Is* (Chicago: Keen and Lee, 1857), 221–23.

42. Ibid., 226–29.

43. Ryder to Crocker, November 8, 1849, *Godfrey Papers.*

44. *Illinois State Register,* January 14, 1851; *History of Sangamon County, Illinois* (Chicago: Inter-state Publishing, 1881), 146.

45. Corliss, *Main Line,* 27.

46. *The Chicago and Alton Railway Company* (Chicago: Ryan & Hart, 1901) 9. The bill was signed on January 29, 1851.

47. *Laws of the State of Illinois,* 1851–1852, 35; *The Chicago and Alton,* 10–16. The Illinois Central Charter was signed February 10, 1851; the Springfield–Bloomington extension, February 11, 1851.

48. Ibid., 16–17.

49. *Joliet Signal,* January 28, 1851.

50. *The Chicago and Alton,* 10–16. The formidable list of 13 incorporators included Thomas Carlin, Alfred Cavarly, Philip Coffman, A. C. Dickson, James Dunlop, W. S. Hurst, Edward Keating, Murray McConnell, Alexander Morean, Samuel Prosser, David Smith, William Warren, and David Woodson. Carlin was a former governor; Dunlop had been the principal contractor on the S&M; Keating had been mayor of Alton and involved with organization of the A&S; and Morean later became associated with other railroads in the region.

51. Ibid., 10.

52. *Illinois Daily Journal,* April 21, 1851.

53. *Illinois State Register,* January 23, 1851.

54. *Alton Telegraph and Democratic Review,* November 22, 1850; "The Story of Alton's First Railroad Station."

55. *Illinois State Register,* March 15, April 8, June 26, 1851.

56. Dan W. Bannister, *Lincoln and the Illinois Supreme Court* (Privately printed, 1994), 74–75.

57. Ibid., 75.

58. Ibid., 75–76.

59. *Illinois Journal,* July 7, 1851; *Peoria Free Press,* July 31, 1851.

60. White, "Captain Benjamin Godfrey," 478–79. The engines were the products of Holmes Hinkley's 10-year-old Boston Locomotive Works.

61. *Alton Telegraph,* August 14, 1851.

62. White, "Captain Benjamin Godfrey," 477.

63. A. D. Russell, *Copy of Certain Proceedings, April, 1858* (New York: Astor, Lenox and Tilden Foundations, 1924), 3.

64. Ibid. The partnership had been given $364,500 in bonds to be used as security to raise cash for supplies—rail, spikes, and lumber—and steamboats and barges. Two-hundred forty-four thousand dollars of those bonds were assigned to Henry Dwight, Jr., in return for a $170,000 loan. The remaining $120,500 was placed with nine other individuals and firms. Cowman's company also held $160,000 face value of stock. Upon completion of the A&S section of the railroad, the partnership was entitled to another $71,104 of the railroad's bonds, $67,902 of the city of Alton's bonds, $41,676 of A&S common stock, and a payment of at least

$226,158 in cash. Godfrey was personally eligible for $50,000 of the company's bonds and $250,000 of common stock.

65. *New York Times,* June 28, 1881; Elizabeth Pearson White, letter to author, March 7, 1995.

66. *Proceedings,* 5. In return for $100,000 payable to Godfrey and $90,000 to James Zacharie of New Orleans for rail and equipment already delivered, Dwight got Godfrey to transfer all of the A. T. Cowman & Co. assets as well as virtually all of Godfrey's personal property to him as security.

67. *Proceedings,* 7.

68. *Illinois State Register,* April 17, 1852.

69. Ibid.; Iles was named for Springfield's first citizen and early participant in the railroad's founding, Elijah Iles.

70. *Illinois State Register,* May 24, 1852.

71. *Illinois Journal,* May 12, 1852.

72. *The Chicago and Alton,* 17–20.

73. *History of Madison County* (Edwardsville, Ill.: W. R. Brink, 1882), 47–48; Frederick Way, Jr., *Ways Packet Directory: 1848–1994* (Athens: Ohio University Press, 1983), 17, 36–37, 47–48, 89, 111, 391.

74. *Illinois Journal,* September 2, 1852; *Illinois State Register,* August 16, 28, 1852.

75. *Illinois Daily Journal,* July 1, 1852.

76. *Illinois State Register,* July 7, 1852.

77. *Illinois Journal,* July 7, 1852.

78. Ibid., July 20, 1852.

79. Angle, *Here I Have Lived,* 162.

80. *Illinois Journal,* October 10, 1852.

81. Ibid.

82. James J. Buckley, Keith E. Sherman, and John D. Stenwyk, "Alton: The Bluff City," *Gulf, Mobile & Ohio Historical Society News,* nos. 47–48 (1987): 5; *History of Madison County,* 46.

83. *Illinois State Register,* July 12, 1852; *Illinois Daily Register,* July 7, 1852.

84. *Illinois State Register,* October 9, 1852.

85. *Alton Telegraph,* December 3, 1852.

86. *Chief Engineer's Report,* October 1852.

87. White, "Captain Benjamin Godfrey," 477–78.

88. *Proceedings,* 8–9.

89. Ibid., 11–12.

Chapter 3: Deception and Default

1. *Illinois Daily Journal,* September 9, August 31, 1852; *Illinois State Register,* August 17, 1852.

2. *Chief Engineer's Report,* October 1852.

3. *Joliet Signal,* June 28, July 20, 1853; *Alton Telegraph,* March 14, 1853.

4. *Illinois Journal,* June 28, 1853.

5. D. W. Yungmeyer, "An Excursion into the Early History of the Chicago and Alton Railroad," *Journal of the Illinois State Historical Society* 38, no. 1 (March 1945): 12.

6. *History of Logan County, Illinois* (Chicago: Donnelley Lloyd & Co., 1878), 263.

7. Raymond N. Dooley, "Lincoln and His Namesake Town" *Journal of the Illinois State Historical Society* 52, no. 1 (spring 1959): 134.

8. Ibid., 134; *History of Logan County, Illinois,* 267. Knapp's bill specified "the northwest quarter of section number 31, in township number 20, range two west," in other words, the Loose property.

9. *History of Logan County, Illinois,* 268.

10. Ibid., 294.

11. *Alton Telegraph,* September 1, 1853.

12. *Bloomington Pantagraph,* October 17, 1853.

13. Ibid., November 12, 1853; *History of McLean County* (Chicago: LeBaron & Co., 1879), 365, 389–90.

14. *Report of the Chief Engineers,* November 7, 1853.

15. *Alton Courier,* June 7, 1854.

16. *Report of the Chief Engineers,* November 7, 1853.

17. White, "Captain Benjamin Godfrey," 480.

18. *Proceedings,* 17. As the nation's credit squeeze worsened, the Massilon Bank closed its doors. Auditors quickly discovered Dwight's deception and demanded return of the bonds. Dwight smugly admitted he had no authority to hold the bonds but claimed he could not get their return. Astonishingly, he told the auditors that if they would transfer ownership of them to him, he would then find a way to return them. Dumbfounded at his audacity, the officials rejected his proposal and sued him successfully for a judgment of $414,261, the value of the bonds with interest. Dwight, however, ignored the judgment and never satisfied it.

19. Ibid., 14–16.

20. Ibid., 12.

21. Ibid., 24.

22. Ibid., 19–20.

23. Ibid. Emboldened by how easily the worthless Benj. Godfrey & Co. paper deceived Peck, Dwight passed off more bogus papers—of equally fraudulent notes of a New York soap manufacturer—to two other banks.

24. Ibid. The Litchfields also controlled the TH&A, which was laying track eastward out of Alton.

25. Ibid., 21.

26. Ibid., 26–27.

27. Ibid., 29–36, schedules xlvi–lii.

28. Ibid., 23–24.

29. Ibid., 36.

30. Ibid., 38–40; *The Chicago and Alton,* 20. Meanwhile, the Illinois legislature amended the company's charter to allow issuance of a new series of 10 percent bonds and, for the first time, 10 percent preferred stock and raised the company's capital limit to $8 million.

31. *Statement of the Directors of the Chicago & Mississippi Railroad Company,* March 15, 1854, 4.

32. *The Chicago and Alton,* 18.

33. Howard, *Mostly Good and Competent Men,* 94–95. St. Louis interests, led by merchant John O'Fallon, had pledged $500,000 of the city's credit for the line's construction, confirming for opponents the O&M's real intent.

34. *Laws of the State of Illinois,* 1849, 63; Ryder to Crocker, *Godfrey Papers,* November 9, 1849.

35. *Carrollton Gazette,* January 15, 1853. It had taken two years just to get stock sales started, and by the beginning of 1853, only $100,000 in subscriptions had been recorded—principally pledged by Greene and Jersey Counties—with

neither Alton nor Jacksonville having pledged anything. In March, 83 percent of Greene County's voters favored the issuance of the county's bonds. Of the 1,992 votes cast, only 330 were negative; all but nine of the negative votes were registered at Greenfield or Athens, both far to the east of the planned route. Only one negative vote was cast in Carrollton. A few weeks later, Jersey County citizens approved their bond issue. After two defeats in special elections, Morgan County passed its bond issue in the general election that November with a comfortable 2,000 majority.

36. Ibid. The J&C commissioners decided to throw a high fast one under Alton's chin by getting state representative Charles Hodges to introduce an amendment that called for the road's southern terminus to be changed from Alton to Illinoistown unless Alton subscribed to $100,000 of stock, the same amount purchased of both the A&S and the TH&A. The city of Alton responded by having Madison County representative Samuel Buckmaster work for the defeat of Hodges's bill. The ploy failed, however, leading Buckmaster to amend Hodges's bill to preclude an Alton investment unless Jersey, Greene, and Morgan Counties each invested $50,000—a measure to which Hodges surprisingly agreed. The prevailing thought in Alton was that, with Buckmaster's amendment added, the counties to the north would oppose the bill, but they did not.

37. *Carrollton Gazette,* September 10, 1853; *Laws of the State of Illinois,* 1849, 93; *Laws of the State of Illinois,* 1852, 114.

38. *The Chicago and Alton,* 26–29.

39. *Statement of the Directors,* 5.

40. *Proceedings,* 39.

41. Ibid., 48.

42. Ibid. Dwight sold the stock for the nominal sum of $10,000, or a little over $2 a share.

43. Dwight owed Wright's Bank of Oswego (which was capitalized at only $200,000) $131,000 for previous personal loans. Wright's nomination was merely a gesture to hold the bank at bay from foreclosing on him.

44. Dwight also owed the New Haven County Bank $318,000 and Hotchkiss $67,000.

45. *Proceedings,* 48. Dwight then appointed himself, Hotchkiss, and Gould to the Executive and Finance Committee, entrusted with supervision of "all the financial concerns of the company, to sell and negotiate the 'Income Bonds' of the company for the purpose of raising cash means."

It didn't take Dwight long to lose patience with Bliss, as he opposed most of Dwight's maneuvers. When hired, Bliss had agreed to serve for an annual salary of $10,000, but in July Dwight, Hotchkiss, and Wright voted to cut his pay to $5,000. This abrogation of his contract wounded Bliss, but it was not enough to remove him. That didn't occur until November, when Dwight and his majority resolved that the president should receive no pay whatsoever. This Bliss could not accept, and he finally resigned the presidency and his board seat in December. To replace Bliss on the board, Dwight recruited Samuel Blatchford, who was induced to leave his Harlem Railroad treasurer's post with the promise that the same position with the CA&St.L would be permanent and liberally paid.

46. *Portrait and Biography of McLean County, Illinois* (Chicago: Chapman Brothers, 1887), 367–71.

47. Fayette B. Shaw, "The Economic Development of Joliet, Illinois" (Ph.D. diss., Harvard University, 1934), 117.

48. Ibid.

49. Ibid.

50. Ibid.

51. Gerhard, *Illinois as It Is,* 221–23.

52. Corliss, *Main Line,* 82–85; Gerhard, *Illinois As It Is,* 221, 398–99.

53. *Illinois Journal,* August 22, 27, 1855.

54. Ibid., January 25, 1855; *Daily Courier,* January 25, 1855; *Illinois State Register,* January 23, 29, 1855.

55. Corliss, *Main Line,* 82–85.

56. *Illinois State Register,* February 1, 1855; *Daily Courier,* February 3, 1855; *Illinois Journal,* August 22, 27, 1855.

57. Ibid., January 25, 1855; *Daily Courier,* January 25, 1855; *Illinois State Register,* January 23, 29, 1855.

58. *Illinois State Register,* February 1, 1855; *Daily Courier,* February 3, 1855.

59. *Daily Courier,* February 3, 1855. The cars' seats and interior paneling were ripped out and broken up to provide fuel for the stoves. Passengers melted snow on the cars' stoves for drinking water and subsisted on the dwindling numbers of cans of oysters they found in the express car, expected by the governor's wife in Springfield for a statehouse reception.

60. Ibid.

61. Ibid.

62. *Daily Courier,* February 14, 1855.

63. *Illinois State Register,* February 1, 1855.

64. Ibid., March 10, 1855.

65. *Illinois Journal,* August 23, 1855.

66. *Carrollton Gazette,* March 31, 1855.

67. Ibid.

68. *Alton Courier,* March 17, 1855.

69. *Illinois State Register,* August 30, 1855.

70. Ibid., September 3, 1855.

71. Angle, *Here I Have Lived,* 167–8.

72. *The Chicago and Alton,* 29–35. Named as incorporators were George Barnett, reputed to be one of the wealthiest men in Will County; William Gooding, the canal's chief engineer and previously part of the team that engineered the Welland Canal; Joel Manning, past secretary of the canal board; Robert Milne, a Scotsman who had built five of the canal's locks and who now had a thriving lumber business in Chicago; and Hiram Norton, founder of Norton & Co. mills and several other commercial enterprises in the region.

73. *Joliet Signal,* January 8, 28, 1851.

74. Linda Legner, comp., *Lockport, Illinois: A Collective Heritage* (Lockport, Ill.: Bank of Lockport, 1980), 11.

75. George H. Woodruff, *Forty Years Ago!* (Joliet, Ill.: Joliet Republican Steam Printing House, 1874), 53.

76. *Portrait and Biographical Album of Will County* (Chicago: Chapman Bros., 1890), 170; Howard, *Mostly Good and Competent Men,* 99–107.

77. *Chicago Press,* July 27, 1856.

78. *Illinois State Register,* August 24, 1855.

79. Ibid., September 6, 1855.

80. *St. Louis Republican,* August 24, 1856.

81. *Illinois State Register,* September 6, 1855.

82. *Daily Courier,* May 9, 1855; *Illinois State Register,* May 2, July 4, 14, 28, August 30, December 13, 14, 1855.

83. White, "Captain Benjamin Godfrey," 483.

84. *Proceedings,* 51–53, 64. Dwight also got the board to pay Hotchkiss $15,000 on the balance of the $20,000 Hotchkiss personally subscribed to as part of the $800,000 loan, even though Hotchkiss only owed $10,000. The company's books later revealed the $15,000 was paid to Dwight, not Hotchkiss.

Dwight next got payment of $140,000 he claimed was interest on unpaid first mortgage bond coupons for debts he incurred in completing the railroad. Though Dwight's claim was unsupported by vouchers and had no validity whatsoever, the board assumed all further claims in return for the bonds Dwight illegally held.

Nevertheless, some of his coupons were redeemed but then pledged to Brown Brothers and a Cleveland bank he owed. When he was asked by his creditors how so large an amount of coupons had remained unpaid for so long and why they were disfigured with holes and marks, Dwight replied, "All you have got to do if my note is not paid, is to present them to the treasurer of the company and they will be paid."

Dwight obviously had no shame, but one has to question the intelligence of those he suckered into his dealings. Canceled coupons detached from bonds offered as security for loans from someone who, at least in New York, was known to be bankrupt and of dubious character, certainly should have provided sufficient reason to reject Dwight's claims.

85. *Proceedings,* 61.

86. Ibid., 61–62.

87. Ibid., 56–57.

88. Ibid.

89. Ibid., 65. Dwight's flagrant attacks on the railroad's treasury were too much for Blatchford, who frequently objected and finally got Dwight to admit his claims were fraudulent; however, it did not stop Dwight.

90. Ibid., 67.

91. Ibid., 69–70.

92. Ibid., 68.

93. Ibid., 71–72.

94. Ibid.

95. Ibid., 72.

96. Ibid.

97. Ibid., 73–78.

98. Ibid., 81.

99. Ibid., 85.

100. Ibid., 91.

101. Ibid.

102. Ibid., 96–97.

103. Ibid., 98–99.

104. Ibid., 99–100. Dwight called for an April 2 meeting in the William Street office, but when the gathering was convened, Dwight did not appear. Instead, he had Hotchkiss announce the meeting would be adjourned until that afternoon and reconvened at Blatchford's residence. Blatchford, unaware he was to be the host, asked Hotchkiss what it was all about, but he got no answer.

Nevertheless, the board reconvened at Blatchford's home. After the forced resignations, Blatchford realized what was happening. Quintard and Alexander, under Dwight's orders, had already begun packing the company's books and papers, but Blatchford intervened, seized the documents, and locked them in his safe. This was something Dwight had not counted on. He insisted they be released, but Blatchford refused and insisted everyone immediately leave his house. It was an ugly scene. After everyone left, Blatchford had the books and papers transferred to a location unknown to the others from which the sheriff, under court order, removed them. Had Blatchford not acted as swiftly as he did, one can only speculate what else Dwight might have done.

105. *Illinois State Register,* January 9, 1856.

106. *Chicago Tribune,* January 23, 1856.

107. *Proceedings,* 105–9. William Fullerton, Henry Brown (a partner of William Platt), and Edward Keating were named trustees.

108. Ibid. When Nathan Peck challenged Dwight, Dwight told him that the Connecticut banks had sued him (the second attempt after Litchfield's was denied on technical grounds) and had caused his indictment. As a result of the assignment, "things were just as he wanted them," and he now "got the whip hand" of them since the banks were the fifth class of creditors under the assignment and since the railroad would be sold. Spencer would gain full control while the banks would get nothing. He further claimed that, as a result of the assignment, Brown Brothers had the railroad in "the hollow of their hand" and could "do with it as they pleased." Dwight ended with the assurance that he had control of the railroad and the management of its affairs and that he had gotten "matters into such shape that the banks would get nothing except through his favor."

Later Dwight repeated his assertions to Stephen Pardee, who represented the New Haven Savings Bank and the St. John estate. He stated that Spencer could not raise the money he needed and that the deed of trust was executed for "the benefit of the creditors" but that the banks that had attacked him were "with the goats" and "would get nothing."

A few days later, two suits were filed in New York Supreme Court against Dwight, one by the County Bank and the other by Hotchkiss for a judgment totaling $108,859 payable by the company and $32,794 payable by Dwight. The total lent either to the company or to Dwight by the County Bank was $461,093—this from an institution whose permanent capital was but $500,000.

109. Ibid., 117–19. Dwight later stated that the replacement of the board of directors in August was the "keenest" thing he had ever carried out. The new directors, he asserted, would do whatever he desired. He also flatly stated that, with the lease in place and the agreements he had with Spencer providing for payments to him, there was no longer a need to pay his debts. In June, at a Bloomington meeting, the board was expanded to nine directors. Added were Uriah

Smith and James Low to represent the New Haven Banks, and James Wright and Hamilton Spencer as Dwight's desinates.

110. Ibid., 119. At the meeting in Bloomington, Alexander was directed to return to New York to seize the company's records from Blatchford. When Alexander learned the sheriff had possession of them, he wired Dwight, who became outraged. A few days later, Dwight directed the board to deny Blatchford any further right to receive monies in the company's name and summarily removed Blatchford as treasurer, despite his lifetime guarantee of employment.

111. Ibid., 119.

112. Ibid., 120.

113. Ibid., 121–25.

114. Ibid., 129. On October 1 the Spencer Lease was turned over to Litchfield and Matteson. Spencer had operated the railroad for 11 months and had paid only those expenses that were absolutely necessary, further weakening the company and, as a result, providing him large payouts. Aside from periodic payments to Dwight and a partial payment to Swinburne, there is no record of any significant payments made. In fact, no records of operations were ever recorded. Later, back in his hometown of Utica, New York, Spencer confided to some of his friends that he had personally realized more than $500,000.

115. *The Chicago and Alton*, 44–46; *Proceedings* 134–36. A nine-man board of directors was named: Matteson; his son-in-law, R. T. Goodall; Samuel Buckmaster of Alton; Hamilton Spencer; Elisha Litchfield; John Stryker; and three of Dwight's creditors—Lorenzo Sanger, John Wilkinson, and Ezekiel Morrison.

Chapter 4: The Courts Decide the Future

1. *Joliet Signal*, September 16, 1856.

2. *New York Times*, September 5, 1856.

3. *Chicago Tribune*, October 16, 1856. In summary, the reorganization plan called for an entire change in the management and control of the company, a union of the creditors in favor of the plan, and a postponement for three years of the payment of interest on the company's bonds.

4. *Circular of Messrs. Matteson & Litchfield, to the Holders of the Third Mortgage (income) Bonds of the Chicago and Mississippi Railroad Company* (New York, 1857).

5. *Report of the Committee of Nine to the Bondholders of the Chicago & Mississippi Railroad Co., now called Saint Louis Alton & Chicago Railroad Co.* (1859).

6. *First Half-Yearly Report of the Receivers of St. Louis Alton & Chicago Railroad,* to the trustees, December 3, 1859–June 30, 1860.

7. Albert A. Woldman, *Lawyer Lincoln* (New York: Carroll & Graf, 1936), 175.

8. *Alton Courier*, April 14, 1854.

9. *Illinois Daily Register*, August 29, 1855.

10. Ibid., August 30, 1855.

11. Bannister, *Lincoln and the Illinois Supreme Court*, 91.

12. Ibid., 92.

13. Woldman, *Lawyer Lincoln*, 176.

14. Among the most important were the broad-gauge O&M running across the state from Illinoistown to Vincennes; the THA&St.L from Alton, through the state, and into Indiana; the Great Western, running from the Illinois River east into Indiana; the Rock Island, through to the Mississippi River with a 47-mile Bureau County Railroad branch running off the main line at Bureau to Peoria; the Burlington, running between Chicago and the Mississippi River across from Burlington, Iowa; the rapidly expanding G&CU running from Chicago to Fulton on the Mississippi River and already double-tracked between Chicago & Turner Junction (later West Chicago) with leased lines operated through Iowa; and the CSt.P&FL, opened between Chicago and Janesville, Wisconsin, and projected to push 360 more miles into the forests of central and northern Wisconsin. Running north and south through the state was the celebrated IC, already the longest, with a line open from Cairo to Dunleith, 454 miles, and a 250-mile branch between Centralia and Chicago, bringing its total length to 704 miles.

15. *Carrollton Gazette*, March 31, 1855. The five named were James Breadan, George Brown, A. B. Morean, Simeon Ross, and George Woodson.

16. Ibid., August 12, 1856.

17. Ibid., March 8, 1856. Edward Eno and J. I. Cassell, both of Jacksonville, and William Shephard of Jerseyville, replaced James Breadan, Simeon Ross, and George Brown. Shephard was elected secretary.

18. Ibid.

19. Ibid., May 2, 1857.

20. Ibid.

21. *Jacksonville Sentinel,* April 10, 1857; *Carrollton Gazette,* May 2, 30, 1857.

22. *Carrollton Gazette*, May 2, June 13, 1857.

23. *The Chicago and Alton*, 46–49.

24. Ibid., 36–44. The incorporators were John Bennett, William Crow, Elijah Farnsworth, Henry Greene, William Greene, Jesse Hammers, Albert Reynolds, Josiah Sawyer, and Richard Yates.

25. Ibid., 36.

26. Ibid., 49–51.

27. *Menard Index*, May 21, 1857; November 14, 1857.

28. *Chicago Tribune*, June 15, 1857; *New York Times*, October 6–7, 13, 28, 30, 1857; Charles R. Geisst, *Wall Street: A History* (New York: Oxford University Press, 1997), 48–49.

29. Andreas, *History of Chicago*, 572–76.

30. *Alton Courier*, October 7, 1857. Nearly all of the corn was from the 1856 crop since farmers were withholding the 1857 yield for higher prices.

31. *Carrollton Gazette*, August 22, 1857.

32. Ibid.

33. Ibid., October 31, 1857.

34. *Joliet Signal*, June 9, 1857.

35. Ibid., October 20, 1857.

36. Ibid., August 25, 1857.

37. Ibid., November 3, 1857.

38. Ibid., December 8, 1857.

39. *New York Herald,* May 8, 1858.

40. *Joliet True Democrat,* March 23, 1858.

41. *Interstate Commerce Commission Reports,* vol. 40 (Washington, D.C.: U.S. Government Printing Office, 1933), 159. The J&C was leased for $120,000 a year—$60,000 less than had been paid the Rock Island for trackage rights.

42. *Carrollton Gazette,* May 1, 1858; *Jacksonville Sentinel,* February 5, 1858.

43. *Joliet Signal,* January 18, 1859.

44. *Laws of the State of Illinois,* 1859. Named as incorporators were Charles Congdon, George Davis, Dennis Kimberly, James Lee, Lewis Von Hoffman, Samuel Tilden, and Samuel White—holders of 7 or 10 percent bonds—and Azariah Flagg, David Hoadley, John Earl Williams, and George Titus—trustees for holders of the third mortgage.

45. *Bloomington Daily Pantagraph,* April 18–19, 1859.

46. Ibid., April 19, 1859.

47. Ibid., April 13, 1859.

48. Howard, *Mostly Good and Competent Men,* 100–2. Hearings continued for another four years, until finally in 1863 a Sangamon County circuit court ruled that the former governor owed the state $253,723. Despite his claims of innocence, Matteson paid the sum with the proceeds of some of his property he sold at auction.

49. Liston Edgington Leyendecker, *Palace Car Prince: A Biography of George Mortimer Pullman* (Niwot: University Press of Colorado, 1992), 17, 24, 26, 29.

50. Ibid., 36–37.

51. Ibid.

52. John H. White, Jr., *The American Railroad Passenger Car* (Baltimore: Johns Hopkins University Press, 1978), 212–15.

53. Leyendecker, *Palace Car Prince,* 37–38; an anonymous account found in company files.

54. Leyendecker, *Palace Car Prince,* 38.

55. Ibid.

56. Ibid., 38–39. Initially, Pullman charged 50 cents a night per occupant above the rail fare for the privilege of extra comfort and semi privacy. Users were attended by the train's brakeman, who made up the beds and collected fares. The idea of porters had not yet been conceived.

57. *Carrollton Gazette,* April 28, 1860.

58. Ibid., July 9, 1860.

59. Ibid.

60. *Jacksonville Sentinel,* November 11, 1859.

61. *Springfield Journal,* July 18, 1859.

62. *Springfield Independent,* September 27, 1859.

63. *Thomas W. Wason vs. Henry Dwight, Jr. et al.; Benjamin Godfrey vs. Thomas W. Wason et al.,* final decree rendered October 21, 1859. The sum Godfrey was found to owe Wason was finally paid after Godfrey's death in 1862, raised from the sale of land his estate inherited, including acreage in Monticello, lots in Alton, and land in Jersey and Macoupin Counties.

64. John H. White, Jr., *A History of the American Locomotive: Its Development, 1830–1880* (New York: Dover Publications, 1968), 24.

65. *Report of the Committee of Nine;* Circuit Court of the United States, Northern Illinois District, no. 572119A.

Chapter 5: From Calamity to Prosperity

1. *Carrollton Gazette,* April 28, 1860.

2. Ibid., September 27, 1860; December 8, 1860.

3. Ibid., December 29, 1860.

4. *Daily Pantagraph,* January 11, 1860.

5. Stover, *History of the Illinois Central,* 39.

6. *The National Cyclopedia of American Biography,* vol. 33 (New York: James T. White & Co., 1940).

7. *First Half-Yearly Report.*

8. *Second Yearly Report of the Receivers of the St. Louis Alton & Chicago Railroad, to the trustees, From January 1, 1861, to December 31, 1861;* William D. Edson, "Locomotives of the Alton Route," *Railroad History,* no. 156 (1987): 61.

9. *Illinois State Journal,* February 27, 1860; White, *A History of the American Locomotive,* 449–50, 456–57.

10. Stover, *History of the Illinois Central,* 65–67.

11. *Illinois Daily Register,* May 11, 1860; Edson, "Locomotives of the Alton," 63; *Second Yearly Report of the Receivers.*

12. *Illinois Daily Register,* April 8, 1860.

13. Clayton, *The Illinois Fact Book,* 38–41.

14. Gerhard, *Illinois as It Is,* 391–400; Cronon, *Nature's Metropolis,* 112–13.

15. Gerhard, *Illinois as It Is,* 391.

16. Malone and Rauch, *Crisis of the Union,* 149–51; David Herbert Donald, *Lincoln* (New York: Simon & Schuster, 1995), 243; Carl Sandburg, *Abraham Lincoln: The Prairie Years and the War Years* (New York: Harcourt, Brace and Co., 1954), 169–74.

17. Sandburg, *Abraham Lincoln,* 169–74.

18. Ibid., 182.

19. Ibid., 184–85.

20. Ibid., 195.

21. *The Chicago and Alton,* 70–75.

22. Victor Hicken, *Illinois in the Civil War* (Urbana: University of Illinois Press, 1991), ix, 50–72, 142–86, 188–215, 240–47.

23. *First Annual Report, 1863,* 16, 18.

24. Stover, *History of the Illinois Central,* 92–96; *First Annual Report of the Receivers.* The Alton's troop revenue was just 16.3 percent of the IC's.

25. *Second Yearly Report of the Receivers,* 5.

26. Ibid., 10–12.

27. *First Annual Report, 1863,* 21–23. At the end of the year, the railroad owned 58 engines. The passenger fleet remained at 35 cars, but the freight roster rose to 711 boxcars, flatcars, and stock cars.

Sixty more miles of track were ballasted; 53 miles of new and 41 miles of rebuilt fence were installed; 22 cattle pens and chutes were constructed; eight new water stations, seven coaling stations, two sand stations, nine depots, and a new coach house were added; a stone roundhouse and turntable were finished at Alton; a brick engine house replaced the wooden one at Springfield; three more stalls were added to the roundhouse; storehouses for iron and lumber were added to the Bloomington Shops; and repairs were made to a score of structures up and down the line.

28. *Bondholders' Agreement of Chicago, Alton & St. Louis Railroad Company, and Finally Amended 25th October, 1862.*

29. Ibid.

30. *The Chicago and Alton,* 80–85. *Carrollton Gazette,* November 6, 1852. There was overwhelming stockholder support of the merger (79 percent of the 6,378 outstanding shares), those opposed presumably being stockholders to the north in Washington, Metamora, and Tonica, who, thus far, had seen nothing of a railroad.

31. Ibid.

32. *Minutes,* April 7, 1862. The seven named were James Robb; John Crerar, a successful industrialist who headed a Chicago-based railroad supply business; John B. Drake, operator and part owner of the Tremont Hotel; Virgil Hickox, the railroad's general agent in Springfield; and Albert Havemeyer, George Robbins, and Isaac Sherman, representing the New York bondholders. To make day-to-day decisions, Robb, Havemeyer, and Robbins were named to an Executive Committee.

33. *Minutes,* April 7, 1863; *First Annual Report, 1863,* 9–10.

34. *Minutes,* April 7, December 31, 1863. It was agreed that 8 percent interest would be paid on the $1.5 million bonds outstanding as well as the principal when it became due in 1882 and that 7 percent dividends would be paid on the outstanding common stock. The purchaser would receive $500,000 of J&C stock. *First Annual Report, 1863,* 9–10.

35. *Interstate Commerce Commission Valuation Reports,* 232. During the first 24 months of consolidated operations, the St.LJ&C had generated revenues of a mere $7,462. After expenses only $882 was left.

36. The PP&J had finished 61 miles of track from Pekin (10 miles south of Peoria) to Virginia, a tantalizing 15 miles north of Jacksonville, before running out of money.

37. *The Chicago and Alton,* 123–27.

38. *First Annual Report, 1863,* 47–50. The assignment to the C&A took effect January 1, 1864.

39. Ibid., 19.

40. *Minutes,* April 7, 1863. *First Annual Report, 1863,* 16, 18. Added to the locomotive roster were two 4-4-0 road engines and two 0-4-0 switchers from Rogers. Bloomington Shops turned out three coaches, a baggage car, a caboose, and 165 freight cars—which raised the freight car total to 846. By the end of the year, nearly three quarters of the ties between Joliet and Alton had been replaced. Most bridges had been renewed. Three coal stations, five water facilities, another sand house, and three stock pens were built. A depot was erected at Normal, and a freight house was built at Chenoa. Bloomington Shops were expanded to include an enlarged foundry, a copper shop, and a rail repair plant; a new 12-stall roundhouse and turntable were finished.

41. *Interstate Commerce Commission Valuation Reports,* vol. 40, 211.

42. L. V. Reavis, *The Railway and River Systems of the City of St. Louis* (St. Louis: Woodward, Truman & Hale, 1879), 79.

43. *The Chicago and Alton,* 51–53. It would turn out to be a very favorable arrangement because the new annual payments were three times less than what the C&A was paying the THA&St.L for trackage rights and the Alton Packet Company for river transfers. *First Annual Report, 1863,* 11. The cost of building the 22 1/2 miles was paid for with the proceeds of a 21,200-share offer, which existing holders bought at $30 per share.

44. *Second Annual Report, 1864,* 20–21. Chanute was a French-born engineer, who, after scoring several major railroad achievements, went on to fame in pioneering aviation advances.

45. Reavis, *The Railway and River Systems,* 250.

46. Ibid., 261–62.

47. Ibid., 266–67.

48. Ibid.

49. *Third Annual Report, 1865,* 21.

50. Ibid.

51. *Minutes,* July 27, 1863 and January 30, 1864. Though Hickox and Sherman had been named two of the reorganized company's first directors, neither participated. Hickox formally tendered his resignation in July 1863, and Sherman did the same six months later. Henry St. John, a major New York investor, was nominated to fill the seat left vacant by Sherman, but he declined. Blackstone was then added.

52. *Minutes,* April 2, 1864.

53. Ida Hinman, *Biography of Timothy B. Blackstone* (New York: Methodist Book Concern Press, 1917); *Chicago Tribune,* May 27, 1900.

54. Leyendecker, *Palace Car Prince,* 74.

55. Ibid.

56. Ibid., 74–75.

57. Ibid., 75–76, 81–84.

58. Ibid., 75.

59. Ibid., 76, 79. The $18,000 cost of the *Pioneer* far exceeded the more typical $4,000 price of competitive cars.

60. Sandburg, *Abraham Lincoln,* 664.

61. Ibid., 690.

62. Ibid., 701–17.

63. Wayne Wesolowski, "Abraham Lincoln's Funeral Train" *Model Railroader* 62, no. 2 (February 1995): 92–97; Sandburg, *Abraham Lincoln,* 736–37.

64. John Carroll Power, *Abraham Lincoln: His Life, Public Services, Death, and Great Funeral Cortege* (Springfield, Ill.: E. A. Wilson & Co., 1875), 122; Sandburg, *Abraham Lincoln,* 740.

65. *Chicago Tribune,* May 3, 1865; J. W. Becker, "The Lincoln Funeral Train," *Illinois Historical Society Journal* 9 (1916–1917): 316; "Lincoln Lore," *Bulletin of the Lincoln National Life Foundation,* no. 895 (June 3, 1946). There are conflicting reports regarding the identity of the funeral train conductor. William Porter, a brakeman who worked the train, recalled 52 years later that the conductor was George Hewitt, but a contemporary *Chicago Tribune* story reported that the conductor was Amos Brinckley. Despite the passage of time, it can be assumed Porter's statement is the more accurate. Porter is the source of the engineer's name although another report stated the engineer was named James Colting.

66. *Chicago Tribune,* May 3, 1865; *Illinois State Journal,* May 5, 1865. The *Chicago Tribune* reported 10 cars in the

train at the Ft. Wayne depot, but the *Illinois State Journal* reported the train's arrival in Springfield "consisted of nine cars beautifully draped in mourning. . . ." Recognizing the confusion that must have prevailed at the Ft. Wayne depot, the author finds the accuracy of the *Illinois State Journal* report more credible and consistent with what is known of the train's Washington-to-Chicago journey.

67. Becker, "The Lincoln Funeral Train," 316.

68. *Instructions Issued by General Superintendent Robert Hale* ("Lincoln Funeral," vertical file, Illinois State Historical Library).

69. Power, *Abraham Lincoln,* 200–204.

70. *Chicago Tribune,* May 6, 1865; *Joliet Republican,* May 13, 1865. Some in Springfield had promoted the idea of having the train pass the C&A's depot and then proceed to Great Western Junction and on to the Great Western depot, from which Lincoln had last left the city, but the military command vetoed the idea. It would have been a very fitting completion to the journey.

71. Ruth Painter Randall, *Mary Lincoln: A Biography of a Marriage* (Boston: Little, Brown & Co., 1953). No known record of those attending the president's remains at Springfield list either Mrs. Lincoln or her sons.

72. *Chicago Tribune,* May 3, 4, 6, 1865; *Joliet Republican,* May 6, 1865; *Illinois State Journal,* May 4, 1865; *Bloomington Pantagraph,* May 5, 1865.

73. Wayne H. Hartwell, "Pullman's Connection with the Lincoln Funeral Train" (notes in preparation for article in *Compton's Pictorial Encyclopedia,* April 15, 1957).

74. *Carrollton Gazette,* August 12, 1865. Though the railroad had no depots, the United States Express Company had appointed agents at stations between Carrollton and Jacksonville within the first month. They were local businessmen who kept the paperwork and parcels they received at their places of business. Once the passing track at Carrollton opposite the planned depot site was added, service to the town's first industry, a lumber yard, began. Within a month or two, 14 new residences were constructed around the depot site. White Hall too saw new construction of substantially better structures than the first rudimentary buildings that had been slapped together there. In October the United States Telegraph Company began sinking poles for its telegraph lines and, by late November, had wires in place from Monticello to Jerseyville and had nearly finished lines from Jacksonville to Carrollton.

75. Ibid., January 6, 13, 1868. To mark the occasion, a special was operated. The train departed Jerseyville for a slow, rough ride to Monticello over Jacksonville track and then entered the C&A's main for a much smoother run to East St. Louis. Those onboard were ferried across the river for a lunch in St. Louis, after which the party returned to East St. Louis and the return to Jerseyville somewhat after nightfall. The first scheduled trip was operated on Friday, January 12. Onboard were Woodson, Greene, and Shephard, all past presidents of the St.LJ&C or its predecessors; George Straut, the current president; R.T. Beckman, the road's superintendent; former state senator and now secretary of the railroad, Charles Hodges; many local investors; and Blackstone.

76. Ibid.

77. *Carrollton Gazette,* January 13, April 14, 1866.

78. *Bloomington Daily Pantagraph,* December 25, 1866, February 2, 1867.

79. Ibid., December 31, 1866. Both the IC and the C&A offered excellent north-south routes, but there was now talk of an east-west road between Danville and Pekin that would pass through Bloomington; the Danville, Urbana, Bloomington & Pekin; and the Lafayette, Bloomington & Mississippi—also an east-west line. The St.LJ&C was given $75,000 by the city and township of Bloomington; others were given as much as $100,000.

80. Though a modest achievement, the event was celebrated on July 4 with the operation of a special train of three coaches filled with a reported 200 celebrants pulled by the *W. G. Greene* up from Jacksonville—a journey that took three hours.

81. *Menard Index,* July 22, 24, 1867.

82. *Bloomington Daily Pantagraph,* September 23, 1867.

83. *History of Grundy County, Illinois* (Chicago: O. L. Daskin & Co., 1882), 346.

84. Modesto Joseph Donna, *The Braidwood Story* (privately printed, 1977), 10, 295.

85. *History of Grundy County, Illinois,* 346.

86. Ibid.

87. *Second Annual Report, 1864,* 13.

88. Donna, *The Braidwood Story,* 57–58.

89. *History of Will County* (Chicago: Wm. LeBaron Jr. & Co., 1878), 752. Not everyone who tried coal mining in the Wilmington Coal Field had Braidwood's success. A mine was started at Gardner in June 1865. The Joint Stock Coal Mining Company sank a shaft southwest of town, along the railroad. A powerful underground stream of water was encountered after a depth of 40–50 feet was reached. Despite the best efforts to void the shaft of water, the mine could not be saved and was abandoned. In 1874 the C&A laid an underground pipe from the shaft to a new water tank, and a continuous supply flowed until the tank was demolished some 68 years later.

90. Richard Patrick Joyce, "Miners of the Prairie: Life and Labor in the Wilmington, Illinois, Coal Field, 1866–1897" (Ph.D. diss., Illinois State University, 1980), 9.

91. *History of Grundy County,* 691.

92. Donna, *The Braidwood Story,* 63–64.

93. Louise Carroll Wade, *Chicago's Pride: The Stockyards, Packingtown, and Environs in the Nineteenth Century* (Urbana: University of Illinois Press, 1987), 5–11.

94. Ibid., 47.

95. John H. White, Jr., *The American Railroad Freight Car: From the Wood-car Era to the Coming of Steel* (Baltimore: Johns Hopkins University Press, 1993), 5–11.

96. *Third Annual Report, 1865.* In 1865, the year the stockyards were opened, the Alton had 53 stock cars of a total roster of 351 freight cars.

97. Ibid., 25.

98. Wade, *Chicago's Pride,* 29.

99. Ibid., 36–41.

100. Ibid., 48–49, 55. Although Joy, as principal owner of the Burlington, had joined with the other railroads in

forming the new corporation, the road's president, John Van Nortwick, refused to abandon the new yard his road had just completed at a cost of $200,000 along Western Avenue, as did the operators of the Western Union Drovers' Yard adjacent to the Bulington's, which served the North Western and the Milwaukee Road. It was crucial for those yards to be shut down for the Union Stock Yards to succeed, but Van Nortwick remained adamant until his board of directors, led by Joy, overruled him. Van Nortwick resigned over the issue, leading to Joy assuming the Burlington's presidency. The Burlington's Western Avenue yard was closed. The owners of Drovers' Yard then capitulated.

101. Ibid., 50–54. Chanute's plan for the infrastructure was to install over 30 miles of drainage tiles, which emptied into two oversized sewers that dumped into the south branch and the south fork of the Chicago River. Freshwater upstream from an outlet on the south fork was drawn, filling six miles of water troughs with 500,000 gallons a day. Alongside the water troughs were constructed 10 miles of feed troughs for the corn and up to 100 tons of hay needed during peak season. Five hundred pens, covering 60 acres, were erected, seemingly more than sufficient for the foreseeable future. Some 75,000 hogs, 22,000 sheep, 21,000 cattle, and 200 horses could be penned simultaneously.

The pens were segregated into four parts—three receiving yards and a yard for shipments east. The B yard, on the north end, served the three eastern roads, while the A yard handled IC and Rock Island traffic. To the west was yard C, which served the Burlington and the C&A, and the D yard, which served the North Western. More than 15 miles of track (including a loop track that connected the yards, affording easy access to each of them) were laid within the Union Stock Yard property.

102. *Fourth Annual Report, 1866,* 40–41.
103. Ibid., 32–33.
104. *Third Annual Report, 1865,* 11.
105. Ibid., 13, 15.
106. Ibid., 16–17. New bridges replaced their worn-out predecessors at Sugar Creek, Macoupin Creek, and Forked Creek. Covered were the bridges at Wood River, Shield Branch, Salt Creek, Archer Road, and the Rolling Mill Bridge in Bridgeport. The bridges at Wolf Creek and Clear Creek were rebuilt, and the company paid the PFt.W&C a share of the costs to rebuild the Chicago River Bridge.
107. Ibid., 17.
108. Ibid., 20–21.
109. *Fourth Annual Report, 1866,* 6.
110. *Fifth Annual Report, 1867,* 8.
111. President Andrew Johnson, New York senator William Seward, and General Ulysses Grant were among the first dignitaries to arrive there within weeks of its opening. Both President Johnson and Senator Seward addressed a crowd in the square opposite the depot before heading to St. Louis by boat. See "The Story of Alton's First Railroad Station."
112. *Bloomington Daily Pantagraph,* November 4, 6, 11, 1867.
113. Ibid., November 5–6, 9, 11, 13, 1867.

114. Ibid., November 26, 28, 1867.
115. Newton Bateman and Paul Selby, *Historical Encyclopedia of Illinois and History of McLean County* (Chicago: Munsell Publishing, 1908), 747.
116. *Sixth Annual Report, 1868,* 14.
117. Leyendecker, *Palace Car Prince,* 81–84. Among the investors was John Crerar, who, on behalf of the C&A, took a 10 percent interest in Pullman's new company and was one of three incorporators. Crerar's association with Pullman went back as far as the building of Pullman's *Pioneer,* in which he had personally invested capital. *Minutes,* May 12, 1869. In May 1869 the C&A purchased 187 more Pullman shares.
118. Leyendecker, *Palace Car Prince,* 85–87.
119. Ibid.
120. *Minutes,* February 12, 1868.
121. *The Chicago and Alton,* 158–77.
122. *Sixth Annual Report, 1868,* 30–33.
123. Ibid., 10.
124. *Sixth Annual Report, 1896,* 27.
125. Ibid., 8–9.
126. Ibid., 19.
127. Ibid., 28.
128. Ibid., 28.
129. *Seventh Annual Report, 1869,* 12–13, 17.
130. White, *The American Railroad Passenger Car,* 563–67.
131. Ibid., 82–85; *Seventh Annual Report, 1869,* 27.
132. Richard C. Overton, *Burlington Route: A History of the Burlington Lines* (New York: Alfred A. Knopf, 1965), 117–19.
133. *Lacon Home Journal,* December 1, 1869.
134. Ibid., March 13, 1867.
135. Ibid., February 19, June 17, 1868.
136. Ibid., August 19, September 19, 1868.
137. If a *Bloomington Daily Pantagraph* report of December 25, 1866, is accurate, there had been some work performed on the line earlier. The paper reported, "It is the desire of the directors (of the St.LJ&C) to build through Washington, Tazewell County, and so on in a northeast direction, to Tonica, on the mainline of the IC, and from there on towards Chicago. Several miles of track are now laid south of Washington, and portions of the road are graded between there and Delevan, and also north through Metamora, in Woodford county. . . ." Up to this point, every request for a branch had been rejected. The citizens of Waverly, in the mid-1850s, wanted to connect at Auburn but were given no encouragement. Interests in Pekin in the early 1860s wanted to connect at Lincoln but were given an equally cool reception.
138. Ibid., October 7, 1868.
139. Ibid., March 9, 1870; *Interstate Commerce Commission Valuation Report,* vol. 40, 227.
140. The C&A received $100,700, the proceeds of a Marshall County bond sale, as payment for its work on the Dwight-Streator portion. When deducted from its own outlays, including the $166,185 paid for the Streator-Wenona line, the 80-mile Dwight-Washington line, with a branch to Lacon, had cost $619,012.

141. *Lacon Home Journal,* November 23, 1870.

142. *Seventh Annual Report, 1869,* 3–4. By now the C&A was delivering the majority of Chicago's coal tonnage, according to the Chicago Board of Trade—51 percent of all the bituminous coal received by rail in Chicago in 1868.

Chapter 6: The Triangle Is Closed

1. Clayton, *The Illinois Fact Book,* 40–41. Joliet had a population of 7,262, Bloomington 14,590, Springfield 17,364, and Jacksonville 9,203.

2. Malone and Rauch, *Crisis of the Union,* 301.

3. See David Haward Bain, *Empire Express* (New York: Viking, 1999), 3–5, 40–42, 115–16, for an excellent telling of the transcontinental railroad story.

4. *Chicago Tribune,* May 10, 1869.

5. Malone and Rauch, *Crisis of the Union,* 294; Tracy Lynch, *Railroads of Kansas City* (Boulder: Pruett Publishing, 1984), 127.

6. The North Western was the first to reach the Missouri River at Council Bluffs, across the river from Omaha. Its trains brought the materials and supplies the UP needed. The Burlington & Missouri River and the Rock Island quickly extended their lines to Council Bluffs as well. The three roads competed for the available traffic. Ever lower rates were offered to attract business. Before long none of the three was making money, and it was realized the rate war would ruin all three. The roads found solution in the creation of a traffic pool where each shared the available business equally. The arrangement became known as the Iowa Pool. It worked. Higher and more stable rates were restored, and for nearly 14 years the three railroads peacefully shared the spoils.

7. Keith L. Bryant, *History of the Atchison, Topeka and Santa Fe Railway* (New York: Macmillan, 1974), 121.

8. Walter Prescott Webb, *The Great Plains* (Lincoln: University of Nebraska Press, 1981), 207–15.

9. Ibid., 223.

10. Ibid., 220.

11. Ibid., 219–23.

12. Lynch, *Railroads of Kansas City,* 127.

13. *Eighth Annual Report, 1870,* 9.

14. *Laws of the State of Missouri,* 1858. The North Missouri Railroad was started at St. Louis with the goal of reaching Ottumwa, Iowa, and the coalfields there. A Kansas City branch off the main line at Moberly was laid in the late 1860s.

15. *The Chicago and Alton,* 195–221.

16. Larry Lawson and Robert Schramm, "Roodhouse: Crossroads of the Western Division," *Gulf, Mobile & Ohio Historical Society News,* nos. 26–27 (1981): 5.

17. *Ninth Annual Report, 1871,* 10.

18. Ibid.

19. Ibid. Mention is made of purchase of only "a Steam Ferryboat" in the annual report. A photo confirms that it was the *J.C. McMullin.* A speech delivered in 1944 by H. B. Voorhess, vice president of the B&O and former president of the C&A, asserts the *W. H. Christy,* a boat of equal size and capacity, inaugurated ferry service. None of the sources referred to revealed anything further about the *W. H. Christy.*

20. *Jacksonville Journal,* October 30, 1871.

21. Ibid., 23.

22. *Eighth Annual Report, 1870,* 12.

23. *Ninth Annual Report, 1871,* 6.

24. Andreas, *History of Chicago,* 703.

25. Ibid., 703.

26. Ibid., 706–15, 718–19.

27. Recollections of E. J. Sanford, Bloomington-based engineer, recorded in 1910.

28. Andreas, *History of Chicago,* 730, 753.

29. Ibid.

30. *Ninth Annual Report, 1871,* 9.

31. Ibid., 11.

32. Ibid., 8, 18; *Tenth Annual Report, 1872,* 9–10.

33. *Tenth Annual Report, 1872,* 8; *Eleventh Annual Report, 1873,* 7.

34. Donna, *The Braidwood Story,* 63–66, 310–12. Two single-trucked, horse-drawn streetcar lines were briefly operated to serve the miners—the Dixon line, which ran from the G mine (on what is now Third Street) to the J, L, and N mines, northwest of the city, and another that ran to the O, P, and R mines.

35. Ibid.

36. George H. Miller, *Railroads and the Granger Laws* (Madison: University of Wisconsin Press, 1971), 59, 67.

37. *Eleventh Annual Report, 1873,* 12–14.

38. Ibid.

39. Miller, *Railroads and the Granger Laws,* 87–88.

40. Ibid., 88–89.

41. Ibid., 90–91.

42. *Lacon Home Journal,* November 12, 1873.

43. Ibid. As an example, the per-100-pound rate at Lacon rose from 11 to 14 cents. Shippers there protested by turning their freight over to riverboats or used railroads only as far as the I&M Canal.

44. Ibid., 13.

45. *Eleventh Annual Report, 1873,* 7.

46. *Joliet Signal,* August 19, 1873.

47. *Eleventh Annual Report, 1873,* 10–11.

48. *The Chicago and Alton,* 235–49. The two companies were then consolidated into a single entity as the Mississippi River Bridge Company with Blackstone, John Mitchell, and John Drake of the C&A; Henry Block of the L&MR; and George Straut of the St.LJ&C as directors.

49. Ibid., 11.

50. Malone and Rauch, *Crisis of the Union,* 302.

51. *Twelfth Annual Report, 1874,* 10. Roodhouse to Quincy Junction returns jumped an impressive 30 percent, and Louisiana-Mexico rose 20 percent, but they were the only segments of the entire railroad that showed increases.

52. Ibid., 14–15.

53. Ibid., 5, 13.

54. *Twelfth Annual Report, 1874,* 11–12.

55. Jean Strouse, *Morgan: American Financier* (New York: Random House, 1999), 197.

56. *Laws of the State of Illinois,* 1867, 756.

57. *Poor's Manual of Railways, 1873.*

58. *The Chicago and Alton,* 290–303; *Interstate Commerce Commission Valuation Report,* vol. 40, 236–38. All of the Illinois River common stock was acquired, with interest payments on the $700,000 of outstanding bonds assumed by the Alton. A month after the transfer of securities, Morris Jesup sold the stock at a 10 percent discount for $426,600.

59. *The Chicago and Alton,* 294.

60. *Railway Age Gazette,* November 28, 1913, 1045.

61. Reavis, *The Railway and River Systems,* 138–44.

62. John M. Barry, *Rising Tide: The Great Mississippi Flood of 1927 and How It Changed America* (New York: Simon & Schuster, 1997), 22–31.

63. Wayne Yenawine, *A History of the Holdings of the Terminal Railroad Association of St. Louis* (privately printed, n.d.); Norbury L. Grant, Hofsommer, and Overby, *St. Louis Union Station,* 15; Wayman, *St. Louis Union Station and its Railroads* (St. Louis: Evelyn E. Newman Group 1987), 19.

64. Barry, *Rising Tide,* 56–66; Reavis, *The Railway and River Systems,* 138–144; H. Roger Grant, Don L. Hofsommer, and Osmund Overby, *St. Louis Union Station: A Place for People, A Place for Trains* (St. Louis: St. Louis Mercantile Association, 1994), 11–12; Wayman, *St. Louis Union Station and Its Railroads,* 15–17.

65. Reavis, *The Railway and River Systems,* 138–144.

66. Wayne Yenawine, *A History of the Holdings,* 27–31.

67. Ibid., 37–38, 43.

68. *Thirteenth Annual Report, 1875,* 15–16.

69. Ibid., 8–10.

70. *Fourteenth Annual Report, 1876,* 7–11.

71. *Fifteenth Annual Report, 1877,* 6–12.

72. *Joliet Weekly Sun,* March 1, 1877.

73. Donna, *The Braidwood Story,* 70–72.

74. *Joliet Morning News,* November 24, 1877.

75. *Fourteenth Annual Report, 1876,* 15–16.

76. *Laws of the State of Missouri,* 1858.

77. *The Chicago and Alton,* 365–77.

78. Ibid. The filing revealed that John Mitchell would hold 155,600 shares; Tansey, Woodson, Straut, and William Mitchell, 1,000 shares each; and the five local organizers, 100 shares each. All but Asbury comprised the first board of directors.

The KCSt.L&C issued $3 million of 25-year 6 percent sinking fund bonds, secured by a mortgage on the property, plus $1.5 million of preferred stock, along with $200,000 of common stock. In November 1877 a $300,000 second mortgage on the L&MR property was drafted, the proceeds of which were used to pay off the creditors and retire half the number of bonds issued in 1870, leaving only $58,900 in the hands of others. To ensure the C&A would not be harmed directly if a failure occurred, $300,000 of Mississippi River Bridge 7 percent common stock and $150,000 of 6 percent bonds the road held was placed in escrow, the proceeds used to pay interest on the outstanding bonds.

79. *Statement of Contract Prices for Grading in Missouri.*

80. H. B. Voorhees, "The First Steel Bridge Recalled," *Railway Age,* February 17, 1945, 343–44; Yungmeyer, "An Excursion into the Early History," 30. Technically, the bridge at Glasgow was the second Hay Steel Process bridge erected; a month before it was opened, the North Western, using the same material, opened a draw span over the Chicago River at Kinzie Street. Because of its length and the danger of the task, however, the Alton's Missouri River bridge became recognized as the first railroad steel alloy bridge.

81. Employee Timetable, 1880.

82. *Eighteenth Annual Report, 1880,* 15. The 160-mile Kansas City extension completed a triangle that joined the three largest railroad terminals of the Midwest—Chicago, Kansas City, and St. Louis. The KCSt.L&C had cost $3.6 million to build, $22,500 per mile, including $475,341 expended on the Missouri River bridge at Glasgow, but after just six months of operation, the extension already generated almost 57 percent of the company's total increase in gross revenues for the year.

83. *Eighteenth Annual Report, 1880,* 9.

84. *Interstate Commerce Commission Valuation Report,* vol. 40, 236–38; *Seventeenth Annual Report, 1879,* 15–16. Made part of the sale was a judgment of $16,364 worth of construction and maintenance costs against the South-Western, which it still owed.

Chapter 7: Defeat at Kansas City, Decline at Braidwood

1. Malone and Rauch, *Crisis of the Union,* 298; Frank N. Wilner, *Railroad Mergers: History, Analysis, Insight* (Omaha: Simmons-Boardman, 1997), 8.

2. Overton, *Burlington Route,* 169.

3. Wilner, *Railroad Mergers,* 9–10.

4. Ibid., 10.

5. *Twenty-Seventh Annual Report, 1889,* 28.

6. *Twenty-Eighth Annual Report, 1890,* 13.

7. *Seventeenth Annual Report, 1879,* 5–8; *Twenty-Seventh Annual Report, 1889,* 6–9.

8. *Twenty-Sixth Annual Report, 1888,* 17.

9. White, *The American Railroad Passenger Car,* 299–300. At the start of the decade, the passenger fleet comprised 105 head-end cars, diners, and coaches, plus 16 sleepers.

10. *Nineteenth Annual Report, 1890,* 13. In 1880 the total freight car fleet numbered 5,271. There were 207 locomotives rostered, all coal-burning, 77 of them equipped with air brakes.

11. Ibid., 14–15.

12. Ibid., 9–10.

13. *Nineteenth Annual Report, 1881,* 14–15; Edson, "Locomotives of the Alton," 59. Sixteen of the oldest engines (4-4-0s and 0-4-0s dating from the 1860s) were sold. An extraordinary demand for locomotives developed in the early 1880s since—short of cash during the depressed 1870s—many roads had deferred purchases. Manufacturers were overwhelmed with orders. Because of the demand, a secondary market developed, and Superintendent J. C. McMullin wisely chose to take advantage of the circumstances by selling some of his castoffs at average prices of $5,100. This was an excellent return. Each of the 11 new, larger engines had cost only

$2,600 more than the older equipment returned.

14. *Nineteenth Annual Report, 1881,* 16; *The Chicago and Alton,* 451–60.

15. *Nineteenth Annual Report, 1881,* 15.

16. George H. Burgess and Miles C. Kennedy, *Centennial History of the Pennsylvania Railroad Company, 1846–1946* (Philadelphia: Pennsylvania Railroad Co., 1949), 123.

17. *Twentieth Annual Report, 1882,* 6.

18. Ibid., 11.

19. Ibid., 9. By comparison, Jacksonville revenues, without benefit of through traffic and dependent on local farm produce, were $1.1 million.

20. *Twenty-First Annual Report, 1883,* 9. The stock car additions increased the number to nearly 2,000 of the type. After retirements, the 1883 freight car fleet totaled 6,429, a 22 percent increase in just two years. Although it isn't certain exactly when they were built and added to the fleet (possibly 1882), for the first time in 1883 10 refrigerator cars bearing C&A markings were rostered.

21. *Twenty-Third Annual Report, 1885,* 7–8; *Twenty-Fourth Annual Report, 1886,* 7–8. White, *The American Railroad Freight Car,* 130. Though neither new engines nor passenger cars were added, the number of freight cars grew by 290 boxcars and 10 more refrigerator cars. Both types were built to supply a highly specialized operation called Blue Line service. The operation was started by the NYC in 1867, patterned on the success of two predecessors, the Red Line and White Line. The service was a cooperative in which the NYC, Burlington, IC, and C&A contributed cars to be freely interchanged for the transfer of high value freight. This was a highly innovative step when introduced, because at the time most freight was still being transloaded from one line to the other. Blue Line revenues were distributed proportionate to the equipment each road contributed. Initially, the company's participation was minimal—just 25 boxcars. The 290 boxcars greatly increased the C&A's participation, as did the 20 refrigerator cars.

22. *Twenty-Fifth Annual Report, 1887,* 7–8.

23. *Twenty-Sixth Annual Report, 1888,* 7–9, 12, 16.

24. Overton, *Burlington Route,* 188; Bryant, *History of the Atchison, Topeka & Santa Fe,* 134.

25. Overton, *Burlington Route,* 190.

26. Ibid. There is no known record of whether Perkins ever engaged in negotiations with Blackstone (one would presume he did), but Blackstone would have given him the same answer.

27. Bryant, *History of the Atchison, Topeka and Santa Fe,* 137.

28. Ibid., 139.

29. *Railway Age,* January 11, 18, 1890.

30. *Twenty-Sixth Annual Report, 1888,* 7–9, 12.

31. Gene V. Glendinning, "When Coal and Braidwood Were Synonymous," *Gulf, Mobile & Ohio Historical Society News,* no. 73 (1994): 18.

32. Ibid.

33. *Wilmington Advocate,* October 16, November 20, 1885.

34. Glendinning, "When Coal and Braidwood Were Syn-

onymous," 21; *Twenty-Seventh Annual Report, 1889,* 59.

35. *Twenty-Eighth Annual Report, 1890,* 11; *Railway Age,* February 14, 1891.

36. *Twenty-Ninth Annual Report, 1891,* 11.

37. Grant, Hofsommer, and Overby, *St. Louis Union Station,* 14.

38. Geisst, *Wall Street,* 110–13.

39. Ibid., 113.

40. *Thirty-First Annual Report, 1893,* 11.

41. *Thirty-Second Annual Report, 1894,* 11–12.

42. Dumas Malone and Basil Rauch, *The New Nation, 1865–1917* (New York: Appleton-Century-Crofts, 1960), 119–22.

43. *Thirty-Second Annual Report, 1894,* 7, *Thirty-Third Annual Report, 1895,* 6, 8. During the year, in a further move to streamline the corporate structure, the Mississippi River Bridge Company was purchased.

44. Grant, Hofsommer, and Overby, *St. Louis Union Station,* 18.

45. Wayman, *St. Louis Union Station and Its Railroads,* 25–26; Grant, Hofsommer, and Overby, *St. Louis Union Station,* 16–18.

46. Wayman, *St. Louis Union Station and Its Railroads,* 29; Grant, Hofsommer, and Overby, *St. Louis Union Station,* 16, 22. The C&A (along with six other roads) was a tenant until 1902, when part ownership was acquired.

47. Grant, Hofsommer, and Overby, *St. Louis Union Station,* 18. The double tracks along St. Louis's waterfront were an eyesore, but, being elevated, they ensured uninterrupted operations when the riverfront flooded.

48. *Thirty-Third Annual Report, 1895,* 10; *Thirty-Fourth Annual Report, 1896,* 11; *Lockport Phoenix,* August 15, 1895; Public Timetable, 1897.

49. *Girard Gazette,* March 26, May 7, 1896.

50. *Thirty-Fifth Annual Report, 1897,* 10.

51. Victor Hicken, "The Virden and Pana Mine Wars of 1898" *Illinois State Journal* 52, no. 2 (summer 1959): 265, 271–78.

52. *Thirty-Sixth Annual Report, 1898,* 12.

53. Strouse, *Morgan,* 396.

54. Wilner, *Railroad Mergers,* 14.

55. George Kennan, *The Chicago and Alton Case* (Garden City, N.Y.: Country Life Press, 19106), 5.

Chapter 8: The Harriman Era

1. Albro Martin, *Enterprise Denied* (New York: Columbia University Press, 1971), 18–19.

2. *Railway Age,* November 18, 25, 1898.

3. *Railway Age,* December 16, 1898.

4. Wilner, *Railroad Mergers,* 14; Maury Klein, *The Life & Legend of E. H. Harriman* (Chapel Hill: University of North Carolina Press, 2000) 250, 321.

5. *Railway Age,* February 24, 1899.

6. Klein, *The Life & Legend of E. H. Harriman,* 172.

7. Kennan, *E. H. Harriman,* 12, 15.

8. Ibid., 66.

9. Ibid., 61–87, 109–38.

10. Ibid., 173.

11. Ibid.

12. Ibid., 174.

13. Ultimately, the syndicate was expanded to include 100 members, including William Rockefeller of Standard Oil—a fellow director with Stillman of the CM&St.P—and fellow bankers Morris Jesup, John Stewart, and John Mitchell—all of whom had a stake in the Alton—plus a consortium of other capitalists.

14. Klein, *The Life & Legend of E. H. Harriman,* 174.

15. *Railway Age,* February 10, 1899.

16. Ibid.

17. Kennan, *The Chicago and Alton Case,* 9.

18. Klein, *The Life & Legend of E. H. Harriman,* 162.

19. Ibid., 170–71. Within a year of Harriman taking control, a rush of crude oil was pushed to the sky at the Spindletop oil patch, just 15 miles north of Port Arthur. The KCS's future was set.

20. For a corporate history of the St.LP&N predecessors, see Richard R. Wallin, Paul H. Stringham, and John Szwajkart, *Chicago & Illinois Midland* (San Marino, Calif.: Golden West Books, 1979). The history of the numerous southern Illinois short lines that were started but failed or were merged into other roads is a fascinating subject, and the *Midland* book is an excellent telling of that story.

21. Martin, *Enterprise Denied,* 7.

22. Wallin, Stringham, and Szwajkart, *Chicago & Illinois Midland,* 24–25; Forrest McDonald, *Insull* (Chicago: University of Chicago Press, 1962) 53, 58, 64–65.

23. *Railway Age,* October 21, 28, November 4, 11, 1898, June 2, 1899.

24. *Railway Age,* November 11, 1898.

25. *Chicago Tribune,* January 4, 1899.

26. *Railway Age,* November 11, 1898.

27. Ibid.

28. Klein, *The Life & Legend of E. H. Harriman,* 163, *Chicago Tribune,* January 4, 1899.

29. *Interstate Commerce Commission Valuation Reports,* vol. 40, 191, 197–203; Paul H. Stringham and Gene Glendinning, "The Sherman Branch: A Dream That Never Came True," *Gulf, Mobile & Ohio Historical Society News,* nos. 36–37 (1984): 41, 43.

30. Robert Fiedler, *The Look Cuss and Wait* (unpublished manuscript, 1993).

31. Ibid.

32. Ibid., 217.

33. *Interstate Commerce Commission Valuation Reports,* vol. 40, 218.

34. Ibid., 218.

35. *The Chicago and Alton,* 497–552; *Railway Age,* July 21, 28, 1899.

36. Kennan, *The Chicago and Alton Case,* 14–15; J. A. Wayland, "The Alton Steal," *Wayland's Monthly* (June 1908): 1–5. Eight million dollars of debt due in 1900 and 1903 comprised bonds bearing 6 and 7 percent interest. Eventually the gold bonds were sold at relatively small profits, after New York State approved them as investment quality for state funds.

37. Klein, *The Life and Legend of E. H. Harriman,* 175; Kennan, *The Chicago and Alton Case,* 10–11.

38. Kennan, *The Chicago and Alton Case,* 10.

39. Ibid., 19–24; Klein, *The Life & Legend of E. H. Harriman,* 176.

40. John Wilson to James Hutchins, March 11, 1899.

41. *The Chicago and Alton,* 553–57. The C&A Railroad continued as a corporate entity with all of its stock owned by the C&A Railway.

42. Ibid., 563–614.

43. *Chicago Tribune,* May 9, 1898. Since the *Tribune* was both the source of the quote and sponsor of the trip, it may be somewhat suspect.

44. Ibid.

45. *Railway Age,* November 17, December 8, 1899.

46. *Railway Age,* November 17, 1899.

47. James Charlton to Charles Chappell, October 4, 1899. Other names suggested were "Admiral," "The Arrow," "Capitol," "Cardinal Limited," "Chicago–St. Louis Limited," "City Belle," "Daylight Express," "Daylight Flyer," "Daylight Limited," "Daylight Special," "Daylight Observation Limited," "Drawing Room Special," "Flying Meteor," "Federal Flyer," "Golden Crown Limited," "Golden Fire," "Great City," "Illinois Limited," "Imperial," "Inter-state Limited," "Interstate Special," "New Century," "Olive Green Limited," "Olive Green Special," "Olympia Special," "Oriental," "Palace Special," "Parlor Car Special," "Peerless Limited," "Prairie State Express" (later used for an Alton train), "Royal Comet," "Royal Crown Limited," "Sunburst," "Sunset Limited," and "Sunshine." More than a few of the suggestions became identified with other roads.

48. *Railway Age,* December 29, 1899. The engines weighed 139,000 pounds and had 73-inch drivers and 19 x 26-inch cylinders with an improved piston design. The firebox had 177 square feet of heating surface. Electric headlights were employed. To ensure smooth, matching lines with the new equipment, Pullman designed the cabs. They were numbered 500–11.

49. Public timetable, 1899.

50. *Scientific American,* March 2, 1901.

51. Ibid.

52. *Railway Age,* April 6, 1900. The railroad's board of directors comprised Harriman, Schiff, W. A. Simonson of the National City Bank (representing Stillman), Felton, and four of Mitchell's lieutenants—R. C. Clowry, J. W. Doane, W. H. Henkle, and J. C. Hutchins. The Railway board of director members were Harriman, Schiff, Stillman, and Gould, plus Felton, Chappell, Mitchell, Rudolph Brand, Norman Ream, Bertram Winston, and other syndicate investors.

53. *Chicago Tribune,* May 27, 1900.

54. *Railway Age Gazette,* August 27, 1909, *Railway Age,* March 15, 1930; H. Roger Grant, *The Corn Belt Route: A History of the Chicago Great Western Railroad Company.* (DeKalb: Northern Illinois University Press, 1996), 76–77.

55. There were a total of 53 passenger engines, all 4-4-0s. The limited tractive effort of the 179 freight engines—made up of 22 small 2-6-0s, 31 4-6-0s, 86 elderly 4-4-0s, and 40 equally inefficient 0-4-0 and 0-6-0 switchers (the oldest of

them dating from the late 1860s)—was no match for the new power other roads employed.

56. *First Annual Report, 1901,* 10; *Second Annual Report, 1902,* 10.

57. *Second Annual Report, 1902, 23.*

58. Ibid., 23.

59. Ibid.

60. Ibid., 10.

61. *First Annual Report, 1901,* 24.

62. Ibid., 10.

63. Ibid.

64. Ibid.

65. The investment made came at a time of a resurgent national economy. The Alton's revenues in 1900 reached $7.8 million, and the road turned a profit of $3.6 million. During 1901 revenues advanced to $9 million, an 87 percent year-on-year increase, and profits climbed to $5 million, 39 percent ahead of the prior year, thanks to an operating ratio of a respectable 62 percent.

66. *First Annual Report, 1901,* 9.

67. Ibid.

68. *Railway Age,* August 24, 1903.

69. *The Flood of 1903* (company-produced promotional brochure).

70. Ibid.

71. Paul H. Stringham, *Illinois Terminal: The Electric Years* (Glendale, Calif.: Interurban Press, 1989), 11–17.

72. Ibid., 18; *Girard Gazette,* August 18, October 6, 1904, April 27, June 22, 1905; *Springfield Journal,* November 5, 6, 14, 26, December 24, 1905.

73. *Fourth Annual Report, 1904,* 10.

74. Richard R. Wallin, "Motor Cars," *Gulf, Mobile & Ohio Historical Society News,* no. 19 (summer 1979): 11–12; *Girard Gazette,* April 27, June 29, 1905.

75. *Fourth Annual Report, 1904,* 11.

76. James L. Windmeier, "Chicago & Alton Atlantics," *Gulf, Mobile & Ohio Historical Society News,* no. 3 (spring 1975): 10–15; *Railway Age,* January 1, 1904; James L. Windmeier, "Chicago & Alton Class I-6 Pacifics," *Gulf, Mobile & Ohio Historical Society News,* no. 6 (spring 1976): 10–15; David P. Morgan, "A Pacific Primer," *Trains* (September 1988): 32–41. The 17 locomotives and 50 passenger cars were purchased through the Chicago & Alton Equipment Association, a financing tool several railroads, including the UP, began using around the turn of the century. The equipment itself was mortgaged for relatively short terms.

77. *Fifth Annual Report, 1905,* 11.

78. *Fourth Annual Report, 1904,* 9; *Girard Gazette,* October 2, 1902.

79. Late in 1905 three miles of track between Eldred and Columbiana were taken up despite local protests. Little purpose was served in keeping that portion of the line open after the announced Quincy extension was abandoned. Thereafter, what traffic was generated came largely from a stone quarry at Eldred.

80. Overton, *Burlington Route,* 269–70.

81. *Railway Age,* July 13, 1904.

82. William W. Baldwin, *Corporate History of the Chicago Burlington & Quincy Railroad Company and Affiliated Compa-*

nies (Chicago, 1921), 1521–33.

83. *Railway Age,* January 1, 1904.

84. Ibid., September 16, 1904.

85. Ibid., October 7, 1904.

86. Ibid.

87. Ibid., November 25, 1904.

88. *Fifth Annual Report, 1905,* 11.

89. *Fifth Annual Report, 1905,* 10–11.

90. Ibid., 6.

91. *Sixth Annual Report, 1906,* 10–12.

92. Malone and Rauch, *The New Nation,* 221.

93. Martin, *Enterprise Denied,* 40.

94. Ibid., 41–45.

95. Malone and Rauch, *The New Nation,* 355.

96. The breakup finally came in late 1909. See Ron Chernow, *Titan: The Life of John D. Rockefeller, Sr.* (New York: Random House, 1998), 541.

97. Kennan, *E. H. Harriman,* 177–227; Martin, *Enterprise Denied,* 84–85.

98. Kennan, *E. H. Harriman,* 229, 242–44.

99. Kennan, *The Chicago and Alton Case,* 21.

100. Kennan, *E. H. Harriman,* 244.

101. Ibid., 247.

102. Martin, *Enterprise Denied,* 118–19.

103. Kennan, *E. H. Harriman,* 247.

104. Carl Snyder, *American Railways as Investments* (Elizabeth, N.Y.: Moody-Barton Press, 1907), 176; *Moody's Manual 1907.*

105. Strouse, *Morgan,* 579.

106. Ibid., 582–86.

107. Martin, *Enterprise Denied,* 118–19.

Chapter 9: The Hawley and Union Pacific Takeovers

1. *Railway Age Gazette,* October 22, 1909, 753.

2. Frank P. Donovan, Jr., "Edwin Hawley," *Trains & Travel* (September 1952): 52.

3. Overton, *Burlington Route,* 233.

4. Klein, *The Life and Legend of E. H. Harriman,* 216.

5. Ibid., 250–51.

6. John A. Rehor, *The Nickle Plate Story* (Milwaukee: Kalmbach Publishing, 1965), 143–67.

7. Klein, *The Life and Legend of E. H. Harriman,* 321, 324. Hawley had earlier offended Harriman by taking a seat on the board of Gould's WP, a line organized to open a route between Salt Lake City and San Francisco, which Gould hoped would bring him control of the first coast-to-coast railroad to compete with Harriman for West Coast traffic.

8. Donovan, "Edwin Hawley," 53.

9. *Railway Age,* August 30, 1907, 299. The 2 percent Clover Leaf bonds had two levels of payment, accelerated after five years. Hawley planned to pay them off with Alton common dividends.

10. *Railroad Age Gazette,* June 5, 1908, 6–7.

11. *Poor's Manual of Railroads,* 1901, 328; *Seventh Annual Report, 1907,* 4.

12. *Poor's Manual of Railroads,* 1909, 343–44, 457–58.

13. *Eighth Annual Report, 1908,* 5–6; *Railway Age,* July 12, 1907, 59.

14. *Seventh Annual Report, 1907,* 6.

15. *Railroad Age Gazette,* August 28, 1908, 847; *Ninth Annual Report, 1909,* 37. The order was financed with a $1.64 million Series E Equipment Trust.

16. *Ninth Annual Report, 1909,* 36. The $250,000 cost of the 15 engines was paid for with the proceeds of a Series F Equipment trust.

17. Lloyd J. Mercer, *E. H. Harriman: Master Railroader* (Boston: Twayne Publishers, 1985), 17.

18. *Railway Age,* August 23, 1907, 482. Besides the holdovers, the new board of directors included the TSt.L&W's Hawley, Hubbard, Shonts, and Ross; Rock Island executive committee chairman Robert Mather and first vice president and general solicitor R. A. Jackson; Felton; and outside directors Joy Morton, F. H. Davis, William Beale, Huntington, Ream, and Mitchell.

19. *Railway Age,* November 29, 1907, 779. Grant, *The Corn Belt Route,* 76. Upon leaving, Harriman wrote Felton a note that read, "Your loyalty & faithfulness has been greatly appreciated & stands as one of the most gratifying results of the . . . Chicago & Alton enterprise." Two years after his Mexican Central stint, he became president of the Chicago Great Western, where he remained until he retired as chairman of the board in 1929.

20. *Poor's Manual of Railroads,* 1908, 363.

21. *Eighth Annual Report, 1908,* 6.

22. Ibid., 7.

23. Ibid., 8–9.

24. Overton, *Burlington Route,* 271–74; *Railroad Age Gazette,* January 5, 1909, 248.

25. *Railroad Age Gazette,* October 22, 1909, 739–41.

26. In 1910, 35–40 carloads of dressed meat were moved daily over the line between Kansas City and the East. But it was the sole example of any sizeable traffic interchange between the roads or between the roads and any of the other Hawley holdings.

27. *Railway Age Gazette,* June 13, 1913, 1327–28.

28. Ibid. Initial plans called for two additional tracks to be laid parallel to the main line as far as Brighton Park and Argo, but instead, crossovers were installed at each end of the yard. Future additions were to include a wye and loop for turning engines or entire trains; 12 repair tracks with a capacity of 145 cars; four bad order storage tracks capable of handling 104 cars; another 12 tracks for the north yard; an additional storage yard of 49 tracks with a separate lead for 1,787 cars; six more storage tracks for the south yard, and a parallel, separate 36-track storage yard; a yard to store 41 cabooses; and 12 radial tracks for outside storage of engines at the roundhouse; but none of these additions were ever made.

29. Public Timetables, 1907–1909.

30. *Tenth Annual Report, 1910,* 6; *Poor's Manual of Railroads,* 1910, 889.

31. Martin, *Enterprise Denied,* 227–28. The author liberally used Martin's definitive narrative of events leading up to the rate application and the subsequent events.

32. *Tenth Annual Report, 1910,* 12. Later the Missouri legislature did the same, and the Missouri Railroad and Warehouse Commission gave notice of its intent to reduce all commodity rates transported within the state by 20 percent.

33. Linn H. Westcott, *Model Railroader Cyclopedia,* vol. 1, *Steam Locomotives* (Milwaukee: Kalmbach Publishing, 1960), 235; John F. Stover, *History of the Baltimore and Ohio Railroad* (West Lafayette, Ind.: Purdue University Press, 1987), 256. The compound, articulated B&O giants had a simple tractive force of 75,200 pounds, more than twice that of the C&A's Consolidations, then the largest freight engines the road owned.

34. Westcott, *Model Railroader Cyclopedia,* 63. The Mallets had Walschaerts valve gear, 22 and 35 x 30-inch cylinders, 66 x 108-inch firebox grates, and 62-inch drivers. The huge 76-foot, 8-inch (with tender) monsters weighed 498,300 pounds and, as delivered, could produce 61,700 pounds of tractive force.

35. The first 10 Mikados, received in April 1910 (the other 20 in September), had all the same features as the Mallets but came with 28 x 30-inch cylinders and Cole header superheaters and, without tenders, weighed 269,000 pounds. The later group of 20 were 4,000 pounds heavier but in all other respects were virtually the same as the first 10. The Mikado became the backbone of Alton freight engines. Eventually, 40 more were added.

36. *Tenth Annual Report, 1910,* 10–11.

37. Ibid.

38. Roderick R. Irwin, "RT&N: The Chicago & Alton's Granville Branch," *Gulf, Mobile & Ohio Historical Society News,* no. 38 (1985): 5–6. C&A control of the road came through purchase of the $97,000 of capital stock and a guaranteed payment of the interest and eventual principal of $225,000 of RT&N 20-year 4 percent bonds.

39. *ICC Evaluation Report,* 245, 243.

40. The year before, the C&A itself entered receivership, unable to pay its own debt and of course that of the RT&N.

41. Irwin, "RT&N," 9.

42. *Eleventh Annual Report, 1911,* 6.

43. Ibid., 11.

44. *Twelfth Annual Report, 1912,* 10.

45. Edson, "Locomotives of the Alton," 79. Presumably the three 2-8-0s were paid for out of retained funds, but the 10 2-6-0s and 10 4-6-2s were financed through issuance of Series G Equipment Trust.

46. *Poor's Manual of Railroads,* 1912, 1994, 1999.

47. *Railway Age,* August 2, 1912, 225; October 4, 1912, 656; July 28, 1934, 461; *Thirteenth Annual Report, 1913,* 5.

48. *Union Pacific, Annual Report,* 1915, 41. The shares were part of a $180 million portfolio in stock, bonds, equipment trusts, and notes the rich and powerful UP held in a number of roads (such as the B&O, North Western, Milwaukee Road, IC, and NYC) strictly for investment purposes.

49. *Railway Age Gazette,* June 14, 1912, 1366.

50. *Thirteenth Annual Report, 1913,* 5.

51. *Twelfth Annual Report, 1912,* 6–7.

52. Ibid.

53. *Thirteenth Annual Report, 1913,* 6–9.

54. Ibid., 13–15.

55. *Brighton News,* April 24, July 17, 31, August 21, September 25, October 2, 23, December 4, 11, 1913.

56. *Railway Age Gazette,* July 17, 1914, 292; ibid., February 26, 1944, 83.

57. See Paul H. Stringham, "A History of C&NW's St. Louis Subdivision," *Northwestern Lines* 20, no. 1 (winter 1993): 37–47, for a complete history of the North Western's St. Louis subdivision.

58. *Fourteenth Annual Report, 1914,* 2.

59. In 1914 the ICC changed the railroad's accounting rules. Using the restated figures back to 1910 would reflect profits instead of deficits for both 1910 and 1911, a slightly lower deficit for 1912, a greater deficit for 1913, and a 48 percent greater loss in 1914. Figures used hereafter are the restated figures.

60. *Fourteenth Annual Report, 1914,* 2–4.

61. *Poor's Manual of Railroads,* 1914, 1164.

62. *Fourteenth Annual Report, 1914,* 11–12. The 50-ton gondolas came from Pressed Steel, the 200 flatcars and work cars from Bettendorf, the 50-ton boxcars from American Car & Foundry, and 500 stock cars from Pullman. The diners and postal cars were also Pullman products.

63. Ibid., 12; Edson, "Locomotives of the Alton," 61, 79; Windmeier, "Chicago & Alton Class I-6 Pacifics," 10–15; James L. Windmeier, "Chicago & Alton Class L-2 Mikados," *Gulf, Mobile & Ohio Historical Society News,* no. 8 (fall 1976): 10–13. The switchers were given B-9 classification, numbered 57–66. They had 19 x 26-inch cylinders and 51-inch drivers and weighed 154,900 pounds. They were the last new 0-6-0s the road ordered.

The Pacifics were classified I-6, numbered 650–659, a part of a 28-engine order from American Locomotive that was divided among the SP, its subsidiary Texas & New Orleans, and the C&A. They were slightly heavier than the 25 already on the property and, as a result, produced greater tractive effort. They too were the last of the type the road received.

The new Mikados were of a new class, L-2, a part of a 94-engine order divided among the Harriman roads. They differed from the previous 30 with smaller (26 x 28) cylinders and 63-inch drivers, rather than the 62-inch size of the two earlier orders. Though they developed more steam pressure, they produced less tractive effort.

Like the rolling stock, the 40 engines were purchased by the Union Pacific Equipment Association and leased to the Alton.

64. *Fourteenth Annual Report, 1914,* 8–11.

65. White, *The American Railroad Passenger Car,* 475.

66. *Brighton News,* November 16, 1916; *Railway Age Gazette,* November 27, 1914, 1016–1017.

67. *Railway Age Gazette,* May 23, 1913, 1111–28, October 30, 1914, 799–804; *New York Times,* February 8, 1998; Peter A. Hansen, "Give the People a Monument," *Trains* (April 1999).

68. *Poor's Manual of Railroads,* 1914, 1153.

69. *Poor's Manual of Railroads,* 1916, 1084.

70. *Annual Report, 1916,* 10.

71. Ibid.

72. Martin, *Enterprise Denied,* 288–92.

73. Stover, *History of the Baltimore and Ohio,* 234.

74. Ibid., 238.

75. Ibid., 239.

76. *Eighteenth Annual Report, 1918,* 2, 4.

77. Stover, *History of the Baltimore and Ohio,* 239; *Eighteenth Annual Report, 1918,* 8. They were built by Standard Steel Car and numbered 43000–43499.

78. Eugene L. Huddleston, "Uncle Sam's Locomotives," *Trains* (March 1991). Alco received the lion's share and built 1,300 engines; Baldwin built 470 and Lima built 160.

79. Edson, "Locomotives of the Alton," 81. The new series of Mikados became the Alton's L-4 class (875–884). They followed the five L-3 class 2-8-2s (860–864) ordered and received earlier in the year. The 500 gondolas and 10 2-8-2s were financed through a 1920 Series Equipment Trust, placed through the Guaranty Trust Company of New York.

80. *Railway Age,* June 17, 1918, 456.

81. V. S. Roseman, *Railway Express: An Overview* (Denver: Rocky Mountain Publishing, 1992), 7.

82. Stover, *History of the Baltimore and Ohio,* 241.

83. Ibid.

84. Ibid.

85. *Poor's Manual of Railroads,* 1917, 1831; *Poor's Manual of Railroad's,* 1918, 1833.

86. *Twentieth Annual Report, 1920,* 5–6.

87. Stover, *History of the Baltimore and Ohio,* 247–248.

88. *Eighteenth Annual Report, 1918,* 6–7.

89. *Brighton News,* February 16, 1918.

90. Chancery Court testimony, box 1653.

91. Edson, "Locomotives of the Alton," 81. Identical in all respects, the engines were built by Alco to USRA design and became the railroad's class L4-A, the suffix added to denote their Standard Oil ownership. They were numbered 885–889 and put in service in January 1921. The gondolas were numbered 501–1000.

92. *Annual Report, 1920,* 10.

93. *Railway Age,* January 7, 1922, 2–3.

94. Clayton, *The Illinois Fact Book,* 361.

95. *Annual Report, 1921,* 7, 9.

96. Ibid.

97. Ibid., 8; Harold M. Mayer and Richard C. Wade, *Chicago: Growth of a Metropolis* (Chicago: University of Chicago Press, 1969), 314. Bierd's prediction proved accurate. After serving the railroad's needs, the freight house became an annex to "the largest mail transfer facility in the world," the central Chicago Post Office, opened in 1932 over two blocks of Union Station's tracks. The raised letters of the name "Chicago & Alton" still appear on the north end of the former freight house portion immediately adjacent to the Eisenhower Expressway bridge spanning the Chicago River, about the last reminder anywhere of what used to be.

Chapter 10: The Long-Anticipated Receivership Arrives

1. Dumas Malone and Basil Rauch, *War and Troubled Peace, 1917–1939* (New York: Appleton-Century-Crofts, 1960), 122.

2. *Twenty-Second Annual Report, 1922,* 10, 29.

3. *Chicago Daily Journal of Commerce,* June 9, 1922.

4. *Railway Age,* July 15, 1922, 98.

5. *Chicago Daily Tribune,* August 23, 1922.

6. *Wall Street Journal,* August 12, 1922.

7. *Chicago Daily Tribune,* August 23, 1922.

8. Ibid., August 28, 1922.

9. Ibid., August 27, 1922.

10. Ibid.

11. Ibid.

12. Ibid.

13. *Wall Street Journal,* August 30, 1922.

14. *Chicago Daily Tribune,* August 31, 1922.

15. *Wall Street Journal,* September 1, 1922.

16. *Chicago Daily Tribune,* August 31, 1922. Receivership brought the removal of the UP management. Bierd replaced Lovett as chairman of the Executive Committee. Named to join him on the committee and as directors were E. M. Richards of the Boston office of Hayden Stone, a brokerage firm representing certain Alton investors; Samuel Moore, general counsel of the KCS; E. F. Swinney, president of the Kansas City National Bank and of the KCSt.L&C and vice president of the L&MR; and William Maffitt of St. Louis. Mitchell, Insull, Morton, Harry Adams, and V. D. Skipworth, all of Chicago, continued as directors.

17. *Wall Street Journal,* August 31, 1922.

18. *Chicago Daily Tribune,* September 1, 1922.

19. *Wall Street Journal,* September 1, 1922; *Railway Age,* September 9, 1922, 487.

20. *Chicago Daily Tribune,* September 2, 1922.

21. Ibid., September 14, 1922.

22. Michael G. Matejka and Greg Koos, eds., *Bloomington's C&A Shops: Our Lives Remembered* (Bloomington, Ill.: McLean County Historical Society, 1987) 4, 12–13.

23. *Twenty-Second Annual Report, 1922,* 3.

24. *Twenty-Second Annual Report, 1922,* 8–10; *Brighton News,* August 3, 1922.

25. *Railway Age,* December 2, 1922, 1069.

26. *Brighton News,* December 21, 1922.

27. *Twenty-Third Annual Report, 1923,* 3, 17, 27.

28. Ibid., 8.

29. Ibid., 7–8.

30. Ibid., 6.

31. Ibid. The newest and best power and equipment on the property had been leased through the Union Pacific Equipment Association over the course of the past 10 years. What was still in use was purchased with the proceeds of a $5.4 million 6 percent Receivers Series A Equipment Trust. Purchased were 20 2-8-2s, 10 Pacifics, 10 0-6-0 switchers, 3,418 freight cars, two steel dining cars, three postal cars, and two sets of *Alton Limited* equipment. Also purchased were 250 steel underframe composite gondolas, 250 steel underframe convertible grain and automobile cars—all from Pullman— and 350 steel center sill wooden gondolas from the Ryan Car Company. Trucks salvaged from retired equipment were used for the gondolas.

32. *Railway Age,* January 9, 1924, 76–77.

33. *Twenty-Fourth Annual Report, 1924,* 10.

34. *Railway Age,* October 4, 1924, 579.

35. *Railway Age,* October 4, 1924, 579–81; William W. Kratville, *Steam, Steel & Limiteds* (Omaha: Kratville Publications, 1967), 228. Two 1903 cafe cars were also rebuilt and steel sheathed as mail storage cars named the *E. L. West* (the postal service's chief clerk at large) and the *Rudolph S. Braver* (superintendent of the sixth division railway mail).

36. Passenger car diagrams, January 1, 1930; memorandum to file, July 13, 1925.

37. *Railway Age,* June 3, 1925.

38. Ibid., 8, 22.

39. Ibid., 7–12.

40. Ibid., 17–19.

41. Ibid., November 3, 1916, 802–5.

42. *Twenty-Fifth Annual Report, 1925,* 11.

43. Why the car was not numbered M2 following the 1905 experimental unit M1 is not known.

44. Wallin, "Motor Cars," 13.

45. Ibid., 11–12.

46. Ibid.

47. *Railway Age,* February 27, 1926, 552.

48. Ibid., March 20, 1926, 1311.

49. Ibid., May 22, 1926, 1400.

50. Ibid., March 13, 1926, 830.

51. Ibid., March 20, 1926, 1431, August 27, 1927, 641, October 27, 1927, 821, December 24, 1927, 1312, January 28, 1928, 289, March 24, 1928, 723, April 28, 1928, 1193.

52. Ibid., August 25, 1928, 398.

53. Ibid., September 28, 1929, 795.

54. Ibid., May 24, 1930, 88, 92, June 21, 1930, 147, July 26, 1930, 216, September 27, 1930, 676, May 20, 1933, 62.

55. *Twenty-Fourth Annual Report, 1924,* 13.

56. Ibid.

57. Ibid.

58. Public timetable, 1927.

59. Consist of passenger trains, no date.

60. *Twenty-Second Annual Report, 1922,* 12.

61. *Twenty-Third Annual Report, 1923,* 11; *Twenty-Fourth Annual Report, 1924,* 10; *Twenty-Fifth Annual Report, 1925,* 11; *Twenty-Sixth Annual Report, 1926,* 10.

62. *Twenty-Seventh Annual Report, 1927,* 9.

63. Ibid., 29.

64. *Moody's Manual of Investments,* 471, 474.

65. *Railway Age,* March 19, 1927, 931.

66. *Twenty-Seventh Annual Report, 1927,* 6.

67. *Chicago Daily Tribune,* October 30, 1927.

68. Ibid. Harry Scullin, president of Scullin Steel Company of St. Louis; James Williams, the road's secretary and treasurer; and Mitchell's son, John J. Mitchell, Jr., who followed his father into banking, replaced the three deceased men.

69. *Twenty-Eighth Annual Report, 1928,* 6.

70. Wallin, "Motor Cars," 16.

71. Ibid., 7.

72. *Railway Age,* July 6, 1929, 241, January 17, 1931, 216.

73. Snyder, *American Railways as Investments,* 170, 172, 617.

74. C. W. Esch to C. M. House, memorandum, October 1, 1929.

75. Ibid.

76. Ibid.

77. *Railway Age,* January 31, 1925, 315.

78. Ibid., January 25, 1930, 231.

79. Ibid., December 28, 1929, 1469.

80. Ibid., January 25, 1930, 234.

81. *William A. Slater vs. The Alton Railroad Company,* civil action case file 1635, 30–33.

82. Ibid., 33–34.

83. Ibid., 34.

84. *Texas Co. vs. Chicago & Alton R.R.,* equity case file 2940, 214–217; *Railway Age,* April 11, 1931, 741.

85. *Railway Age,* September 9, 1932, 1332.

86. *William A. Slater vs. The Alton Railroad Company,* 37–38.

87. *Texas Co. vs. Chicago & Alton R.R.,* 1–3.

Chapter 11: The B&O and the War Years

1. Malone and Rauch, *War and Troubled Peace,* 183.

2. Ibid., 185.

3. Ibid.

4. Ibid., 188.

5. Ibid.

6. Ibid., 190–91.

7. Stover, *History of the Baltimore and Ohio,* 280.

8. Ibid.

9. *Annual Report, 1932,* 10.

10. Ibid., table 6.

11. Employee timetable, 1932.

12. Consolidation hearing, examiner testimony, *William A. Slater vs. The Alton Railroad Company,* 37–38.

13. Locomotive Diagrams, January 1, 1931, revised February 9, 1933.

14. *Annual Report, 1932,* table 10.

15. Ibid., table 11.

16. Ibid., table 11. In 1933 a surplus MK&T Brill motor car and trailer were purchased. The motor unit was converted to a trailer. A year later four head-end cars were retired, reducing the total fleet to 84 cars.

17. Ibid., table 1.

18. Robert Schramm, "Cabooses, C&A/Alton," *Gulf, Mobile & Ohio Historical Society News,* nos. 40–41 (1985): 22–23.

19. *Railway Age,* February 27, 1932, 384.

20. Ibid., June 18, 1932, 1045.

21. Ibid., June 4, 1932, 426.

22. Ibid., April 4, 1932, 519.

23. Dave Randall, "Abe 'n Annie," *Gulf, Mobile & Ohio Historical Society News,* no. 21 (winter 1979): 11; White, *The American Railroad Passenger Car,* 163. Because the industry was tradition-bound and starved for capital, by 1946, 85 percent of all passengers cars operated on American railroads were still heavyweights. Six hundred thousand man-hours of much needed employment resulted from the contract. The cars were paid for with the proceeds of a $900,000 loan from the newly created Public Works Administration.

24. The two train sets remained in service for almost 35 years, running daily Chicago–St. Louis round-trips. In 1970, all cars but steel car 5750—reconfigured as a combine from a straight baggage car—were still on the property though out of service.

25. Randall, "Abe 'n Annie," 12–13.

26. Ibid., 16. On test runs in Ohio, the *Lady* was clocked at 94.5 mph; similar speeds were reached by the *Lord.* Though such speeds were not needed in regular runs, it was clear these two engines were designed to make up time when needed.

27. Ibid., 13, 16. The tests of the power would be on a fast three-and-one-half-hour schedule between Washington, D.C., and Jersey City on the popular *Royal Blue.*

28. Kratville, *Steam, Steel & Limiteds,* 235.

29. Belin Bodie, interview by Stephen T. Parsons, October 1989.

30. *Railway Age,* May 18, 1935, 461.

31. Randall, "Abe 'n Annie," 16.

32. *Railway Age,* December 19, 1936, 923.

33. Randall, "Abe 'n Annie," 16, 19; *Railway Age,* July 17, 1937, 727.

34. *Railway Age,* June 15, 1935, 948; July 16, 1938, 672.

35. *Annual Report, 1938,* table 11.

36. Ibid., table 9.

37. Ibid., table 6. The average passenger revenue per mile in 1938 was just $1.08, but the *Abraham Lincoln* averaged $2.79 per mile.

38. Public timetable, 1937.

39. *Railway Age,* October 7, 1944, 541–542.

40. Stover, *History of the Baltimore and Ohio,* 298.

41. Ibid., 301.

42. Ibid., 304.

43. Ibid., 302.

44. *Moody's Manual of Railroads,* 1942.

45. Ibid., 314.

46. *Railway Age,* December 5, 1942, 1612. The reorganization plan proposed that all fixed charges (except the leased line rentals) be canceled and the 6 percent interest payable on the KCSt.L&C preferred shares be reduced to 3 percent. Bondholders would receive income bonds totaling $24,205,562, receiving annual interest at 4 percent, $968,222. The bondholders would receive the outstanding 242,055 shares of common stock, less some shares that would be turned over to the RFC as security for current claims against the Alton.

47. Gardner proposed a capitalization of the new company of $57,784,562. Of the total, $30 million was to be in common stock and the remainder in bonds that would mature in 2018, bearing interest in varying payouts of from 4 to 7 percent. Stockholders were to receive bonds equal in value to their present holdings. Creditors with secured claims would get one share of common stock for each $100 of claims. Unsecured creditors were to be paid a pro-rated share of the company's limited unpledged assets in common stock at a 25 percent discount of claims.

48. Douglas B. Nuckles and Thomas W. Dixon, Jr., *Baltimore & Ohio E-Unit Diesel Passenger Locomotives* (Lynchburg, Va.: TLC Publishing, 1994), 29; Randall, "Abe 'n Annie," 19. The order was the first to be constructed at Electro-Motive's

LaGrange, Illinois, plant.

49. Alton Board of Director minutes, October 7, 1941; C. M. House, memorandum to file, October 7, 1941.

50. House to Voorhees, memorandum, January 26, 1942.

51. J. F. Whittington to Voorhees, memorandum, February 2, 1942.

52. R. B. White to Voorhees, memorandum, March 6, 1942. The units originally were to be numbered 85–90, but after Voorhees was advised that the separate numbers might encourage claims for double-heading—as was the case when two steam engines were employed—Voorhees ordered the units numbered 85A and 85B through 87A and 87B.

53. Stover, *History of the Baltimore and Ohio,* 303. Though the need was evident, over the course of the war only 40 percent of the freight and passengers cars and 60 percent of locomotives the roads asked for were produced.

54. Smith to Voorhees, April 15, 1942; WPB General Limitation Order L-97.

55. Ibid.

56. House to A. Chinn, March 16, 1944.

57. John Szwajkart, "The Salutary Switchers," *Gulf, Mobile & Ohio Historical Society News,* nos. 83–84 (1997): 4, 7, 9–14. They were numbered 50–59 and were the only units of the type painted in an Alton scheme and Alton lettering.

58. Esch to House, memorandum, January 3, 1947. The last class D-40 0-6-0, no. 146, was sold to the Chicago Gravel Company in December 1947. The last Mogul, class K-18, no. 2422, used in switching service, was scrapped in August 1948. The last Consolidation switcher, class E-49, no. 2990, was scrapped in August 1950.

59. Esch to House, memorandum, August 4, 1945.

60. *Railway Age,* March 10, 1945, 429, 444–47, April 14, 1945, 743. Before the new equipment arrived, only 2,752 cars were rostered. Only 95 flatcars were all steel, the rest—100 hoppers, 101 stock cars, 397 drop bottom gondolas, 246 automobile cars, and 1,815 boxcars—had steel underframes and, in the case of the boxcars, steel ends but were otherwise of wood (919 were built in 1906, 894 others in 1913).

61. *ICC Statistics.*

62. R. A. Pearce to House, memorandum, August 12, 1943.

63. Memorandum in file C-276, March 21, 1944.

64. *Railway Age,* May 8, 1943, 1321.

65. *ICC Statistics.*

66. *Annual Report, 1943,* 7; *Railway Age,* October 9, 1944, 1162.

67. *Annual report 1943,* 11.

68. Randall, "Abe 'n Annie, 21, 23. The units were paid for with $838,128 of promissory notes, taken by the American National Bank & Trust.

69. House to Chinn, memorandum, August 7, 1943.

70. Edson, "Locomotives of the Alton," 79.

71. *Moody's Manual of Investments,* 1944, 807.

72. Arthur W. Baum, "The Hesitant Hero of Jackson," *Saturday Evening Post,* March 11, 1947, 1–4.

73. Ibid.

74. Ibid.

75. Overton, *Burlington Route,* 515–516.

76. *Railway Age,* April 28, 1945, 572.

77. James Hutton Lemly, *The Gulf, Mobile & Ohio: A Railroad That Had to Expand or Expire* (Homewood, Ill.: R. D. Irwin, 1953), 185.

78. *Railway Age,* September 29, 1945, 513–515, 528.

79. House, memorandum, July 31, 1945.

80. G. P. Brock to I. Tigrett and F. M. Hicks, memorandum, June 28, 1945.

81. House to R. H. Gray, memorandum, May 31, 1945. The cars were the GM&O's numbers 140–141, 144, 209–10, 212, 214, 216–18.

82. Hicks to Voorhees, June 19, 1945.

83. Gene V. Glendinning, "When the Alton Route Went Shopping for a Passenger Fleet, Part I," *Gulf, Mobile & Ohio Historical Society News,* no. 15 (summer 1978): 9–15. The coaches were numbered 3050–3060; the parlor cars were named the *Alton, Bloomington, St. Louis,* and *Springfield.*

84. Glendinning, "When the Alton Route Went Shopping," 5–6.

85. *GM&O News,* July 19, 1950.

86. Hicks to Tigrett, memorandum, September 7, 1945.

87. Memorandum of conference, March 26, 1943. The F3s were to be numbered 400A and 400B through 419A and 419B, but before the first were delivered in December 1946, the composition of the order was changed. The number of boiler-equipped units was increased one to nine units and numbered 880A and 880B through 882A and 882B plus 883A through 885A. The units without boilers were numbered 800A and 800B through 811A. EMD was making rapid improvements to their models, and, before the last of the Alton order was delivered in 1949, four new model F7s instead of F3s appeared, numbered 811B, 812A, 812B, and 813A.

88. Memorandum to file S-30-92, August 31, 1946.

89. Ibid.

90. *Railway Age,* August 30, 1947, 32 (350)–35 (353).

91. Brock to General Chairmen, memorandum, May 3, 1947.

92. *Chicago Tribune,* June 1, 1947.

93. Ibid.

Epilogue

1. *GM&O News,* August 15, 1947, 1.

2. Overton, *Burlington Route,* 516.

3. *Railway Age,* June 29, 1946, 1278.

4. Ibid., November 22, 1947, 46.

5. Ibid., 47.

6. Ibid., December 7, 1946, 966.

7. Ibid.

8. Ibid.

9. Ibid., November 22, 1947, 46.

10. Brock, memorandum for file, July 18, 1948.

Bibliography

Newspapers and Periodicals

Alton Courier
Alton Telegraph
Alton Telegraph and Democratic Review
Bloomington Pantagraph
Bloomington Daily Pantagraph
Brighton News
Carrollton Gazette
Chicago Daily Journal of Commerce
Chicago Daily Tribune
Chicago Democrat
Chicago Press
Chicago Tribune
Daily Courier
Girard Gazette
Illinois Daily Journal
Illinois Daily Register
Illinois Journal
Illinois State Journal
Illinois State Register
Jacksonville Journal
Jacksonville Sentinel
Joliet Morning News
Joliet Republican
Joliet Signal
Joliet True Democrat
Joliet Weekly Sun
Lacon Home Journal
Lockport Phoenix
Menard Index
New York Herald
New York Times
Peoria Free Press
Railway Age
Railway Age Gazette
St. Louis Republican
Sangamo Journal
Sangamon Journal
Springfield Independent
Springfield Journal
Wall Street Journal
Wilmington Advocate

Government Documents

Benjamin Godfrey vs. Thomas W. Wason et al. Madison County Circuit Court 1859.
Chancery Court, box 1653, testimony. National Archives and Records, Chicago.
Interstate Commerce Commission Reports, vol. 40, Valuation Reports, Decisions of the Interstate Commerce Commission of the United States, May 1932–March 1933.
Laws of the State of Illinois.
Laws of the State of Missouri.
Report of the Committee of Nine, Circuit Court of the United States, Northern Illinois District, no. 572119A.
Texas Co. vs. Chicago & Alton R.R. Equity Case file 2940.
Thomas W. Wason vs. Henry Dwight Jr. et al.
William A. Slater vs. The Alton Railroad Company. Civil Action Case, file 1635.

Chicago & Alton Railroad Documents

Annual Reports, 1863–1877, 1879–1883, 1885–1891, 1893–1896, 1898, 1901–1902, 1904–1906, 1907–1914, 1916, 1918, 1920–1928, 1932, 1938, 1943.
Bondholders' Agreement of Chicago, Alton & St. Louis Railroad Company, and Finally Amended 25th October, 1862.
Chief Engineer's Report, October 1852.
Circular of Messrs. Matteson & Litchfield, to the Holders of the Third Mortgage (income) Bonds of the Chicago and Mississippi Railroad Company (New York, 1857).
Consist of Passenger Trains, circa 1920s.
Employee Timetable, 1880, 1932.
First Half-Yearly Report of the Receivers of St. Louis Alton & Chicago Railroad, to the trustees, December 3, 1859–June 30, 1860.
The Flood of 1903 (company-produced promotional brochure)
GM&O News, August 15, 1947, July 19, 1950.
Instructions Issued by General Superintendent Robert Hale, vertical file "Lincoln Funeral," Illinois State Historical Library.
Locomotive Diagrams, January 1, 1931, revised February 9, 1933.
Minutes, April 7, 1862; April 7, 1863; July 27, 1863; December 31, 1863; January 30, 1864; April 2, 1864; April 12, 1864; February 12, 1868.
Passenger Car Diagrams, January 1, 1930.
Public Timetables, 1897, 1899, 1907–1909, 1927, 1937.
Report of the Committee of Nine to the Bondholders of the Chicago & Mississippi Railroad Co., now called Saint Louis Alton & Chicago Railroad Co. (1859).
Report of Survey, Alton & Sangamon R.R., From Alton to City of Springfield, August 18, 1848.
Report of the Chief Engineers, November 7, 1853.
Second Yearly Report of the receivers of the St. Louis Alton & Chicago Railroad to the trustees, January 1, 1861–December 31, 1861.

Statement of Contract Prices for Grading in Missouri.

Statement of the Directors of the Chicago & Mississippi Rail Road Company, March 15, 1854.

Union Pacific Annual Report, 1915.

Papers, Correspondence, Interviews, Memorandums, and Pamphlets

Bode, Belin. Interview with Stephen T. Parsons, October 1989.

Brock to General Chairmen, memorandum, May 3, 1947.

Brock, memorandum to file, July 18, 1948.

C. M. House, memorandum to file, July 31, 1945.

Crocker to Ryder. November 9, 1849, Godfrey Papers Collection.

C. W. Esch to House, memorandum, October 1, 1929.

Esch to House, memorandum, August 4, 1945.

Esch to House, memorandum, January 3, 1947.

F. M. Hicks to H. B. Voorhees, memorandum, June 19, 1945.

G. P. Brock to Hicks, memorandum, June 31, 1945.

Hicks to I. Tigrett, memorandum, June 31, 1945.

Hicks to Tigrett, memorandum, September 7, 1945.

House to A. Chinn, memorandum, August 7, 1943.

House to R. H. Gray, memorandum, May 31, 1945.

James Charlton to Charles Chappell, memorandum, October 4, 1899.

John Wilson to James Hutchins, March 11, 1899.

Memorandum to file, July 13, 1925.

Memorandum of conference, March 26, 1943.

Memorandum to file C-276, March 21, 1944.

Memorandum to file S-30-92, August 31, 1946.

R. A. Pearce to House, memorandum, August 12, 1943.

Ryder to Crocker, November 8, 1849, Godfrey Papers Collection, Illinois Historical State Library.

"The Story of Alton's First Railroad Station." Pamphlet by Jean Floss Paul. Alton Area Landmarks Association, December 1970.

Suttles, Dennis E. Untitled biography of Benjamin Godfrey. Godfrey Papers Collection, Illinois Historical State Library, 1989.

White, Elizabeth Pearson. Letter to author, March 7, 1995.

Books and Articles

Ackerman, William K. "Early Illinois Railroads" (paper presented at the Chicago Historical Society, Chicago, Ill., February 1883). Fergus Historical Series No. 23. Chicago: Fergus Printing, 1884.

Allen, Frederick Lewis. *Only Yesterday: An Informal History of the Nineteen-Twenties.* New York: Harper & Row, 1931.

Andreas, A. T. *History of Cook County.* Chicago: A. T. Andreas, 1884.

———. *History of Chicago.* Chicago: A. T. Andreas, 1884.

Angle, Paul M. *Here I Have Lived: A History of Lincoln's Springfield, 1821–1865.* Springfield, Ill.: Abraham Lincoln Association, 1935.

Atlas Map of Morgan County Illinois. Davenport, Iowa: Andreas Lyter & Co., 1872.

Auffart, A. M. *The Elgin Joliet and Eastern Railway Company: A History of the Early Development of a Regional Railroad.* Privately printed, 1988.

Aylesworth, Thomas G., and Virginia L. Aylesworth. *Chicago: The Glamour Years (1919–1941).* New York: W. H. Smith, 1986.

Bach, Ira J. *Chicago on Foot: An Architectural Walking Tour.* Chicago: Follett Publishing, 1969.

Bain, David Haward. *Empire Express.* New York: Viking, 1999.

Baldwin, William W. *Corporate History of the Chicago, Burlington & Quincy Railroad Company and Affiliated Companies.* Chicago, 1921.

Bannister, Dan W. *Lincoln and the Illinois Supreme Court.* Springfield, Ill., 1994.

Barry, John M. *Rising Tide: The Great Mississippi Flood of 1927 and How It Changed America.* New York: Simon & Schuster, 1997.

Basler, Roy P., Lloyd A. Dunlap, and Marion Dolores Pratt, eds. *The Abraham Lincoln Association Collected Works.* New Brunswick, N.J.: Rutgers University Press, 1953.

Bateman, Newton, and Paul Selby. *Historical Encyclopedia of Illinois and History of McLean County.* Chicago: Munsell Publishing, 1908.

Baum, Arthur W. "The Hesitant Hero of Jackson." *Saturday Evening Post,* March 11, 1947.

Becker, J. W. "The Lincoln Funeral Train." *Illinois Historical Society Journal* 9 (1916–1917).

Beebe, Lucius, and Charles Clegg. *The Trains We Rode.* 2 vols. Berkeley: Howell-North Books, 1965.

Bishop, Jim. *The Day Lincoln Was Shot.* New York: Harper & Brothers, 1955.

Bryant, Keith L. *History of the Atchison, Topeka and Santa Fe Railway.* New York: Macmillan, 1974.

Buckley, James J., Keith E. Sherman, and John D. Stenwyk. "Alton: The Bluff City." *Gulf, Mobile & Ohio Historical Society News,* nos. 47–48 (1987).

Buisseret, David. *Historic Illinois from the Air.* Chicago: University of Chicago Press, 1990.

Burgess, George H., and Miles C. Kennedy. *Centennial History of the Pennsylvania Railroad Company, 1846–1946.* Philadelphia: Pennsylvania Railroad Co., 1949.

Burns, James MacGregor. *The Vineyard of Liberty.* New York: Alfred A. Knopf, 1982.

Campbell, E. G. *The Reorganization of the American Railroad System: 1893–1900.* New York: Columbia University Press, 1938.

Casey, Robert J., and W. A. S. Douglas. *Pioneer Railroad: The Story of the Chicago and North Western System.* New York: Whittlesey House, 1948.

Chernow, Ron. *Titan: The Life of John D. Rockefeller, Sr.* New York: Random House, 1998.

Chicago: A Century of Progress, 1833–1933. Chicago: Marquette Publishing, 1933.

The Chicago and Alton Railway Company. Chicago: Ryan & Hart, 1901.

Clayton, John. *The Illinois Fact Book and Almanac: 1673–1968.* Carbondale: Southern Illinois University Press, 1970.

Collias, Joe C. *The Last of Steam.* Berkeley: Howell-North Books, 1960.

Commager, Henry Steele. *Herndon's Life of Lincoln.* New York: Da Capo Press, 1983.

Corliss, Carlton J. *Mainline of Mid-America.* New York: Creative Age Press, 1950.

Costello, Mary Charlotte Aubry. *Climbing the Mississippi River Bridge by Bridge.* Privately printed, 1995.

Cronon, William. *Nature's Metropolis: Chicago and the Great West.* New York: W. W. Norton, 1991.

Cunningham, Eileen Smith. *Rural Railroads.* Carrollton, Ill.: Eileen Smith Cunningham Reprints, 1956.

Davidson, A., and B. Stuve. *A Complete History of Illinois from 1673 to 1873.* Springfield, Ill.: H. W. Rooker, 1874.

Donald, David Herbert. *Lincoln.* New York: Simon & Schuster, 1995.

———. *Lincoln's Herndon.* New York: Alfred A. Knopf, 1948.

Donovan, Frank P., Jr. "Edwin Hawley." *Trains & Travel,* September 1952.

Dooley, Raymond N. "Lincoln and His Namesake Town." *Journal of the Illinois State Historical Society* 52, no. 1 (1959).

Dorin, Patrick C. *Everywhere West: The Burlington Route.* Seattle: Superior Publishing, 1970.

Droege, John A. *Passenger Terminals and Trains.* New York: McGraw-Hill, 1916.

Drury, George H. *The Historical Guide to North American Railroads.* Milwaukee: Kalmbach Publishing, 1985.

Dubin, Arthur D. *Some Classic Trains.* Milwaukee: Kalmbach Publishing, 1964.

———. *More Classic Trains.* Milwaukee: Kalmbach Publishing, 1974.

Dukes, Brian. "Reaching the Goal." *Illinois History* 34, no. 3 (1980).

Duff, John J. *Prairie Lawyer.* New York: Bramhall House, 1960.

Edson, William D. "Locomotives of the Alton Route." *Railroad History,* no. 156 (1987).

Fiedler, Robert. "The Look Cuss and Wait." Unpublished manuscript, 1993.

Filson, Lester F. *From Whence Came a City.* Privately printed, 1957.

Ford, Thomas A. *A History of Illinois from Its Commencement as a State in 1818 to 1847.* Chicago: Lakeside Press, 1854.

Gandy, Joan W., and Thomas H. Gandy. *The Mississippi Steamboat Era in Historic Photographs.* New York: Dover, 1987.

Gates, Paul Wallace. *The Illinois Central Railroad and Its Colonization Work.* Cambridge, Mass.: Harvard University Press, 1934.

Geisst, Charles R. *Wall Street: A History.* New York: Oxford University Press, 1997.

Gerhard, Frederick. *Illinois as It Is.* Chicago: Keen and Lee, 1857.

Glendinning, Gene V. "When the Alton Route Went Shopping for a Passenger Fleet, Part I." *Gulf, Mobile & Ohio Historical Society News,* no. 15 (summer 1978).

———. "When the Alton Route Went Shopping for a Passenger Fleet, Part III." *Gulf, Mobile & Ohio Historical Society News,* no. 18 (spring 1979).

———. "When Coal and Braidwood Were Synonymous." *Gulf, Mobile & Ohio Historical Society News,* no. 73 (1994).

Gould, Maury. *The Life and Legend of Jay Gould.* Baltimore: Johns Hopkins University Press, 1986.

Grant, H. Roger. *The Corn Belt Route: A History of the Chicago Great Western Railroad Company.* DeKalb: Northern Illinois University Press, 1996.

———. *The North Western: A History of the Chicago & North Western Railway System.* DeKalb: Northern Illinois University Press, 1996.

Grant, H. Roger, Don L. Hofsommer, and Osmund Overby. *St. Louis Union Station: A Place for People, A Place for Trains.* St. Louis: St. Louis Mercantile Library, 1994.

Greenberg, Dolores. *Financiers and Railroads, 1869–1889: A Study of Morton, Bliss & Company.* Newark, N.J.: University of Delaware Press, 1980.

Gross, Joseph. *Railroads of North America.* Privately printed, 1986.

Hall, Jennie. *The Story of Chicago.* New York: Rand McNally, 1911.

Hansen, Peter A. "Give the People a Monument." *Trains* (April 1999).

Hartwell, Wayne H. "Pullman's Connection with the Lincoln Funeral Train." Notes in preparation for article in *Compton's Pictorial Encyclopedia,* April 15, 1957.

Heimburger, Donald J. *Wabash.* Forest Park, Ill.: Heimburger House, 1984.

Hicken, Victor. "The Virden and Pana Mine Wars of 1898." *Illinois State Journal* 52, no. 2 (summer 1959).

———. *Illinois in the Civil War.* Urbana: University of Illinois Press, 1991.

Hinman, Ida. *Biography of Timothy B. Blackstone.* New York: Methodist Book Concern Press, 1917.

Historical Encyclopedia of Illinois. Chicago: Minsell Publishing, 1902.

History of Grundy County, Illinois. Chicago: O. L. Daskin & Co., 1882.

History of Logan County, Illinois. Chicago: Donnelley Lloyd & Co., 1878.

History of McLean County, Illinois. Chicago: Wm. LeBaron & Co., 1879.

History of Madison County, Illinois. Edwardsville, Ill.: W. R. Brink, 1882.

History of Sangamon County, Illinois. Chicago: Inter-state Publishing, 1881.

History of Will County, Illinois. Chicago: Wm. LeBaron & Co., 1878.

Howard, Robert P. *Mostly Good and Competent Men.* Springfield: Illinois Historical Society, 1988.

Huddleston, Eugene L. "Uncle Sam's Locomotives." *Trains* (March 1991).

Hunter, Louis C. *Steamboats on the Western Rivers.* Cambridge, Mass.: Harvard University Press, 1949.

Husband, Joseph. *The History of the Pullman Car.* Grand Rapids, Mich.: Black Letter Press, 1974.

Illinois Atlas & Gazetteer. Freeport, Maine: Delorme Printing, 1991.

Irwin, Frederick R. "RT&N: The Chicago & Alton's Granville Branch." *Gulf, Mobile & Ohio Historical Society News,* no. 38 (1985).

Joyce, Richard Patrick. "Miners of the Prairie: Life and Labor in the Wilmington, Illinois, Coal Field, 1866–1897." Ph.D. diss., Illinois State University, 1980.

Keiser, John H. *Building for the Centuries: Illinois 1865 to 1898.* Urbana: University of Illinois Press, 1977.

Kennan, George. *Misrepresentations in Railroad Affairs.* Garden City, N.Y.: Country Life Press, 1919.

———. *The Chicago and Alton Case.* Garden City, N.Y.: Country Life Press, 1916.

———. *E. H. Harriman: A Biography.* 2 vols. Boston: Houghton Mifflin, 1922.

Kirkland, E. C. *Industry Comes of Age: Business, Labor and Public Policy, 1860–1897.* New York: Holt, Rinehart & Winston, 1961.

Klebaner, Benjamin J. *American Commercial Banking: A History.* Boston: Twayne Publishers, 1990.

Klein, Maury. *The Life and Legend of Jay Gould.* Baltimore: Johns Hopkins University Press, 1986.

———. *The Life & Legend of E. H. Harriman.* Chapel Hill: University of North Carolina Press, 2000.

Kogan, Herman, and Lloyd Wendt. *Chicago: A Pictorial History.* New York: Bonanza Books, 1958.

Kratville, William W. *Steam, Steel & Limiteds.* Omaha: Kratville Publications, 1967.

Krenkel, John H. *Illinois Internal Improvements: 1818–1848.* Cedar Rapids, Iowa: Torch Press, 1958.

Lawson, Larry, and Robert Schramm. "Roadhouse: Crossroads of the Western Division." *Gulf, Mobile & Ohio Historical Society News,* nos. 26–27 (1981).

Legner, Linda, comp. *Lockport, Illinois: A Collective Heritage.* Lockport, Ill.: Bank of Lockport, 1980.

Lemly, James Hutton. *The Gulf, Mobile and Ohio: A Railroad that Had to Expand or Expire.* Homewood, Ill.: R. D. Irwin, 1953.

Leyendecker, Liston Edgington. *Palace Car Prince: A Biography of George Mortimer Pullman.* Niwot: University Press of Colorado, 1992.

"Lincoln Lore." *Bulletin of the Lincoln National Life Foundation,* no. 895 (June 3, 1946)

Lord, Walter. *The Good Years.* New York: Harper & Row, 1960.

Lowe, David. *Lost Chicago.* New York: Random House, 1975.

Lynch, Tracy. *Railroads of Kansas City.* Boulder: Pruett Publishing, 1984.

McDonald, Forrest. *Insull.* Chicago: University of Chicago Press, 1962.

Maiken, Peter T. *Night Trains.* Baltimore: Johns Hopkins University Press, 1989.

Malone, Dumas, and Basil Rauch. *Crisis of the Union, 1841–1877.* New York: Appleton-Century-Crofts, 1960.

———. *The New Nation, 1865–1917.* New York: Appleton-Century-Crofts, 1960.

———. *The Republic Comes of Age, 1789–1841.* New York: Appleton-Century-Crofts, 1960.

———. *War and Troubled Peace, 1917–1939.* New York: Appleton-Century-Crofts, 1960.

Martin, Albro. *Enterprise Denied.* New York: Columbia University Press, 1971.

Masters, Edgar Lee. *The Tale of Chicago.* New York: G. P. Putnam's Sons, 1933.

———. *The Sangamon.* New York: Farrar & Rinehart, 1942.

Matejka, Michael G., and Greg Koos, eds. *Bloomington's C&A Shops: Our Lives Remembered.* Bloomington, Ill.: McLean County Historical Society, 1987.

Mayer, Harold M. and Richard C. Wade. *Chicago: Growth of a Metropolis.* Chicago: University of Chicago Press, 1969.

Mercer, Lloyd J. *E. H. Harriman: Master Railroader.* Boston: Twayne Publishers, 1985.

Middleton, William D. *The Interurban Era.* Milwaukee: Kalmbach Publishing, 1961.

Miller, Donald L. *City of the Century: The Epic of Chicago and the Making of America.* New York: Simon & Schuster, 1996.

Miller, George H. *Railroads and the Granger Laws.* Madison: University of Wisconsin Press, 1971.

Miller, Rev. R. D. *Past and Present of Menard County, Illinois.* Chicago: S. J. Clarke Publishing, 1905.

Modesto, Joseph Donna. *The Braidwood Story.* Braidwood, Ill.: privately printed, 1977.

Moody's Manual.

Moody's Manual of Investments.

Morgan, David P. "A Pacific Primer." *Trains* (September 1988).

Morgan, Ted. *A Shovel of Stars: The Making of the American West, 1800 to the Present.* New York: Simon & Schuster, 1995.

Morison, Samuel Eliot. *The Oxford History of the American People.* New York: Oxford University Press, 1965.

Morrison, Olin Dee, and E. M. Morrison. *Illinois, "Prairie State," Social, Economic, Geographic, Political.* Vol. 1, *History of Illinois.* Athens, Ohio: E. M. Morrison, 1960.

———. *Illinois, "Prairie State": Social, Economic, Geographic, Political.* Vol. 3, *Historical Atlas.* Athens, Ohio: E. M. Morrison, 1963.

The National Cyclopedia of American Biography. Vol. 33. New York: James T. White & Co., 1940.

1928 Handy Railroad Atlas of the United States. Milwaukee: Kalmbach Publishing, 1973.

Nuckles, Douglas B., and Thomas W. Dixon, Jr. *Baltimore & Ohio E-Unit Diesel Passenger Locomotives.* Lynchburg, Va.: TLC Publishing, 1994.

Olmsted, Robert P. *GM&O North.* Privately printed, 1976.

Overton, Richard C. *Burlington Route: A History of the Burlington Lines.* New York: Alfred A. Knopf, 1965.

Pease, Theodore C. *The Frontier State: 1818–1848.* Springfield: Illinois Centennial Commission, 1918.

———. *The Story of Illinois.* Chicago: University of Chicago Press, 1949.

Poor's Manual of Railroads.

Poor's Manual of Railways.

Poppeliers, John C., S. Allen Chambers, Jr., and Nancy B. Schwartz. *What Style Is It?* Washington: Preservation Press, 1983.

Portrait and Biographical Album of Will County. Chicago: Chapman Bros., 1890.

Portrait and Biography of McLean County, Illinois. Chicago: Chapman Bros., 1887.

Pratt, Harry C. *Lincoln, 1840–1846.* Springfield, Ill.: Abraham

Lincoln Association, 1939.

Prince, Ezra M., and John H. Burnham. "History of McLean County." Chicago: LeBaron & Co., 1908.

Power, John Carroll. *Abraham Lincoln: His Life, Public Services, Death, and Great Funeral Cortege.* Springfield, Ill.: E. A. Wilson, & Co., 1875.

Rand McNally Handy Railroad Atlas of the United States. Chicago: Rand McNally, 1971.

Randall, Dave. "Abe 'n Annie." *Gulf, Mobile & Ohio Historical Society News,* no. 21 (winter 1979).

——. "Abe 'n Annie." *Gulf, Mobile & Ohio Historical Society News,* no. 22 (spring 1980).

Randall, David W., and Alan R. Lind. *Monarchs of Mid-America.* Park Forest, Ill.: Prototype Publications, 1973.

Randall, J. G. *Lincoln the President.* Vol. 1, *Springfield to Gettysburg.* New York: Da Capo Press, 1997.

Randall, Ruth Painter. *Mary Lincoln: A Biography of a Marriage.* Boston: Little, Brown & Co., 1953.

Reavis, L. V. *The Railway and River Systems of the City of St. Louis.* St. Louis: Woodward, Truman & Hale, 1879.

Rehor, John A. *The Nickle Plate Story.* Milwaukee: Kalmbach Publishing, 1965.

Ripley, William Z. *Railroads: Finance & Organization.* New York: Longmans, Green, 1915.

Roseman, V. S. *Railway Express: An Overview.* Denver: Rocky Mountain Publishing, 1992.

Russell, A. D. *Copy of Certain Proceedings, April, 1858.* New York: Astor, Lenox and Tilden Foundations, 1924.

Samuel, Ray, Leonard V. Huber, and Warren C. Ogden. *Tales of the Mississippi.* Gretna, La.: Pelican Publishing, 1955.

Sandburg, Carl. *Abraham Lincoln: The Prairie Years and the War Years.* New York: Harcourt, Brace & Co., 1954.

Schramm, Robert. "Cabooses, C&A/Alton." *Gulf, Mobile & Ohio Historical Society News,* nos. 40–41 (1985).

Scientific American. March 2, 1901.

Shaw, Fayette B. "The Economic Development of Joliet, Illinois: 1830–1870." Ph.D. diss., Harvard University, 1934.

Sheriff, Carol. *The Artificial River: The Erie Canal and the Paradox of Progress, 1817–1862.* New York: Hill & Wang, 1996.

Simon, Paul. *Lincoln's Preparation for Greatness.* Urbana: University of Illinois Press, 1971.

Snyder, Carl. *American Railways as Investments.* Elizabeth, N.J.: Moody-Barton Press, 1907.

Spearman, Frank H. *The Strategy of Great Railroads.* New York: Scribner's Sons, 1904.

Starr, John. W., Jr. *Lincoln and the Railroads.* New York: Dodd, Mead & Co., 1927.

Stratton, H. J. "The Northern Cross Railroad." *Journal of the Illinois State Historical Society* 28, no. 2 (1977).

Stringer, Laurence. *History of Logan County, Illinois: A Record of Its Settlement, Organization, Progress, and Achievement.* Evansville, Ind.: Unigraphic, 1978.

Stringham, Paul H. *Illinois Terminal: The Electric Years.* Glendale, Calif.: Interurban Press, 1989.

——. "A History of C&NW's St. Louis Subdivision." *North Western Lines* (Chicago & North Western Historical Society) 20, no. 1 (winter 1993).

——. *Toledo, Peoria & Western: Tried, Proven & Willing.* Peoria, Ill.: Deller Archive, 1993.

Stringham, Paul H., and Gene Glendinning. "The Sherman Branch: A Dream That Never Came True." *Gulf, Mobile & Ohio Historical Society News,* nos. 36–37 (1984).

Stover, John F. *History of the Illinois Central Railroad.* New York: Macmillan, 1975.

——. *History of the Baltimore and Ohio Railroad.* West Lafayette, Ind.: Purdue University Press, 1987.

Strouse, Jean. *Morgan: American Financier.* New York: Random House, 1999.

Sunderland, Edwin S. S. *Abraham Lincoln and the Illinois Central Railroad.* Privately printed, 1955.

Sutton, Robert M. *The Heartland: Pages from Illinois History.* Lake Forest, Ill.: Deerpath, 1975.

Swanson, Leslie C. *Canals of Mid-America.* Privately printed, 1984.

Szwajkart, John. "The Salutary Switchers." *Gulf, Mobile & Ohio Historical Society News,* nos. 83–84 (1997).

Thomas, Benjamin P. *Lincoln Day by Day: 1847–53.* Springfield, Ill.: Abraham Lincoln Association, 1936.

Traxel, David. *1898: The Birth of the American Century.* New York: Alfred A. Knopf, 1998.

Urdang, Laurence, ed. *The Timetables of History.* New York: Simon & Schuster, 1981.

Valle, James E. *The Iron Horse at War.* Berkeley: Howell-North Books, 1977.

Voorhees, H. B. "The First Steel Bridge Recalled." *Railway Age,* February 17, 1945.

Wade, Louise-Carroll. *Chicago's Pride: The Stockyards, Packingtown, and Environs in the Nineteenth Century.* Urbana: University of Illinois Press, 1987.

Wallin, R. R. "Dick." *Gulf, Mobile & Ohio Color Pictorial.* La Mirada, Ca.: Four Ways West Publications, 1996.

Wallin, Richard R. "Motor Cars." *Gulf, Mobile & Ohio Historical Society News,* no. 19 (summer 1979).

Wallin, Richard R., Paul H. Stringham, and John Szwajkart. *Chicago & Illinois Midland.* San Marino, Ca.: Golden West Books, 1979.

Way, Frederick, Jr. *Ways Packet Directory, 1848–1994.* Athens: Ohio University Press, 1983.

Wayland, J. A. "The Alton Steal." *Wayland's Monthly* (June 1908).

Wayman, Norbury L. *St. Louis Union Station and Its Railroads.* St. Louis: Evelyn E. Newman Group, 1987.

Webb, Walter Prescott. *The Great Plains.* Lincoln: University of Nebraska Press, 1981.

Wesolowski, Wayne. "Abraham Lincoln's Funeral Train." *Model Railroader* (February 1995).

Westcott, Linn H. *Model Railroader Cyclopedia.* Vol. 1, *Steam Locomotives.* Milwaukee: Kalmbach Publishing, 1960.

White, Elizabeth Pearson. "Captain Benjamin Godfrey and the Alton and Sangamon Railroad." *Illinois Historical Journal* 67, no. 5 (1974).

White, John H., Jr. *A History of the American Locomotive: Its Development, 1830–1880.* New York: Dover Publications, 1968.

——. *The American Railroad Passenger Car.* Baltimore: Johns

Hopkins University Press, 1978.

———. *The American Railroad Freight Car: From the Wood-car Era to the Coming of Steel.* Baltimore: Johns Hopkins University Press, 1993.

Wilner, Frank N. *Railroad Mergers: History, Analysis, Insight.* Omaha: Simmons-Boardman, 1997.

Windmeier, James L. "Chicago & Alton Atlantics." *Gulf, Mobile & Ohio Historical Society News,* no. 3 (spring 1975).

———. "Chicago & Alton Class I-6 Pacifics." *Gulf, Mobile & Ohio Historical Society News,* no. 6 (spring 1976).

———. "Chicago & Alton Class L-2 Mikados." *Gulf, Mobile & Ohio Historical Society News,* no. 8 (fall 1976).

Woldman, Albert A. *Lawyer Lincoln.* New York: Carroll & Graf, 1936.

Woodruff, George H. *Forty Years Ago!* Joliet, Ill.: Joliet Republican Steam Printing House, 1874.

Yenawine, Wayne. *A History of the Holdings of the Terminal Railroad Association of St. Louis.* Privately printed, n.d.

Yungmeyer, D. W. "An Excursion into the Early History of the Chicago and Alton Railroad." *Journal of the Illinois State Historical Society* 38, no. 1 (March 1945).

Index

A Book in the
RAILROADS IN AMERICA
Series

H. Roger Grant and James A. Ward

General Editors